T5-BQB-606

BUILDING MID-REPUBLICAN ROME

BUILDING MID-REPUBLICAN ROME

Labor, Architecture, and the Urban Economy

Seth Bernard

Oxford University Press is a department of the University of Oxford. It furthers the University's objective of excellence in research, scholarship, and education by publishing worldwide. Oxford is a registered trade mark of Oxford University Press in the UK and certain other countries.

Published in the United States of America by Oxford University Press
198 Madison Avenue, New York, NY 10016, United States of America.

Library of Congress Cataloging-in-Publication Data
Names: Bernard, Seth (Classicist), author.
Title: Building Mid-Republican Rome : Labor, Architecture,
and the Urban Economy / Seth Bernard.
Description: New York : Oxford University Press, 2018. |
Includes bibliographical references and index.
Identifiers: LCCN 2018001370 | ISBN 9780190878788 (hardcover) |
ISBN 9780190878801 (epub)
Subjects: LCSH: Urbanization—Rome—History. | Rome—Economic conditions—
30 B.C.–476 A.D.
Classification: LCC HT169.I8 B464 2018 | DDC 307.760937/63—dc23
LC record available at https://lccn.loc.gov/2018001370

CONTENTS

FIGURES

MAPS

ACKNOWLEDGMENTS

This book uses the archaeological remains of architecture in combination with a wide range of other sources and documents to describe a chapter of Rome's socioeconomic and urban history. The interdisciplinary nature of this project has required that I rely time and again on the help and expertise of friends and colleagues in the decade or so since I began the University of Pennsylvania doctoral thesis from which this book has grown. I am happy to acknowledge the community who has given encouragement, taken time to answer questions, read and commented on drafts, or facilitated access to archaeological sites. Several people fit into several of those categories: Margaret Andrews, Dirk Booms, Christer Bruun, Monica Ceci, Robert Coates-Stephens, Cynthia Damon, Penelope Davies, Janet DeLaine, Dan Diffendale, Joe Farrell, Lisa Fentress, Harriet Flower, William Harris, Lothar Haselberger, John Hopkins, Marie Jackson, Nathaniel Jones, Matthew Karp, Ann Kuttner, Lynne Lancaster, Jeremy Lefkowitz, Susann Lusnia, Marco Maiuro, Lisa Mignone, Dan-El Padilla Peralta, Jordan Pickett, Gianni Ponti, Anna Maria Ramieri, Andrew Riggsby, Brian Rose, Walter Scheidel, Christopher Smith, James Tan, William Turpin, Michael Waters, Kevin Wilkinson, Mark Wilson Jones, Ulrike Wulf-Rheidt, Rita Volpe, and Stephan Zink. I am sure this list is too short. Research has been generously supported by a Rome Prize Fellowship at the American Academy in Rome, a Postdoctoral Fellowship jointly sponsored by the Archaeological Institute of America and the Deutsches Archäologisches Institut in Berlin, and a Connaught New Researcher Grant from the University of Toronto. In Toronto, Susan Dunning ably assisted in assembling the catalog in appendix 2, and John Fabiano helped with the bibliography. At Oxford Press, Sarah Humphreville contacted me years ago with interest in seeing a manuscript and then waited with remarkable patience until I had one to share with her. My wife Alexa has been my lifeline from this project's beginning, and my children Livia and Jonathan have brought much-needed levity and perspective to the journey. I dedicate this book to my parents Stephen and Shula for their unwavering support.

MAPS

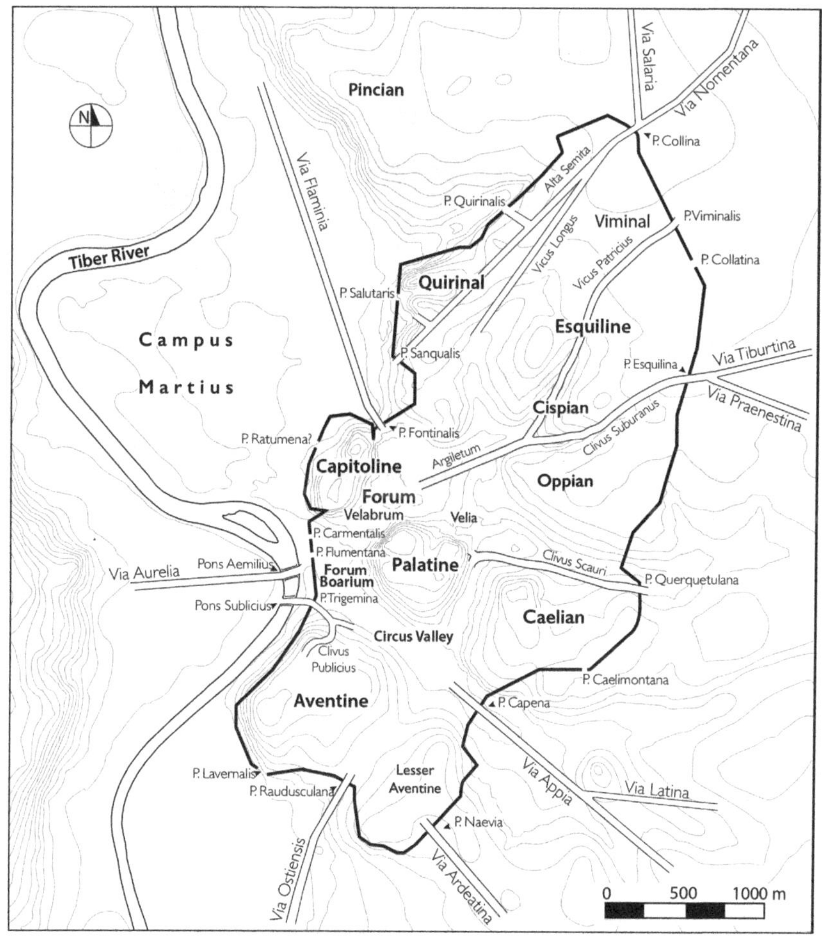

MAP 1 Mid-Republican Rome. Walls, routes, gates, and physical terrain.
Map © S. Bernard.

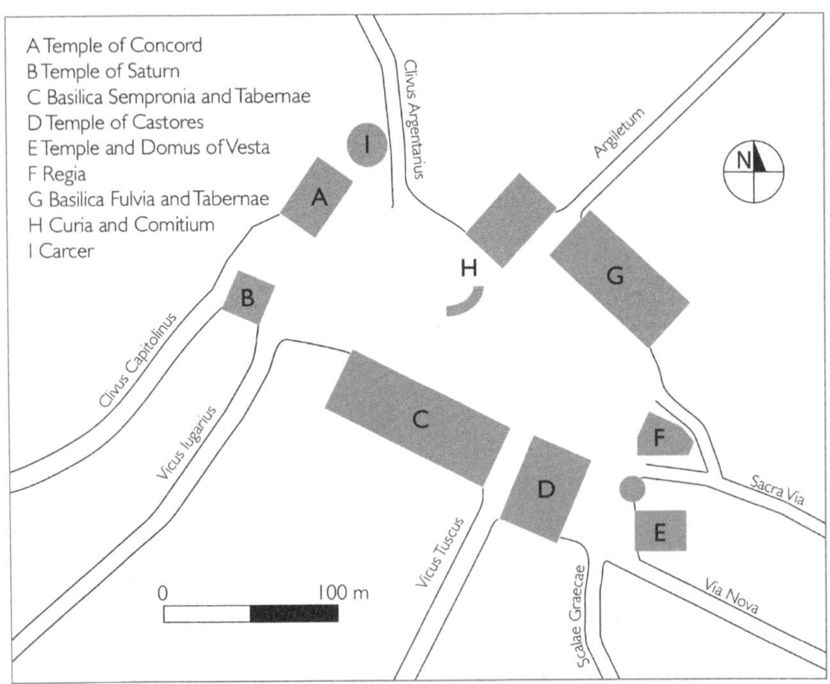

MAP 2 The Mid-Republican Forum and its surrounding area.
Map © S. Bernard.

BUILDING MID-REPUBLICAN ROME

1 INTRODUCTION

BUILDING AS HISTORICAL PROCESS

The senate is in charge of what is by far the greatest and most considerable public expenditure, namely what the censors contribute every five years to the construction or upkeep of public works.

—POLYBIUS, *6.13.3*

This book describes the physical and socioeconomic processes that contributed to the formation of the Republican city of Rome during the Mid-Republican period. In political terms, the study is bounded by the conquest of Veii in 396 and the end of the Third Macedonian War in 168 BCE, and it thus encompasses one of the most intense phases of Rome's imperial expansion across the Italian peninsula and throughout the Mediterranean.[1] The massive influx of manpower and wealth from the tributary empire transformed Rome from a prominent Central Italian city-state into the principal urban center of its world. The final result of this urban transformation is well known: by the early principate, Rome's architectural density and population of perhaps a million people had reached levels of magnitude not seen again in any Western city until the eighteenth century. However, Rome was quickly becoming an exceptional city already by the Mid-Republic. The Greek historian Polybius, cited above, highlighted the outsized portion of public funds allocated by the Republican state to the construction and upkeep of the capital city. This was certainly true at the time he was writing in the first half of the second century BCE, when in some years half or even all public income was budgeted for building projects.[2] But even a century

1. For the periodization of Republican history, see Flower 2011; for the fourth and third centuries BCE as fundamental for Republican society, see Hölkeskamp 2004: 14. Translations are my own unless otherwise noted.

2. According to Livy, the entire *vectigal* was earmarked for construction in 179 (40.46.16), and half in 169 (44.14); see Tan 2017: 31–32.

or more before that date, we may detect the application of imperial wealth to urban infrastructure on a grand scale. In 312 BCE in the midst of the Samnite Wars, Appius Claudius Caecus was said to have drained the state coffers building the city's first aqueduct and highway (A21–22). In 272 BCE, Manius Curius Dentatus initiated the costly project to build Rome's second aqueduct explicitly "from the spoils" (*de manubiis*) of his military campaigns in Italy (A44).[3] In quantitative terms, the number of attested public building projects rose notably in the decades around 300 BCE, just as Rome embarked on a century of largely uninterrupted imperial expansion. In other words, the process of building Mid-Republican Rome began with great energy during the period of the conquest of Italy. Moreover, as is argued here, the creation of the Republican city resulted not only from the spoils of empire, but from fundamental changes in the fourth and third centuries to the way in which such wealth was allocated and to the economic institutions with which imperial tribute was transformed into urban infrastructure.

The Mid-Republican city was distinguishable both for its dense urban fabric and for the particular socioeconomic structures it contained.[4] In some sense, all cities are distinctive as both built *and* human environments, and it is an overarching goal of urban studies to find ways to combine these separate but related aspects. The following study attempts to do this by using architecture and urbanism as a point of entry into a synthetic discussion of the city's historical development during a formative period. Certainly, Mid-Republican Rome saw several novelties from a purely architectural standpoint: Rome's first aqueducts, public roads, basilicas, arches, and porticoes all appeared during this period, and these building types were subsequently carried beyond the city as markers of *Romanitas* throughout the expanding empire. Many of these formal developments have already received significant attention from architectural historians.[5] Here instead I pursue a different set of questions designed to highlight these buildings' broader historical (rather than simply physical) dimensions. Granting that the transformation of Republican Rome into an imperial capital was highly costly, how did the Roman state and its residents meet such costs? How were supplies of material

3. Throughout, cross-references are included to appendix 2 containing a catalog of public building projects with further bibliography.

4. Morley 1996 provides an excellent overview of the economic features which distinguished the ancient capital; for labor in particular, see Hawkins 2013.

5. Gros 1996; Gros and Torelli 2007; Palombi 2010.

and labor organized? What effects did sustained urban construction have on the structures of Rome's society and economy?

Along with warfare, construction regularly represented the costliest productive activity undertaken by pre-industrial states, while most complex societies built monumental architecture, if for various reasons. Such costliness and commonality have given the building process a prominent place in the economic histories of pre-modern and early-modern states, including recent work on Imperial Rome.[6] For more recent periods of the past onward, the prominence of building within the broader productive economy has often lent greater visibility to builders in comparison to other urban workers, and a number of studies have used building wages or material prices to inform broad inquiries about the movement and structure of labor through time.[7] While potentially useful, such an investigation has not yet been undertaken for the earlier phases of Rome.

1.1. Previous Approaches

To date, the two dominant ways of studying the Mid-Republican city's urban development may be termed formalist and topographical. The formalist approach has already been alluded to: architectural historians mark this period as a moment in which several new Roman building forms appeared in the city for the first time. As many of these new building types such as the fornix or basilica are relatable to similar and perhaps earlier structures in the Greek East, discussion of their appearance at Rome links into larger debates of Hellenization and the Roman adoption of Greek culture.[8] This debate has less of a place in this study, first of all because the object here is to view architecture not discretely, but for what it reveals about socioeconomic trends. I am also more broadly resistant to the concept of Hellenization as a useful way of understanding developments in the Mid-Republican city. Recent scholarship insists on a more fluid and interactive Mediterranean world in which contacts between East and West were very longstanding.[9]

6. For Rome, see DeLaine 1997; 2001. Otherwise, Goldthwaite 1980; Clarke 1992; Woodward 1995.

7. Phelps Brown and Hopkins 1981; Allen 2001; Özmucur and Pamuk 2002; some caveats in Dyer 1989: 220–22. For Roman Imperial builders' wages, see Bernard 2016a.

8. Delbruck 1907–12; Zanker 1976; Hölscher 1978.

9. Horden and Purcell 2000.

With regard to urbanism and architecture, strong links between Rome and the Greek East appeared as early as the sixth century BCE.[10] Focus on moments of cultural interaction within a framework of more longstanding Mediterranean contacts, or "connectivity" as Horden and Purcell put it, tends to deemphasize rigidly separated cultural categories like Greek and Roman. The appearance of supposedly "Greek" architectural styles at Rome seems less radical, and Rome's participation in wider Mediterranean architectural styles seems less derivative. In this light, the search for the first appearance of this or that Hellenistic form in Republican Rome's architecture is unproductive, as Rome and Central Italy—and indeed the entire Hellenistic West—may be seen as holding more agency in the creation of architectural style within the connected Mediterranean world after the death of Alexander the Great.[11]

While such formalist studies of Roman architecture tend to look outward for models, Roman topographical research is by contrast strongly introspective. The venerable attempt to reconstruct the layout of ancient Rome may be traced back to Quattrocento Humanists, if not all the way to Late Republican antiquarians like Varro. Motivating such inquiries was often a self-conscious assertion that Rome was the center of its world, either in the early years of the Augustan regime or after the end of the Great Schism and the reestablishment of the Roman papacy in the fifteenth century.[12] From such beginnings, topographical research took on great energy in the late nineteenth and early twentieth centuries in response to large-scale excavations prompted by the designation of Rome as the capital of the new nation of Italy in 1861. The first comprehensive work on Roman topography by Jordan and Hülsen appeared in 1871–1907, and the first topographical dictionary by Platner and Ashby was published in 1929. Up-to-date summaries of topographical research accounting for recent archaeological discoveries can be found in the dictionary by Richardson, Jr. (1992) and in guidebooks by Coarelli (2007) and Claridge (2010). A fundamental reference to any work on ancient Rome is the multivolume *Lexicon Topographicum Urbis Romae* edited by Steinby. Specific to the Mid-Republic, an important exhibit on *Roma medio repubblicana*, organized at Rome in 1973, brought together much of the archaeological material from

10. Hopkins 2016.

11. Prag and Crawley Quinn 2013.

12. Bernard 2014–15.

previous excavations and sought to repair a general neglect for the city's material culture between the Archaic and later Republican periods. The show stimulated scholarly interest, which has done much to enrich our understanding of the layout of the Mid-Republican city.[13]

1.2. The Topographical Approach: A Case Study from Largo Argentina

The results of all of this topographical work are valuable, but the method also reaches a point of diminishing returns where intense topographical debate sometimes dominates other lines of inquiry. To illustrate this, I present a case study of the four Republican temples uncovered at Largo Argentina in the southern Campus Martius. This requires entering into a degree of detail, but the concentration of Mid-Republican architecture on this site is fundamental to any understanding of the city during the third and second centuries BCE. The modern archaeological zone results from excavations begun in 1926 under the direction of Marchetti Longhi (figure 1.1). At that date, at least two of the four Roman temples were already known to exist beneath the modern city block: Temple A (A54) to the north was incorporated into the medieval church of San Nicola ai Cesarini, while the circular colonnade of Temple B immediately to its south was still visible. The subsequent destruction and clearing of the entire block down to its Roman layers exposed two additional Mid-Republican temples, C (A29) and D (A119) along with a number of other ancient structures (figure 1.2).[14]

Which four temples were found at Largo Argentina? Even before evaluating various answers to this question, it is important to note that a great deal about each temple's chronology can be established independently on the basis of related finds and building techniques.[15] The oldest structure, Temple C, dates to the first quarter of the third century. To its north, the earliest iteration of Temple A was built shortly after as a small, prostyle temple still partly visible beneath the cella of the later temple (figure 1.3).

13. Castagnoli 1974; Dondero, Pensabene, and Campus 1982. By far the most important work is that of Coarelli in a series of monographs and articles.

14. As one of Mussolini's earliest projects in Rome, the excavation is of historical interest in its own right; Painter 2005: 7–9.

15. The following relies on Coarelli 1981.

FIGURE 1.1 The archaeological site of Largo Argentina viewed from the north.
Photo © S. Bernard.

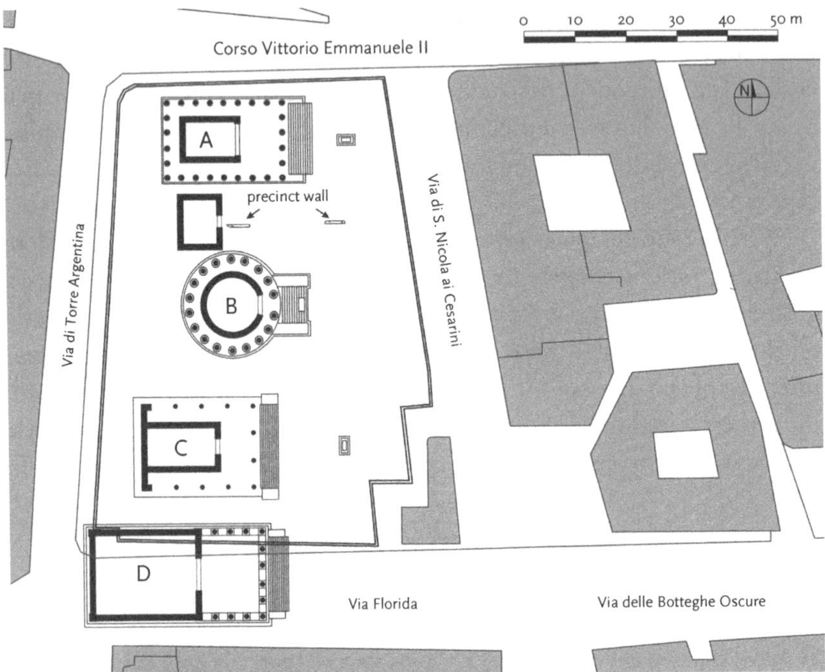

FIGURE 1.2 Hypothetical reconstruction of the four Republican temples at Largo Argentina showing their location in relation to the modern streets.
Plan © S. Bernard.

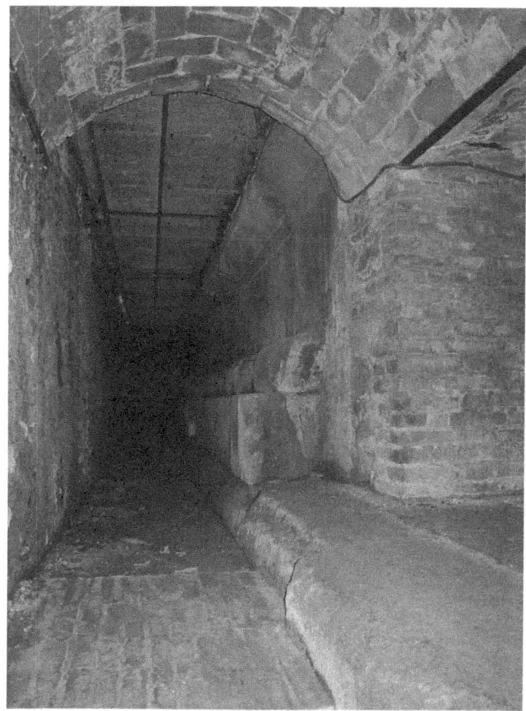

FIGURE 1.3 Molded podium wall of the second phase of Temple A viewed from beneath the podium of the later temple. The lowest course of blocks represents the temple's earliest phase.

Photo © S. Bernard.

Temple D was built around a half century later to the south. These three temples sat directly upon the ground of the Campus Martius. Sometime later the surrounding area was paved in tuff slabs, and Temple B was built on top of this pavement. Its round plan, Corinthian capitals in travertine, and marble frieze relate it to urban religious architecture of the late second century.

Equipped with a notion of each temple's initial construction, we may now turn to the tools employed for topographical research. The religious topography of the southern Campus Martius depends on a wide array of evidence. Parts of the Largo Argentina temples are visible, for example, on fragments of the so-called *Forma Urbis Romae*, a Severan-period map of the city inscribed on marble slabs on a wall of the Temple of Peace (figure 1.4). Also vital are several inscribed Roman calendars (*fasti*) recording the date of sacrifices to urban cults, often with details of a cult's location. These *fasti*

FIGURE 1.4 Fragment of the Severan marble plan (*FUR* 37a) showing Temples A and B at Largo Argentina.

Photo © Stanford Digital Library/Ufficio Fotografico dei Musei Capitolini.

locate a Temple of Fortuna Huiusce Diei ("Fortune of this very day"), vowed by Q. Lutatius Catulus in 101 BCE, on the Campus Martius, while Varro (*Res Rust.* 3.5.12) notes that the temple was round in plan. Date, location, and style correspond to Temple B, making the identification of this monument as that built by Catulus secure.[16]

Identifying the earlier temples A, C, and D proves more difficult. At least Temples A and C were built in a period in the mid-third century when Livy, normally the best guide for Mid-Republican temple dedications, is lost and extant sources are fragmentary. Many of the dozen or so cults in the Campus Martius whose foundation can still be identified in this period can then be ruled out for various reasons. Temples for Fons or Juturna are arguably located elsewhere in the Campus. The Temple of Fortuna Equestris had no Imperial

16. Boyance 1940; Leach 2010; Caprioli 2011; Mattei 2014; cf. *LTUR* II s.v. "Fortuna Huiusce Diei" 269–70 (P. Gros).

phases, while the Temple of Jupiter Fulgur had an unroofed cella, and these qualities do not match any of the Largo Argentina temples. For cults such as Juno Curritis or Feronia, evidence is limited and cannot confirm the existence of an actual temple as early as the third century. By this process of elimination, some half dozen cults remain possibilities.

Coarelli presents the most coordinated attempt to make sense of this confusing situation. He begins from the suggestion that the present archaeological zone of Largo Argentina was architecturally unified already in antiquity as a triumphal portico, which he identifies as the "old" (*vetus*) Porticus Minucia built by M. Minucius Rufus in 107 BCE. This Porticus Minucia served as the center for the distribution of state-subsidized grain, the *annona*, until a new porticus of the same name was built in the Early Empire. Asserting a physical connection between the distribution of the *annona* and the *statio aquarum*, the office in charge of Rome's water supply,[17] he then argues that Largo Argentina contained a series of cults connected not only architecturally but by their deities' custody of Rome's water and grain supplies: Temple A housed the water nymph Juturna, Temple C the agricultural goddess Feronia, and Temple D the Lares Permarini, tutelary marine deities whose temple, dedicated in 179, is located by the Praenestine *fasti* in the Porticus Minucia BCE.

This rapid overview hardly does justice to the complexity of Coarelli's reconstruction, which would identify a remarkably stable locus in the ancient city for the provision of food and water. However, several issues must be accounted for. One problem is how to relate Largo Argentina's temples to the wider topography of the southern Campus Martius. For example, Ovid's *Fasti* associated Juturna's temple with the area "where the Aqua Virgo washed the Campus" (1.463–4). The Aqua Virgo terminated beside the Saepta in an area physically separated in Ovid's day from Largo Argentina by a long portico called the Hecatostylum.[18] Read closely, Ovid's text thus makes it difficult to associate Juturna's cult with the temples of Largo Argentina. Of course, Ovid may have been gesturing to the general confluence of water infrastructure in the central Campus Martius. But an identification between Juturna and Temple A is only made by assuming a certain looseness to the poet's otherwise specific topographical description.

17. Coarelli identifies the *statio aquarum* with a brick building between Temples A and B, but see Bruun 1989: 138–41.

18. Cf. Front. *de Aq.* 22.

Another problem is that Largo Argentina does not resemble other triumphal *porticus* built in the Mid-Republic.[19] As Zevi and others point out, the area lacked a unified colonnade running around its sides, a feature which typically defined such structures.[20] Moreover, the pavement in front of the temples seems to have extended further south beneath via Florida, outside the space defined by modern excavation, and there was at least one other temple located south of Temple D.[21] Finally, new excavations have revealed a precinct wall running south of Temple A, delimiting the temple's sanctuary within the confines of Largo Argentina (cf. fig. 1.2) and making it highly unlikely Temple A was conceived of as sitting within the same architectural space as the three temples to its south.[22] In short, there are good reasons for thinking that the modern site did not correspond to an architecturally unified area in antiquity. If we are looking to explain Largo Argentina's shape, another explanation is easily found in the limits of modern excavation determined by the housing block destroyed in 1926.

Still, rejecting the identification of Largo Argentina with the old Porticus Minucia leaves the question of where that structure was located, and alternative proposals are not without their own problems. The Imperial Porticus Minucia has reasonably been located in the area south of Largo Argentina, but the earlier porticus was almost certainly not in the same place.[23] One prominent theory locates the earlier structure east of Largo Argentina, along the north side of via delle Botteghe Oscure, where fragments of the Severan marble plan show a temple within a portico inscribed with the label *MINI*, perhaps [*porticus*] *MINI*[*cia*].[24] A temple podium excavated in this exact spot would then be the aforementioned Temple of the Lares Permarini, built in 179 BCE and later incorporated into the Porticus Minucia vetus in 107 BCE. However, the via delle Botteghe Oscure temple's construction employed

19. For the typical form, see Gros 1996: 95–99.

20. Zevi 1993: 678 n. 31; 2007: 378; for the area's confines, see Santangeli Valenzani 1994: 60.

21. Additional temple: Rodriguez Almeida 1991–92: 6; pavement: Santangeli Valenzani 1994: 60 n. 14.

22. Ceci and Santangeli Valenzani 2012.

23. Key is the listing *Minucias duas veterem et frumentariam* within *Regio IX Circus Flaminius* in the *Notitia regionum urbis Romae*, a late antique catalog of Rome's buildings; this implies that two separate porticus Minuciae still stood in the lower Campus in the Constantinian period; on the Imperial portico's location, see Zevi 1993: 704; 2007: 369; Tucci 1994–95; *LTUR* IV s.v. "Porticus Minucia Frumentaria" 132–37 (D. Manacorda).

24. Cozza 1968.

cement in its earliest phase, and this technique would seemingly point to a later second-century date and precludes an identification with the earlier temple in the Porticus Minucia vetus.[25]

In sum, Largo Argentina's topographical study permits mutually exclusive but internally coherent reconstructions, each with their own problems to explain away. On a broader level, this discussion demonstrates how rapidly the approach can descend into minute detail and, at times, into speculation. No perfect solution integrates the archaeology with the motley historical evidence for the ancient Campus Martius. It is entirely possible, although rarely admitted, that we simply cannot know the identification of these ancient structures on the basis of the evidence at hand. Admittedly, I have focused on an especially fraught area of the city. More confidence seems justified in the case of three temples beneath the church of San Nicola in Carcere, for example, while the layout of the Forum and the course of Rome's walls are reasonably understood in this period. But with Largo Argentina, the great scholarly energy that goes into questions that may ultimately be unanswerable is frustrating, especially because these temples' archaeology would seem to speak volumes about Republican Rome's urban image through time, even if the temples cannot be decisively named.

1.3. The Urban Economy of Mid-Republican Rome

Thus, my critique of the topographical approach is not that it lacks utility, but that it should not be an end in and of itself. In part, the work of employing topographical data to answer historical questions is underway. The religious implications of temple building in this period are well studied by Ziolkowski and others.[26] Hölkeskamp demonstrates that the Mid-Republican city's architecture was not a passive backdrop, but monumental space could be activated in support of the competitive politics of the period.[27] What scholarship has not looked into are the economic implications of the production of Mid-Republican Rome's physical topography. Indeed, the Roman economy

25. Marquez and Gutierrez Deza 2006; Zevi 2007: 457–58; for the late second-century date of concrete's introduction at Rome, see Mogetta 2015.

26. Ziolkowski 1992; also Pietilä-Castrén 1987; Aberson 1994; Orlin 1997.

27. Hölkeskamp 2004, esp. chs. 1 and 5; 2010: 57–67; Hölkeskamp and Stein-Hölkeskamp, eds. 2006; Steinby 2012a; Davies 2013; Popkin 2016.

prior to the Second Punic war remains generally neglected.[28] Meanwhile, the broader study of the Roman economy has advanced considerably in recent years. Fundamental is the publication of the *Cambridge Economic History of the Greco-Roman World* (2007), edited by Scheidel, Morris, and Saller, which follows the analytical framework of new institutional economics by investigating how the ancient economy's structure shaped its performance. In other words, the editors redefine the goals of ancient economic history as the study of both (i) the character of ancient economic institutions, those formal and informal constraints that structured economic interactions, and (ii) the way in which antiquity's institutional framework led to particular outcomes in terms of the production, distribution, and consumption of wealth over time.[29]

The new institutional focus provides a useful way forward from the older debate in the wake of Finley's *Ancient Economy* over the essentially primitive or modern character of the ancient economy. Finley held that ancient societies subordinated economic activity to social structures; they were therefore largely incapable of economic growth and were primarily composed of cellular, relatively unchanging household economies. That is, the ancient economy's structure left little to say about its performance.[30] It is undoubtedly correct that over the long run ancient Mediterranean economies, like all "organic economies" prior to the industrial revolution, cannot have experienced significant and lasting rates of growth above demographic expansion as ancient societies never seem to have completely outrun the risk of Malthusian checks.[31] This alone precludes some recent modernizing work, which insists on analyzing Rome's economy as a massive market containing disembedded individuals acting in search of profit, and there are further reasons for rejecting this sort of view.[32] By positing growth with little regard

28. Works by Frank 1933; Clerici 1943; De Martino 1979 are out of date, particularly in regard to the archaeology. See Kay 2014 for the period after the Second Punic War; Viglietti 2011 for Archaic Rome; Panella 2010 on the Mid-Republic from the perspective of Roman ceramics.

29. North 1981: 3. As with much study of the ancient economy, informal (behavioral norms, conventions, codes of conduct) rather than formal (rules, laws, constitutions) institutions are more important in this book, although a more purely legal history of the early Roman economy is not impossible, and might resemble Capogrossi Colognesi 2012.

30. For Finley's "relentless emphasis" of structure over performance, see Morris, Saller, and Scheidel 2007: 5.

31. The phrase is from Wrigley 2010: 9; see also Piketty 2014: 72–109; for similar acknowledgment among Romanists, see Saller 2005: 229–33; Scheidel and Friesen 2009: 64; Scheidel 2012: 11; for technical discussion of pre-industrial growth, see Persson 2010: 60–71.

32. Temin 2013. Problematically, evidence for extensive markets often comes from contexts in which the state loomed large: army-run quarries and mines, or the grain supply. It thus becomes

for the ancient economy's distinguishing features, this modernizing perspective is no less unbalanced than primitivism, even if it reverses the problem by emphasizing performance while overlooking structure. The view of a disembedded Roman market economy also seems out of step with current economic scholarship, which allows great room for social structure and ideology in determining economic outcomes. As North and especially economic sociologists like Granovetter point out, the laws governing economic behavior are neither ergodic nor universal, but the supposedly "rational" incentives that motivate economic actors in turn depend upon an informational background arising from social networks or belief systems, and this is true even in modern economies.[33]

While the priority assigned by recent economic sociology to culture, religion, ideology, or social organizations may resemble Finleyan substantivism, where it differs is in allowing for divergent outcomes. The embeddedness of economic behavior in non-economic activities need not result in stasis, but frequently produces change: as a result of their structure, economies expand and contract, grow and fail. Even if such change does not necessarily resemble modern growth, it remains historically significant. Thus, by eschewing both primitivist and modernist stances, current economic discourse gives space to both structure and performance and returns a welcome balance to the conversation.[34] This is all relevant because the Mid-Republic should be recognized as a moment of change in terms of both economic aspects, structure and performance. A major reorganization of Rome's sociopolitical hierarchy during this time, the emergence of the patricio-plebeian *nobilitas*, was closely linked to new modes of production and consumption as the Roman state's initial steps toward empire began to enrich the ruling elite as never before. As Fabius Pictor claimed, only at this time did Romans "first come to know the meaning of wealth."[35]

---

hard to disentangle redistribution or reciprocity from markets, while the question remains of the extent to which individual examples of profit-seeking behavior ever characterized the Roman world as a whole. See the very different views of Bang 2008; Hobson 2014. Tchernia 2016 provides an excellent overview of Roman trade that is not modernizing.

33. North 2005: 23–37; Granovetter 2017; for economic sociology, see Smelser and Swedberg 2005; for the subjectivity of rationality, see Simon 1983.

34. Morris, Saller, and Scheidel (2007: 2) note that Weber espoused similar views in the early twentieth century.

35. Fabius Pictor *FRH* F24 = Strabo 5.3.1, tying the statement to the conquest of the Sabines without further specification, although the quip fits the traditions surrounding M.' Curius Dentatus' campaigns in the 290s, when sources contrasted elite *frugalitas* and *paupertas* to the wealth of those whom Rome was conquering.

Recognizing the Mid-Republic as a fundamental moment of change for the economy of Rome as both city and emerging empire is important, as an outpouring of recent work concentrates almost entirely on the economic history of the Late Republic and Empire, when the expansion and stabilization of trade networks across the Mediterranean supported an economic efflorescence. This focus carries its own sort of implicit modernism by insisting that the Roman economy only becomes historically interesting when its level of production was highest and, for that reason, most comparable with the modern European world, a point of reference I am resistant to for reasons mentioned above. Moreover, there is often a latent misunderstanding of what constitutes economic growth. Even if the Imperial economy's level of production was comparatively high, it was also relatively stable. Since *growth* is a dynamic process implying change over time, scholarly interest in structure and performance should emphasize periods of expansion and contraction, when the rate of change was highest, rather than the more stable, if impressive, period of Imperial rule itself.

It is therefore more than a simple matter of complementing current study with that of other less well-known periods like earlier Rome. The Mid-Republican economy deserves attention in its own right. Indeed, several indications suggest that the decades before and after 300 BCE were fundamental to the institutional structure of the later Roman economy.[36] If we look, for example, to the city's hinterland, it was in that moment that fine-wares and amphorae produced at Rome or in Roman contexts were first exported around the Italian peninsula and into the Western Mediterranean. Closer to the city, the concomitant proliferation of proto-villae or large farmsteads in the *suburbium* indicates increasingly intensive agriculture in response to rising urban demand. Coinage, one of the essential ingredients of the Roman economy, began around that time and marked a new chapter for an economy that turned to metallic wealth for novel purposes. And, finally, the organizational mode of production appears to shift with the decline of older forms of dependency-based labor and the rise of slavery and wage labor. At the same time, the city experienced physical as well as demographic and economic development; the overlapping of all of these trends was hardly coincidental.

This book situates developments in the city within the context of broader economic change by arguing that the features of an urban economy emerged at Rome in this period. It is necessary to justify what is meant by urban

36. Morel 2007.

economy, since by many measures Rome had been a city for centuries prior to the Mid-Republic.[37] The Archaic Roman state certainly built on a large scale, particularly in the sixth century in the period traditionally associated with the Tarquinian monarchy.[38] However, a key difference between the Archaic city and the city of the Republic and Empire can be seen in the essential division between agricultural and non-agricultural labor.[39] Since urban workers did not grow their own food, their material well-being depended upon both the creation of an agricultural surplus and the exchange of that surplus between town and countryside, implying costs of transporting and transacting commodities. Such qualities imply that urban labor was necessarily more costly than rural labor, and urban work therefore speaks to economic complexity and growth. These aspects make urbanism important to any understanding of overall Roman economic performance, while Rome's emergence as a major urban center seems in and of itself to problematize the notion that the Roman peasant economy was entirely cellular and autarkic.[40]

However, the situation is complicated by the fact that the division of labor between agricultural and non-agricultural production in antiquity was not always identical to the division between rural and urban labor. As Erdkamp points out in an important paper, in many peasant economies including Rome's, farming households found themselves for structural and seasonal reasons with surpluses of labor, which they deployed in activities beyond food production. This allowed workers whose primary location remained in the countryside to contribute meaningfully to the labor supply of urban centers.[41] Meanwhile, rural estates in Italy often drew on nearby urban populations for periods of high demand, such as the harvest, or for building work on rural estates.[42] Thus, at certain times and places in antiquity, there were regular flows of labor between towns and countryside, and this problematizes categories of "rural" and "urban" from an economic perspective. A fluid location of labor was typical of parts of Classical Greece, where high rates of urbanization have been postulated on the basis of citizens who politically and administratively

37. Fulminante 2014.

38. Hopkins 2016; Lulof and Smith 2017.

39. The study of pre-modern cities has focused on labor at least since Childe 1950, if not from Adam Smith, as see Finley 1999: 192; cf. Bairoch 1988: 9.

40. Finley 1999: 192–96 was not unaware of this; generally, Morley 2011; Wilson 2011.

41. Erdkamp 1999.

42. E.g., Cic. *Att.* 14.3.1 with Virlouvet 1995: 176.

identified with central *poleis*, but who mostly worked in the countryside or *chora*.[43] These Greek *poleis* conform well to Weber's model of agrarian towns or *Ackerbürgerstädte* (farmer-citizen cities), where many "urban" citizens were in fact primarily engaged in agricultural production beyond the city walls, and where citizen farmers came together in urban centers for political activity.[44]

There is little reason to doubt that such overlap between urban and rural labor persisted to varying degrees in many communities throughout antiquity. It is reasonable to think that Archaic Rome was a Weberian farmer-citizen city.[45] What is important for present concerns is that, while fluidity characterized the labor supply of many Roman towns, the characterization hardly applies to the Late Republican and Imperial capital. Some of Rome's free urban population may have found occasional work on suburban estates, of course, but the balance of production and labor decidedly tilted toward the city itself. Evidence for urban craftsmen, merchants, and other specialized non-agricultural workers in Rome makes it impossible to deny that a very large number of people resided and worked in the *urbs*. It is axiomatic to think that Rome was home not only to this growing skilled working population, but also to a large group of unskilled and underemployed residents who depended for their livelihood on casual employment in the urban labor market. Brunt famously argued that Imperial building programs were a primary source of casual employment for such residents.[46]

This book dates to the Mid-Republican period the transition of Rome's labor supply from that of a Weberian farmer-citizen city to that of a more urban-centered working population. Consequently, I argue that the division of labor at Rome between agricultural and non-agricultural work began to conform more consistently to the geographical division between rural and urban during the Mid-Republic. The evidence for craft and other non-farming productive activities at Rome increases considerably at that time, and a similar pattern is observed in evidence pertaining to commercial agents and relevant institutions. As this discussion suggests, the economic changes detailed in this book were by no means limited to building, and other productive

43. Hansen 2006 with De Ligt 2012: 200.

44. Weber 2000: 5, 88; cf. Scheidel 2007: 82; for the utility of Weberian urban categories to antiquity, see Hansen 2000.

45. Bradley (2017: 131) argues that Tarquinian Rome was not a farmer-citizen city, but the indications he gives for this (trade, migration, large-scale construction) can also be found at Archaic Athens, which conformed well to the farmer-citizen model.

46. Brunt 1980; Bernard 2016a.

activities frequently enter into this study. However, building represents one of the best means of accessing these developments, both because of the outsized costs implied, and because the activity presents historians with several forms of useful evidence.

1.4. The Evidence

The study of the dynamics of urban production in more recent societies often depends upon information for real incomes drawn from prices and wages. Obviously, this sort of material is lacking for our period, not only because we no longer possess documents that may have contained price information, but because, more fundamentally, we are looking at the very earliest moments of a monetized Roman economy. Instead, this book depends largely on archaeological and textual evidence. Other materials also feature prominently: considerable attention is paid to the nature of early Roman coinage as it sheds light on the urban economy, while important epigraphic documents exist, even if not in the same quantity as for later periods.

Since archaeology and textual sources require different approaches, some introductory remarks will be useful. In total, there are about two dozen sites, which are dateable on the basis of building technique, material, or in some cases related finds, to the Mid-Republic; a list may be found in the catalog in appendix 2. That the majority of these sites appear to relate to public monuments is not coincidental, since public financing normally allowed for more costly and less perishable building materials. The corpus includes larger complexes such as the Forum, Largo Argentina, or the sanctuary beneath the Capitoline beside the church of Sant' Omobono. Sections of the Republican walls are found in several locations around the city. By contrast, the material record of private housing in Republican Rome is extremely thin prior to the second century BCE, and not especially full after that. Some important tomb complexes, such as the famous monument of the Cornelii Scipiones, also provide important information.

The evidence that exists consists of those parts of monuments built in non-perishable materials, particularly the stone podia and foundations of various structures. Terracotta roof tiles also fall in this category, although this class of material has received more detailed study for the Archaic period than for the Republic.[47] The general state of preservation does not shed

47. Winter 2009; Hopkins 2016; see Strazzulla 1981.

FIGURE 1.5 Interior podium wall of Temple A at Fosso dell'Incastro, Ardea, Latium. Holes visible on blocks are for the insertion of lifting tongs.
Photo © M. Waters.

light on certain topics. There is only a speculative idea of what architectural elevations looked like in this period, as we do not actually know how tall a single building built at Rome was prior to the mid-second century. Still, the available evidence remains useful if particular questions are asked of it. Several blocks in various monuments around the city, for example, preserve holes cut for the attachment of lifting machines (figure 1.5). Close observation also reveals a great deal about the stonemasonry techniques employed in different monuments throughout the city. The existence of these and other indications of the building process, while much other material evidence for architecture has been lost, promotes the study of labor and economics, since such evidence speaks to the practices of workers responsible for producing the city's urban fabric.

It is sometimes put forward that the archaeological evidence for the period is more objective and thus holds greater historical utility than its textual counterpart. This insistence on a "buildings-first" approach is not new and appeared, for example, already in the late nineteenth century, when the British archaeologist John Henry Parker proclaimed that his "work is avowedly grounded upon the existing remains and not made out of other books; and the existing remains are my evidence of the truth of its statements their reconstructions."[48] Before this, a similar discourse arose in the context of eighteenth-century Pyrrhonist criticism of ancient sources, which led to the

48. Parker 1878: xix.

elevation of (initially) antiquarian research on non-textual sources, and the development of ancillary disciplines like numismatics and epigraphy.[49]

The insistence on the objectivity of archaeology gained great force as scholars became increasingly aware of problems contained in the textual record. Historians of the Republic will be very familiar with the typical criticisms applied to the period's literary sources. The problem is essentially this: those extant witnesses to the historical tradition such as Livy, Dionysius of Halicarnassus, and Diodorus Siculus wrote during the Late Republic, long after the events they described. Moreover, the historiographical tradition they transmitted did not exist prior to the Second Punic War, since it was only then that Fabius Pictor wrote the first Roman history. Perhaps we may allow that the problem becomes less acute the further we move into the living memory of our earliest historians.[50] And an emphasis on the innovation of Fabius Pictor tends to imply an overly narrow view of what Roman history entailed.[51] It is not true that there were no records or mechanisms of recording events prior to Fabius Pictor. From the later fourth century, there was rising interest among Greek historians and intellectuals in gaining familiarity with Rome. We may also point to a variety of non-historiographical forms of writing about the past in the Mid-Republic, from historical epics by Ennius and Naevius, to the performance of historical dramas, to the antiquarian investigations of Varro.

Nevertheless, we must still admit that the fullest available ancient accounts accessed their information through the filter of several centuries' of transmission, and so the question of how to use textual evidence is as important as the information it contains. In this book, I operate under the assumption, necessary but to my mind justified, that our extant sources ultimately derived information about the city from a core of authentic documentary information. But I also maintain that we must contend with the fact that such information was subject to a process of interpretation and elaboration already in antiquity. Oakley provides the best exposition of the forms of information underlying the Roman annalist tradition, and his analysis leaves little doubt that some of our surviving record depended on archival material.[52] Nonetheless, Polybius' comments on the document containing the first Roman-Carthaginian treaty,

---

49. Momigliano 1950.

50. Poucet 2000: 117–29.

51. Purcell 2003.

52. Oakley 1997–2005 vol. I, 21–108.

dated to 509 BCE, should be considered more broadly (3.22.3): by Polybius' day in the second century BCE, the treaty's arcane language made its interpretation difficult even in the hands of Roman specialists.[53] The linguistic obscurity of epigraphic documents from Archaic Rome and its surroundings like the *Lapis Niger* inscription or the Pyrgi tablets give a real sense of how strange this material must have seemed even in the time of Fabius Pictor to those who were then using it to access the Roman past. Thus, modern historians should not dismiss the literary sources, while caution is also necessary as the treatment of the authentic material upon which ancient accounts depended was difficult then as it remains now.

An ongoing debate also concerns the extent to which the annalists' "expansion of the past," the creation of fuller narratives from meager archival material, has distorted the accuracy of historiography for the sake of its literary merits.[54] While scholars are right to point out that writing history was considered in Roman antiquity to be a literary practice, I side with Damon in noting that historiography's rhetorical register still operated within the limits of the genre's stated aim to transmit a record of events.[55] Famously, Aristotle stated that poets and historians were not distinguished by their respective uses of meter and prose, but by the fact that poets wrote of potentialities, "things that might happen," while historians wrote "things that have happened" (*Poet.* 9). This highly schematic division does not describe all ancient historiography, but it does confirm the existence of a basic ancient expectation that historical writing in some sense strives to conform to the shape of real events.

The approach sketched out here that authentic material can be drawn with due caution from the extant sources is not new, and readers may look to any number of studies for fuller discussion.[56] Perhaps it may be complained that this method does not provide a truly objective or mechanical way of determining the merits of a particular episode in Livy or other authors, but one might ask whether that standard is ever fairly applied. The written record of Mid-Republican Rome has taken on fabrications and manipulation over the course of its formation and transmission and must therefore be treated

53. See Richardson 2008.

54. The phrase from Badian 1966. Wiseman 1979; Woodman 1988 foreground rhetorical and literary; Lendon 2009 offers a strident rebuttal.

55. Damon 2007.

56. Cornell 1986; 2005; Oakley 1997–2005 I; for skeptical views, see Millar 1989; Forsythe 2005; Raaflaub 2005. Wiseman (2008: 15) acknowledges the fourth century as a turning point for the sources' reliability.

critically on a case-by-case basis with a constant and deep awareness of context; but surely this describes the responsibilities of historians of any period of antiquity to some extent. In the spirit of Hopkins, while I submit that individual arguments drawn here from the literary evidence may be susceptible to criticism at the margins, I hope nonetheless that this book's overarching model of Mid-Republican Rome best incorporates all evidence at hand.[57]

With particular regard to the evaluation of literary evidence for the developing city's form, the most valuable material are those notices of urban building projects vowed, contracted for, or dedicated by various magistrates. While information about the Republican city comes down to us in other ways, such notices constitute the primary basis of the book's catalog of building projects and are an indispensable source of data for urban history, particularly as a reflection of public monuments and state investment in infrastructure. The best source for such notices is Livy who commonly lists building projects in the annalistic notices that conclude his record of each year's events. We are rarely as well informed of the scope and extent of public construction as when we possess such lists: it may partly be an artifact of their existence that we see, for example, such a large spike in known construction projects in the first quarter of the second century BCE (cf. figure A2.1 in appendix 2). How reliable are these notices? There are reasons to think that certain pressures independent of Livian or broader historiographical tradition stimulated the commemoration and transmission of information about Roman public monuments, and this encourages a degree of optimism. Temple foundations, for example, held importance for marking festivals or rites, and such dates therefore could serve communal purposes. Purcell emphasizes the importance of such information to Mid-Republican historical consciousness by noting Cn. Flavius' anchoring of his foundation of the shrine of Concord in 304 BCE to the 204th year "after the foundation of the Capitolium."[58] Aristocratic competition also played a role in promoting the preservation of valuable information. The construction of almost all public building projects in this period was overseen by magistrates who were senators and thus members of the ruling elite. Because of this, contributing to the city's built landscape was an important way of making a magistrate's accomplishments and offices visible to his peers, but personal involvement in a monument's history needed to be made explicit to create any political effect.

---

57. Hopkins 2002, esp. 191–93.

58. Plin. *NH* 33.19; Purcell 2003: 26–33.

It is in the context of political promotion and the competition for individual *gloria* that notices of building projects first appear in some epigraphic or otherwise non-historiographical contexts from the Mid-Republic. The funeral *elogium* of L. Cornelius Scipio (consul 259 BCE) inscribed on his sarcophagus from the Tomb of the Scipios, for example, recorded his offices, his military accomplishments in Corsica, and then concluded with the notice that "he gave a temple deservedly to the Tempestates." This inscription was likely composed in the late third century, contemporary with the career of Fabius Pictor. It thus provides proof that the act of adding to the city's monumental landscape was recorded in the archival record.[59] Similar pressures may have motivated the eventual practice of inscribing one's name and, sometimes, accomplishments directly onto an actual building. Livy shows his use of this sort of record in citing the lengthy historical inscription above the doors of the Temple of the Lares Permarini, while his reports of censorial building have been demonstrated to show similarities with the language of Republican building inscriptions.[60]

Thus, a record of Roman building projects, particularly public construction, plausibly existed from some point in the Early Republic, when its creation and transmission were supported by various religious or political motivations. And there are reasons to think that historians like Livy drew from this source of information. This does not mean the record is unimpeachable or can be read uncritically. Indeed, the same aristocratic competition that encouraged commemoration also sometimes produced distortion as Roman elites tried retroactively to claim historical actions for their family or for their ancestors.[61] However, *a priori* skepticism about public building projects is unwarranted.

At the same time, this discussion emphasizes the limitations of the literary evidence for urban history. It goes without saying that the magistrates who "built" temples, basilicas, aqueducts, and roads credited to them normally did little of the actual designing and building, and there are exceedingly few cases of senatorial magistrates taking direct interest in Republican architecture as a practice. In this case, while the extant textual evidence is plausibly based on authentic material, it is also of a particular quality. As an authentic notice of

---

59. *CIL* I² 9; for date and context, see *LTUR* IV s.v. "Sepulcrum (Corneliorum) Scipionum" 281–85 (F. Zevi), esp. p. 284.

60. For the Lares Permarini, see Liv. 40.52.4–7 with Briscoe 2008: 551; censorial lists: Gast 1965.

61. Wiseman 1986.

building from the third century BCE, the aforementioned elogium of L. Cornelius Scipio is indicative: the inscription only says that Scipio "gave" (*dedet*) a temple to Tempestates. The vague verb does not relate whether Scipio vowed or dedicated the temple, nor how it was paid for or built. In short, very little technical information can be expected from either this sort of material or sources dependent upon it. Meanwhile, Vitruvius' statement, explored in greater depth in chapter 7, that Republican builders were generally disinclined to commit their trade to writing also will have limited the technical information on building available to our extant sources (*De Arch.* 7.*pr.* 18).

There is in this case a potential complementarity between the textual and physical evidence for building in Mid-Republican Rome. The literary record provides useful data about the chronology, overall authorship, and location of urban building projects at Rome. The material evidence speaks to how those buildings were built, but reveals little specific information about a monument's sociopolitical or historical context. Such complementarity promotes a method of combining two different sets of material in a way that does not simply seek to corroborate or disprove one set of evidence with the other, but rather hopes to build a more complete narrative of urban change from the combination of different forms of material.

1.5. The Structure of the Book

This study is arranged in six analytical chapters and two technical appendices. Chapter 2 introduces the organization of the supply of various building materials to Roman construction. The chapters that follow then take up different themes relating to the economic development of building in the city over time. The arrangement of topics progresses in roughly chronological fashion, but rather than give a narrative of building projects or architectural developments in Mid-Republican Rome, these analytical chapters are intended to be read as self-standing but related monographs. Chapter 3 investigates the effects of the Gallic sack on the city and its economy, while chapter 4 uses a quantitative model to explore the labor cost of the Republican walls. The subject of chapter 5 is the large-scale reorganization of urban production in the late fourth century in the hands of an emerging Roman political elite. Chapter 6 details the resulting growth of slave and free wage-labor in the city as seen from the wider viewpoint of urban production, and chapter 7 looks at similar themes from the more focused perspective of building technology. Collectively, the narrative traces the shifting productive mode of Rome's economy and its relationship to the urban supply of labor.

The first appendix discusses the quantification of labor costs for construction in the sort of building techniques typically attested for this period and is meant to be used in tandem with cost analyses presented in several chapters. The second appendix serves the study as a whole by presenting a catalog of attested public building projects at Mid-Republican Rome.

2 MATERIALS AND SUPPLY

Cities were impressive consumers of building materials, and the production of urban architecture entailed supply chains of great complexity. Writing in the Early Empire, Strabo compared Roman architecture's constant demand for timber and stone to the city's voracious consumption of grain, and he noted Rome's fortunate situation in respect to respective supply routes:

> The city, although it has grown to such an extent, holds out in the way it does, not only in respect to food, but also in respect to timber and stones for buildings. . . . . To meet these requirements, the Romans are afforded a wonderful supply of materials by the large number of mines, by timber, and by the rivers which bring these down.[1]

The passage suggests that, at that time of Strabo's writing, most building resources still arrived to Rome from inland down the Tiber, rather than up from the seaport at Ostia. That is, even into the Early Empire, building supply remained largely focused on Central Italy. In this regard, Rome benefitted not only from its location, but from its political ability to extract materials from the quarries, mines, and forests of Italy, a situation directly resulting from the conquest of the peninsula. This context directs our attention to the development of supply routes during the Mid-Republican, when Rome expanded its power into Italy.

While most of this book examines the mobilization of human resources at Rome, this chapter introduces the material resources used by Mid-Republican builders prior to the start of

---

1. 5.3.7: ἐπὶ τοσοῦτον αὐξηθεῖσα ἡ πόλις ἀντέχει τοῦτο μὲν τροφῇ τοῦτο δὲ ξύλοις καὶ λίθοις πρὸς τὰς οἰκοδομίας . . . πρὸς ταῦτ᾽ οὖν τό τε τῶν μετάλλων πλῆθος καὶ ἡ ὕλη καὶ οἱ κατακομίζοντες ποταμοὶ θαυμαστὴν παρέχουσι τὴν ὑποχορηγίαν.

marble and concrete architecture in the mid-second century BCE. I start with stone, which is best attested archaeologically, before turning to what is known about the supply of other materials. Discussion closes with some evidence for the institutional frameworks that surrounded the city's supply of building materials. In general, the chapter reveals the unsurprising importance of imperialism to the shifting geography of supply, but also the complex relationship between territorial expansion and the city's use of natural resources.

2.1. Stone

Prior to 146 BCE, when the city's first marble temple was built of imported Greek stone, Rome's builders relied exclusively on the stones of Central Italy. Since the appearance of ashlar masonry at Rome in the early sixth century, Republican masons worked predominately with dressed rectangular blocks for the foundations, and eventually the elevations, of both public and elite private architecture until the expanded use of mortared aggregate in the second century.[2] In this case, we confront a nearly four hundred year development of an architectural practice exclusively involving Central Italian cut-stone. Fieldstone is rare in public construction of this period, while polygonal masonry, popular from an early period in Latium, mostly does not appear at Rome, no doubt because the capital lacked the ready supplies of limestone employed for polygonal construction by Latin masons.[3]

While a later chapter takes up the socioeconomic implications of Rome's evolving supply of stone, here it will be helpful to review the physical characteristics and provenance of stones typically employed by Mid-Republican stonemasons. In doing so, it is important to acknowledge that such discussion is greatly enhanced through recent geological research.[4] There is little doubt that future work, including ongoing petrochemical study, will continue to expand our understanding.[5] The geology of the district around Rome, shown in the maps in figures 2.1 and 2.2, is dominated by rocks erupted from nearby

---

2. For early ashlar masonry at Rome, see Cifani 2001; 2008: 238–39; Hopkins 2016: 39–65.

3. I owe this observation to F.M. Cifarelli. While unknown in the urban core, polygonal masonry appears beyond Rome's walls along the Via Tiburtina; see Helas 2016: 592–93.

4. Fundamental earlier works are Frank 1924; Blake 1947; Lugli 1957. See now Funiciello 1995; Marra and Rosa 1995; Jackson et al. 2005; Jackson and Marra 2006; Panei and Dell'Orso 2008; Panei 2010.

5. Marra et al. 2011; Farr, Marra, and Terrenato 2015.

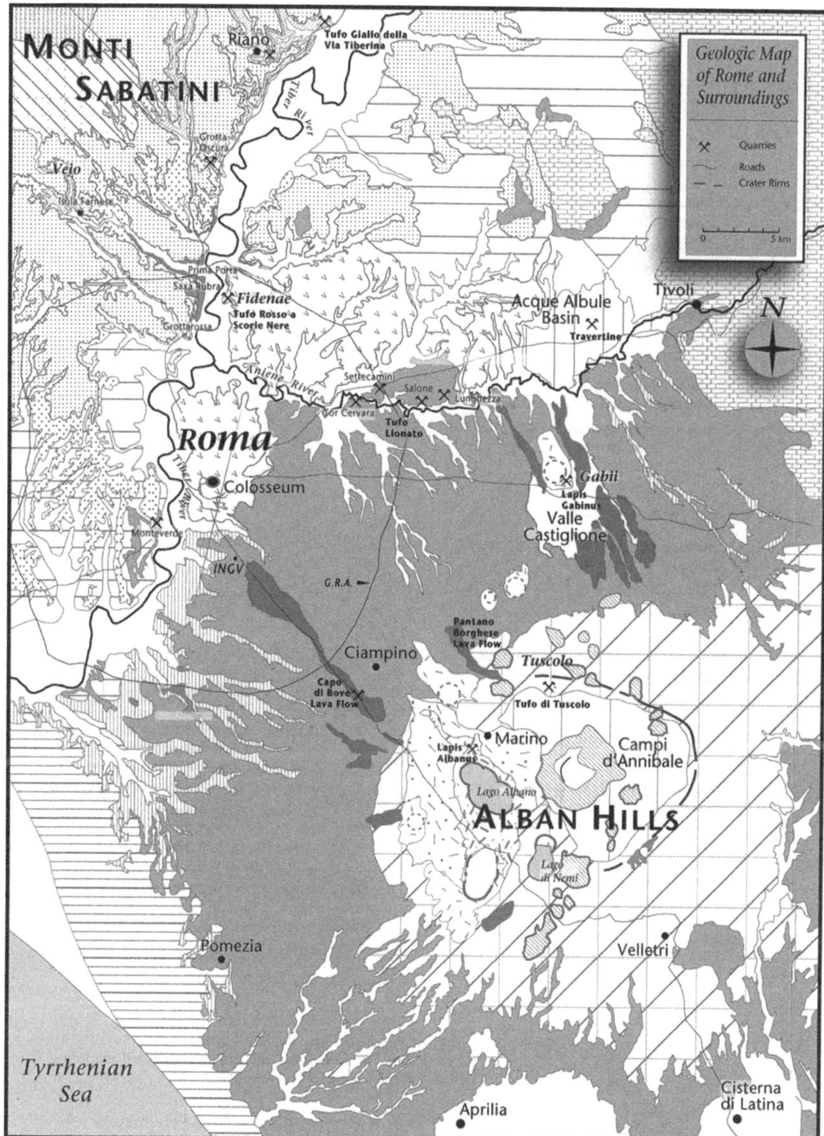

FIGURE 2.1 Geological map of Rome and its surroundings showing the disposition of different deposits of tuff and the location of ancient quarry zones.

Map reproduced with permission from Jackson and Marra 2006.

volcanoes and exposed to human quarrying by the erosive power of the Tiber and Anio rivers. The stone most commonly employed for Mid-Republican ashlar masonry was tuff, in Italian *tufo*, the product of welded pyroclastic material deposited by at least seven different volcanic eruptions in the Monti

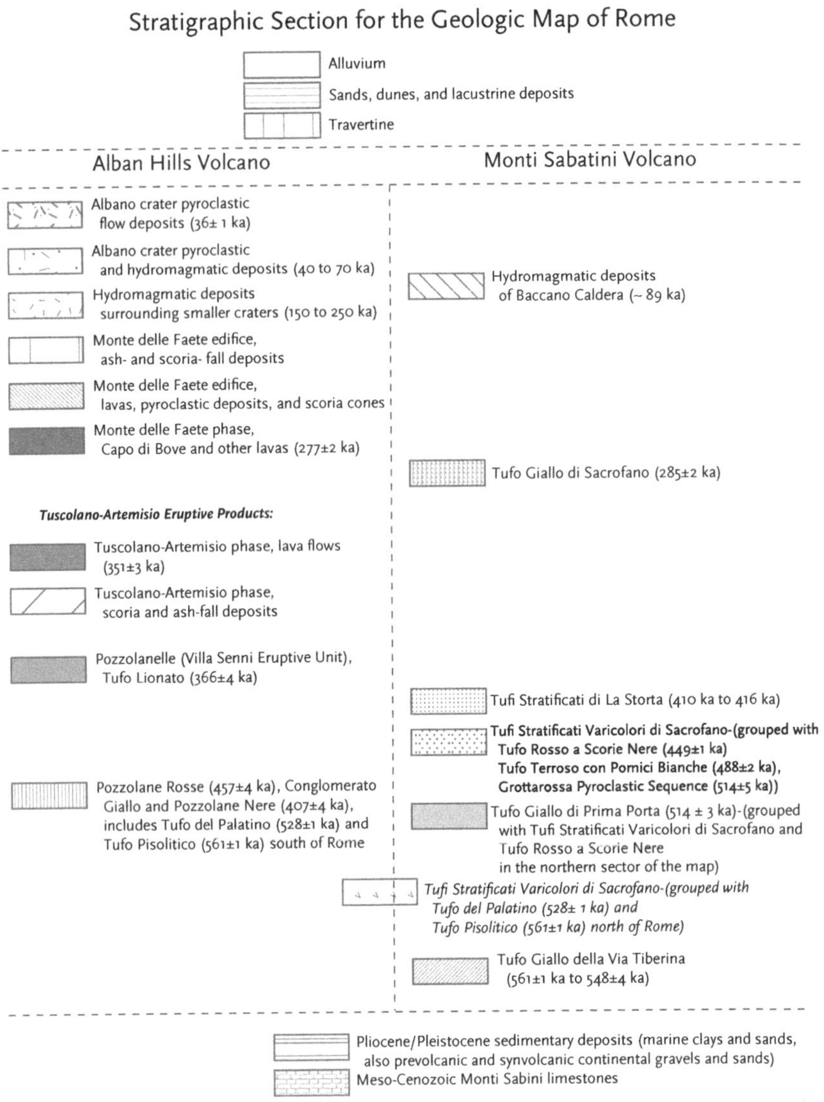

Stratigraphic Section for the Geologic Map of Rome

Alluvium
Sands, dunes, and lacustrine deposits
Travertine

Alban Hills Volcano

Albano crater pyroclastic flow deposits (36± 1 ka)
Albano crater pyroclastic and hydromagmatic deposits (40 to 70 ka)
Hydromagmatic deposits surrounding smaller craters (150 to 250 ka)
Monte delle Faete edifice, ash- and scoria- fall deposits
Monte delle Faete edifice, lavas, pyroclastic deposits, and scoria cones
Monte delle Faete phase, Capo di Bove and other lavas (277±2 ka)

Tuscolano-Artemisio Eruptive Products:

Tuscolano-Artemisio phase, lava flows (351±3 ka)
Tuscolano-Artemisio phase, scoria and ash-fall deposits
Pozzolanelle (Villa Senni Eruptive Unit), Tufo Lionato (366±4 ka)
Pozzolane Rosse (457±4 ka), Conglomerato Giallo and Pozzolane Nere (407±4 ka), includes Tufo del Palatino (528±1 ka) and Tufo Pisolitico (561±1 ka) south of Rome

Monti Sabatini Volcano

Hydromagmatic deposits of Baccano Caldera (~ 89 ka)
Tufo Giallo di Sacrofano (285±2 ka)
Tufi Stratificati di La Storta (410 ka to 416 ka)
Tufi Stratificati Varicolori di Sacrofano-(grouped with Tufo Rosso a Scorie Nere (449±1 ka) Tufo Terroso con Pomici Bianche (488±2 ka), Grottarossa Pyroclastic Sequence (514±5 ka))
Tufo Giallo di Prima Porta (514 ± 3 ka)-(grouped with Tufi Stratificati Varicolori di Sacrofano and Tufo Rosso a Scorie Nere in the northern sector of the map)
Tufi Stratificati Varicolori di Sacrofano-(grouped with Tufo del Palatino (528± 1 ka) and Tufo Pisolitico (561±1 ka) north of Rome)
Tufo Giallo della Via Tiberina (561±1 ka to 548±4 ka)

Pliocene/Pleistocene sedimentary deposits (marine clays and sands, also prevolcanic and synvolcanic continental gravels and sands)
Meso-Cenozoic Monti Sabini limestones

FIGURE 2.2 Stratigraphic section and key for the geological map of Rome. Map reproduced with permission from Jackson and Marra 2006.

Sabbatini to the north and the Alban Hills to the south. As Rome lies at the juncture between these two areas of volcanism, the surrounding subsurface geology is relatively complex, and rocks with sometimes very different physical properties can be found within a small area. The earliest varieties of tuff employed by Roman architects were found within the area of the city itself from the Monti Sabbatini eruptions. From the fifth century, tuffs from the Alban Hills also appeared in Roman monuments. In general, the Monti Sabbatini tuffs contain more glass fragments and are more porous and less well-cemented, making them of poorer quality for building. Alban Hills tuffs are more compact and better cemented and are thus more durable for architectural uses.[6]

The local rock found in Rome's earliest stone architecture is *tufo del Palatino*, often called *tufo grigio* or *cappellaccio* in scholarship. This olive-gray tuff is among the softest of the class of tuffs erupted from the Alban Hills.[7] Quarries on the Palatine give the stone its geological name, and galleries on the hill's western side extending for approximately 4.5 km were explored in the nineteenth century. Surface quarrying also took place near the area of the later Temple of Victory.[8] Ancient quarries of similar material have been discovered on the Esquiline hill near the course of the *agger*, as well as in extensive underground galleries found along the Via Nomentana to the northeast.[9] An ancient toponym "quarries" (*lautumiae*) associated with an area at the foot of the Capitoline may indicate the presence of early quarries on that hill (Varr. *Ling.* 5.151; Fest. Paul. 104 L).

Tufo del Palatino was used to build substantial Archaic monuments such as the platform of the Temple of Jupiter Optimus Maximus, the podium of the Temple of the Castores, or the Archaic *agger* wall. With the introduction of other, more durable tuffs, the use of this particular stone became less dominant, although *tufo del Palatino* continued to appear in public monuments, typically in hydraulic structures or below-ground foundations, into the second century BCE.

The next most significant stone in terms of the quantity employed by Mid-Republican builders was *tufo giallo della via Tiberina*, the yellow friable material used in copious quantities to build the Mid-Republican circuit walls (A6). The stone is often called Grotta Oscura tuff after its best-known quarries along the right bank of the Tiber about 15 km from the city. The stone, erupted from the Monti Sabbatini, is porous, friable, and poorly cemented, making it of limited quality as a dimension stone even as it dominated urban architecture in the fourth and third centuries BCE. The southern extension

---

6. Jackson and Marra 2006.

7. Jackson and Marra 2006: 419–20; the stone is fairly consistent in Archaic architecture, but see Diffendale et al. 2016 on a variant used in the early temple at Sant' Omobono.

8. Tomei 1998.

9. Cifani 2008: 221–34; material from the city's east and northeast tends to be of better quality, as see Jackson and Marra 2006: 420.

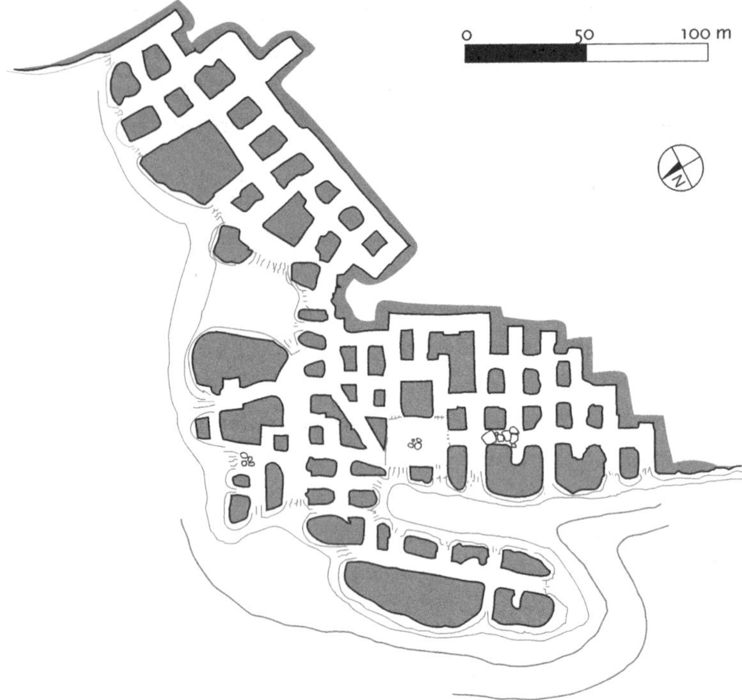

FIGURE 2.3 Plan of the *tufo giallo della via Tiberina* quarries at Grotta Oscura. Plan © S. Bernard after Ashby 1929.

of the *tufo giallo* deposit in the area of Prima Porta produced a more lithified stone, but these quarries were not exploited in great quantity during the Mid-Republic. There is some evidence of surface quarrying, but *tufo giallo* was mostly extracted in extensive underground galleries as at Grotta Oscura, where galleries were formed by carving out crisscrossing channels and a central chamber, open to the sky, facilitated the raising of quarried material to ground level where it could be conveyed to the river for transport to Rome (figure 2.3).[10]

Using Ashby's plan of Grotta Oscura, it is possible to estimate that this quarry provided some 43,000 m^3 of building stone.[11] Nowhere near sufficient

10. Ashby 1924: 134–38.

11. To form this estimate, I traced the plan in Google SketchUp and created a 3D model assuming after Ashby 1924: 136 that the galleries' original height was approximately 2.5 m, while the large central chamber reached a height of 10 m. The resulting area is 43,021.5 m^3. These quarries were damaged by WWII bombing, as cf. Carbonara and Messineo 1996: 294–95.

for the city's building industry, this volume represents slightly more than a tenth of the total material required to build the Republican walls.[12] Thus, these gallery quarries, even as they appear of considerable size, must have been only part of a much larger operation.[13] That no other *tufo giallo* quarry of equivalent size has been identified suggests that the overall operation relied on multiple small- to medium-sized quarry zones throughout the district, rather than on a few massive quarries, and the implications of this system are revisited in this chapter's closing section.[14]

Along with *tufo del Palatino* and *tufo giallo*, other stones in Mid-Republican architecture include *lapis Albanus* or *peperino di Marino*, the hard green tuff quarried from the crater of the Alban Mount. Recent study of the building materials of the Early Republican phases of the twin temples at Sant' Omobono confirms the use of this stone at Rome by the early fifth century BCE.[15] Access to these quarries was perhaps facilitated through nascent political relationships between Rome and other city-states in Latium during the early years of the Latin League. Notably, *peperino* was the only stone from beyond Rome's immediate environs brought in large quantities to the Republican city by land, presumably along the Via Latina, rather than by waterway. In the late nineteenth century, Ashby documented large gallery quarries for *peperino* near the train station of Marino.[16]

By the fourth century BCE and possibly earlier, Roman builders employed *tufo rosso a scorie nere*, or Fidenate tuff, in public monuments.[17] This Monti Sabbatini tuff from near Fidenae on the right bank of the Tiber is easily recognizable for its reddish-brown matrix and frequent, sometimes large, inclusion of gray scoria and lava. Also from the right bank of the Tiber, but closer to the city, were quarries of *tufo lionato di Monteverde*, or Monteverde tuff. This more lithified tuff appears in Roman architecture from the fifth century onward, but not regularly or in large volumes, though the reasons for its

12. For the tuff needed to build the walls, see p. 97.

13. Similar evidence consisting of multiple small quarries, one of which is firmly dated to the Mid-Republic, reported by Buccellato and Coletti 2014 from Mezzocammino in the *suburbium*.

14. The other *tufo giallo* quarry of noteworthy size at Fosso del Drago is smaller than Grotta Oscura. Numerous other single gallery quarries or smaller pits along the Via Tiberina are noted by Carbonara and Messineo 1996.

15. Farr, Marra, and Terrenato 2015.

16. Buranelli and Turchetti 2003: 99.

17. E.g., in the Temple of Juno Moneta (A14). For limited earlier use, see Cifani 2008: 223.

sparing use are unclear. A large underground quarry, perhaps a main source for this stone, has recently been identified in the area of Stazione Trastevere, but the site has yet to see scholarly publication.[18]

Two harder and higher quality stones from Latium first appear at Rome toward the very end of the period under consideration. The first is *tufo lionato di Aniene*, the well-lithified red tuff first used in great quantity for the construction of the Aqua Marcia (144 BCE). Several large quarries of this stone remain visible along the Via Flaminia on the north bank of the Anio.[19] The second is travertine, the white durable limestone found in great quantities near Tivoli. The quarrying of this sedimentary rock for architecture in Rome started in the second century and continued throughout antiquity. Strabo notes that travertine arrived at Rome via the Anio river, which ran by the quarries (5.3.11). The long life of the Tivoli quarries continues today, and little evidence remains of the ancient quarry pits.[20]

Before turning from the topic of stone, we should note the supply of ingredients for plaster. There is little evidence from Rome itself, but enough to demonstrate that here, as elsewhere in Latium, ashlar masonry was often plastered over, presumably for a mix of aesthetic and protective reasons, and traces of plaster can still be seen in some contemporary contexts outside the city (figure 2.4).[21]

The practice of covering exposed mud-brick with simple clay slip appears in evidence from the Archaic period.[22] More complex surface preparations involved a calcium carbonate base such as lime, and limestone for making plaster was available in Central Italy.[23] In 179 BCE, the censors contracted out for covering the columns of the Temple of Jupiter Optimus Maximus (A116) with "white," presumably lime-based plaster.[24] Writing around the same time,

---

18. 150,000 m³ in size, noted in *Corriere della Sera*, 28 November 2013, Maria Rosaria Spadaccino, "Monteverde, sotto la catacomba una antica cava di tufo."

19. Quilici 1974.

20. Mari 1983.

21. At Largo Argentina, Marchetti Longhi (1932: 298–99) found traces of light plaster coating the podium of Temple C and incised with lines coinciding with masonry joins so as to retain the external appearance of stonemasonry, similar in appearance to Pompeian first style wall painting; see also Marchetti Longhi 1936: 107 on Temple A; Nielsen and Poulsen 1992: 78 for the Temple of the Castores.

22. Brown 1967: 54–59 on the Regia.

23. Lancaster 2005: 16; see Christensen 1992.

24. Liv. 40.51.4: *poliendas albo*.

FIGURE 2.4 Plaster preserved on the podium of Temple B at Fosso dell'Incastro, Ardea, Latium.

Photos © S. Bernard (inset) and M. Waters.

Cato gave detailed instructions for the construction of a limekiln (*fornax calcaria*), although he probably intended it to produce lime for fertilizer.[25] Lime preparations were often painted. Scientific analysis of plaster on architectural elements from a Mid-Republican farmhouse in Trastevere confirms the use of ochre for yellow and red pigments by the third century.[26]

2.2. Clay Resources

The use of fired brick for walls began at Rome only in the Late Republic and related closely to the development of *opus caementicium*. Brick structures can be found as early as the third century in Italian contexts, especially in Magna Graecia but also in the Roman colony of Fregellae, although the technology does not seem to have circulated to the capital.[27] Fired tile, however, first appeared in roofs at Rome by the early sixth century BCE at a very similar

25. *De Agr.* 38; Kay 2014: 230.

26. Filippi 2008: 51; similar compounds in second century frescoes from the Temple of the Castores noted by Christensen 1992; for the supply of exotic pigments, see Gliozzo 2007.

27. Fregellae: Diosono and Battaglini 2010; cf. Manzelli 2000 on the brick walls of Ravenna, the date of which is debated. For Magna Graecia, see Johannowsky 1982.

date to the earliest stone foundations.[28] This coincidence makes sense as the two technologies related to each other: firmer foundations were necessary to support heavier roofing systems. Tile roofs quickly became regular for public and larger private architecture. A fragment of the Late Republican author Cornelius Nepos, cited by the Elder Pliny, states that Roman (private?) buildings were roofed in wooden shingles up to the time of the Pyrrhic War. However, as tiles commonly appear earlier, this cannot be entirely true, and it has been suggested that the passage relates to a prohibition during the Pyrrhic War of wooden tiles in favor of clay ones in an attempt to make urban housing more fire resistant in an increasingly dense city.[29] If true, tile production at Rome must have picked up considerably in the early third century. So little evidence for the size of urban residential architecture in this period exists that an informed guess as to the scale of this increase is impossible. Some general indication for the requirements of an aristocratic house's roof may, however, be found in the Caesarian *lex coloniae genetivae*, which specified that colonial *decuriones* own houses of a minimum size of 600 tiles, and other *coloni* own a minimum size of 300 tiles.[30] Cato paid a worker two *nummi* per tile for installing a roof (*Agr.* 13.4). If *nummus* here refers to the bronze *as*, then this rate was notably high, and installing the roof of a non-elite house of 300 tiles cost half a soldier's annual wage in the same period.[31]

The two main ingredients in Republican tiles were clay and chaff; according to Lucilius, tilemakers never owned much more than mud and wheat husks.[32] Recent petrochemical analysis shows developments in the supply of one of these ingredients: the city's very earliest tiles employed clay beds in the Velabrum, while clay from areas outside Rome was used for the fabric of tiles of the sixth to the second century BCE. The exurban fabric also represented a technological improvement with the addition of inclusion material to

28. Hopkins 2016: 39.

29. Plin. *NH* 16.36: *scandula contectam fuisse Romam ad Pyrrhi usque bellum annis CCCCLXX Cornelius Nepos auctor est.* Cf. Ogilvie 1965: 750–52; Robinson 1992: 29.

30. Caballos Rufino 2006: 219–23.

31. This assumes a date before the re-tariffing of the denarius, and that a soldier received 120 denarii per year; see Kay 2014: 287. Two *nummi* was the daily wage for a drover at *Agr.* 22.3.

32. 9.352–53 Warmington = Non. 445.13: "He who makes bricks never has more than common clay and chaff, mixed mud and grain-husks," *lateres qui ducit habet nihil amplius numquam quam commune lutum ac paleas caenumque aceratum.*

limit cracking and shrinkage.[33] This shift may find parallel in the literary record. In his extensive discussion of Rome's topography, Varro located several toponyms relating to the production of clay artifacts in the *argiletum* just to the north of the Forum (5.157), in two areas identified as potters' quarters (*in* or *inter figlinis*), one on the Oppian spur of the Esquiline (5.50), and another in the circus valley between the Palatine and Aventine (5.154). Notably, by the time of Varro's writing in the Late Republic, one and perhaps two of these areas were occupied by activity other than clay working: the *argiletum* was the site of the *macellum* (A80), while the circus probably replaced any previous industry in its location.[34] By contrast, the Esquiline *figlinae* remained active into the Mid-Republic, as confirmed by a kiln found in the area in the late nineteenth century. The potential dislocation of Esquiline tile makers from clay resources around the Forum may reflect increasing complexity in both the spatial and economic organization of production, with greater specialization between those responsible for extracting clay and other additives and those involved in producing finished objects.

Important as they must have been to both public and private Mid-Republican architecture, vernacular technologies like unfired mud-brick, rammed earth, and *pisé de terre* have left little trace in Rome's archaeological record and are likely to have depended on local materials. [35] This does not mean that such techniques were crude. From a third-century BCE residential context in Trastevere, we find fragments of a Doric frieze and a faux-masonry wall decoration fashioned out of stuccoed-over clay mixed with chaff.[36]

2.3. Plant Resources

The perishable nature of timber and other plant resources limits discussion of the supply of such materials to Republican builders. Still, the scarcity of extant evidence conceals what were probably extraordinary demands for building timbers, as well as for tools, scaffolding, and also for fuel for metal or tile production.

---

33. Ammerman et al. 2008; Winter et al. 2009. Their sample concentrates on Archaic tiles, and further work on Mid-Republican material may change this picture.

34. It is also possible that the circus *figlinae* still existed on the eastern side of the valley near the *porta Capena*.

35. Fentress and Russell 2016.

36. Filippi 2008.

The best trees for construction produced long and hard but relatively light timbers.[37] Pine and especially silver fir, native to the Apennines, produced long beams prized in antiquity for architecture and shipbuilding. Fir represents almost 60% of timbers preserved from structures at Pompeii and Herculaneum.[38] Other species of trees native to Italy were recognized by writers such as Pliny and Vitruvius to have particular utility: cypress was resistant to decay, alder was good for use in wet ground, while dense but heavy oak was excellent for foundations or for tools.[39] Such ancient discussions imply that different species of tree were used, when available, for different parts of a building in a manner attentive to their respective physical properties. Confirmation of this practice appears in the so-called *lex Puteolana parieti faciendo*, an inscription dating to 105 BCE from Puteoli recording the contract for building an addition onto a temple. The document stipulates the use of oak for the structure's doorpost, lintel, and corbel, while fir was to be used for the components of the roof (*CIL* X 1781).

The sources reveal the evolving urban timber supply. Pliny was struck by the fact that numerous toponyms in the built-up area of his contemporary Rome reflected the earlier presence of stands of trees (16.15):

> At all events (Rome's) different regions used to be denoted by designations taken from the woods: even now the Precinct of Jupiter of the Beech Tree (*Fagutalis Iovis*) is where there was once a grove of beeches, the Oak-forest Gate (*Porta Querquetulana*), Willow Hill (*Viminalis*) in which willows were sought, and all the groves, certain ones named from two types of trees. When the plebs seceded to the Janiculum, it was on Chestnut Hill (*Aesculatum*) that the dictator Quintus Hortensius carried the law that what the plebs ordered should be binding on all citizens.[40]

The availability of trees within the city itself is attested here, but, as urban resources were progressively exhausted or built over, Rome turned to Central

37. Meiggs 1982; Ulrich 2007.

38. Ulrich 2007: 242; cf. Vitr. 2.9.2.

39. Meiggs 1982: 240; see Vitr. *De Arch.* 2.9; Plin. *NH* 16.213–30.

40. *NH* 16.15.37: *silvarum certe distinguebatur insignibus, Fagutali Iove etiam nunc ubi lucus fageus fuit, Porta Querquetulana, Colle Viminali in quem vimina petebantur, totque lucis, quibusdam et geminis. Q. Hortensius dictator, cum plebes secessisset in Ianiculum, legem in Aesculeto tulit ut quod ea iussisset omnes Quirites teneret.*

Italian forests often praised by ancient authors and made available by conquest. In several instances, sources closely tie Republican expansion in Italy to the acquisition of new timber resources. Livy recalled how, in 310 BCE, the brother of the consul was sent to gather information about the Ciminian forest "in those days more impenetrable and frightening than until recently were the forests of Germany" (9.36). In the early third century, the submission of the Bruttii brought half their territory into Roman hands, including significant forestland. According to Dionysius of Halicarnassus, Bruttium was full of timber "suitable for building houses and ships and all kinds of construction." Large timbers, he went on to say, were brought down to the coast, while inland forests provided smaller timbers transported overland (20.15.5–6).

Considering the visibility and importance of forestlands in the narrative of Italian conquest, it may even be asked whether some of Rome's expansionist activity was undertaken in part with the intention to acquire better access to timber. A remarkable notice in this regard comes from Theophrastus' *Historia Plantarum*, written in the late fourth century BCE. Theophrastus appended a notice on the prodigious size of fir trees in Corsica with a story of a Roman attempt to colonize the island and, failing that, to carry away some of its excellent timber (5.8.2). Shipbuilding, not construction, seems to have been Rome's primary motivation in seeking Corsican timber, but fir was important to both productive activities, and the aforementioned passage on the forests of Bruttium in Dionysius reinforces how closely related the respective supply chains were.

Rome never seems to have exhausted the timber resources of Central Italy, as Strabo states more than once that most of the city's building timbers came inland down the Tiber (5.2.5, 5.2.7). However, building in the Mid-Republic may have sometimes strained this region's supply. In the fourth century, Theophrastus described Latium as being essentially forestland, with bay, myrtle, and excellent beech at low elevations, and fir at higher altitudes (5.8.3). By the early second century, these resources may have had difficulty meeting the demands of urban consumption. Frank suggested that several reports of bad flooding in Rome around 200 BCE reflected deforestation for shipbuilding and construction.[41] Related to this may have been the fact that a "portico among the wood-workers" (*porticus inter lignarios* A96) was built along the Tiber in 192 BCE by the *porta Trigemina* by the foot of the Aventine, in a position better suited to receive timber from Ostia, rather than

41. Frank 1933: 174–75.

downriver from the Tiber Valley.[42] As this might attest, the third and early second centuries may have seen some short-term deforestation owing to the timber demands of shipbuilding and increased urban construction.

Besides timber, the construction industry demanded great quantities of rope, especially as cranes became more complex and heavy loads of stone were lifted to higher levels. Even high quality ropes could survive only a finite amount of stress, and ropes for lifting heavy loads needed to be replaced frequently.[43] Rope-making is a little studied topic for all periods of Roman construction owing to an almost total lack of evidence.[44] The identity of at least one Republican rope-maker is known: Mark Antony apparently taunted Octavian that his great-grandfather was a rope-maker.[45] The agronomists provide some useful information: Varro lists hemp, flax, rush, and esparto as useful for making rope (*Rust.* 1.23.6). Pollen analysis from Lake Nemi confirms that hemp was cultivated probably for rope-making in Latium during the Roman period.[46] Cato specifies that lifting ropes (*funes subductarios*) be made from esparto (*spartum*), and that the best such ropes were bought in Capua (*De Agr.* 135.3). Esparto was associated with Spain, where it grew wild, and Pliny knew it as a product mostly of that province (*HN* 19.7.26–27).

2.4. Metal

As with plant resources, material evidence for the metal used in Mid-Republican architecture is lacking. Metal is an often overlooked component of building supply but was of importance not only for nails, door hinges, architectural sculpture and ornament, and so forth, but also for the manufacture of shovels, pickaxes, and other tools used in clearing and excavating building sites, or processing and shaping stone and wood, among many other tasks. Metalworking was thus closely linked to building, and the production of metal sometimes even took place at construction sites, as attested, for

42. Meiggs 1980: 186; 1982: 246–47; Diosono 2008: 90–91; Harris 2013: 178.

43. Fitchen 1986: 118–19.

44. White 1975: 29–38 for rope in Roman agriculture.

45. Suet. *Div. Aug.* 2. Gell. *NA* 10.17.2 cites D. Laberius, a contemporary of Caesar, who wrote a mime about a *restio*. *CIL* VI 9856 records an imperial *collegium restionum*.

46. Mercuri, Accorsi, and Bandini Mazzanti 2002.

example, by a forge discovered adjacent to the Capitoline Temple of Jupiter Optimus Maximus.[47]

The Republican city's chief source of iron and bronze was most likely Tyrrhenian Italy and its adjacent islands, particularly Sardinia. The fame of these areas as sources of metal may have played a role in attracting the earliest seaborne exploration from the Eastern Mediterranean to Italy.[48] Rome itself had no native metal resources; however, traces of metallurgy in late Bronze Age layers on the Capitoline confirm that trade links with mining districts were longstanding.[49] Republican military expansion into the mineral-rich areas of Etruria and Sardinia will have helped meet demand for metal, and this lends importance to the period of Italian conquest for the development of the urban supply of metal.[50] Roman interests in Sardinia are apparent already in mention of the island in the first Roman-Carthaginian treaty of 509 BCE (Polyb. 3.22.9). Torelli detects an early but failed attempt by Rome to establish a colony on the island in the mid-fourth century BCE.[51] Ultimately, the conquest of the Central Tyrrhenian coastline in the early third century, and particularly the metal rich area around Populonia, brought significant mining districts under Roman control. Recent work downdates much of Populonia's Hellenistic architecture, including its fortification walls, to the period after the Roman conquest of the region.[52] Meanwhile, signs of a flourishing mining industry appear at Populonia and Elba starting c. 300 BCE, shortly after Rome's conquest of the Etruscan coastline.[53] It seems plausible that connection with Roman markets encouraged the growth of this mining district. Beyond Italy, Spain was not only important for precious metals like silver and gold, but was noted by Cato as a source of iron.[54]

High demand for Italian metal supported the emergence of a factor market of sorts in which unprocessed ore from Elba was shipped to Puteoli,

47. Lugli 2001: 314–17; Cifani 2010: 45.

48. Pallottino 1991: 59; Ridgway 1992: 5.

49. Giardino and Lugli 2001.

50. According to Pliny (*NH* 3.138; 33.78), at some point, perhaps in the second century BCE, the working of *metalla* in Italy was forbidden by an otherwise obscure *senatus consultum*; see Harris 1971: 110 n. 7.

51. Torelli 1981.

52. Mascione and Salerno 2013; C. Mascione pers. comm.

53. Dallai 2009; Firmati 2009: 187–88.

54. Gell. *NA* 2.22.28–29 = Cat. *Orig. FRH* M. Porcius Cato F116.

where craftsmen formed it into finished products. Diodorus, who described the shipping of ore from Elba to Campania, noted that, while some of this production related to weapons, Puteoli's metalworkers produced agricultural implements and other tools for sale in Italian markets (5.3.1). While Diodorus described this system of production in the context of the late Republic, Corretti argues that the practice existed by the third century. He bases his argument on Livy's list of donations made by Etruscan cities to Scipio's fleet on the eve of the invasion of North Africa: while Populonia provided Rome with iron ore (*ferrum*), weapons and armor came from Arrezzo.[55] As with other extractive activities discussed above, little is known about those individuals involved. The Roman name Aulus Vettius inscribed on an early third-century BCE black-gloss cup from the port of Elba has been identified as an early *negotiator* in the metal trade, but this is merely speculation.[56]

2.5. The Question of Organization

The supply of material to private building seems easy enough to envision: landowners might rely on what resources existed on their own property or else use various forms of exchange to acquire additional material from elsewhere.[57] However, the organization of supply to public construction in the city was different, both because public architecture's monumentality implied higher demand for materials, and because the responsibility of provision ultimately fell to the Republican state. One way in which the state could arrange supply was through the direct control of mines, forests, and quarries. Such an arrangement implied additional needs to provide labor for extracting and processing materials, as well as to organize transport. This arrangement appeared, for example, in the imperial granite quarries at Mons Claudianus, which seem to have been worked largely by military labor and with public funds. However, the imperial state held a monopsony on massive granite columns, and Russell stresses that this sort of state-run quarrying represented only a small portion of the total extractive activity in the Imperial Mediterranean. More often, state and private concerns overlapped.[58] One way to knit

55. Corretti 2009; Liv. 28.45.15.

56. Firmati 2009: 188.

57. Cf. Cato *Agr.* 14.3, according to which the owner was responsible for supplying builders working on his estate.

58. Russell 2013.

together public and private exploitation was to shift public arrangements to private contractors, who also supported private demand and took on the responsibility of supplying capital and labor within their larger portfolio. Such contractors were ubiquitous throughout Italy by the second century BCE (Polyb. 6.17), and the use of contractors pertained, for example, to Rome's earliest supply of Greek marble to public architecture in close connection with private demand.[59]

There are reasons to think that private supply also figured importantly into Mid-Republican construction when masons relied on local tuffs. Consumption patterns between private markets and public needs intersected, something observable in the appearance of the same stones in Mid-Republican public architecture and monuments identified as private residences. Moreover, the fact noted above that one of the largest *tufo giallo* quarries at Grotta Oscura were insufficient to meet urban demand suggests a diffuse pattern of extraction, drawing from resources on both public and private land. DeLaine notes the proximity of villas to some tuff quarries, particularly the *tufo lionato di Aniene* quarries on the Via Flaminia, where one villa was even built atop quarry waste.[60] Elsewhere in Latium, other villas have been found in close proximity to smaller quarries, and a relationship between private property and stone quarrying has been suggested.[61] In the *Res Rusticae,* Varro considered the possibility that stone quarries might be worked on private land as part of an estate's larger productive portfolio (1.2.23).

Mixed private and public organizational modes also pertained in the manufacture of tiles and bricks. Mingazzini argued for the Late Republican state's dominance over brick production in continuation of Mid-Republican practice.[62] He based this argument largely on a passage of the Caesarian *lex coloniae genetivae* regulating the operation of tile kilns:

> No one is to have tile kilns (*figlinae teglariae*) of a greater capacity than 300 tiles or tile-like objects within the walled area of the colony. Anyone who will possess one, let this building become public property,

59. Bernard 2010.

60. DeLaine 1995.

61. Buccellato and Coletti 2014. See Pensabene, Gasparini, Gallocchio, and Brilli 2015 on the villa and quarries of Cottanello.

62. Mingazzini 1986.

and let whoever is legally in charge of this building pay the money (from its operation) without deceit into the public treasury.[63]

The passage hardly supports the idea of state domination of this industry. While Mingazzini interpreted the law as indicating the prohibition of private ownership of such sized kilns, in fact the opposite is implied, as the *lex* sought to regulate the location and scale of private production. If anything, the passage confirms the existence of kilns operated on both private and municipal levels, albeit on different scales. The 300-tile capacity describes a medium-sized tile kiln, so that this law encompassed most, but not all, production.[64] Also noteworthy is the clause's final stipulation implying the continued state production of tiles within the colony's walls, since it addresses the collection of profits from such activity. Thus, no attempt is made here, as sometimes argued, to exclude tile-making from the *urbs* for fear of fire or pollution.[65] Instead, the text points to kilns of mixed ownership within urban sites like Rome.[66]

The *lex coloniae genetivae* places us in the context of the last decade of the Republic, although the law's content probably derives from some indeterminately earlier date. Still, what evidence there is for earlier Italian tile production suggests a similar overlap of organizational interests. Both Livy and Diodorus reported that, in the wake of the Gallic sack of Rome, the senate provided residents repairing their houses with tiles at public expense. Diodorus recorded that "up to the present time these [sc. roof tiles] are known as *politikai*" (14.116.8). For reasons discussed in the following chapter, these statements are highly rhetorical and the emphasis on the role of the senate is untrustworthy. Nothing from Rome corroborates Diodorus' reference to "public tiles" (*politikai*), as the vast majority of Roman stamped bricks from the Late Republic and Empire relate to privately owned *officina*. However, by the fourth century BCE more than a dozen communities in southern Italy and

---

63. *RS* vol. I no. 25 §76: *figlinas teglarias maior<e>s tegularum (trecentarum) tegulariumq(ue) in oppido colon(iae) Iu(iae) ne quis habeto. qui habuerit, it{a} aedificium isque locus publicus colon(iae) Iul(iae) esto, eiusq(ue) aedificii quicumque in c(olonia) G(enetiva) Iul(ia) i(ure) d(icundo) p(raerit), s(ine) d(olo) m(alo) eam pecuniam in publicum redigito.*

64. Harari (2002: 277–79) estimates the large east tile kiln at Corinth (7.5 × 5.5 × 2.0 m) could "easily fire ca. 900" tiles. Based on this, most Italian examples noted by Cuomo di Caprio 1971–72 fall within the law's restrictions.

65. Sensible discussion in Goodman 2007: 106–8.

66. For the essentially Roman character of municipal laws, see Frederiksen 1965.

Sicily are known to have stamped tiles and bricks with a mixture of both private names and indications of public ownership such as *poleôs, basilikos*, and *dêmosios*. This early practice of stamping bricks and tiles was not restricted to Greek-speaking communities of Italy, as examples with Oscan stamps, again including a mixture of both the names of private individuals and indications of public ownership, have been found dating to the same general timeframe.[67]

Insisting on fluidity in Rome's supply of building materials between state and private involvement also helps accommodate the dynamics of property ownership through this same period. So far, this discussion has assumed a clear division between private and public ownership of resource-rich territory and productive capital. Of course, the situation was far more complex and seems particularly fluid in the period concerned. Private property as a category existed by the Archaic period, or at least by the time of the Twelve Tables.[68] The early development of communal or publically held land remains much debated. At issue is the supposed ownership of land by extended family structures such as the *gens*, and how this form of ownership somehow gave way to the development of *ager publicus*, or land considered the property of the state but available to individual cultivation.[69] While this development is too complex to be treated here in its entirety, it is noteworthy that sources portray the Mid-Republic and particularly the early fourth century as a moment of innovation in Roman conceptions of property, as well as one of tension between private and collective ownership.[70] After some alleged attempts to secure the viritane distribution of land in the late fifth century, territory within the newly conquered *ager Veientanus* was distributed individually to Roman citizens in the 390s. *Ager publicus* became an issue at the same time with the first law limiting its possession passed in 367. All of this is relevant because it alerts us to the fact that the institutional framework surrounding access to productive land in Rome's widening territory was changing rapidly at the start of the Mid-Republican period. Thus, it would be incautious, and probably unrealistic, to say that either public or private interests dominated the supply of material resources at this time.

67. Vecchio 2009–12.

68. Roselaar 2010: 21–22.

69. Smith 2006: 235–50; Roselaar 2010; Viglietti 2011; Capogrossi Colognesi 2012; Carafa 2017: 60.

70. Capogrossi Colognesi 2012: 32–33.

In sum, those quarries, forests, mines, and clay beds responsible for supplying the Mid-Republican city's builders were likely under diverse ownership. In turn, the organization of building supply depended upon a spectrum of arrangements from this early point. Undoubtedly, imperial expansion mattered to the shape of supply: successful warfare brought new forestlands or mining districts within Roman control. However, the complex management of newly acquired territory meant a concomitantly complex system of supply in the wake of conquest.

One final aspect to reemphasize is the chronological importance of the fourth and third centuries BCE to Roman architecture from the perspective of supply. Expanding Roman power entailed territorial gains into the Ciminian forest, the woodlands of Bruttium, or the metal-rich Tyrrhenian coastline. By the early empire, as Strabo attests, Central Italy continued to provide Rome's builder with much of their necessary material, and this speaks to the importance of the Mid-Republican period of Italian conquest for the enduring shape of the city's supply of building materials.

3 ROME FROM THE SACK OF VEII TO THE GALLIC SACK

According to our sources, the most important event for the formation of the Republican city was the burning of the earlier city by invading Gauls sometime around 390 BCE. It is well known that the sack shaped both Roman history and historical memory in important ways, and this chapter focuses on the fire's particular effects on Rome's physical form. The sack's impact was expressed in dramatic terms by the Imperial epitomator Florus:

> I thank the immortal gods for the very fact of so great a disaster. For that fire concealed the houses of shepherds, and the flame hid the poverty of Romulus. What else did that conflagration accomplish, but that a city, destined to be home to men and gods, should seem not destroyed or overturned, but rather cleansed and purified?[1]

This idea of urban discontinuity was widely reported: the Archaic city founded by Romulus and developed by successive kings was destroyed completely by fire (*incendium*), allowing the Republican city to emerge as if from nothing. Not only this, but the sack's effects were closely linked to Rome's labor supply. The tremendous physical effort required to create the new *urbs* was held to have played a significant role in the formation of a new Republican society. Livy gives the fullest account of the fire's social and economic consequences, placing reconstruction at the center of his domestic history for several decades after the sack. The labor cost of rebuilding

---

1. Flor. *Epit.* 1.7, *agere gratia dis inmortalibus ipso tantae cladis nomine libet. Pastorum casas ignis ille et flamma paupertatem Romuli abscondit. Incendium illud quid egit aliud, nisi ut destinata hominum ac deorum domicilio civitas non deleta nec obruta, sed expiata potius et lustrata videatur?*

Republican Rome caused a debt crisis among the plebs, in turn leading to the collapse of the Roman state, which was reconstituted only through the radical admission of the plebs to the consulship. Upon closer inspection, Livy's text contains the usual mixture of more and less credible components. While there are reasons to uphold specific elements of his account, the overarching narrative of sack, rebuilding, debt, and political collapse is less sound. In particular, the destructive *incendium*, which set this chain of events in motion, finds little basis in the archaeological record, even accounting for some recently published excavation.

The critical view of the *incendium* taken here is not new, and scholarship has found reason to critique ancient accounts of the sack since the eighteenth century.[2] However, this source criticism holds broader if insufficiently considered implications. One question that remains difficult to answer is why the conquest of Veii in 396 BCE and the subsequent increase of Roman territory did not ameliorate the problems that seem to have hampered Rome's economy since at least the mid-fifth century. Despite a significant expansion in its territory, Rome shows few signs of economic growth for several decades. Herein lies the issue: the sources blamed continuing difficulties on the costly effort to repair the city after the sack, but if a devastating Gallic *incendium* is untenable, it follows that the idea of rebuilding all Rome is as well, and we must reassess the continuing pressures on the Roman economy of the early fourth century.

In offering such a reassessment, this chapter insists that a historiographical discussion of the sack holds important historical implications. I evaluate the Gallic sack's repercussions for Roman urbanism while also seeking to understand the broader historical implications of a minimalist interpretation of the sack's physical effects. After discussing the traditional narrative of Rome's destruction and reconstruction, this chapter turns to the development of the early fourth-century economy and argues for increasing pressures on Rome's labor supply, as labor became a rising concern to Roman landholders after Rome's conquest of Veii. This discussion intends to be read in tandem with the following chapter, which focuses on the labor cost of the largest monument built at Rome in the Mid-Republic, the new circuit walls dated by Livy to 378 BCE.

2. For modern historiography, see Ampolo 1983; Briquel 2008: 34; Delfino 2009: 340.

3.1. Livy's Account

While multiple sources document the sack itself, Livy's sixth book provides the only extant continuous narrative from the sack to the passage of the Licinio-Sextian laws in 367 BCE, and the work thus takes on central importance. Rebuilding Rome dominates the domestic history of the first half of Livy's sixth book, picking up on a theme emphasized in the final chapter of book five, which covered Rome's conquest of Veii and the Gallic sack and the repair effort in its immediate aftermath:[3]

> The city began to be rebuilt indiscriminately. Brick was provided at public expense, and it was made legal for anyone to quarry stone and other material wherever they wished, so long as they made guarantees that they would complete construction within the year. Haste removed their concern for arranging the streets, while, after any discretion had been set aside for what was their own or belonged to another, they built up the open spaces. This is the reason that the old sewers that once ran through public space now here and there run under private houses, and the form of the city resembles one occupied rather than distributed.[4]

Any understanding of this passage must begin by recognizing its artificiality. The idea that rapid city-foundation resulted in a chaotic urban plan makes little sense, as irregular streets were more likely to arise from long-term settlement accretion and continuity. Orthogonal street plans already appeared in Latium from the fifth century, and there is no reason to think that a city laid out in that period would not have followed a similarly ordered pattern.[5] Livy himself was sensitive to the fact that something unusual was required to produce an irregularly planned *urbs* in this manner, hence the passage's final claim that the urban form was more *occupata* than

---

3. This section draws from Bernard forthcoming a.

4. 5.55.3–5: *promisce urbs aedificari coepta. Tegula publice praebita est; saxi materiaeque caedendae unde quisque vellet ius factum, praedibus acceptis eo anno aedificia perfecturos. Festinatio curam exemit vicos dirigendi, dum omisso sui alienique discrimine in vacuo aedificant. Ea est causa ut veteres cloacae, primo per publicum ductae, nunc privata passim subeant tecta, formaque urbis sit occupatae magis quam divisae similis.*

5. Mogetta and Becker 2014. Ostia's rectangular *castrum* belongs in the fourth century (Coarelli 1990b: 136–43; Martin 1996; Zevi 1996); other fourth-century *castra* at Lavinium (Jaia 2013) and Ardea (Di Mario 2009).

divisa, contrary to expectations. *Dividere* was the verb for the partitioning of land accompanying the establishment of a Roman colony.[6] The denial of Mid-Republican Rome as an *urbs divisa* may intend to contrast the new plebeian city with the divinely ordered Archaic *Roma quadrata* of Romulus and Numa, and this is not the only place where Livy's account of the refoundation of Rome in book six used the monarchic foundation of Rome in book one as a point of comparison.[7]

One important question for present concerns, and one that has played a central role in Livian studies in general, is the degree to which Livy transmitted or reinterpreted his sources. At first glance, Livy's "reading" of his contemporary Rome's urban form as attributable to post-sack repairs might argue for autopsy and originality. However, Diodorus Siculus appended a similar observation on the rapid construction and chaotic urban form to his account of the sack, adding the further detail that publically supplied roof tiles continued to be known in his day as *politikai* (14.116.8). These slightly different versions of the same episode suggest that both authors drew from an earlier source. Still, Livy's attention to the placement of this passage within his larger narrative design is clear. Before and throughout the sack narrative in book five, Livy highlighted the physical nature of the *incendium*.[8] The theme of urban construction continued immediately at the start of book six when, after his prefatory remarks, Livy described the plebs "engaged in the constant work and effort of rebuilding the city."[9] However, at this point Livy started to change his tone, and the plebeian rebuilding effort that began innocuously enough started to play a role in rising social friction. At 6.4.5, a *senatus consultum* had to be passed to recall those plebeians who, tired of rebuilding Rome (*pigritia Romae aedificandi*), had begun to migrate to Veii.[10] Rebuilding was thus no longer something that the state encouraged by easing restrictions on building materials, but the senate now compelled a reluctant populace to participate. After the requisite labor returned from Veii to Rome, the repair of the city came to an end, again with state intervention (6.4.6):

6. *TLL* s.v. *divido* §I.C.1.a.

7. Luce 1971; Kraus 1994; and below.

8. Ruins appear even before the Gauls arrive (5.39.12); later, the Gauls wage war upon Rome's buildings themselves (5.43.1); rubble impedes Camillus in the Forum (5.49.4).

9. 6.1.6: *cum civitas in opere ac labore assiduo reficiendae urbis teneretur.*

10. Kraus 1989: 217–19.

> Rome swelled with the crowd and the whole city grew at once with buildings, with the state defraying the expense and the aediles urging on work as if it were public, and with private citizens themselves hastening to have finished their work. . . . Within the year, a new city stood.[11]

While this concluded the effort to rebuild the city post-sack, it did not mark the end of the theme of building in Livy's narrative. After the election of the next year's consuls, Livy placed the first annalist notice of public construction in book six (6.4.12):

> In the same year, lest the city grow so much only with private buildings, the Capitoline was fortified in ashlar masonry, a work worth seeing even in the present magnificence (*magnificentia*) of the City.[12]

Notices of public construction are rare in this part of Livy's work, and this makes this passage, coming after the conclusion of the post-sack rebuilding, striking.[13] There are other signs here of attention to larger narrative designs: the Capitoline *substructio* was not the first time in Livy's work that earlier Roman structures compared favorably to the architecture of his contemporary city. At 1.56.2, Livy remarked similarly on the Tarquinian work on the circus and cloaca, "two works which are scarcely rivaled by any recent magnificence (*magnificentia*)."[14] *Magnificentia* as a word to describe architecture served to tie together Tarquinian Rome, these Mid-Republican projects, and the works of Livy's own day, presumably the projects of the triumvirs or Augustus and Agrippa. Livy had praised the *magnificentia* of the king's building projects immediately following his description of the onerous effort (*haud parvus . . . labor*) coerced from the Roman citizens to construct them. As would also be the case in book six, Tarquin's public works came at great

11. *et Roma cum frequentia crescere tum tota simul exsurgere aedificiis et re publica impensas adiuvante et aedilibus velut publicum exigentibus opus et ipsis privatis (admonebat enim desiderium usus) festinantibus ad effectum operis; intraque annum nova urbs stetit.*

12. *eodem anno, ne privatis tantum operibus cresceret urbs, Capitolium quoque saxo quadrato substructum est, opus vel in hac magnificentia urbis conspiciendum.*

13. Two other notices in book six: circuit walls (6.32.1–2) and T. Quinctius' Temple of Mars (6.5.8). The *substructio* is the first notice since the Villa Publica at 4.22.7.

14. *quibus duobus operibus vix nova haec magnificentia quicquam adaequare potuit.*

social and political cost, as Brutus would cite the oppressive labor corvées in the service of Tarquin's building program in inciting the Roman people to revolt.

The allusion in book six to the role of building in Tarquin's oppressive tyranny lent building activity an increasingly sinister and destructive characterization, which increased as the narrative unfolded. The tribunes found difficulty calling the plebs, who were preoccupied with construction, to assembly.[15] Concern for building made the plebs scarce in the Forum and forgetful of their land (*immemorem agri*), that is, forgetful of agricultural production. By the middle of book six, the collective effort to build Rome had become a means of political manipulation. The plebs' preoccupation with building interfered with their sensitivity to the monarchic designs of Manlius, who emphasized the debts taken on by the plebeians through their construction efforts, calling building a "most ruinous thing" (*res damnossisma*).[16] In so doing, Manlius' speech recalled Livy's version of Brutus' revolutionary speech at the end of book one, in which reference was made to the coercive building labor required from the plebs by the king.[17] An association between Manlius' seditious speech and Brutus' aforementioned denouncement of Tarquin's public works was facilitated by the fact that, in book six, the Mid-Republican aediles encouraged plebeian construction "as though it were a public work" (6.4.6), transforming private rebuilding after the sack into a sort of public concern. In both cases, Livy portrayed costly building as a rallying point for political revolution.

At the conclusion of Manlius' trial at 6.20, Livy resumed a more recognizable annalist pattern for the next five years. However, construction and its potentially disastrous social effects resurfaced when the building of circuit walls around the city in 378 BCE pushed plebeian debt to disastrous levels (6.32.1–2):

> Although there was a brief space to breathe given to the debtors, after there was quiet from the enemies, legal proceedings were again frequent, and hope of alleviating existing debt was so absent that new debt was accumulated from an assessment for a wall contracted by

15. 6.5.1: *civitate aedificando occupata.*

16. See further Bernard forthcoming a; 6.11.9: *et erat aeris alieni magna vis re damnosissima etiam divitibus, aedificando, contracta.*

17. 1.59.9: *labores plebis in fossas cloacasque exhauriendas demersae.* Dion. Hal. 4.81.2 focuses on extracting materials presumably, but not explicitly, for building.

> the censors to be built in ashlar masonry; the plebs were compelled to submit to this burden because the tribunes had no levy to obstruct.[18]

Unnamed here are the censors Q. Cloelius Siculus and Sp. Servilius Priscus, both from major patrician families, and both with relatives attested as military tribunes in the same year.[19] These censors' construction of the walls was the final explicit mention of building in book six, but the episode had far-reaching consequences. Debt caused by this project forms the last detail of domestic history reported by Livy before the background to the Licinio-Sextian rogations two chapters later, with only a minor campaign against the Volsci in between. This sequence suggests that Livy intended the reader to relate his extended narrative on construction and debt with the anarchy caused by the patrician-plebeian conflict concerning the laws proposed in 376 BCE.

This close reading has shown Livy promoting construction as the engine behind the larger movement of domestic history, well beyond the rebuilding following the Gallic *incendium*. For Livy, rebuilding the sacked city set off a chain of events connecting two fundamental episodes of early fourth-century history: the Gallic sack and the struggle over the admission of the plebs to Rome's highest office. Within this narrative, without the destructive *incendium*, the social problems of the period would have been avoidable.

3.2. The Historiographical Background to Livy's Account

How original was Livy's arrangement, and how far back can the story of a destructive *incendium* be traced? Certain individual elements in the story appear more or less credible: Livy's notices of particular public building projects—the Capitoline *substructio* (A3), the Temple of Mars (A4), and the censors' walls (A6)—more likely than not rested on some documentary basis, and all three find support in the archaeological record.[20] The crucial importance of debt to the early Republican economy, a topic taken up at greater length later

---

18. *Parvo intervallo ad respirandum debitoribus dato postquam quietae res ab hostibus erant, celebrari de integro iuris dictio, et tantum abesse spes veteris levandi fenoris, ut tributo novum fenus contraheretur in murum a censoribus locatum saxo quadrato faciundum. Cui succumbere oneri coacta plebes, quia quem dilectum impedirent non habebant tribuni plebis.*

19. Cf. Liv. 6.31.2; several consular Cloeli Siculi of the fifth century have the cognomen Structus, perhaps relating to building, but see below p. 186 for problems with occupational cognomina in this period.

20. For the *substructio* and walls, see chapter 4. For the Temple of Mars, see Dubbini 2016.

in this chapter, seems credible for many reasons. But what can be said of the narrative framework within which these elements were embedded? On the one hand, Livy's effort to fit the sack into the architecture of his larger history speaks to his own compositional arrangement, as do allusions in book six to his version of monarchic Rome in book one. On the other hand, we may also detect potential influences: in the opening chapter of book six Livy alluded to the claim of the Sullan-period annalist Claudius Quadrigarius that the *incendium* destroyed Rome's pontifical archives and thus rendered Roman history prior to the sack obscure.[21] The parallel claims were not entirely precise, since Quadrigarius apparently denied even the possibility of writing early Rome's history and started his own history with the sack. Livy made the attempt, of course, speaking of the new ability post-sack to give a "clearer and more accurate" (*clariora deinceps certioraque*) account, rather than of the inability to tell earlier history at all (6.1.2). Nonetheless, one is led to think that Quadrigarius' emphasis on the sack as a point of historical rupture may have served to emphasize the story's destructive elements in later versions.

Also influential on the Late Republican elaboration of the *incendium* may have been famous depictions of other city-sacks such as the Roman sack of Corinth and especially the Persian sack of Athens.[22] Parallels between the destructions of Rome and Athens were noted in antiquity. Dionysius of Halicarnassus observed that the rediscovery of Romulus' *lituus* on the Palatine mirrored the regrowth of Athena's olive beside the Erechtheion on the Acropolis (14.2.1–2). Dionysius knew the latter episode from Herodotus, and modern scholarship has focused on Roman allusions to Herodotus' account. But an overlooked passage of Thucydides on the Persian sack of Athens seems particularly relevant to Livy, since Thucydides, not Herodotus, described in fullest detail the rebuilding that followed (1.89.3):

> The Athenian people, after the barbarians had departed from their territory, at once proceeded to convey their children and wives and whatever property they had left from the places where they had deposited them, and they prepared to rebuild their city and the walls, for only a

21. Oakley 1997–2005: I.381–2. Frier's (1979: 122–4) identification of Clodius cited at Plut. *Num.* 1.2 with Quadrigarius is not certain, as cf. Beloch 1926: 104–5; Briscoe in *FRH* I.264–5. Even if these are different writers, however, they share a distinct conception of Roman history.

22. Corinth: Wolski 1956: 43; Athens: Sordi 1984; Williams 2001: 150–54; Richardson 2012: 130–39 with earlier bibliography.

> short part of the circuit remained standing and most of their houses were destroyed.[23]

Thucydides spent an inordinate amount of the *Pentakontaetia*, his narrative of the interim period between the Persian and Peloponnesian wars which this passage starts, describing the construction of Athens' new walls.[24] The Greek historian's attention to wall building at Athens shows striking similarity to Livy's narrative, which closed a narrative of urban rebuilding by focusing on Republican Rome's wall-building efforts.[25] Again, by noting this parallel in the structure of these two historian's work, my intention is not to invalidate the historicity of Livy's notice of a Mid-Republican wall-building project, something for which further corroborating evidence is discussed in the next chapter, but rather to point to possible literary models for Livy's incorporation of the Republican walls into a larger narrative framework of urban destruction and regeneration following the Gallic sack.

As Oakley observes, although the paucity of comparative material makes firm conclusions difficult, so far as we can tell Livy gave one of the fullest treatments of the period after the sack as compared to other Roman annalists.[26] The best extant parallel account of the period is Plutarch's *Life of Camillus*. At *Cam.* 31.1, Camillus guided the plebs in rebuilding Rome; their exhaustion from these efforts led them to consider colonizing Veii until the senate intervened. At Plut. *Cam.* 32.3, immediately after Camillus convinced Romans to remain in their own city, the episode concluded:

> The inclinations of the multitude were marvelously changed. They exhorted and incited one another to the work, and pitched upon their several sites, not by any orderly assignment, but as each man found it convenient and desirable. Therefore the city was rebuilt with confused and narrow streets and a maze of houses, owing to their haste and

23. Αθηναίων δὲ τὸ κοινόν, ἐπειδὴ αὐτοῖς οἱ βάρβαροι ἐκ τῆς χώρας ἀπῆλθον, διεκομίζοντο εὐθὺς ὅθεν ὑπεξέθεντο παῖδας καὶ γυναῖκας καὶ τὴν περιοῦσαν κατασκευήν, καὶ τὴν πόλιν ἀνοικοδομεῖν παρεσκευάζοντο καὶ τὰ τείχη: τοῦ τε γὰρ περιβόλου βραχέα εἱστήκει καὶ οἰκίαι αἱ μὲν πολλαὶ ἐπεπτώκεσαν.

24. See Hornblower 1997: 135.

25. While Quintilian named Livy the Roman Herodotus (*Inst. Orat.* 10.1.101), Thucydidean influence is increasingly acknowledged in modern scholarship: Rodgers 1986; Champion 2014 on the Third Decade; Cornell 2004: 128 sees Thucydides in Livy's account of the Samnite wars.

26. Oakley 1997–2005: I.112.

speed. Within a year's time, it is said, a new city had arisen, with walls to guard it and homes in which to dwell.[27]

This sequence of events contains *in nuce* most of those elements found in Livy: the debate over Veii resolved by Camillus, the harmonious but chaotic rebuilding effort post-sack, new private housing, even new walls. If Plutarch did not use Livy's account, a common source seems likely.[28] However, Plutarch confined the entire sequence to the span of a single year. This corresponds to Livy's declaration that *nova urbs stetit* at 6.4.6, but Plutarch did not return to the theme of building any further in his work, despite some overlap in subject matter with Livy's consequent narrative. If anything, then, this divergence points to Livy's originality in relating the sack's aftermath.

Because the sack was perhaps the most widely attested event in Republican history prior to the Hannibalic War, the questions of precedence and novelty are different for Livy's account of the sack itself than for its aftermath. Modern source-criticism on pre-Livian accounts of the Gaul's invasion has continued unabated since the nineteenth century.[29] Part of the reason for this is a certain degree of ambiguity, and the very fragmentary earlier sources do not always lend themselves to the confident conclusions sometimes made about them. For example, it is often pointed out that the sack was a rare episode in Mid-Republican history known almost contemporaneously in Greece.[30] From various sources, we learn that Heraclides Ponticus, Aristotle, and Theopompus all knew of the Gaul's invasion of Rome by the fourth century. However, the context in which each of these early writers' awareness of the sack is transmitted explicitly emphasized that their information was erroneous or superficial, or else discrepant with the later tradition—not one early Greek account is cited

27. Text and translation from B. Perrin (ed.), Loeb Classical Library edition. θαυμαστὴ δὲ καὶ τὸ πλῆθος ἔσχε μεταβολὴ τῆς ὁρμῆς, ἀλλήλους παρακαλούντων καὶ προτρεπομένων πρὸς τὸ ἔργον, οὐκ ἐκ διανομῆς τινος ἢ τάξεως, ἀλλ᾽ ὡς ἕκαστος ἑτοιμότητος ἢ βουλήσεως εἶχε τῶν χωρίων καταλαμβανομένων. διὸ καὶ τεταραγμένην τοῖς στενωποῖς καὶ συμπεφυρμένην ταῖς οἰκήσεσιν ἀνήγαγον τὴν πόλιν ὑπὸ σπουδῆς καὶ τάχους, ἐντὸς γὰρ ἐνιαυτοῦ λέγεται καὶ τοῖς τείχεσι καινὴ καὶ ταῖς ἰδιωτικαῖς οἰκοδομαῖς ἀναστῆναι πάλιν.

28. Plutarch's use of Livy in the Camillus life is a "hopeless question" (Momigliano 1942: 111 n.2). For contrasting opinions, see Mommsen 1879: 346 n. 91; Thouret 1880: 117; Theander 1951: 72–78; Briquel 2008: 365–67.

29. Mommsen 1879; Thouret 1880; Pais 1918; Roberts 1918; Wolski 1956; Ogilvie 1965; Torelli 1978; Sordi 1984; Williams 2001: 140–84; Briquel 2008; Delfino 2009: 345–56; Richardson 2012: 114–38.

30. Williams 2001: 146.

as useful or accurate. [31] That is, there is no reason to privilege any information simply for its chronological priority, and these early witnesses to the tradition instead serve to underscore the extraordinary degree to which the record of the sack was manipulated in its retelling even by comparison to the surrounding narrative of Republican history. It is impossible to be confident that a stable or even monolithic tradition *ever* existed for an event that was retold more often than any other in Mid-Republican history.

With specific regard to the development of a destructive fire in the sack tradition, it is often held that, since Polybius, who (presumably) followed Fabius Pictor, made no mention of the *incendium*, Fabius Pictor himself was unaware of that aspect, which was only later added to the story.[32] While this argument is appealing, it necessarily contains a degree of speculation: Polybius' two mentions of the Gaul's invasion of Rome are extremely compact, and it is hard to be sure that his lack of detail is not owed to abbreviation. Problematically, we know nothing otherwise about Fabius' treatment of the event, while there remains the possibility that he treated it, like all events after the foundation of the city, "summarily."[33]

I would suggest that an alternate tradition depicting a more violent *incendium*, which destroyed parts of the city, had started to circulate already by the time Polybius was writing, if not earlier. This more destructive version of the sack is hinted at by several authors. One possible early witness is the famous *augusto augurio* line of Ennius' *Annales*, which Skutsch assigns to Camillus' speech to convince the plebs to abandon their plans to move to Veii and to set about rebuilding Rome. If this conjecture is correct, the line's context assumes the destruction of Rome, since this is what was held to have prompted the plebeian debate over colonizing Veii.[34] A second possible witness comes from the annalist Cassius Hemina's report of the bravery of the

31. Plut. *Cam.* 22.3 dismissed Heraclides Ponticus as exaggerated and unreliable; Aristotle gave Rome's savior's praenomen as Lucius, which confused Plutarch; cf. Sordi 1960: 49–52, *contra* Luce 1971: 291 n. 43. Plin. *NH* 3.57–8 cited Theopompus' report as an example of superficial Greek attention to Roman events; cf. Badian 1965. Thus, these citations' brevity hardly implies that failure to mention the *incendium* proves its nonexistence, *contra* Delfino 2014: 229. The attempt of Delfino 2009: 347; 2014: 229 n. 37 to revive a suggestion that Aristotle derived information from Roman pontifical records is unconvincing: even if *annales maximi* contained such information, how did Aristotle access them?

32. Polyb. 1.6.2–3; 2.18.1–3; cf. Walbank 1957–79: I.185.

33. Dion. Hal. 1.6.2: κεφαλαιωδῶς, on which see Richardson 2012: 137 n. 108; *FRH* I.169–73 (E. Bispham and T. J. Cornell).

34. Enn. *Ann.* 4.154–55 (Skutsch); Skutsch's argument is not unproblematic, as cf. Elliott 2013: 65.

priest "Dorso," known to Livy as Fabius Dorsuo, who climbed down from the Capitol, made his way through the enemy in the Forum to perform the rites of Vesta, and then returned to the Roman Capitol unharmed.[35] Dorso found the Temple of Vesta burned down but performed the rites in the customary location. Notably, the temple's destruction was secondary to the story, whose focus instead was on the impression Dorso's brave piety made on the Gauls, and so the burning of the Temple of Vesta was unlikely to have been created for this particular episode. Hemina was a contemporary of Cato and appears not to have been widely read by historians of the late Republic, and there is little reason to think that he invented the *incendium* himself.[36] It is more likely that Hemina derived details from already extant accounts circulating by the early second century.[37] Again, we are not dealing with the sort of evidence that yields firm conclusions. However, if it is possible that Fabius Pictor did not mention the *incendium*, it is just as possible that his near contemporaries already knew alternate versions of the sack legend that included a fire and the destruction of some of Rome's monuments.

The possible existence of an early account of the Gaul's destructive *incendium*, but in any case the general variability of the sack legend from its earliest renditions, calls into question the idea that the sack narrative as it related to the city's development was shaped by a simple process of expansion over time. Instead it is likely that the tradition developed, almost from its beginning, as alternate versions circulating contemporaneously.[38] Read closely and in this light, it is possible to see Livy himself working to integrate competing depictions of the violence of the *incendium*. At 5.42.1–3, he noted the unusual restraint of the Gauls on the first day after their capture of the city. A chapter later, and without any intervening explanation, the Romans are said to look down from the Capitoline to see

35. Majority opinion assigns the fragment to Hemina: Peter (F19), Chassignet (F22), Beck and Walter (F22), and *FRH* (F22). The citing authority App. *Gall.* 6 reads *Kausios*, emendable to *Kassios*, but permitting diverse opinions: Forsythe 1990: 342–43 argues for Cassius Dio; Richardson 2004 considers Quadrigarius.

36. Thouret (1880: 111) suggests Cato's awareness of the *incendium*, but misinterprets Fest. 277 L. Pliny the Elder is the earliest extant author to cite Hemina (*NH* 13.27, etc.).

37. Wiseman (2004: 129–30) thinks that the Dorsuo story was created in 345 BCE when M. Fabius Dorsuo was consul, but the implications for the *incendium* story are unknowable.

38. This concords with Skutsch 1953; 1978; Horsfall 1981 on simultaneously circulating ideas of the capture/safety of the Capitoline. See also Williams 2001: 142; Richardson 2012: 128–29. This is not to be confused with the more mechanical theory of F. Münzer *RE* VII (1910) coll. 334–45 s.v. "Furius" (44) that the tradition divides into "official" and "vulgate" versions.

"nothing surviving amidst the fires and ruins of the captured city" (5.43.1). The situation had already changed from calm to destruction by 5.42.7 when, as if from nowhere, the city appeared destroyed (*omnia flammis ac ruinis aequata*). Within this chapter, Livy made no attempt to reconcile the discrepancy.

Thus, characteristic multiplicity and instability diminishes the value in attempting to delineate any precise path by which Livy's version of the violent *incendium* may have developed. However, two general conclusions about the earlier, pre-Livian narrative of the Gallic *incendium* do emerge from this discussion. First, what we can observe about the historical record of the period following the sack does not preclude innovation on Livy's part in fitting the sack into a coherent narrative with otherwise available information on public works projects or socioeconomic problems. It is in this sense possible to see the author working to fit authentic but disparate events into a more fluid, but ultimately artificial, narrative framework. Second, the story of the sack itself is likely to have been multilinear from a very early point, containing as it did highly disparate accounts of the Gauls' effects on the city. If these observations do not themselves negate the validity of the destructive *incendium* and its impact on Rome's urban development, there are other reasons to do so, and I turn to these in the next section.

3.3. The Archaeology

A violent fire as described by the sources should have left traces in the city's archaeology. Stratigraphic deposits relating to the Neronian fire in Rome of 64 CE, or to the Persian sack of Athens to which ancient authors compared the Gallic sack, suggest what we are looking for: a thick stratum of carbonized material and building rubble deposited extensively and consistently across the city.[39] Gjerstad attempted to find just such a stratum by assembling a number of previously excavated contexts, which he suggested contained both evidence of destruction and diagnostic material indicative of an early fourth-century date. He connected deposits on the southwest Palatine near the *scalae caci* and around the Forum on the Via Sacra near the Vestals' complex, at the Regia, in the area of the *equus Domitiani* base, and at the *comitium*. The destruction fill under the *comitium* paving in particular had been associated with the Gallic sack since the early twentieth century, as Boni himself hoped his

39. Athens: Shear 1993.

stratigraphic excavations in that area would help in assessing the sack's historical merits.[40] Gjerstad noted that excavations at Sant' Omobono at the foot of the Capitoline failed to produce any parallel material relating to destruction, but he took the positivist view that such absence displayed the Gaul's respect for Roman sanctuaries.[41]

Gjerstad's reconstruction of the sack's archaeology was refuted by Coarelli, who restudied the material from Boni's excavations of the *comitium* and found that ceramics from the destruction layer underneath the *comitium*'s second pavement give a *terminus ante quem* of the late sixth century, not the early fourth.[42] The destruction deposit at the *comitium* could not therefore be associated with the period of the Gallic sack, and Coarelli correlated the deposit instead with the late sixth-century destruction of the Archaic temple at Sant' Omobono and a similarly dated deposit at the Regia. Rather than cohere around the *incendium Gallicum*, these destruction deposits were related by him with the violent upheaval at the time of the expulsion of the Tarquins.[43]

From a purely archaeological basis, Coarelli's dating of the *comitium* stratigraphy remains sound.[44] Once this important context at the *comitium* is removed from the sack's archaeology, Gjerstad's case falls apart, since the other relevant deposits, which he collected around the Forum, were mostly assigned relative dates on the basis of similarities with the *comitium* stratigraphy. Likewise, recent work on the Regia and the Vestals' complex, as well as Lacus Curtius area and the Temple of the Castores, show no signs of fourth-century destruction.[45] Only Gjerstad's early fourth century BCE date for the destruction stratum on the southwest Palatine, related with the *incendium* already by Vaglieri, has not been seriously challenged.[46] This context was

40. Boni 1900: 340; Pinza 1905: 47.

41. Gjerstad 1953–74; III.462.

42. Coarelli 1977b; 1978; 1983: 129–30.

43. Coarelli 1983: 138–139; also Steinby 2012b: 30–31.

44. A revised chronology by Carafa (1998: 43–46 n. 28) largely does not affect this conclusion, and cf. Hopkins 2010: 34–38.

45. Regia: Carnabuci 2012: 64; Vestals: Scott 2009: 18–32. The attempt by Arvanitis (2010: 57) to distinguish an early fourth century phase to the *domus Vestae* is unconvincing considering that the supposed phase has no related architecture and belongs within the same cut and orientation as the next phase.

46. Vaglieri 1907: 205; Gjerstad 1953–73: III. 79–80; Ampolo 1976: 144; Delfino 2009: 343–44.

excavated above one of the Archaic huts near the *scalae caci*, and the topographical situation of this part of the Palatine prior to the creation of the Temple of Victory (294 BCE) (A33) is not entirely clear.[47]

At present, no public monument can be demonstrated to have been destroyed by fire in the early fourth century, and it would be hard to imagine a violent fire that destroyed all Rome's houses in the central area around the Forum, but selectively left adjacent monumental architecture untouched. Until very recently, this view of the absence of archaeological evidence for a widespread *incendium* has gone unchallenged. However, excavation of two Archaic houses beneath the piazza of the Forum of Caesar at the foot of the Capitoline now reopens this debate.[48] Both houses, divided by a small alley and facing onto a street leading from the Forum, were destroyed violently by fire. Debris from their destruction was swept into several wells, and the structures were quickly rebuilt. Pottery relating to these phases as well as radiocarbon dating suggest that the houses were built in the late sixth century, their destruction took place in the early or mid-fourth century, and the reorganization of the area took place in the mid-fourth century.[49] Di Giuseppe and Delfino note how well this sequence corresponds to the literary tradition of the Gallic sack and the subsequent repair effort. A similar correspondence between signs of destruction and repair has now been suggested for Mid-Republican strata from the northeastern slopes of the Palatine in the area of the Velia, although this material's architectural context remains more difficult to discern.[50]

Do these excavations beneath the Forum of Caesar at the foot of the Capitoline and on the Velia near the Palatine provide positive evidence for the *incendium* described by our sources? Two issues urge caution. First, in the case of the evidence from the Forum of Caesar, the fire that destroyed the two houses must not have spread very far as it did not seem cross the *argiletum* into the central area of the Forum, and the nearby *comitium* remained undamaged. Just to the west of the Velia, toward the central area of the Forum, those aristocratic houses along the Via Sacra excavated in the 1990s likewise

---

47. Pensabene (1998: 25; 2001: 119) suggests cult structures; Ampolo (1976: 143) argues for private housing.

48. Delfino 2009, 2010, 2014.

49. Pottery: Di Giuseppe 2010; radiocarbon dating: Delfino 2014: 74.

50. Zeggio 2006: 70; Panella, Zeggio, and Ferrandes 2014: 179–86.

seem not to have been damaged by fire in the early fourth century.[51] Thus, taking into account all of this new evidence for both the presence and absence of destruction deposits, the resulting picture remains that of patchwork, rather than holocaustic, destruction.

The second issue is methodological and poses a more fundamental question of how to reconcile archaeological and textual evidence. The previous section's emphasis on the labile nature of the sack tradition argues *prima facie* against the possibility of any straightforward alignment with the archaeological record. That is, because of the exceptionally variable tradition on the sack, we cannot ask the material evidence to prove or disprove the sources without first establishing which of the various, often contradictory, layers of the tradition we aim to prove. To put this problem in more concrete terms, it is noteworthy that, as mentioned, the one deposit studied by Gjerstad, which remains datable to the early fourth century BCE, comes from the southwest Palatine. Descriptions of a violent fire on the Palatine appeared in the tradition, but only in relation to the story of Camillus' recovery of Romulus' *lituus* among the ashes.[52] In turn, this story of the rediscovery of the *lituus* was programmatic to the conception of Camillus as second founder of Rome, while an Attic literary model for the whole episode emerges clearly in Dionysius' aforementioned comparison of the *lituus'* discovery to the regrowth of Athena's olive tree on the Athenian acropolis after the withdrawal of the Persians. That is, it is easy to see how this story might have entered artificially into the tradition. By contrast, Livy did not mention the *lituus* at all despite focusing closely on Camillus, and he never mentioned any destruction on the Palatine. Diodorus went so far as to specify that "the Gauls pillaged the city except for a few dwellings on the Palatine" (14.115.6). In sum, the archaeological context of destruction on the southwest Palatine may be reconciled with *some* versions of the sack, but only by disregarding or otherwise arguing away other versions.

To his credit, Delfino does not suggest that the results of his excavations beneath the Forum of Caesar overturn prevailing opinion on the *incendium* in its totality. He raises the idea that the houses beneath the Forum of Caesar support

---

51. Carandini and Carafa 1995: 253–54; although, when Gualandi returns to the same house in Papi and Carandini 1999: 18, reference is given without explanation to restorations following the *incendium*.

52. Cf. Verrius Flaccus citing Lutatius in the *Fasti Praenestini, CIL* I^2 p. 234 = *Insc.Ital.* 13.2 pp. 122–3 = Lutatius *FRH* F10 (Smith): *ruina Palati incensi a Gallis*; Dion. Hal. 14.2.1–2; Cic. *de div.* 1.30, 2.80; Plut. *Rom.* 22.1–2; *Cam.* 32.4–5; Val. Max. 1.8.11.

a minimalist interpretation of the original *incendium*: while the fire destroyed some private buildings, it was not as violent as later authors suggested. He attributes the more violent version of the *incendium* to amplification and exaggeration by later authors, particularly after the model of the Neronian fire in 64 CE.[53] This idea is plausible and may well be correct, but it still requires us to assume that the *incendium* underwent a more linear pattern of expansion over time than can otherwise be detected. As Delfino recognizes, the clearest evidence for Roman historians using the Neronian fire to think about the Gallic *incendium* comes from Tacitus' statement that some Romans in 64 CE noted a synchronism between the start of *incendium Neronis* and "the day in which the Gauls burned down the captured city."[54] However, Tacitus' understanding of the Gallic sack was by no means monolithic. In comparing the sack to the fire that destroyed the Temple of Jupiter Optimus Maximus during the civil war of 69 CE, Tacitus seems to have implied that the Capitolium escaped the Gauls unscathed, as it did not escape the armies of Vespasian and Vitellius (*Hist.* 3.72.1). Elsewhere, when discussing the debate over admitting the leading men of Gallia Comata into the senate, Tacitus made the emperor Claudius respond to an opposing senator's protest that Rome should "preserve the memory of those who died slain by the Gauls on the Capitoline," seemingly alluding to the capture of the citadel (*Ann.* 11.23.7). The plainly contradictory nature of these two passages' conception of the sack's effects shows Tacitus' awareness of contrasting accounts with his choice to deploy one interpretation of the sack or the other being largely rhetorical.[55]

To summarize, there is new evidence of the destruction by fire of some domestic structures in the center of the city in the early fourth century BCE, but it remains difficult to relate this evidence to the tradition in any straightforward manner, or to determine which layer of the complex tradition we ought to relate it to in the first place. Something seems to have happened in early fourth-century Rome, but the evidence does not overturn Coarelli's general conclusions on the sack's effects. There remains no sign of extensive violent fire nor of the destruction of any public monuments. As a test of Livy's particular reconstruction, archaeology militates against the idea of total urban destruction, which played a catalytic role in his narrative.

---

53. Delfino 2009: 359; 2014: 236–39.

54. Tac. *Ann.* 15.41: *fuere qui adnotarent XIIII Kal. Sextiles principium incendii huius ortum, quo et Senones captam urbem inflammaverint.*

55. Horsfall 1980–1: 301–2; cf. Skutsch 1973.

This is not to deny the Gallic sack's historical consequences for the city's development, even including some physical destruction. The motivations for the expansion and elaboration of the *incendium*'s violence in Roman collective memory were certainly multiple.[56] I have noted how convenient a destructive sack would have been to Claudius Quadrigarius' insistence that the deep Roman past was inaccessible to historical inquiry, and this view was shared at least in part by the later Republic antiquarians. An emphasis on rupture with the deep Roman past had a certain rhetorical value: by touting the great darkness (*non mediocres enim tenebrae*) that shrouded Early Rome, Varro, for example, could promote his skill in recovering and reconstructing this past for his readers (*Ling.* 5.5). Whatever the case may be, since the fire described by Livy and his sources does not match the material evidence, we are encouraged to endorse those views of the sack's effects as above all psychological.[57] Indeed, the fear of another Gallic invasion exerted great force on Republican society in the centuries following the sack.[58] While the Gauls may not have destroyed Rome entirely, the Romans' decision to maintain the city's safety often entailed extraordinary measures, and at least three times in the later Republic Romans resorted to human sacrifice to ward off the Gauls' approach.[59] Also among those extraordinary measures was the decision to renew the city's defenses with a massive fortification project begun in the decades after the sack, and I return to this topic in the next chapter.

3.4. The Historical Context: Rome From the Fifth to Fourth Centuries

It is now time to consider the broader implications of this minimalist interpretation of the *incendium*'s effects on the city of Rome and the Roman economy. In other words, what happens to the overall understanding of Rome's development if we remove the first link from Livy's interconnected sequence of events: destruction, rebuilding, debt, anarchy? The first thing to note is the persistence of economic difficulties following the sack. As with other periods, the record of construction in the city forms a helpful index for tracing the Roman state's output during the Early and Mid-Republic.

---

56. Richardson 2012.

57. Cornell 1995: 318.

58. Bellen 1985; Wiseman 1995: 118–9; Williams 2001: 171–82.

59. Wiseman 1995: 206 n. 92.

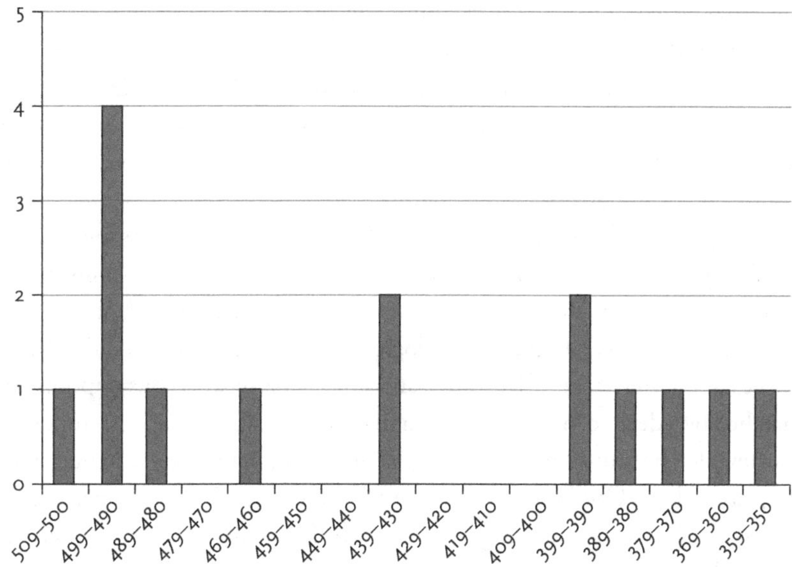

FIGURE 3.1 Public building projects by decade, 509-350 BCE

Since it was increasingly customary to apply war spoils to the construction of temples, temple building is a good indicator not only of state expenditure, but of overall income.[60] Temples predominate among the building projects charted in figure 3.1. Some unattested projects could perhaps be added: the construction of the massive platform beneath the Republican temples at Sant'Omobono in all likelihood belongs to the early fifth century.[61] I also exclude some limited evidence for repair, discussed below, and some minor projects mentioned by our sources, such as an altar to Pater Dis perhaps discovered, but not built, in the context of the first Ludi Saeculares, or an altar dedicated to Aius Locutius (A5) after the Gallic sack.[62] However, nothing changes the overall picture in which building activity spiked at the beginning of the fifth century with a number of temples either initiated by

60. For public construction as proxy for economic performance, see Ampolo 1990; generally, Wilson 2009: 74–77; 2011.

61. Pisani Sartorio 1977: 59–60; Pisani Sartorio and Virgili 1979: 44; Poucet 1980: 293. Coarelli (1988a: 216–19) assigns the project to Camillus in the early fourth century; however, new study of the complex refutes this: Regoli 2012: 93; Terrenato et al. 2012: §4.2 (I. Cangemi); Diffendale et al. 2016: 21–25.

62. Cf. Fest. 440 L; Paul. Fest. 479 L; *LTUR* II s.v. "Dis Pater et Proserpina, Ara" 19 (F. Coarelli). The Villa Publica dedicated in 435 BCE may not have entailed actual building, as cf. Richardson 1976a.

the kings or vowed in the wars following the expulsion of the Tarquins.[63] The rise in the 390s and early 380s comprised several dedications related to the sack of Veii, while the cessation of building activity during the central decades of the fifth century appears to indicate economic decline, a trend supportable through other classes of archaeological material, especially inscriptions and pottery.[64]

This picture of economic decline in fifth-century Rome aligns with general instability and socioeconomic transformation across the Italian peninsula.[65] In south Etruria, several urban sites contracted or were abandoned.[66] Attic pottery largely disappeared from the archaeological record of Etruria, as it did at Rome, by the last quarter of the fifth century, and shifts in patterns of consumption were matched by a decline in new construction of both sanctuaries and necropoleis.[67] Meanwhile, the sources record several disruptive population movements around Italy: transalpine Gauls into the Po Valley, Samnites into the Campanian cities of Capua and Cumae, and possibly Volsci into the Liris Valley and the Latin coast.[68]

By the very end of the fifth century, successful military campaigning seems to have begun to reverse Rome's fortunes, starting with the captures of Fidenae in 426 BCE and Labici in 418. Following on these gains, the crucial event of the period was the Roman conquest of Veii in 396.[69] Even within the much-elaborated tradition, we discern that the capture of the Etruscan capital brought a number of fundamental changes to Rome's economy and society. There is no reason beyond *a priori* skepticism, for example, to discredit reports that the prolonged Roman siege, perhaps the first of its kind, led to the innovation of military pay (*stipendium*),

---

63. Note Hopkins 2016: 32, 126–37 for some unattributed terracotta architectural elements belonging to this period and a possible mid- or late fifth-century date for the initial canalization of the cloaca.

64. Inscriptions: Salomies 2014: 158–59; pottery, particularly the disappearance of Attic red figure at Rome c. 425 BCE: Meyer 1980.

65. The key studies for this trend appear in *Crise et Transformation.*

66. Colonna 1990: 9–12.

67. Meyer 1980; Rendeli 1989: 555–56; changes may not have been purely economic as Colonna 1977 correlates decline in lavish burial to anti-sumptuary restrictions relating to funerals in the Twelve Tables (tb. X.2–6); cf. Cornell 1995: 106–8.

68. Celts: Williams 2001; Campanian Samnites: Cornell 1974 for the sources with Pontrandolfo and D'Agostino 1990 for the archaeology; Volsci: Coarelli 1990a; *contra* Cifarelli and Gatti 2006.

69. This is Livy's Varronian date; for the chronological problem, see Harris 1971: 41–49.

likely in the form of commodities weighed out against a bronze standard.[70]

Above all, the potential economic changes that the conquest of Veii stimulated related to two primary factors of production, labor and land. Starting with the labor supply, Livy reports that all captured Veians were sold into slavery (5.22.1). No source helps to quantify the sale of slaves, but Harris supposes the number reached into the tens of thousands.[71] While the tradition tends to equate Veii with Rome in manpower and physical size (cf. Dion. Hal. 12.15), especially by contrast to the diminished later city (cf. Flor. 1.12.11), each city's respective circuit walls suggest that the Etruscan settlement was smaller than contemporary Rome, and therefore less populous. One estimate puts its total population at fewer than 32,000 people.[72] Still, some increase in the supply of labor to Roman production seems indisputable.

With the newly conquered Veian territory, the *ager Veientanus*, Romans acquired some 50,000 ha across the Tiber.[73] Exceptional land grants and sociopolitical innovations revolving around landholding frequently appeared in the sources of the period. Livy recorded a *senatus consultum* after the conquest that granted land to all free adult males in Roman households, and not simply to heads of families, *patres familias*.[74] This was the first reported distribution of conquered land to individuals as private property (*viritim*), and the seven-iugera (1.75 ha) plots supposedly distributed by the Roman state were still modest, but nonetheless over three times larger than typically granted before and afterwards.[75] More land measures reportedly followed. Following the subsequent captures of the Faliscan centers of Capena, and then Nepet and

70. Diod. 14.16.5; Liv. 4.59–60; in favor of this view, see Boren 1983; Crawford 1985: 22–24; Massa-Pairault 1986: 40–43; Harris 1990: 507 (although giving too much room to the *aes rude* theory); Cornell 1995: 187–89; Gabrielli 2003a: 84; Rosenstein 2004: 54–55. There is no evidence for the use of unstandardized *aes rude* as a medium of exchange, while the Twelve Tables describe values in bronze and sale *per aes et libram*. That Romans were paid in lumps of bronze is more fantastical than the notion of pay made with a bronze standard.

71. Harris 1990: 498.

72. Cristofani 1984: 31. The Etruscan settlement was about 190 ha. (Cascino, di Giuseppe, and Patterson eds. 2012: 349), whereas Rome's walls enclosed approximately 364 ha. (Fulminante 2014: 101–2).

73. Beloch 1926: 620; Afzelius 1942: 190; cf. Roselaar 2010: 33–4 for problems with such estimates. De Martino (1974: 188) notes that non-arable land remained productive for timber and other uses.

74. 5.30.8; Diod. Sic. 14.102.4 records a single distribution.

75. Liverani 1984: 36–37; Roselaar 2010: 41–42, 55; Livy reports 7 *iugera*, while Greek sources give different figures.

Sutrium (Liv. 6.9.4), Rome was able to award citizenship and land to those former citizens of Veii, Capena, and Fidenae who had gone over to Rome during campaigns against their respective cities. Shortly after, the creation of four rural tribes marked the first expansion of the popular tribal system since the first years of the Republic.[76] There has been much debate about the viability of land grants of 1.5 ha to individual settlers in this period, and consequently about the reliability of the sources.[77] Roselaar notes that *viritim* allotments of seven iugeras of land appear in the sources not only after the sack of Veii but in the context of Late Republican colonies. The plot size thus seems historical, as it would be hard to think that the Roman state regularly set up new settlers for failure.[78] Meanwhile, survey archaeology is supportive of the idea that this point in time saw the significant reorganization of landholding and exploitation patterns in the Tiber Valley.[79]

The siege and sack of Veii thus seems to have offered Rome the potential for expansion and economic growth. This makes it all the more notable that any signs of growth turned out to be short lived. By the early 370s, Rome returned to a pattern of limited military success and minimal urban expansion. Cornell argues for Rome's undiminished rise and rapid recovery from the Gallic sack in the early decades of the fourth century. I am sympathetic with his desire to respond to extremely critical positions, like that of Beloch, who rejects the period's sources altogether and holds that Rome accomplished next to nothing at this time; however, the evidence does not support much optimism for Rome's economic performance in the early fourth century.[80] We need not go so far as to dismiss the sources entirely to recognize a reduced Roman state, especially by comparison to the late monarchy or the later fourth century BCE. For one thing, problematic debt dominated the domestic history of the period and seems to have persisted despite multiple legislative attempts to resolve the issue.[81] The first attested debt law at Rome, the

76. Liv. 6.4.4, .5.8; Taylor 2013: 47–49.

77. See Roselaar 2010: 204 n. 204 for bibliography.

78. Roselaar 2010: 204–7; Bernard 2016b: 331–32.

79. Patterson, Di Giuseppe, and Witcher 2004: 5–13; Cifani 2015; the British School survey detected major change between the Classical and Hellenistic periods, although the lack of diagnostic ceramics for the early fourth century hampers visibility at the precise moment of the sack; cf. Di Giuseppe 2012: 359.

80. Cornell in *CAH* VII.2[2] Ch. 7; 1995: 318–22; 2000: 44; cf. Ziolkowski 1999: 377.

81. Hölkeskamp 1987: 96–97; Bernard 2016b.

lex Licinia Sextia de aere alieno of 367 BCE, was followed in close succession by at least five more similar measures in the next half-century. [82] In terms of Rome's external affairs, there seems to have been only tentative interest in expansion in the decades after the sack, and without much success. While it remains hard to discern what Roman colonization may have actually entailed in this period, the process was remembered by later sources as largely unsuccessful: the colonies at Sutrium and Nepet were Rome's final recorded colonial attempts until the first Latin colony at Cales in 334 BCE, and there are hints of failed efforts to establish Roman outposts in Sardinia or Corsica, while colonies closer to the city were said to revolt.[83]

Meanwhile, warfare after the sack of Veii, as Harris points out, remained limited in scope into the mid-fourth century BCE.[84] According to the sources, this was not an impressive period for Roman armies. Livy saw no exceptional military leader emerge after Camillus until the time of L. Papirius Cursor in the Second Samnite War (9.15.9-10). The army rarely ventured outside Latium and operated mostly on an ad hoc basis, sometimes reportedly taking the same city twice in what has been interpreted as a pattern of annual raiding rather than programmatic imperialism.[85] Temporary change in Roman military policy may have come in the early 350s, although again with mixed success. In 358 BCE, one consular army ventured north into Etruscan territory as far as Tarquinii, only to suffer defeat. The other consul defeated the Hernici, and the annexation of Hernician land in the Sacco valley prompted the creation of two new tribes for the first time since the annexation of the *ager Veientanus*. However, the same year also saw renewed conflict with Gauls, whose advance as far as Praeneste and Pedum drew Rome away from Etruria for the time being.[86]

---

82. On debt in the Early Republican economy, see Bernard 2016b. Catalogs of debt laws: Rotondi 1962; Savunen 1993; Elster 2003; Gabrielli 2003a. On the *lex Licinia Sextia de aere alieno*, see Oakley 1997–2005: I. 659–61.

83. The nature of Rome's Early Republican colonies remains highly debated, and recent work such as that by Bispham (2006) or Stek and Pelgrom (2014) tends to view them as uneven and motivated by different reasons. Terrenato (2014) goes so far as to view much of this phase of colonization as serving the private interests of individual families. Generally, see Torelli 1988: 68; Termeer 2010. On the Sardinian colony, Torelli 1981. On Corsica, Theophr. *Hist. pl.* 5.8.3. For revolt, Liv. 6.21.

84. Harris 1971: 47.

85. E.g., Satricum in 386 BCE and again in 346, and Velitrae in 380 and 367; the authenticity of these doublets has been doubted, but need not be, as see Oakley 1997–2005 I.352 n. 73.

86. Harris 1971: 48–49.

This picture of the relatively limited scope of Roman warfare agrees with the reconstructed triumphal *fasti*, which record only one *ovatio* and five triumphs between 396 BCE and the passage of the Licinio-Sextian laws in 367.[87] Meanwhile, we know of several military setbacks, such as defeat to the Volsci in 379 and disaster in 362, when the Hernici killed a consul.[88] Of course, the appraisal of the period is subject to the distortion produced by the annalists' record of an anarchy of some length between the proposal and passage of the Licinio-Sextian laws.[89] However, Cornell's characterization of the period from 376 to 363 as "one of comparative peace" poorly describes a moment of extreme duress in Rome's political system, and the lack of campaigning during those years is just as easily ascribed to internal crisis as to the absence of enemies.[90]

In the city itself, there were few construction projects other than the fortifications (A6) of 378 BCE. Three temples were dedicated from 396 to 367, and I reiterate that these projects clustered in the decade after the capture of Veii, when Camillus dedicated temples to Mater Matuta (396, A1) and Juno Regina (392, A2), and T. Quinctius Cincinnatus Capitolinus dedicated a temple to Mars outside the city walls (388, A4). No temples were reported for the entirety of the 370s. A fourth temple may have been repaired: a fragment of Cn. Gellius noted that L. Furius *tribunus militum*, perhaps L. Furius Medullinus, military tribune in 381 and 370 BCE, carried out a senatorial decree to build the Temple of Saturn, *ut aedes Saturni fieret* (A8). This is normally interpreted as work on the fifth-century temple to Saturn at the foot of the Capitoline.[91] Otherwise, the altar to Aius Locutius (A5) at the base of the Via Nova was established to expiate a prophetic voice warning of the impending Gallic invasion, but does not seem to have included substantial architecture. A problematic (see below) Temple of Concord attributed to Camillus in 367 BCE (A10) was the only public monument attested in the

87. Triumphs: L. Valerius Potitus over Aequi (392 BCE), M. Furius Camillus over Volsci, Aequi, and Etruscans (389 BCE), A. Cornelius Cossus over Volsci (385 BCE), Q. Quinctius Cincinnatus Capitolinus over Latins (380 BCE), M. Furius Camillus over Gauls (367); *ovatio*: M. Manlius Capitolinus over Aequi (392 BCE).

88. Liv. 6.30; Liv. 7.6.

89. Von Fritz 1950: 9–10; Oakley 1997–2005: I.646–51; Pellam 2014. While the implausible five-year anarchic period was likely produced by later attempts to reconcile competing chronologies, a total denial of political crisis in this period is unconvincing.

90. Cornell 1995: 322.

91. *FRH* 14 Cn. Gellius F27 = Peter *HRR* Gellius F24; cf. *LTUR* IV s.v. "Saturnus, Aedes" 234 (F. Coarelli).

360s. Sources note no further building projects until 353 BCE, when Livy recorded that soldiers were employed to repair the city's walls (A11), and a temple to Apollo was dedicated (A12). This produces a total of five temples, some repair to a sixth, and an altar, built at Rome in the span of fifty years from 400 to 350 BCE. Again, it is not unlikely that some unattested repair work belongs to this period.[92] However, the picture remains one of reduced state expenditure on public monuments at home, and this reinforces the picture of limited warfare and military income abroad.

Since M. Furius Camillus was personally responsible for two triumphs and three temples, any interpretation of Rome's capacity in the early fourth century hinges on an assessment of this figure. The artificiality of his career has been noted since Mommsen, who dismissed Camillus as the "most deceptive of all Roman legends."[93] There are two options for evaluating his career, since few scholars would accept all of Camillus' accomplishments at face value. We can deny Camillus' achievements altogether and thereby remove his activities from the history of the period.[94] Alternatively, we can uphold the veracity of some of Camillus' achievements, but allow for the retroactive attachment of these actions, originally carried out by other magistrates, to the singular career of a largely fictitious character. This is the position of Bruun, who plausibly reconstructs the manner through which some of Camillus' deeds came to be disassociated with other members of the *gens Furia* and associated with Camillus.[95]

How far Bruun's solution might be extended to Camillus' three building projects is difficult to say. There is no positive archaeological evidence for the Camillan Temple of Juno Regina (A2), although inscriptions attest to the cult on the Imperial Aventine. Meanwhile, any understanding of Camillus' Temple of Mater Matuta in the *forum boarium* (A1) rests upon the complex stratigraphy of the structures at Sant'Omobono, where there is little to no evidence for a substantial Camillan phase.[96] Only Ovid and Plutarch make reference

92. Including the Domus Vestae (A13), as see Scott 2009: 21–33; Arvanitis 2010: 54–59; also see A9.

93. Mommsen 1899: 1018 n. 2; Cornell in *CAH* VII.2[2] 306, 310 asserts that Camillus is "certainly historical, and there is no good reason to doubt that he dominated affairs in the years after the Sack," but elsewhere acknowledges several ways in which the Camillus legend was manipulated to suit later purposes; 1995: 317.

94. Beloch 1926: 318–19.

95. Bruun 2000; also Coudry 2001.

96. Diffendale et al. 2016: 23–24.

to Camillus' temple to Concord (A10). Livy's silence on the dedication is noteworthy, as he was otherwise attentive to Camillus' temple foundations. The discrepancy led Momigliano to deny the Camillan temple's existence altogether and to interpret Ovid and Plutarch's mentions as either confusion with Cn. Flavius' *aedicula* to Concord built in 304 BCE (A24), or as rhetorical invention relating to L. Opimius' construction of a temple to Concord in 121 BCE.[97] In his study of the Tiberian temple to Concord *in arce*, Gasparri describes ashlar walls of *tufo lionato* belonging to Opimius' temple beneath the *caementa* of the imperial temple's podium, but explicitly reports no physical evidence of any earlier phase.[98] By contrast, exploration in the 1990s of the temple's podium claim to have revealed some fragmentary walls beneath the later temple. The discovery remains unpublished outside of a brief note in the *LTUR*, which raises the possibility of a fourth-century phase.[99] On this basis, Cornell returns the temple to the period of Camillus. However, without better information on the nature of the remains beneath the later temple, it is hard to controvert Gasparri's report, and it is not clear where in relation to the imperial podium these newly reported remains belong.[100] In light of this uncertainty, it seems safest to understand the sources' tally of five new temples in the period, including three attributed to Camillus, as something of a maximum.

Thus, while the annexation of Veii's territory and its consequent reorganization in the hands of Roman landholders represented a potential trigger to Roman economic growth through the infusion of additional land and labor, the record does not support any sustained Roman recovery for the first half of the fourth century. The sources pinned Rome's failure to follow up on the gains of Veii on the disaster of the Gallic sack and, at least in the Livian conception, on the high cost of rebuilding Rome, but we have seen that this reconstruction of events is untenable, and therefore we continue to seek an explanation for Rome's development in the early fourth century BCE.

---

97. Momigliano 1942: 116–20 followed by Levick 1978; Ziolkowski 1992: 22–23; Heyworth 2011: 60.

98. Gasparri 1979: 61.

99. *LTUR* I 317 s.v. "Concordia, Aedes" (A. M Ferroni); fragments of *tufo giallo* in the concrete core of the Tiberian temple were noted by Momigliano 1942: 116.

100. Cornell 2000a: 44.

3.5. The Socioeconomic Context: Land and Labor

The argument of the last section for the continued limitations of Rome's economy after the conquest of Veii was made on the basis of trends in the textual and archaeological records. Further nuance is gained by turning to a less empirical discussion of how the capture of Veii and its territory may have altered the structures of the Roman economy. The topic takes us beyond the limits of the city into an investigation of agricultural production in Rome's expanding hinterland, but we should bear in mind that, at this point, Rome's urban production largely still overlapped with agriculture on the *ager Romanus*. Since, as noted above, Veii appears to have offered gains to Roman production through the increase of two productive factors, land and labor, the crucial question is whether such gains were commensurate: did Rome add sufficient new labor to cultivate its new territory, or sufficient land for its expanding population?[101]

The details of the increase in slaves following Rome's conquest of Veii do not permit quantification since so little is known about the respective populations of Rome and Veii at this time.[102] What can be said is that cultivating the *ager Veientanus* implied the movement of some portion of existing Roman population onto new land, to some extent lowering the overall proportion of Romans to territory. If Livy's depiction of the viritane land assignations of seven *iugera* not only to existing *patres familias* but to non-inheriting children is historical, this would have further removed labor from existing households of Roman landowners and spread it thinly over the newly acquired territory.[103] The creation of four new tribes may attest to the amount of Roman citizens who now became landed in the new territory, as the tribe members were unlikely to have been predominantly new citizens.[104]

Rosenstein's useful model of the labor requirements of Republican agriculture permits some idea of how successful new Roman farms of seven *iugera* in the *ager Veientanus* may have been. He suggests that families on seven *iugera* estates would have needed to cultivate additional land, perhaps

---

101. See further Bernard 2016b.

102. See above p. 65.

103. Liv. 5.30.8; Livy here employs rhetoric used elsewhere to describe the Gracchan land reforms (cf. App. *BC* 1.10), and this leads Evans 1981 to dismiss both Livy's explanation and the *senatus consultum* itself, but it may simply be that Livy used later Roman history to interpret the earlier land measure. The argument of De Martino 1974: 169 that land went to *proletarii* and poor plebs presupposes an anachronistic view of the urban population in this period.

104. Livy 5.30.7–9; Ziolkowski 1999: 378.

through tenancy, and the resulting manpower this required would have pushed them much closer to household labor shortfalls. Rosenstein's figures leave only 11–18 days of work beyond subsistence costs, a dangerously thin margin of success.[105] If they were called upon to contribute military power, something which seems likely, new Roman farms would have found their labor supplies stressed even further. I note here some suspicions that Rosenstein's model of agricultural labor demands may underestimate the necessary labor requirements for Republican agriculture making the potential for household labor shortages all the more real, although this is not the place for an extended critique.[106]

To make up for labor shortfalls, Roman households on the *ager Veientanus* might have increased their family through childrearing, with all the short-term risks that implied. Alternatively, they could have looked to take on labor from outside their estates through debt-bondage or slavery. This scenario thus returns us to the question of the commensurability of the number of newly enslaved Veians to the demand for labor on land now controlled by Romans. Importantly, as Rome captured both Veii's territory and its population, those Veians working on new Roman estates in the *ager Veientanus* will not have changed their productive location, but only their status: free to slave. This fundamentally distinguishes the conquest of Veii from later Roman imperial expansion where subsequent control of conquered territory was not regularly pursued. Instead, in later periods slaves were imported from provincial territories to the imperial core where they intensified production. While the labor of Veian slaves could be utilized brutally and efficiently by Roman masters, there were not more total workers on Roman and Veian territory after the war than before. If anything, accounting for military casualties, the total population may have been lower. Logically, then, even as the conquest of Veii increased both Rome's supplies of land and labor, the annexation of the *ager Veientanus* to some extent thinned the overall Roman labor supply relative to demand.

---

105. Rosenstein 2004: 71, subtracting cost of cultivating wheat, plus legumes and garden, plus two oxen, and sharecropping from the total labor available to a family of father, mother, daughter. A smaller family configuration accords with Livy's report that land grants were made to all *liberi*, not only to eldest sons, as see Bernard 2016b: 332–33.

106. Two reasons in brief: first, he may underestimate food processing costs, which often exceeded production and collection costs, especially for the preferred hulled wheats of the period (cf. Halstead 2014: 182–83). Second, his low figures for family caloric requirements may not suffice for those engaged in strenuous labor required by many agricultural tasks; compare Muldrew 2011: 129–32.

We should not exaggerate the effects of this shift, and the conquest of Veii did not in and of itself spell disaster for the Roman peasant economy. However, the rapid gain in territory, and the need to put sufficient labor to work on that new territory, may have begun to cast previous economic pressures in a different light, shifting the potential point of tension in the Roman economy from land hunger, well-attested in the Early Republic, to a thinned supply of labor. Indeed, several pieces of evidence may be interpreted as speaking to pressures on the Roman labor supply in the mid-fourth century BCE. For example, we may observe the continuation of problems of debt, and particularly debt-bondage, which remain highly visible in the sources for several decades after the sack of Veii until the legal curtailment of *nexum* by the *Lex Poetelia de nexis* in 326 or 313 BCE.[107]

Another relevant feature may be an observable move toward slavery. The mid-fourth century was an important moment for the development of the Roman slave economy into one of the "genuine slave societies" in world history. Finley brilliantly connected the decline of debt-bondage at Rome with the rise of slavery in the fourth century BCE, and the middle of that century was a time when both *nexi* and, increasingly, slaves would have been available to Roman elites.[108] Along with the eventual suppression of debt-bondage, which presumably required the availability of an alternative labor source, slavery's deepening economic importance is indicated variously. A tax on manumission, the *vicesima libertatis*, was established in 357 BCE.[109] Another sign appears in clauses relating to slave-raiding in Polybius' second Roman-Carthaginian treaty, dated sometime in the later fourth century, whereas such language was not contained in the earlier treaty of 509 BCE.[110]

Manpower shortages and competing labor demands on households would also serve to explain a number of political measures in the period. The Roman state's desire to maintain a sufficient free population on the *ager Romanus* may, for example, have been behind aforementioned land grants to Veientines, Capenates, and Fidenates who had been loyal to Rome in recent wars (Liv. 6.4.4). Similar interests may have motivated Rome's decision to force the senators of Velitrae, after that town's revolt in 340 BCE, to relocate onto land

107. Lo Cascio 2009: 23; for the *Lex Poetelia Papiria de nexis*, see Elster 2003: 63–71; for *nexum*, see Cornell 1995: 282–83; Bernard 2016b: 322–23.

108. Finley 1964; 1998: 77.

109. Liv. 7.16.7; Bradley 1984: 175–76.

110. Compare Polyb. 3.24.6–7 to 3.22.

"across the Tiber" and ostensibly onto the *ager Veientanus* (Liv. 8.14.5), and comparable action was taken against the local senators of Privernum in 320 BCE (Liv. 8.20.9). In these instances, the Roman state may be seen to act as though it held a surplus of land but was anxious to supply the requisite manpower to maintain production.

3.6. Conclusions

This chapter began by noting both historiographical and archaeological problems with the annalists' reconstruction of a new and costly Republican city built in the ashes of the Gallic *incendium*. A critical reading of the history of this period leads us to uphold certain aspects of the sources' account of the fourth century while rejecting others, above all the violent destruction of the *incendium*. The resulting historical picture poses further questions for the Roman state's overall economic performance. Rome's economy appears on several indices to have stalled in the early fourth century despite Rome's expansion into the *ager Veientanus* and consequent innovations in landholding. If the putatively massive cost of rebuilding Rome after the violent Gallic *incendium* was not responsible for counteracting the gains made by conquering Veii, then we are left to ask what was. This discussion has suggested the changing supply of labor within the complex balance of the Republican economy as a potential point of friction, as the conquest of Veii brought new land and labor under Roman control, but not necessarily in sufficiently equal proportions.

4 A COST ANALYSIS OF THE REPUBLICAN CIRCUIT WALLS

Roman farms were not the only centers of demand for labor in the newly conquered territory of Veii. The early fourth century BCE saw the beginning of the large-scale extraction of *tufo giallo della Via Tiberina* from quarries in the *ager Veientanus*. In the decades after the annexation of Veii, and with few other attested monuments, this extractive activity primarily served to provide building material for the construction of Rome's massive walls. As a counterpart to the previous chapter's discussion of socioeconomic developments in Rome and its territory in the early fourth century BCE, I turn here to the historical implications of a single monument, the Republican circuit walls built shortly after the Gallic sack. These ashlar-masonry walls with their associated earthen mound and ditch, the *agger* and *fossa* respectively, constituted the largest man-made addition to the city of Rome during the Republic. With the help of a quantitative estimation of the labor-cost of the walls' construction, this chapter models the effects of the Roman state's decision to undertake the single greatest productive activity of the period.

Remains of Rome's pre-Imperial walls are archaeologically identifiable around the modern city (figure 4.1). Frank first pointed out that long stretches of walls were built of *tufo giallo* supplied from the quarries of Grotta Oscura in the *ager Veientanus*.[1] Although there may have been some limited earlier use of *tufo giallo* at Rome, the first large-scale reliance on the stone converges with Livy's notice of the construction of a *murus*

1. Frank 1918: 181–83; see above, pp. 29–30.

FIGURE 4.1 The Republican walls of the *agger* in Piazza dei Cinquecento beside the entrance of Termini station.
Photo © S. Bernard.

in saxo quadrato two decades after Rome's annexation of Veii's territory (6.32).[2] This helps to secure the identification of the monument, particularly of those stretches of *tufo giallo*. Topographical reconstruction of the walls' archaeological remains has been the center of scholarship since the nineteenth century. However, the evidence affords little certainty in this debate as parts of the old circuit were overbuilt or destroyed already by the time that it was described by Livy and Dionysius of Halicarnassus.[3] Ultimately, then, this chapter encourages scholarship to move beyond the walls' topography, and to understand the monument's construction as an historical phenomenon.

2. Volpe 2014 argues for earlier use.

3. Liv. 1.44.4; Dion. Hal. 4.13.5. No detailed study of the walls' later transformations exists, but useful information is found in Oliver 1932; Wiseman 1998; Haselberger 2007: 204–7; Barbera 2008: 26–29; Fabbri 2009; Bernard 2012: 2–3.

4.1. Cost-Analysis of Republican Architecture

The physical evidence leaves little doubt that the Republican walls were an enormous undertaking, and their eleven-kilometer circuit finds few parallels in Italy or the western Mediterranean. To complement this impression, this chapter quantifies the walls' cost by applying standard work rates to a volumetric reconstruction of the original monument. That is, if it normally took x days to produce a single block of stone, and the walls required y blocks, we can extrapolate the project's total cost in person-days (PD) of human effort as $x \times y$. This reconstruction is facilitated by the modular and repetitive *opus quadratum* technique employed by the walls' builders. Romanists will be most familiar with this quantitative approach to architecture from DeLaine's work on brick structures at Rome and Ostia. Her publications have inspired a number of imitative studies of Imperial architecture.[4] Meanwhile, New World archaeologists since the 1960s employ a similar "energetics" approach, as Abrams terms it, toward the study of architecture as the sum of human energy expended in its creation.[5] Different sources provide these studies with standard work rates: DeLaine draws on figures found in nineteenth-century European engineering manuals, while New World archaeologists have employed ethnographic experiments including interviews with modern masons and timed experiments replicating various building tasks. Some recent work derives labor costs by working backwards, so to speak, from epigraphic evidence for prices and wages.[6] For thinking about the time and manpower needed to build the Mid-Republican walls, a valuable comparandum appears in the form of Diodorus Siculus' detailed description of the workforce assembled by Dionysius I to build part of Syracuse's wall in 401 BCE. Not only was this fortification project closely contemporary to Republican Rome's walls, but the more general influence of Syracuse on Rome in this period is variously recognized, and the relationship is explored further below.[7]

While DeLaine's work has sparked much subsequent study of the economics of Roman architectural production, there has been little interest

---

4. DeLaine 1997, 2001.

5. Erasmus 1965; Abrams 1989, 1994; Carrelli 2004.

6. Barresi 2003; Pakkanen 2014.

7. Diod. Sic. 14.18.3–8. Pinza (1897: 260–61) already suspects Syracusan influence, while Diodorus' numbers are used by Cifani 2010 and Volpe 2014; for social relationships between Rome and Syracuse, see Gabrielli 2003a: 33–56.

in revisiting the theoretical parameters of this approach.[8] Recent historical research into energy and labor necessitates some preliminary remarks. Fundamental to the application of comparative data however derived is the assumption that human physiology was sufficiently uniform over time for Mid-Republican builders to produce architectural forms at rates roughly similar to workers in other times and places. However, workers' output can change, with technology and energy contributing most of all to such change.[9] As far as possible the model here seeks to account for the sort of tools that were used in the walls' construction.[10] The issue of energy, however, is more problematic: recent scholarship on consumption in early modern Europe stresses that modern workers began to consume more daily calories than in the past, and that this measurably raised their productive abilities.[11] It is now commonly held that, before the technological breakthrough of the industrial revolution, a preceding "industrious" revolution saw economic growth facilitated by rising household consumption.[12] The upwards of 6,000 calories consumed in an eight-hour workday by some early modern builders engaged in strenuous work seems unrealistic for the Roman economy where malnourishment is held to have been widespread.[13] Replicative experiments show that a builder's productivity drops off sharply in the sixth hour of labor-intensive activity. Thus, workers may have stayed on-site for longer periods of time, but their effectiveness was constrained by their level of consumption, and there is some evidence to suggest that Roman authors were well aware of nutritional constraints on work.[14] It is therefore necessary to differentiate between time spent productively, something which is physiologically determined, and time spent by workers on a worksite, something which is more often culturally determined.[15] With such qualifications in mind, this chapter's

8. DeLaine 1997: 105–6 remains the fullest explicit theorization for the Roman world; see also Barker and Russell 2012.

9. Trigger 1990.

10. Cf. Säflund 1998: 115–20 and below.

11. Fogel 2004; Scheidel 2007: 61.

12. Allen 2001; De Vries 2008; Muldrew 2011.

13. Muldrew 2011: 131–32; Garnsey 1998 on Rome.

14. Erasmus 1965: 283–84; see Barker and Russell 2012: 85; cf. Cato *de Agr.* 56; at Liv. 5.19.11, Camillus' soldiers work in six-hour shifts; Plaut. *Capt.* 721–38 implies a working day coinciding with daylight hours; for later periods, see Le Goff 1980: 47; Goldthwaite 1980: 291.

15. Pickett et al. 2016: 104.

model follows Abrams in using a shorter five-hour workday for more arduous tasks, while retaining a twelve-hour day for less intensive activity.

The model generated in this chapter represents a hypothetical magnitude of cost, but this figure should not be taken as an end in and of itself. Whereas some previous attempts have been made to calculate a rough total of the manpower consumed in building the Republican walls, by themselves the resulting numbers reveal little more than an initial impression: the walls were big and costly.[16] Instead, the present exercise intends to test the plausibility of a larger historical reconstruction of the flow of labor in the Republican economy in the absence of data on wages and prices.[17] We want to know whether and, if so, to what extent the construction of the Republican walls contributed to the slowed performance otherwise observable for early fourth century Roman economy and described by the previous chapter. In order to check this hypothesis, the model selects for minimum inputs as far as possible.

4.2. The Scale of the Project

This section reconstructs the basic dimensions of the Republican walls in order to calculate the volumes of various building materials. Before setting out the evidence, it is important to account for the fact that the Republican circuit walls were not Rome's first fortification project. The discovery in the late 1980s of a wall at the foot of the Palatine, which possibly served to protect that hill already in the mid-eighth century, and, more recently, the discovery of a similarly ancient wall at the base of the Capitoline suggest that defenses on some of the hills predated the Republic by several centuries.[18] Such confirmation was probably not needed: literary sources attribute walls to Rome's successive kings, who were held to have amplified the circuit to some extent by including one or another hill, or by closing gaps between hills. The relationship of the Republican circuit to these earlier fortifications remains debated, the central question being when the system expanded from a network of hilltop fortifications to encompass the full course of hills and valleys.[19] Two basic positions in this debate emerged already by the middle of

16. Cornell 1995: 462 n. 11; Cifani 2010: 37–38; Volpe 2014: 61–62.

17. This approach owes much to Padilla Peralta 2014, even if our results are different.

18. Palatine wall: Carandini and Carafa 1995; for criticism of the interpretation of its defensive purpose, see Fontaine 2004. Capitoline wall: Catalano, Fortini, and Nanni 2001.

19. Bernard 2012.

the twentieth century: Säflund argued that the circuit dated no earlier than the fourth century BCE, with the earlier city's defenses reliant on natural terrain and, in some places, an earthen *agger*.[20] By contrast, Lugli argued for two different circuits, each distinguishable by the use of different materials: sixth-century walls of *tufo del Palatino*, and Republican walls of *tufo giallo*.[21] While Säflund's thesis prevailed through the early 1990s, rising recent interest in the archaeology of sixth-century Rome has led a number of scholars to support Lugli's idea of two distinct circuits, with some putting forward the idea that the sixth-century walls ran on an identical course to the *tufo giallo* walls of the fourth century.[22]

For the purposes of this chapter, it is worth emphasizing the scale of the fourth-century building project, whether or not the new walls replaced an earlier defensive circuit. Some regions of the city like the Caelian lack any remains of an Archaic wall whatsoever. On the Aventine, where some stretches of wall consist of *tufo giallo* blocks superimposed directly onto courses of *tufo del Palatino*, the underlying *tufo giallo* wall is only three or four courses high, while the Aventine's *tufo giallo* walls reach a height of almost ten meters and represent a construction project of an entirely different magnitude.[23]

Moreover, I might challenge the basic idea that different building stones represent different chronological phases, and the model presented in this chapter considers some *tufo del Palatino* in the Esquiline *agger* to be part of the fourth-century building project. If this requires justification, we may first of all note that the combination of multiple types of tuff within a single phase of construction was a widely observable feature of Mid-Republican construction.[24] While *tufo del Palatino* typifies earliest Roman ashlar construction, the stone appears in public architecture into the second century, and there is no reason to believe that the urban quarries of *tufo del Palatino* were inaccessible by the early fourth century.[25] More specific to the Republican walls, there is indication of the continued use of *tufo del Palatino* in the earthen *agger* on the Esquiline, which was contained between two stone walls, an exterior

20. Säflund 1998; earlier skepticism in Richter 1901: 43; Delbrück 1907–12: I.16; Carter 1909: 136–41

21. Lugli 1933.

22. Coarelli 1995a; Cifani 1998, 2008, 2013; Barbera 2008; Fabbri 2008, 2009.

23. Cf. Quoniam 1947.

24. Bernard 2012: 9 n. 32; see ch. 7.

25. Cf. Cifani 2008: 232–34 for quarries.

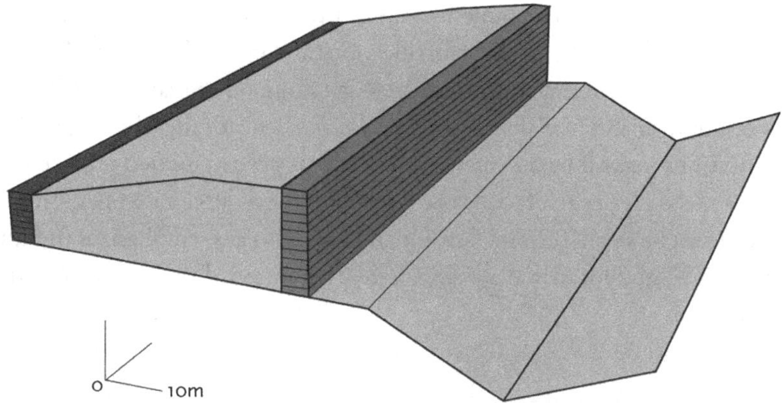

FIGURE 4.2 Reconstruction of the Esquiline *agger* and *fossa*.
Drawing © S. Bernard.

wall of *tufo giallo* and an interior wall of *tufo del Palatino,* as reconstructed in figure 4.2.

Some suggest that this situation represents two phases; as I understand the argument, the *agger*'s interior containment wall of *tufo del Palatino* would have continued in use from the Archaic period to the Mid-Republic, while the exterior wall of *tufo giallo* replaced an earlier one of *tufo del Palatino.* [26] The reasons for the need to replace one face of the *agger* entirely but not the other would in that case be obscure. More problematically, several signs of an older, dismantled *agger* in this area of the city lend little support to the idea that the Mid-Republican *agger* incorporated or reused existing earlier fortifications in this way. Lugli noted sections of a *tufo del Palatino* wall backed with earth to the west of the larger Republican *agger.*[27] In 1999, a similar wall of *tufo del Palatino* backed with earth, perhaps a continuation of the same structure, was excavated beneath a train platform of Termini station in an area directly below the fourth-century *agger*, whose construction apparently involved the earlier wall's partial dismantling and burial.[28] A similar situation appears nearby beneath the modern church of San Vito. Here, the *tufo del Palatino* wall of the Archaic *porta Esquilina* was buried beneath several meters of fill below the course of the Republican walls. Even as the Republican *porta*

26. Cifani 2008: 51–3; not all proponents of the sixth-century circuit share this view, as see Menghi 2008: 32.

27. Lugli 1933: 27; Bernard 2012: 15.

28. Menghi 2008: 34 also notes differences in construction technique.

Esquilina maintained the same location as the earlier gate, the Republican builders dismantled the Archaic fortifications and raised the terrain above the earlier gate, constructing an entirely new structure on the same spot.[29] These sections of dismantled walls of *tufo del Palatino* beneath the Mid-Republican fortifications make it best to envision the later *agger* as a unified project, even though the walls of each face of the *agger* employed different stones. This evidence from beneath Termini Station and San Vito also emphasizes the scale of the Mid-Republican walls even where it maintained the course of earlier fortifications.

4.2.1 Width and Height

While the original height of the Republican walls cannot be established with certainty, the highest preserved section of *tufo giallo* wall in Piazza dei Cinquecento outside Termini Station rises to 17 courses, with the lowermost courses being somewhat taller than the typical block height (0.63 as opposed to 0.59 m), producing a total extant height of 10.20 m. Originally, this section may have been taller, but this represents a minimum dimension. The circuit size of Rome's walls puts them in a class with the fortifications of Sicilian *poleis*, but they were comparatively tall: Gela's walls in their first ashlar phase were only 5.50 m high, Selinunte's walls were 8 m high, and Syracuse's walls appear to have been somewhat shorter.[30] At least part of the Roman walls were below ground level, presumably to stabilize the structure. A flaring profile and a different finish to the lowest five courses of walls at via di Sant' Anselmo on the Aventine suggest that about 3 m of the walls' height were originally below ground (figure 4.3).[31] The lowermost courses of the wall are 4.50 m wide, implying the need to excavate a foundation trench of around 3 × 5 m for the length of the walls.

In thickness, the *tufo giallo* walls display a slightly trapezoidal profile in section, thicker toward the base. Their median width is 3.60 m, and the decrease in thickness at the upper courses is roughly similar to the increase at the lower courses; the walls may be treated as a roughly rectangular polygon measuring $10.20 \times 3.60 = 36.72\ m^2$ in profile. The external wall of the *agger* included a series of buttresses at 36 m intervals. These are not precisely

29. Andrews and Bernard 2017.

30. Mertens 2002: 251.

31. Säflund 1998: 20–21.

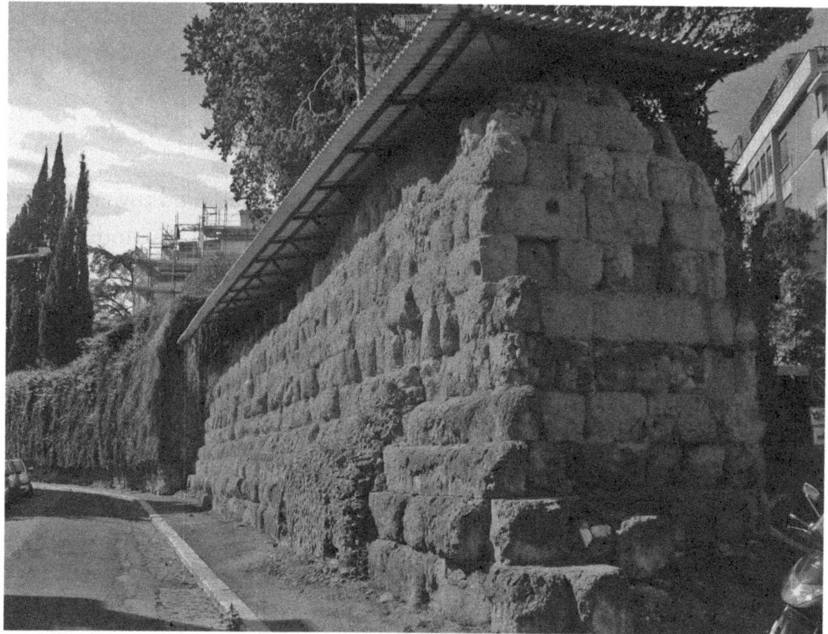

FIGURE 4.3 A section of the fortification walls on via di Sant' Anselmo on the Aventine. Note the wall's trapezoidal profile with wider lower courses.
Plan © S. Bernard.

regular, but the two best-preserved examples on the Esquiline average 3.70 m × 2.70 m, and a maximum preserved height of 4.80 m.[32] Thus, for every 36 m of the Esquiline *agger*, there is a need to account for an additional 47.90 m^3 of *tufo giallo* construction.

The interior wall of *tufo del Palatino* excavated in Piazza dei Cinquecento preserves eight courses in height, and Aurigemma suggests the possibility in some areas of a ninth course, bringing the height to 2.48 m.[33] The continuation of this wall in Largo Montemartini reaches a maximum extant height of 2.75 m, or ten courses.[34] The average width is 1.40 m, making the wall 3.85 m^2

32. The *tufo giallo* wall was not doubled in width along the *agger*, but the confusing depiction of these buttresses in profile by Aurigemma (1961–62: fig. 4) may have misled A. G. Thein (in *MAR* s.v. "*Agger*" 43) and Coarelli (1995a: 23 fig. 17). Cf. Säflund 1998: 57–58.

33. Aurigemma 1961–62; Cifani 2008: 51.

34. Säflund (1932: 69) records 12 courses and a 2.75 m height, although 12 courses would measure 3.3 m if these blocks of *tufo del Palatino* were cut on a 0.275 m foot; see Cifani 2008: 49–50.

in profile. In all cases, the *agger* was steeply graded: even a 15% grade over 42 m from an external wall of 10.20 m would require an internal wall of 3.90 m.

4.2.2 Gates and Towers

While literary sources commonly refer to the city's "walls and towers" (*muri turresque*) and "crenulations" (*pinnae*), and Strabo specifically notes towers along the *agger* (5.3.7), there is no archaeological evidence for these features whatsoever.[35] We may exclude a curvilinear wall of *tufo giallo* blocks disposed in a radial manner and projecting into the space of the *agger* at Piazza Manfredo Fanti, although this structure's function remains obscure.[36]

While at least twenty-two gate names are known, mostly from antiquarian discussions of various *portae*, the corresponding archaeological data are not easy to interpret.[37] The evidentiary problem may in part be owed to the Augustan reconstruction of many of the city's entranceways, which in several cases destroyed earlier structures.[38] The understanding of the physical layout of the Mid-Republican city's gates rests on four examples: the Collina at the northernmost corner of the circuit, the Sanqualis on the southern spur of the Quirinal, and the Viminalis and Esquilina on the Esquiline (figure 4.4). We may consider each case in turn:

i. The *porta Collina*, re-excavated in 1996–97, was laid out already in the Archaic period with two rectangular bastions on either side of its entranceway. A similarly formed entranceway with a small courtyard between two bastions is found in fourth-century fortifications at Ostia, Herdonia, and Ardea, but the Collina would represent the earliest example of this type.[39]
ii. A similar courtyard and bastions layout has been proposed for the *porta Sanqualis* based on the disposition of various fragments of wall uncovered

35. Säflund 1998: 265; cf. Varr. *apud* Cens. 1.17.8.

36. Volpe and Caruso 1995; Volpe suggests to me that this may have been a sort of sentry post.

37. See several entries in *LTUR* III 324–34 (F. Coarelli). In a confusing passage, Pliny states that the number of gates in his day was 37 (*NH* 3.66); cf. Hülsen 1897; the interpretation of Säflund 1998: 191–92 is unconvincing.

38. For the Augustan intervention on some city gates, see Coarelli 1988a: 54–59; Haselberger 2007: 204–7.

39. Brands 1988: 17–19, 196–97.

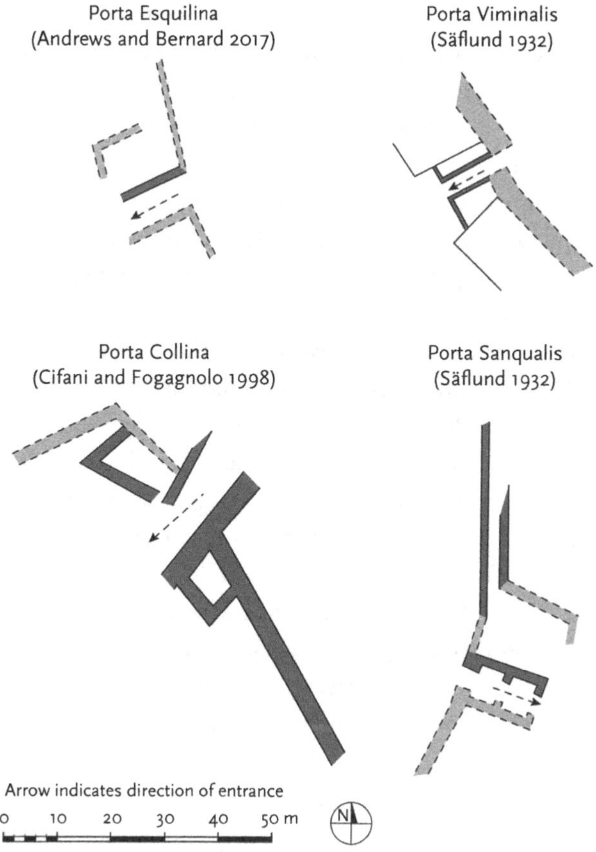

FIGURE 4.4 The gates of the Mid-Republican circuit walls shown to scale. Plan © S. Bernard.

in the nineteenth century in and around Piazza Magnanapoli.[40] This reconstruction includes the wall still visible in the traffic circle of the piazza that Lanciani attributed to the interior wall of the gate's northern bastion. In his view, the gate consisted of an entranceway oblique to the walls' path entering a small vestibule with two interior rooms. The walls' course southeast of the gate is very poorly known, so that the reconstruction is a guess, although not an impossible one.[41]

40. The proposal by Carafa 1993 that this is the *porta Fontanalis* does not sit easily with the *porticus ab porta Fontinali ad Martis aram* built in 194 (Liv. 34.44.5); see *LTUR* III 332 s.v. "'Murus Servii Tulii': Mura repubblicane: Porta Sanqualis" (F. Coarelli).

41. Bernard 2012: 28–31 with earlier literature.

iii. The *porta Viminalis*, situated by Strabo at the center of the Esquiline *agger* between the *porta Collina* and the *porta Esquilina* (5.3.7), is identifiable with the opening in the walls still visible on the north side of Piazza dei Cinquecento.[42] Two ashlar walls of *lapis Gabinus* form the sides of the entranceway as it made its way through the *agger*; the material indicates repairs of some later date.[43] The entranceway's corridor became narrower toward the exterior, forming a triangular room within the *agger*, which limited access and provided defense. There is no evidence of towers or an oblique entranceway.

iv. The location of the *porta Esquilina* beneath the modern church of San Vito presents a logical choice in the natural terrain, as the gate sat where the east-west *subura* valley running between the Cispian and Oppian hills up from the Forum basin crossed over the north-south ridge of the Esquiline. Unfortunately, while the Archaic and Augustan phases of the gate are at least partly known, nothing remains of the interim Mid-Republican phase, the construction of which entailed the dismantling and burying of the earlier phase. The Archaic gate had what appears to have been a rectangular bastion flanking the passageway. The situation recalls the *porta Collina*, although the architecture here is more fragmentary, and only a section of one wall of the northern bastion preserves.[44]

It has been suggested that Rome's Republican city gates provide early examples of a two-tower layout with a courtyard entranceway, as found in better states of preservation at several Latin colonies of the third century, but the theory finds firm archaeological support only in the *porta Collina*.[45] Even if the *Collina*'s plan is extrapolated to the more fragmentary evidence of other gates, it is hard to argue that Rome's defenses paid any attention to the use of large-scale siege artillery. The *porta Collina*'s better-preserved southern bastion is 7.50 m wide, possibly large enough for a torsion artillery engine, but small by comparison to fourth-century Hellenistic fortification towers.[46] The *porta Collina* bastions also do not project from the wall, as was typical for Hellenistic towers so as to provide better artillery range.

42. Lanciani 1876: 168–70; Säflund 1998: 63–65; Aurigemma 1961–62: 35.

43. Bernard 2012: 14–5; Farr 2014: 132–3.

44. Andrews and Bernard 2017.

45. Sewell 2010: 35–36.

46. Winters 1997: 285–86.

Instead, they were built directly into the *agger*.[47] It is also noteworthy to find installed into the fortification circuit at some later point two artillery arches in Anio tuff built within the thickness of the wall near, but not adjacent to, two gates: at Piazza Albania on the Aventine near the *porta Raudusculana*, and under Palazzo Antonelli on the Quirinal near the *porta Sanqualis*. If later engineers retrofitted the walls' course, rather than its towers, to accommodate artillery, then it seems likely that the fourth-century defenses never had towers appropriate for artillery in the first place. In thinking about the development of fortifications in Italy and Rome, much is made of Dionysius I of Syracuse's siege of Motya in 397 BCE using newly invented artillery engines.[48] However, while potential technological links between Syracusan and Mid-Republican Roman builders are discussed shortly, the material evidence for Rome's Republican defenses shows no awareness whatsoever of contemporary Syracusan poliorcetics. In the early third century, Roman colonial defenses did start to feature projecting towers for artillery. Cosa's fortifications, built in 272 BCE, display one of the earliest examples of projecting towers, while towers were retrofitted onto circuits in other Central Italian cities to defend against torsion artillery engines.[49] However, Rome's Mid-Republican walls should play no part in this discussion.

4.2.3 Agger and Fossa

Rather than western Hellenistic *poleis*, the poliorcetic context reflected by Rome's walls was that of Central Italy. This is nowhere more evident than in the complex system of earthen mound fronted by trench, the *agger* and *fossa*. Similar *aggeres*, often faced with stone, appear in Latium as early as the eighth century BCE.[50] At Rome itself, the Palatine wall excavated by Carandini lacked an earthen mound, which has led some to question whether it held a defensive purpose.[51] An earthen fortification does seem discernible on the

---

47. Fogagnolo in Cifani 1998: 385–86; as Cifani (2008: 48) notes, Juv. *Sat.* 6.291 and Sidon. Apoll. 7.132 refer to towers near the gate.

48. Cifani 2013: 206; 2016: 90.

49. Benvenuti 2002; the earliest *a cortile* gate may now be found at Castrum Inui, depending on the date, see Di Mario 2012.

50. Guaitoli 1984; Quilici 1994; Ziolkowski 2005. Adamsteanu 1956 for Sicilian *aggeres*; Fontaine (2008: 213–14) suggests that where *aggeres* appear outside of Latium, their presence may indicate Romanization.

51. Hurst and Cirone 2003: 54; Fontaine 2004; Ampolo 2013: 254.

Quirinal by the later Archaic period.[52] Otherwise, toponyms in the early city such as the "earthen wall" (*murus terreus*) in the Carinae, or the "ditches" (*fossae*) of Cluilia or of the Quirites, may relate to early *aggeres* in the city and its environs.[53]

Dionysius describes the Republican *agger* and *fossa* in full detail:

> One section which is the most vulnerable part of the city, extending from the Esquiline Gate, as it is called, to the Colline, is strengthened artificially. For there is a ditch excavated in front of it more than one hundred feet in breadth where it is narrowest, and thirty in depth; and above this rises a wall supported on the inside by an earthen rampart so high and broad that it can neither be shaken by battering rams nor thrown down by undermining the foundations. This section is about seven stades in length and fifty feet in breadth.[54]

While Dionysius' fortifications on the Esquiline and Quirinal are archaeologically attested, their measurements are somewhat different than he reports. In Piazza dei Cinquecento, the *fossa* measured 36 m in width at its top and 8 m at its base. The *fossa*'s depth of 17.10 m is consistent with nineteenth-century reports from Piazza Manfredo Fanti just to the south, where the *fossa* extended 18.00–19.60 m beneath modern ground level.[55] In profile, the Piazza dei Cinquecento *fossa* formed a trapezoid with an area of 376.20 m^2. Apparently, the sloping walls of the *fossa* were typical of Italian *fossae*, whereas *fossae* with vertical sides were "Punic."[56]

The earthen mound of the *agger* measured 42 m between the two stone walls and sloped down from outside to inside.[57] Riemann offers a solution for the significant discrepancy in the width of the excavated *agger* (about 140

---

52. Boni 1910: 510–12 with Bernard 2012: 33–34.

53. Varr. *Ling.* 5.48 with Quilici 1994: 147; Liv. 1.23.3 and 1.33.5-7 with *LTUR* II s.v. "Fossae Quiritium" 360 (F. Coarelli); Fest. 304L.

54. Dion. Hal. 9.68.3–4, ἓν δὲ χωρίον, ὃ τῆς πόλεως ἐπιμαχώτατόν ἐστιν, ἀπὸ τῶν Αἰσκυλίνων καλουμένων πυλῶν μέχρι τῶν Κολλίνων, χειροποιήτως ἐστὶν ὀχυρόν. τάφρος τε γὰρ ὀρώρυκται πρὸ αὐτοῦ πλάτος ᾗ βραχυτάτη μείζων ἑκατὸν ποδῶν, καὶ βάθος ἐστὶν αὐτῆς τριακοντάπουν: τεῖχος δ᾽ ὑπερανέστηκε τῆς τάφρου χώματι προσεχόμενον ἔνδοθεν ὑψηλῷ καὶ πλατεῖ, οἷον μήτε κριοῖς κατασεισθῆναι μήτε ὑπορυττομένων τῶν θεμελίων ἀνατραπῆναι. τοῦτο τὸ χωρίον ἑπτὰ μέν ἐστι μάλιστ᾽ ἐπὶ μῆκος σταδίων, πεντήκοντα δὲ ποδῶν ἐπὶ πλάτος.

55. Säflund 1998: 47.

56. Ps.-Hyg. *De munit. castr.* 40.

57. Aurigemma 1961–62: 21.

Roman feet) and Dionysius' claim of an *agger* width of 50 feet, arguing that the *agger* was flat for 50 Roman feet nearest the exterior wall, from which point it sloped sharply down to the interior wall.[58] In profile, an *agger* of these dimensions has an area of 1167.30 m^2.

The Esquiline *agger* extended south beyond the *porta Esquilina* at least as far as the gardens of Maecenas, as confirmed by Horace's comment that Maecenas' estate transformed the *agger* into a pleasant park (*Sat.* 1.8.15–16), while the so-called Auditorium of Maecenas was inserted directly into the external *agger* wall. The *fossa* must have terminated somewhere near the *porta Esquilina*, as burials on the Esquiline dating from the fourth century sit just east of the Horti Maecenatis, where the *fossa* would otherwise have run.[59] The total length of the Esquiline *agger* was around 1,400 m, making it among the longest in Latium.[60]

Away from the Esquiline, signs of a smaller *agger* appear widely around the city. On the Quirinal and to the west of Dionysius' limit of the *porta Collina*, traces of an *agger* have been identified near the church of Santa Susanna, while a large section of *agger* was excavated in 1907 during the construction of the offices of the Ministero di Agricoltura on via Antonio Salandra.[61] A fragmentary wall of *tufo del Palatino* north of Piazza Magnanapoli has been identified as a containment wall, and this might indicate that an *agger* circled almost the entire Quirinal around to the *porta Sanqualis*.[62] The Aventine walls also included an earthen *agger*, which has been identified near Piazza Albania and on the lesser Aventine between the churches of San Saba and Santa Balbina.[63] In the last case, a small *fossa* was found measuring 7.50–8.20 m deep, but the breadth was not recorded.[64] Based on the Quirinal *agger*, Riemann reconstructed the city's smaller *agger*'s dimensions with a sectional area of 297.30 m^2.[65] For the purpose of the model, I restore the complex Esquiline

58. Riemann 1969: 108.

59. *MAR* s.v. "Agger" 43 (A.G. Thein); Bodel 1994: 40–47; Lanciani's *puticuli* (cf. Varr. *Ling.* 5.25; Fest. 241L) are north of the Horti Maecenatis on via Napoleone III.

60. Quilici 1994, Anzio's *agger* was 2.5 km long.

61. Säflund 1998: 82–84; Riemann 1969: 104.

62. Bernard 2012: 29–30.

63. Säflund 1998: 22, 28.

64. Lanciani 1892: 284.

65. Riemann 1969: 108; *MAR* s.v. "Agger" 43 (A. G. Thein) suggests the *fossa* was unnecessary on the steeper Quirinal.

agger and *fossa* for 1.40 km from the *porta Collina* to the *porta Esquilina*, and a smaller *agger* with neither *fossa* nor interior stone wall on the Esquiline south of the *porta Esquilina*, on the western Quirinal, and on the Aventine, totaling 7.20 km. For the walls' remaining 2.40 km on the Caelian, from the Quirinal to the Capitoline, and through the *forum boarium*, the model reconstructs a simple ashlar wall of *tufo giallo*. There may have been an *agger* in these other sections, and there was a *fossa* on some part of the Aventine, but available evidence leaves these aspects difficult to quantify, and they are therefore excluded from my model in further interests of minimizing the resulting extrapolation of costs.

4.3. Building Techniques and Process

The walls were built in dry-set masonry of squared stone blocks without the use of ties or cramps. A section on the Esquiline destroyed in 1907 had blocks joined with iron clamps, but the use of *peperino* suggests this was later repair.[66] Blocks were coarsely dressed and show only minor anathyrosis, while some well-preserved blocks display axe marks. The lack of evidence for plaster or stucco, particularly in a few places where later ancient structures are built immediately against the walls' exterior surface and should therefore have preserved any original finish, suggest that the Republican walls were undecorated.[67] Courses were laid either entirely in headers or in stretchers, a style that was common practice in Central Italian ashlar masonry, and perhaps what Vitruvius referred to as stonemasonry *in alternis coriis*.[68] This differs from the Greek *emplekton* technique of in-facing blocks (*diatonoi*) bonding courses to the core, as appears widely in fortifications of Magna Graecia.[69]

---

66. Säflund 1998: 54–55; Coarelli 1995a: 25 fig. 19.

67. E.g., on via di Sant'Anselmo, an *opus reticulatum* wall is built immediately against the *tufo giallo* of the circuit walls with no trace of plaster between; beneath Santa Sabina, an *insula* built against the circuit walls has frescoes applied directly to the surface of *tufo giallo* blocks. Note that walls in other periods of antiquity could be decorated extensively. Bidwell 1996 notes plaster on sections of Hadrian's Wall and elsewhere in Britain and Germany, which lends support to Aelius Aristides' reference to city walls "gleaming with stucco" (*Orat.* 26.83). I thank J. DeLaine for bringing this evidence to my attention.

68. *De Arch.* 2.3.4; Lugli 1957: 181–83; Castagnoli 1974: 431–32; Säflund 1998: 119.

69. Cf. Vitr. *De Arch.* 2.8.7; also Plin. *NH* 36.22.51; Karlsson 1992: 67–86; Gros 2003: 119–20.

4.3.1 Material, Module, Block-Weight

The primary material of the fourth century wall, as mentioned, were blocks of *tufo giallo* from the Grotta Oscura quarries cut on an ideal module of 2 × 2 × 4 Roman feet on a foot of 29.50 cm, thus 0.59 × 0.59 × 1.18 m = 0.41 m^3. As this tuff has a standard weight of 1,520 kg/m^3, each block weighed an average 624 kg. Because of the material's friability and the relatively inexact method of its extraction, block length was somewhat variable with some blocks reaching 1.50 m in length and weighing upwards of 850 kg. Meanwhile, *tufo del Palatino* weighs 1,890 kg/m^3 and was one of the heavier tuffs employed in Roman architecture. The material was cut consistently from the first use of squared-off *tufo del Palatino* in the sixth century BCE on a smaller module, ideally 1 × 2 × 3 Roman feet with a foot of 27.50 cm, thus 0.27 × 0.54 × 0.83 m = 0.12 m^3. Individual blocks of this stone weighed 229 kg on average.[70]

4.3.2 Metrology

Observing the size of the *tufo giallo* blocks, the wall in *tufo giallo* appears to show a basic unit of a foot of approximately 0.295 m, a unit which appears in the architecture of late fifth and early fourth-century Syracuse.[71] The unit appeared at Rome in architecture earlier than the walls, but inconsistently, and Cifani suggests that Roman metrology was fluid and transitional in the Early Republic.[72] The 0.295 m foot appeared more consistently in architecture employing *tufo giallo*, and the wall was, of course, the first major monument built of that stone. Looking at the walls' plan, Säflund first noted that the 36 m distance between two masonry seams in the long stretch of wall at Piazza dei Cinquecento equaled roughly 120 Sicilian feet, or one *actus*.[73] This stretch of wall does not bond to the walls' extension on either side, as shown in figure 4.5, and this separate panel plausibly relates to a division in the organization of the walls' construction.

Diodorus reports that Dionysius I of Syracuse divided up the workers for his fortification project into *plethra* (100 feet), and the panel reflects similar Roman organizational practice. When divided into 36 m, the slightly smaller Oscan-Italic foot results in an inexact division into more than 130 feet, a

70. Specific weights from Jackson et al. 2005: 502.

71. Säflund 1998: 232ff.; Lugli 1957: 193. It was slightly smaller than the Attic foot of Periclean builders, 0.3083 m according to Hültsch 1882: 66–67.

72. Cifani 2008: 239–40.

73. See Bernard 2012: 9–10.

FIGURE 4.5 *Agger* walls in Piazza dei Cinquecento. Masonry seam indicated by arrows. Photo © S. Bernard.

number that does not mesh well with known Roman metrological systems. Again, using the same measurement, the width of the *agger* from the wall in *tufo giallo* to the wall in *tufo del Palatino* is recorded by Aurigemma as 42.00 m: 140 Syracusan feet, but about 153 Oscan-Italic feet.

The appearance of a foot of Syracusan rather than Italian origin in the planning of the *agger* and elsewhere suggests the participation of Syracusan masons in the engineering of Rome's walls, but it is interesting that this observation comes mostly in relation to measurements of the plan of the *agger*, a feature that is not part of Syracuse's own defenses. The technological background is thus complex: while influence of Syracusan technology appeared in the walls' layout and design, the overarching poliorcetic context remained Italian.

4.3.3 Masons' marks

Letters or marks appear semi-regularly on blocks of *tufo giallo*, and almost only on this stone.[74] Early discussion of these mason's marks has been

74. Zeggio 2006: 69 notes marks on *tufo del Palatino* from the *curiae veteres* sanctuary below the Palatine.

linguistic and concerned with supporting various theses of influence in the walls' plan. Thus, Säflund argued for Greek letters employed by Syracusan masons, while Castagnoli suggested the alphabet was Archaic Latin in support of his view of a more autochthonous design.[75] Since the early epigraphic Latin alphabet is a Greek alphabet, perhaps brought via Etruria to Latium, this discussion is unhelpful. Moreover, marks continue to appear almost exclusively on *tufo giallo* at Rome as late as the second century BCE. Unless we are prepared to suggest these later instances are all reused blocks from a stockpile two centuries old, and this seems doubtful, then the long practice hardly attests to cultural influence at any single moment in time. Volpe recently takes a more productive approach: noting the large number of construction sites implied by a project of the wall's scale, as well as at least ten other monuments in which marked blocks appear around Rome, she argues that such marks relate to the organization of the complex system that delivered massive quantities of material from quarries to worksites around the city. Since the stone arrived at Rome on the Tiber by raft, she furthermore suggests that each mark may correlate to single boatloads of material.[76]

Further information may be gleaned by looking more closely at the distribution of various marks on specific sections of the walls. For example, fifteen of the nineteen marks observed on the apse-like structure at Piazza Manfredo Fanti have the same **E** letter-form. The aforementioned 36 m panel of wall in Piazza dei Cinquecento is similarly interesting in this regard. Although the monument's degradation has left few marks visible today, Säflund's drawings show that two marks (**H** and **T**) make up 21/26 examples in the lowest eight courses (figure 4.6). On the upper eight courses, however, no **T** and only one **H** appear, and instead 23 of 25 marks are **Π**. In the continuation of the wall north and south of this central 36 m panel, however, all three marks are extremely rare, while the northern extension shows predominantly (marks and the southern extension shows over a dozen arrow-shaped marks similar in form to an Etruscan *kh*. Since the 36 m panel was built separately from its abutting southern and northern extensions, and since it was built from the bottom up, this distribution of marks should relate to the progressive supply of material to the worksite.

75. Säflund 1998: 104–14; Castagnoli, 1974: 432; see also Richter 1885; Frank 1924; *RMR* 12–14 (Lazzarini); Lugli 1957: 199–207; Bernard 2012: 11; Volpe 2014: 66–70.

76. Volpe 2014.

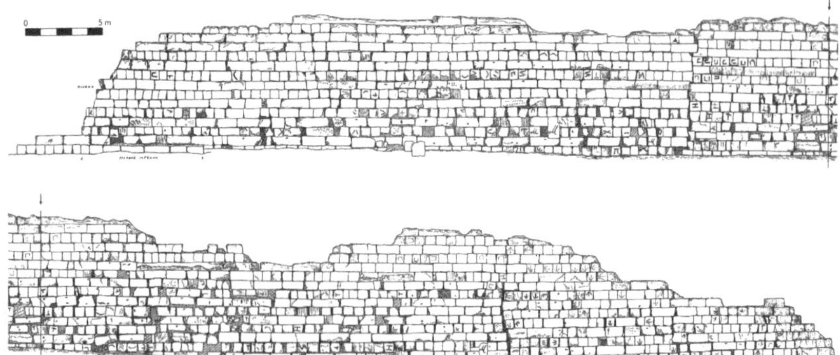

FIGURE 4.6 Säflund's drawing of the Piazza dei Cinquecento *agger* walls showing the eastern (interior) face. Visible are both masons' marks and lifting tong holes.
Image reproduced with permission from Säflund 1932 (repr. 1998), table 25.

Marks are unattested on other tuffs such as *tufo lionato di Aniene* delivered to Rome by boat. If this means that marks do not relate to the riverine delivery of stone *per se*, how else might we understand their function as connected to the supply of stone? An important detail is provided by Vitruvius and Pliny, who discuss the need to cure local tuffs before using them in urban construction. Both writers specify that, after quarrying, this stone needed to rest two years exposed to the elements; only stone that had passed this period uninjured was suitable for use in load-supporting walls.[77] Since no masons' marks have been found at the quarries themselves, it is possible that marks relate to this intermediary proofing stage and served to indicate that a block or stockpile of blocks had proven of sufficient quality.

4.3.4 Lifting Machines

Blocks of *tufo del Palatino* show no evidence of any mechanisms for attaching ropes from cranes. This does not mean that cranes were not involved in the construction of walls of *tufo del Palatino*, and it is not impossible that blocks were maneuvered with rope-cradles suspended from cranes. But it is also possible that builders placed these blocks, smaller in size than those of *tufo giallo*, using sledges and earthen ramps, and the latter technique is attested in Roman architecture from the Archaic period.[78]

77. *De Arch.* 2.7.5; Plin. *HN* 36.50.170; see further pp. 195–6.

78. Ioppolo 1989: 31; Cifani 2008: 241–42.

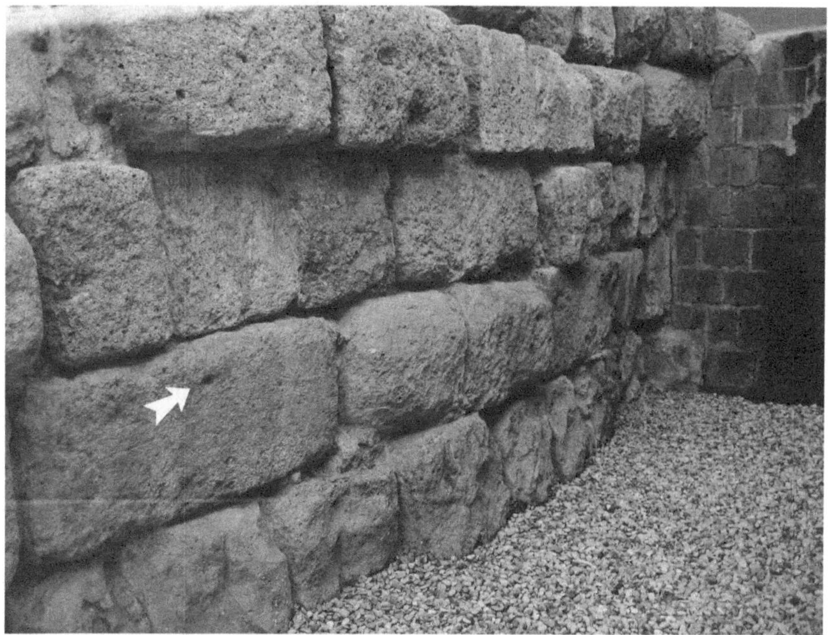

FIGURE 4.7 Section of walls in the entranceway of a modern apartment building at via Mecenate no. 35. Hole for insertion of iron lifting tongs indicated by arrow.
Photo © S. Bernard.

Many blocks of *tufo giallo*, however, show the earliest identifiable evidence of lifting machines in Roman architecture in the form of small indentations on the lateral sides of some blocks (figure 4.7). These holes were carved for the insertion of lifting tongs referred to by Vitruvius as "iron forceps" (*ferrei forfices*).[79] Etruscan architecture presents some rare examples of holes for *ferrei forfices* in the sixth century.[80] It may be that the technology was brought to the city from Etruria, and this idea is attractive when we consider the wall used copious amounts of stone quarried in the territory of the conquered Etruscan capital of Veii.

The walls' evidence for lifting tongs is not straightforward, however. In several places, blocks display indentations for tongs on the lower margins of a block's face. This is true not only in the walls' lower courses, but in its upper

79. Vitr. 10.2.2; for general discussion of lifting tongs, see Schröck 2012; Bernard 2013a: 101–2; below pp. 212–20.

80. Colonna 1986: 430, 448; Cifani 2008: 242.

courses as well. The implications for the walls' assembly stem from how tongs work: the forceps- or scissors-like configuration of the tongs drives their tips into the block, locking them into the indentations when they are loaded with the block's weight. The tong holes are therefore carved above a block's center of gravity. If loaded below its center of gravity, a block will swivel until it hangs from the tongs, thereby loading and locking the tong's points into the block. Thus, a block found with indentations on its lower margins was not placed with tongs. In architecture of other periods, one sometimes finds lifting-tong holes consistently upside-down, so to speak, as blocks are manually revolved or flipped into place after being lifted to a required height. This is often the case in structures that are several blocks thick, since lifting tongs must be disengaged before setting blocks flush against each other. However, the Roman walls show no such consistency, and the random distribution of tong holes suggests instead that cranes and tongs were used at *some* stage of the building process, but not in a systematic manner for the final task of placing blocks into courses. I would suggest that the division relates to the supply of *tufo giallo* to Rome, as tong holes appear only on that material and never on *tufo del Palatino*. Since *tufo giallo* arrived on the Tiber, cranes may have been used to offload blocks at the port and then load them onto carts for intra-urban transport. Loading stone on and off boats at the Tiber banks was an awkward step in the supply chain. Once offloaded, however, stone could be maneuvered around the city and placed into the walls using traditional means. When we remember that much of the stone walls were built directly against an *agger*, the use of an earthen ramp for positioning blocks seems logical. Indeed, excavators have sometimes noted a correspondence between the stratified layers of the *agger* and courses of the walls' blocks.[81]

4.4. The Labor Cost of the Republican Walls

Based on the foregoing discussion, the walls required volumes of building materials as summarized in table 4.1. To extrapolate from these figures to total labor-cost, we need to know how much the production of each component cost in terms of working time. Abrams usefully breaks down total cost into four primary construction phases: 1) extraction of materials, 2) processing of materials, 3) transport of materials from source to site, and 4) assembly on site. Table 4.2 sets out the labor requirements for

81. Lanciani 1871: 61; Boni 1910: 510–14.

Table 4.1. Volumetric measurements of materials for the walls' construction

Component	Volume/Quantity
Blocks of *tufo giallo*	405,568 m^3 = 989,190 blocks
Blocks of *tufo del Palatino*	5,390 m^3 = 44,917 blocks
Earth excavation for *fossa* and foundation trench	691,680 m^3
Earth for the *agger*	3,774,780 m^3

Table 4.2. Work rates for the production of the wall

Operational phase	Specific task	Rate in person-days (PD) with skill specified where applicable
Extraction	Quarrying	0.92 skilled + 1.84 unskilled per block of *tufo giallo* 0.33 skilled + 0.66 unskilled per block of *tufo del Palatino*
Processing	Squaring and facing of blocks	1.0 skilled per block of *tufo giallo* and 0.43 skilled per block of *tufo del Palatino*
Transport	Transport of *tufo giallo* to Rome on the Tiber	Each shipment of 18 blocks required 6 PD unskilled.
	Movement of material to building sites	0.13 unskilled per block of *tufo giallo* and 0.02 unskilled per block of *tufo del Palatino* with 0.1 skilled + 0.1 unskilled per cartload for loading
Assembly	Stone masonry, lifting and maneuvering blocks into place	0.39 PD skilled + 0.52 PD unskilled per block of *tufo giallo* 0.06 PD skilled + 0.08 unskilled per block of *tufo del Palatino*
	Earth excavation and removing earth in baskets	0.28 PD unskilled per m^3
	Earth mounding	0.34 PD unskilled per m^3

Table 4.3. Cost analysis of the Republican walls

Construction stage	Cost breakdown	Cost in person-days (PD)
I. Extraction (41%)	Quarrying stone	930,917 skilled + 1,861,832 unskilled
II. Processing (15%)	Shaping stone	1,008,195 skilled
III. Transport (9%)	a. River shipment of *tufo giallo*	38,469 skilled + 368,199 unskilled
	b. Intra-urban movement of stone	41,412 skilled + 170,589 unskilled
IV. Construction (35%)	Ashlar walls	388,436 skilled + 517,915 unskilled
	Earth excavation	193,670 unskilled
	Earth assembly	1,283,425 unskilled
Total cost		6,803,059 PD

each phase in person-days (PD); more detailed discussion can be found in appendix 1.

For simplification, the model considers all labor for activities such as transport not related to building unskilled. Applying these rates to the volumetric measurements produces the costs detailed in table 4.3. While the interior *agger* wall is included in this calculation, I note that the argument assigning all *tufo del Palatino* to a supposed Archaic phase sheds only about 1–2% of total cost. This further emphasizes the magnitude of the Mid-Republican project, whatever previous fortifications it is held to have replaced. In seeking a minimum cost, the model ignores several variables that would increase the project's overall labor needs, among them site clearance including the removal of parts of the old *agger* on the Esquiline, and cost of manufacturing tools, cranes, scaffolding, and so forth.

The resulting quantification produces a large number, and the remainder of the chapter turns to situate this figure in its socioeconomic context. Before doing so, it will be valuable to keep in mind some aspects of this total cost. First, approximately 65% of all labor was unskilled. Second, the model can be decomposed into the relative costs of each stage of the construction process (figure 4.8). The resulting proportion of off-site to on-site costs (65:35) is not atypical of pre-modern building projects where the labor expended on extraction and transport often far exceeded that for on-site assembly.

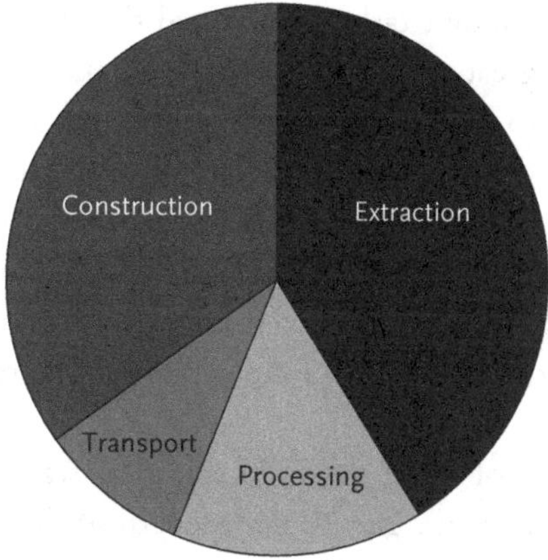

FIGURE 4.8 Pie chart showing the breakdown of total cost into construction stages

4.5. A Cost Comparison with the Syracusan Wall

Several further aspects of the cost model emerge when compared more closely to Diodorus' description of wall building under Dionysius I of Syracuse in 401 BCE. Here is the full passage:

> Sending, therefore, for his master-builders, in accord with their advice he decided that he must fortify Epipolae at the point where there stands now the Wall with the Six Gates . . . Wishing to complete the building of the walls rapidly, he gathered the peasants from the countryside, from whom he selected some sixty thousand capable men and parcelled out to them the space to be walled. For each stade he appointed a master-builder and for each plethron a mason, and the laborers from the common people assigned to the task numbered two hundred for each plethron. Besides these, other workers, a multitude in number, quarried out the rough stone, and six thousand yoke of oxen brought it to the appointed place. And the united labor of so many workers struck the watchers with great amazement, since all were zealous to complete the task assigned them. For Dionysius, in order to excite the enthusiasm of the multitude, offered valuable gifts to such as finished first, special ones for the master-builders, and still others for the masons and in turn for the common laborers; and he in person, together with his friends, oversaw the work through all the days required, visiting every section and ever lending a hand to the toilers. Speaking generally, he laid aside the dignity of his office and reduced himself to the ranks. Putting

> his hands to the hardest tasks, he endured the same toil as the other workers, so that great rivalry was engendered and some added even a part of the night to the day's labor, such eagerness had infected the multitude for the task. As a result, contrary to expectation, the wall was brought to completion in twenty days. It was thirty stades in length and of corresponding height, and the added strength of the wall made it impregnable to assault; for there were lofty towers at frequent intervals and it was constructed of stones four feet long and carefully joined.[82]

This was the second of three major fortification walls undertaken by the long-lived Syracusan tyrant. The 30 *stade* length of the stretch described by Diodorus accords well with the distance between the Epipolai Gate and the area east of the Hexapylon Gate along the north of the Epipolai plateau, to the west of the city of Syracuse itself. The walls' remains can be traced for most of this extent, about 5.70 km.[83] Diodorus' account is highly detailed and, in many ways, should be taken as reliable. His source here was the *Peri Dionysiou* of Philistus, an author who had the advantage of being an eyewitness to the building project, but the disadvantage, so far as we are concerned, of being a court historian.[84] Philistus' treatment of the Syracusan tyrant was wholly positive, going so far as to describe the king's personal willingness to

82. Diod. Sic. 14.18.3–8: 3. διόπερ τοὺς ἀρχιτέκτονας παραλαβών, ἀπὸ τῆς τούτων γνώμης ἔκρινε δεῖν τειχίσαι τὰς Επιπολάς, ᾗ νῦν τὸ πρὸς τοῖς Εξαπύλοις ὑπάρχει τεῖχος. 4. . . . βουλόμενος οὖν ταχεῖαν τὴν κατασκευὴν τῶν τειχῶν γίνεσθαι, τὸν ἀπὸ τῆς χώρας ὄχλον ἤθροισεν, ἐξ οὗ τοὺς εὐθέτους ἄνδρας ἐλευθέρους ἐπιλέξας εἰς ἑξακισμυρίους ἐπιδιεῖλε τούτοις τὸν τειχιζόμενον τόπον. 5. καθ᾽ ἕκαστον μὲν οὖν στάδιον ἀρχιτέκτονας ἐπέστησε, κατὰ δὲ πλέθρον ἐπέταξεν οἰκοδόμους, καὶ τοὺς τούτοις ὑπηρετήσοντας ἐκ τῶν ἰδιωτῶν εἰς ἕκαστον πλέθρον διακοσίους. χωρὶς δὲ τούτων ἕτεροι παμπληθεῖς τὸν ἀριθμὸν ἔτεμνον τὸν ἀνέργαστον λίθον: ἑξακισχίλια δὲ ζεύγη βοῶν ἐπὶ τὸν οἰκεῖον τόπον παρεκόμιζεν. 6. ἡ δὲ τῶν ἐργαζομένων πολυχειρία πολλὴν παρείχετο τοῖς θεωμένοις κατάπληξιν, ἁπάντων σπευδόντων τελέσαι τὸ τεταγμένον. ὁ γὰρ Διονύσιος τὴν προθυμίαν τοῦ πλήθους ἐκκαλούμενος μεγάλας προέθηκε δωρεὰς τοῖς προτερήσασι, δίχα μὲν τοῖς ἀρχιτέκτοσι, χωρὶς δὲ τοῖς οἰκοδόμοις καὶ πάλιν τοῖς ἐργαζομένοις: καὶ αὐτὸς δὲ μετὰ τῶν φίλων προσήδρευε τὰς ἡμέρας ὅλας τοῖς ἔργοις, ἐπὶ πάντα τόπον ἐπιφαινόμενος καὶ τοῖς κακοπαθοῦσιν αἰεὶ προσλαμβάνων. 7. καθόλου δ᾽ ἀποθέμενος τὸ τῆς ἀρχῆς βάρος ἰδιώτην αὑτὸν ἀπεδείκνυε, καὶ τοῖς βαρυτάτοις τῶν ἔργων προσιστάμενος ὑπέμενε τὴν αὐτὴν τοῖς ἄλλοις κακοπάθειαν, ὥστε πολλὴ μὲν ἔρις ἐγίνετο καὶ τοῖς τῆς ἡμέρας ἔργοις ἔνιοι προσετίθεσαν καὶ μέρη τῶν νυκτῶν: τοσαύτη σπουδὴ τοῖς πλήθεσιν ἐνε πεπτώκει. 8. διόπερ ἀνελπίστως ἐν ἡμέραις εἴκοσι τέλος ἔσχε τὸ τεῖχος, τὸ μὲν μῆκος κατασκευασθὲν ἐπὶ σταδίους τριάκοντα, τὸ δὲ ὕψος σύμμετρον, ὥστε τῷ τοίχῳ τῆς ὀχυρότητος προσγενομένης ἀνάλωτον ἐκ βίας ὑπάρξαι: τοῖς γὰρ πύργοις διείληπτο πυκνοῖς καὶ ὑψηλοῖς, ἔκ τε λίθων ᾠκοδόμητο τετραπέδων φιλοτίμως συνειργασμένων.

83. Drögemüller 1969: 97–103; Karlsson 1992: 14; Mertens 2002; 2006: 424–33.

84. On Philistus' relationship with Dionysius, see Diod. Sic. 16.16.3 with Jacoby *FrGH* III.B.496–502; Meister 2002.

join in the building effort. Likewise, although neither citizen labor forces nor short building times are unparalleled, the size of the labor force assembled (60,000) and the rapidity of the construction project (twenty days) serve to compliment the king's abilities and are therefore suspect to rhetorical exaggeration. As Mertens notes, a workforce of 60,000 men parceled out along a 5.70 km wall implies a logistical nightmare, with over ten workers assigned to each linear meter of wall.[85] If it can be at all trusted, perhaps the 60,000 figure encompassed both actual assembly and the unspecified number of workers involved in supplying material. In this case, the Syracusan wall had a maximum cost of 1,200,000 PD. This project was half the length of the Roman Republican circuit and a little over half its height. It lacked an *agger* and *fossa*, and, rather than solid masonry, its stone walls were built in *emplekton* style with two ashlar faces and a core filled with rubble. There are moreover signs of quarrying along the walls' course, so that material was probably supplied on-site if not very near to it.[86] All of these aspects reduced the Syracusan walls cost by comparison to Rome's walls. Still, I note that, if we take the total cost of Rome's walls less shipment of material and divide by four to account in a simplistic manner for the difference in each walls' dimensions, the resulting figure of 1,331,491 PD is strikingly close to the Syracusan walls' costs according to Diodorous.

Diodorus' figures for the number and organization of skilled masons are less likely to show rhetorical manipulation, as the ratio of skilled to unskilled laborer had little bearing on Dionysius' effectiveness as a ruler as presented by Philistus. Dionysius was famous for attracting skilled military engineers to his kingdom, and besides Syracuse he was involved in fortifying several sites in south Italy and Sicily, and the king's investment in fortification technology gives further confidence to Philistus' report.[87] The ratio that Diodorus reports is 1 master-builder to 6 masons to 200 laborers, or 7:200 skilled to unskilled workers per *stade* of wall. This not only confirms the plausibility of the 7:13 ratio of skilled to unskilled workers in the model of Rome's walls but suggests that, if anything, the model exaggerates the need for skilled labor at Rome.[88] In comparative terms, the low demand for skilled labor at both Rome

85. Mertens 2002: 251.

86. Karlsson 1992: 107.

87. Mertens 2006: 433–34.

88. Pegoretti's figures describe skill levels in industrialization-era workforces, and this may have some effect on the model. Relevant is Saller 2012 on low Roman investment in human capital formation.

and Syracuse is remarkable. In early modern Europe, fortification projects could entail ratios of 3:2, and typically over half of building workforces were skilled.[89]

One last aspect that Diodorus' description emphasizes is the high number of oxen required, even if the 6,000 yoke counted by Diodorus is inflated to some extent. The cost model for the Republican walls, for which stone was transported a farther distance and by a more complex supply chain, counts one team of oxen to tow each boat back up the Tiber from Rome to the Grotta Oscura quarries after it had delivered stone to Rome. I also count on the movement of stone from Tiber port to construction site by oxen cart, with carts likely unable to move loads larger than one block at a time at a rate of about seven out-and-back trips per day. Focusing only on *tufo giallo*, that extrapolates to a cost for the Roman Republican walls of 196,268 "yoke-days" and stresses the non-human demands the project placed on the larger Roman economy, surely raising the Roman walls' real costs above those modeled here.

4.6. Organizing the Project

As the walls were a public monument, the project was organized by the Roman state. To consider what this means, I start by suggesting a range of *per capita* cost before turning to the organizational structure by which the state met that cost. One advantage to a project reliant mostly on unskilled labor was its ability to draw from a larger proportion of Rome's available labor force. In relation to the quarrying and processing of relatively soft tuff, many of the tasks considered here to have been "skilled" were in actuality semi- or low-skilled and could be learned relatively quickly. Thus, I consider the *per capita* cost starting from the potential population of the *ager Romanus* in the early fourth century BCE. This is not an easy task and presents two particular problems: first, the slave population is unknowable in any direct manner for this or any other period in Roman history; second, the precise understanding of the free population at this moment depends almost entirely on a single census report of dubious historical value.

First, the slave population. The last chapter argued that it is likely that exploiting the newly conquered *ager Veientanus* required a significant proportion of the enslaved population of Veii to be put to work on that land, as Roman expansion put pressure on labor relative to landholding. The

89. Woodward 1995: 99; generally, Goldthwaite 1980: 348.

production of stone from Veian territory must be viewed in this context. It is suggestive that the first large-scale exploitation of Veian tuff followed the conquest of Veii and the enslavement of its population. Quarries were regular destinations for war slaves in antiquity, and it is reasonably suggested that much of the walls' extraction costs were met by slave labor.[90] The sudden acquisition of a large labor force close to quarry zones moreover may help in part to explain the longstanding question of why Rome relied so heavily on a less durable tuff like *tufo giallo della via Tiberina*.

If slaves bore the burden of extracting stone, 41% of the project's total cost was not exactly costless, but slaves could be maintained at closer to starvation rates, and, if they were state-owned, the cost of their maintenance could be distributed across the entire Roman economy. For some idea of what maintaining slaves may have entailed in the early Republic, the Twelve Tables (tab. 3.3) specify that imprisoned debtors received a minimum of one *libra* (327 g) of *far* (emmer wheat) per day.[91] Scarcely more than a thousand calories, this was well below starvation level and implausible for someone involved in strenuous work, but it suggests an absolute minimum wheat-cost of slaves involved in quarrying stone for the walls of 913,228 kg distributed across the Roman economy.

This leaves for the free population the remaining 59% of the cost of processing and transporting material, and on-site assembly, equivalent to 4,010,310 PD. If the remainder of the eligible workforce was roughly equivalent to the military force, and further reasons for this equation are noted below, then model life tables suggest that men aged 17–45 made up 21.75% of the total population.[92] The next required ingredient is a notion of the citizen population at the time. Determining this is no easy matter, but we may start from the much-discussed Roman census returns, and particularly the temporally closest figure of 152,573 "free Romans" (*capita libera*) for 392 BCE, reported by Pliny (*NH* 33.16). Problematically, what proportion of Romans these Republican census figures reported, and how accurately they did so, are highly controversial topics. Census figures for the period are provided in table 4.4.

90. Frank 1918: 183; for quarries and captives, see Varr. *Ling.* 5.151.

91. Ampolo 1980: 24–25.

92. Coale and Demeny 1983 West level 3 (0% growth); for the methodology, see Hin 2008: 198–99.

Table 4.4. Mid-Republican census reports down to the Hannibalic War*

Year	Number
392	152,573
340	165,000
c. 323	150,000 (or 250,000)
294	262,321
289?	272,000
279	287,222
275	271,224
265	292,234 (382,223)
251	297,797
244	241,712
240	260,000 (250,000)
233	270,712

* For sources, see Brunt 1971: 13–4.

In approaching these figures, it is first of all important to recognize that Roman population changes in this period are normally interpreted as institutional and arising from the extension of Roman territory and citizen status, or from changes to the census' mechanics, rather than from natural demographic phenomena.[93] In this case, if the numbers are to be trusted, then the consistency between 392 and 340 BCE followed by a sharp rise in population by 294 BCE must be understood as reflective of either a major change in total citizenship or in the way Rome counted its citizens. Consequently, Coarelli follows Frank in finding an explanation for the demographic trend in the significant citizenship extensions of the late fourth century, with six new tribes founded from 339 to 299.[94] However, Brunt notes that the figures reflected no similar rise in population in correlation to the doubling of Roman territory between 293 and 264, or the founding of two new tribes in 241, and he considers all data prior to the later third century unreliable.[95] Meanwhile, the census'

93. Brunt 1971: 28, although figures plausibly reflect mortality owed to military casualties to some extent.

94. Coarelli 1988c: 338–9; Frank 1930.

95. Brunt 1971: 31; as noted by Ampolo 1980: 27, the apparent reflection of historical events in the movement of the census figures is interpretable as the product of later, annalistic reconstruction of numbers to fit those events.

mechanics changed at some point in this period, although it is difficult to say when or why: Pliny suggested the census of 392 counted all free Romans, possibly including free women and even children, whereas later, and possibly also earlier, censuses seem to have counted only those capable of bearing arms.[96] Problems of these sort have largely led recent debate on Republican demography to set the earlier figures aside.[97]

Even beyond the issue of historical merit, there are questions concerning the feasibility of Pliny's census figure for 392 BCE. It is unlikely that 150,000 citizens lived at that date in the area represented by the Republican circuit walls. The implied urban density of approximately 400 persons/ha would make Rome by far the most populous city in Central Italy at a time when one estimate puts most other settlements' densities at around 150 persons/ha.[98] Rome would in this case have been as dense as, for example, Imperial Alexandria, which was significantly more extensive and contained multi-story housing.[99] In the early fourth century, before aqueducts were built, and over a century before the first possible signs of Roman *insulae*, Rome was unlikely to have been so densely settled.[100] Obviously, disposable labor to urban production was not limited in this period to the *urbs* itself for reasons discussed in the introductory chapter. Bradley, following Hansen's work on Greek *poleis*, suggests that Archaic Rome may have had 33% of its population within its walls, while noting that similarly large cities typically saw settlement on 33% of intramural land.[101] Applying these figures to the Mid-Republican city and assuming a relatively high urban density for that time of 200 persons/ha., the urban population would have been 24,267 and total Roman population on the order of 73,000. Roman territory in the early fourth century was

---

96. Lo Cascio 1994: 32 defends an interpretation of *capita libera* as only adult males, against the view of Frank 1930: 314 n. 5; Coarelli 1988c: 320, that Pliny refers to all free Romans, but the implied total population of almost 700,000 seems exceedingly high and would require an urban population alone in this period of about 140,000, which is unlikely for reasons discussed below. Generally on the census' changing purpose, Lo Cascio 2001, esp. 575; Hin 2008. Complicating matters, the Servian census already reputedly counted Romans able to bear arms (Liv. 1.44, citing Fabius Pictor).

97. Cf. e.g., De Ligt 2012; Hin 2013.

98. Cristofani 1984: 31.

99. Bagnall and Frier 1994: 54.

100. See below, pp. 165–6.

101. Bradley 2017: 130 following Hansen 2006; Bradley uses a larger figure for Rome's intramural area, but see Fulminante 2014: 101–2.

Table 4.5. Matrix of *per capita* cost of building Rome's walls on the free population

Total population	Potential labor supply (males aged 17–45)	*Per capita* burden less extraction.
75,000	16,313	246 PD/person
100,000	21,750	184
125,000	27,188	147
150,000	32,616	123

significantly enlarged by the *ager Veientanus*, such that the urban population may have represented a much smaller portion of total Roman population. An overall urbanization rate for the *ager Romanus* on the order of 20%, for example, would put the total population closer to 125,000. This would make a Roman population of 150,000 in 392 BCE in accordance with Pliny's census tally possible, but also highlights the implications of such a figure, which should be treated cautiously as a sort of maximum. Consequently, I present a matrix of estimates for *per capita* cost based upon a total population ranging from 75,000–150,000 people (table 4.5). Depending on total population, the direct burden on eligible male Roman citizens ranged from 123 to 246 days' work. To understand what the subtraction of this many days per eligible worker from Roman households entailed, we need to consider several aspects of the project's organization.

4.6.1 Project Duration and Schedule

The length of the project closely corresponded to its impact since a longer project whose costs were amortized over several years would be less disruptive to other demands for labor. No clear evidence exists for the time it took to build the walls. The relevant literary sources discussed in the last chapter are as follows: Livy gives two notices for censorial fortification efforts after the sack in 390 BCE, a Capitoline *substructio* of 388 (A3) and a *murus* in 378 (A6), and it is reasonable to think that these two projects represented different stages of a larger effort. Meanwhile, the statement in Plutarch's life of Camillus that Rome was standing with new buildings and walls a year after the sack seems merely rhetorical. The only other directly relevant passage is Livy's notice that the legions in 353 BCE, after raiding Faliscan territory, returned to Rome where they spent the duration of the year repairing walls and towers.[102] This is sometimes interpreted as evidence for the continuation of the original project, but for what it's worth Livy explicitly describes repair (*reficiendis*).[103] Like Volpe, I find it hard to believe that Romans left the project incomplete for so long with the continuing threat of Gauls in Latium. In 358, a Gallic army was said to have encamped at the third mile of the Via Salaria "not too far from the *porta Collina*."[104] Unfortunately, archaeology is not in a position to provide further resolution. If there were repairs on the walls in these decades, there are no detectable variations in building technique or material to distinguish them.

Helpfully, the model points to several bottlenecks that would have constrained the overall schedule, particularly during the project's supply phases. The transport of *tufo giallo* down the Tiber required a total of 54,955 boat trips downriver, assuming a capacity of 18 blocks (7.38 m^3 of stone) per boat. A team of four laborers would take almost four hours to load each boat.[105] Let us say 100 workers assisted by 50 yokes of oxen were retained at the quarry solely for loading boats, and each team of four workers loaded two boats a day, with fifty boats shipping per day. Even in this scenario, the supply chain still required 1,000 days of active shipment to deliver the requisite stone. A minimum lead time of three or four years for the quarrying and delivery of material to Rome seems likely if not necessary. A second bottleneck was produced by the aforementioned practice of quarrying and curing tuff for a period of several years. Vitruvius expressly discouraged quarrying tuff in the winter, probably because he recognized its propensity to retain water and therefore be of inferior quality for building. If quarrying was limited to the dryer months, then the supply chain was constrained even further.

By comparison, the assembly phase of construction at Rome itself could move quickly so long as a large enough work force was provided. If we consider the 36 m panel of wall visible on the Esquiline *agger* as a typical unit for a single working team, then each team was responsible for 1,369 m^3 of stone or 3,339 blocks of *tufo giallo*. Leaving aside the *agger* and *fossa*, the stone wall of the panel required 1,302 skilled and 1,736 unskilled PD to assemble. If the wall were supplied with 200 workers, as Diodorus reports was the case for

---

102. 7.20.9: *legionibus Romam reductis reliquum anni muris turribusque reficiendis consumptum.*

103. *Contra* Cornell 1995: 462 n. 11; Coarelli 1995a: 22–23 suggests repair and ongoing construction.

104. Liv. 7.9 and 7.11.6 with Volpe 2014: 63; see also Polyb. 2.18.6.

105. DeLaine 2001: 258.

each *plethron* of Dionysius' Syracusan wall, then the work could be accomplished in about fifteen days, ignoring the breakdowns between skilled and unskilled labor.

Thus, the speed of on-site construction was relative to the supply of labor, while production and transportation of materials were constrained by other factors. It seems plausible, therefore, that the actual construction of the wall proceeded in rapid fashion, while it was the supply phase instead that was liable to delay the overall project. In light of this, I see no reason to think that Rome spent twenty or more years on the project unless they were confronted with serious manpower shortages. It goes without saying that a circuit wall best serves its purpose when complete, and it makes sense to see the Roman state investing in the project's rapid completion. The attempt to shore up the Capitoline with a *substructio* in 388 BCE may indicate the first efforts at the construction phase of the project. Coming a little over a year after the Gallic sack, the report of the *substructio* could be an indication of the time necessary to compile the requisite amount of building stone. The decade's time between the Capitoline *substructio* and the censorial project of 378 would have been sufficient for all the required material to be brought to Rome and cured, and there is nothing in the nature of the project itself to prevent the actual construction from advancing in rapid fashion after 378 BCE.

4.6.2 Forced Labor

The only literary evidence attesting to the project's organization is Livy (6.32), who recorded that the plebeians were compelled to meet the cost (*succumbere oneri coacta plebes*). The salient features of his report are as follows: in the absence of a levy (*dilectus*) that year, there was no mechanism for resisting the burden of building the walls, as otherwise the tribunes may have been able to disrupt the levy (*quem dilectum impedirent non habebant tribuni plebis*).[106] The walls were contracted for by the censors (*locatum a censoribus*), and the verb *locare* suggests that Livy envisioned a *locatio-conductio* contracting process. He otherwise referred to the arrangement as a tax (*tributum*) imposed upon the indebted plebs.[107]

106. Tribunician interference with the *dilectus* is commonly attested, e.g., Liv. 3.10, 4.5; Liv. *Per.* 48.16, 55.3; Mommsen *StR* II.1 290–97.

107. Niebuhr (1827 I.296–97) already noted problems with the applicability of *tributum*, normally a property tax, to Romans already in debt.

The conglomeration of tax, coercion, and debt suggests that Livy understood the project as a form of compulsory labor imposed by the state directly upon its citizens, as a corvée, and the theme of coercion spilled into the next chapter, when the plebs were politically coerced (*coacta*) to elect an entirely patrician slate of military tribunes (6.32.3). Payment for work and forced labor could coexist, although they are not otherwise attested together for Rome, and it is more likely that the corvée envisioned here meant that workers went unremunerated. This puts such compulsory labor at odds with Livy's suggestion that the walls were arranged by censorial *locatio*, which involved a bidding process and private contractors. Moreover, the idea of *locatio* does not harmonize with the assertion that the project caused economic problems, since Roman building contracts entailed remuneration, and there is no other recorded instance of a Republican censorial contract causing widespread private debt.

In Livy's day, Rome rarely if ever used forced labor for urban public works, and the potential anachronism of his description of corvée confirms for some that Livy's details of coercion should be privileged over those of censorial contracting.[108] The use of citizen labor is often related to similar corvées for public building attested by sources for the reigns of the despotic Tarquins, as well as for Ancus Marcius.[109] I find the idea that the walls were built using corvée labor very plausible, but it is unnecessary to base this assertion on either the tradition for the monarchy, or on Livy's internally contradictory description of the Republican walls' building process. Instead, corvée makes general sense in consideration of the broader context of the organization of labor in this period, and of the appropriateness of citizen labor for wall building found throughout antiquity.

Starting with the economic structures of labor in the early Mid-Republic, it is uncontroversial to suggest that Roman society in the eighth century followed a similar social and economic development to those communities of Latium, where Iron Age burial patterns appear to reflect the emergence of "princely" elites who, we assume, extracted wealth from beyond their immediate family through forms of obligation and dependency.[110] When, somewhat later, these kings or king-like figures began to produce monumental

108. Coarelli 1990a: 146–48; Cornell 1995: 431 n. 55.

109. For sources, see Milazzo 1993; Palombi 1997a; Tarquinian corvée appeared already in Cassius Hemina (*FRH* 6 L. Cassius Hemina F19); for Ancus Marcius, see Fest. 304 L.

110. Colonna 1988; Smith 2006: 144–63.

architecture, it is difficult to see how they accomplished this other than through similar means. While market labor cannot be discounted entirely, it seems to have been restricted in this period to skilled workers: sources, for example, reported Etruscan artisans summoned to produce the fine terracotta sculptures for the Capitolium, while the larger workforce was "coerced craftsmen and commanded workers" (*coactis fabris operisque imperatiis*).[111]

A productive mode based upon ties of obligation and coercion persisted beyond the overthrow of the monarchy, when it seems less likely that economic institutions themselves were transformed, and more likely that power passed from a single *rex* into the hands of a larger, although still limited, group of aristocrats. The continued economic importance of dependency and obligations in the Early Republican patrician state is attested to by the prominence of clientage and debt-bondage, *clientela* and *nexum*, in the Twelve Tables, as well as by the multiple stories of fifth-century military *coniurationes* (e.g., those followers of Attius Clausus, Coriolanus, or the Fabii at Cremera).[112] These stories of war-bands find support in some well-known archaeological finds, including a cache of 125 helmets from Vetulonia, many of which are inscribed with the same Etruscan gentilicium *Haspnas*, and the famous Satricum inscription recording a dedication to Mars by the *suodales* of Poplios Valesios.[113] As this material suggests, social hierarchies based upon dependency emerge in the record most clearly in relation to warfare, and the entire Early Republican army has been characterized as a loose coalition of *condottieri* and clients.[114] It seems simplest to envision similarly structured arrangements at work in other costly state activities.

Some evidence suggests in particular that an economy of civic obligations extended to the construction of fortifications. Consider Varro on the Latin word *munus* or "duty":

> *munus*, something commanded for the cause of fortification (*muniendi*), from which word also citizens (*municipes*) are called, as those who must jointly perform a *munus*.[115]

---

111. Cic. *Verr.* 2.5.48; Milazzo 1993: 24–5; Palombi 1997a: 7–10.

112. Among the vast literature on the social structure of the Early Republic, see Richard 1990; Cornell 1995, 2003; Smith 2006: 168–76.

113. Vetulonia: Egg 1986: 207; *lapis Satricanus*: Stibbe et al. 1980 and much since.

114. On Early Republican warfare, see Adam and Rouveret 1988; Smith 2006: 281–98.

115. *Ling.* 5.179: *munus, quod muniendi causa imperatum, a quo etiam municipes, qui una munus fungi debent, dicti*; cf. Pinsent 1954; Bispham 2007: 15–16.

Varro's assertion of a relationship between defensive walls and citizen obligations finds support in many other authors.[116] It is also worth emphasizing how Romans of later periods distinguished between different types of buildings on the basis of utility, and how such distinction affected the organization or financing of a building's construction. Cicero classified walls along with *navalia*, ports, and aqueducts as "better expenditures" (*impensae meliores*) because, unlike theaters, porticoes, or temples, they served the public good (*De Off.* 2.60). A similar class of *impensae meliores* including roads, ports, and irrigation systems were grouped together and associated with citizen *munera* in legal documents, and several Imperial inscriptions testify to the use of corvée for the construction of these sorts of buildings.[117] Since walls like these other monuments normally demanded more than could be provided by a community's own labor market, they frequently required the use of non-market labor to some extent. There is remarkable continuity between, for example, Thucydides' report of all Athenians helping to build the city's long walls and frequent accounts of medieval Italians participating *en masse* in the construction of their town's fortifications.[118]

Considering how commonly wall building was associated with compulsory citizen labor in antiquity, the idea that Rome distrained the costs of building the walls onto its populace makes historical sense. We might even ask whether the Republican state in the early fourth century yet possessed alternative means of raising sufficient amounts of labor. At some point, the forms of dependency and obligation typical of the Archaic state were replaced by a labor market and by slavery, as corvée seems to have formed only a trivial part of the later Roman economy. While, as mentioned, later Republican and Imperial Roman communities utilized *munera* to some extent for particular types of monuments, normal practice in such cases was an assessment on the order of five days (*operae*) per adult male. This burden was very light by comparison to other societies where corvée was more common and annual levies of 25 or even 40 days were not unheard of.[119]

---

116. Fest. 128L; Lucilius I.9 (Warmington); Serv. *ad Aen.* 11.567; Isid. *Orig.* 15.2.18.

117. Cf. *CJ* 8.11.7 and inscriptions cited by Duncan-Jones 1990: 175.

118. Thuc. 1.90 with Epstein 2008: 111–12; Goldthwaite 1980: 122 for medieval Italy.

119. See Duncan-Jones 1990: 160, five days appears in the *Lex coloniae genetivae* (*RS* no. 26, ch. XCVIII) and in *penthemeros* certificates from Egypt, on which see Sijpesteijn 1964. Twenty-five days appear Han dynasty corvées (Loewe 1968: 75), forty days in Medieval England (Goldthwaite 1980: 121–22).

The near disappearance of corvée from the Roman economy would seem to confirm that the labor systems of the Archaic economy at some point became more or less obsolete, but when? As the next chapter argues, nascent signs of market labor appear at Rome in the third century, and competitive contracting for state building projects was standard by at least the First Punic War. The appearance of coinage in the third century facilitated wage labor, as discussed in chapter 6, although attestation of corvées in several monetized Hellenistic states shows that coinage did not itself preclude forced labor.[120] Most important may be the expansion of slavery in the Roman economy beginning in the fourth century, a trend discussed in the previous chapter. Scheidel suggests that the absence of forced labor in the Roman empire related to the state's reliance on slave labor instead.[121] By this logic, if increasing state investment in slavery gave it a competitive advantage over corvée, then we might mark the beginning of forced labor's decline with the Roman economy's increasing reliance on slavery. This topic of the overall shift in the Roman mode of production is noteworthy and will be taken up in later chapters.

The idea that the Roman state used forced labor to build the Republican walls also finds support from the material evidence. The use of ramps rather than cranes for laying blocks and the relatively high reliance on unskilled labor speak to the traditional technologies employed in the project and the continuity with earlier workforces, at least from the viewpoint of composition and specialization. The actual mechanics of a large corvée at Rome are unknown, although the procedure of the Republican military draft or *dilectus*, where Roman citizens assembled on the Capitoline and were divided into fighting units, would have served both to gather the requisite workforce and to break them into appropriate work teams envisioned by Diodorus for the Syracusan walls and suggested by the wall panel in the Esquiline *agger*.[122] The army was employed in activities other than warfare in the Mid-Republic, and legions built walls and *aggeres* on campaign.[123] Problematically, however, Livy insisted that the walls were built in the absence of the *dilectus*. This is not an atypical theme in his first Decade whereby military service and large-scale

120. Ptolemaic corvée labor noted by von Reden 2007: 136–38; Kosmin 2014: 168 notes Seleucid corvée. Obligations in the Macedonian economy: Arr. *Anab.* 1.16.5 with Shipley 2000: 113.

121. Scheidel forthcoming.

122. For the Republican *dilectus* see Polyb. 6.19–20 with Brunt 1971: App. 20.

123. Gabrielli 2003b; see Liv. 8.16.8 for soldiers building an *agger*.

construction competed for citizen labor. Tarquin Superbus turned to building projects only after concluding a Sabine war "so that there be no more rest for the people at home than there was on campaign" (1.37.5), while Brutus inveighed against the tyrant that public works had added no small amount of effort to military service. Meanwhile, Livy was careful to point out that the Republican walls were built or repaired in the absence of military action or after its conclusion.[124]

The problems caused by corvée labor on the flow of labor in an economy are well attested in other pre-modern societies. In Imperial China, where great reliance on corvée labor has left rich documentation, anxieties emerged on the part of rulers and subjects over the careful calibration of corvée with other demands for household labor. Government officials were acutely aware that ill-timed labor taxes could ruin a harvest and lead to widespread unrest.[125] Similar desires to allocate construction work outside of high-labor periods of the agricultural season appear widely in other societies.[126]

Seasonality played a role in the flow of labor in the Republican economy as well. In the Mediterranean climate with wet winters and dry summers, Roman building followed particular rhythms. I have already noted the prescription of ancient authors that volcanic tuff be cut in the summer, and earthmoving would have likely waited for the dry season to avoid moving heavier waterlogged soil. Meanwhile, the agricultural schedule of Roman Italy is well-enough established: crops were planted in the fall and harvested in early June in warmer areas and as late as August in some higher elevations.[127] The seasonality of warfare in the Early Republic and into the fourth century is more difficult to trace. Until Rome's incursion into Campania in the 340s, more localized warfare may have sought to time attacks to correspond with an enemy's harvest, so that the army could make up part of their subsistence costs by seizing produce and flocks.[128] The one date extant for the fourth century suggests that the consuls then entered office on the kalends of July, a date which corresponds well enough with the grain harvest.[129] Thus, at the time of the walls' construction, Roman agriculture and perhaps also warfare

124. 6.32.2; 7.20.9.

125. Chan 1992: 634–41; Barbieri-Low 2007: 217.

126. Padilla Peralta 2014: 42 n. 89; Richardson 2014: 295–96.

127. Spurr 1986.

128. Rosenstein 2004: 27–28.

129. Pina Polo 2011: 13–15.

demanded manpower during the same dry summer months in which building also took place, and this raises the potential that multiple demands came into conflict.

4.7. Meeting the Cost

Considering the overlapping schedules of demand for building and other productive activities, is it possible that a labor corvée for the walls upset the balance of the early fourth century Roman economy? To answer this question, we need to contextualize the walls' cost within the larger flow of labor in the Roman economy.[130] Under normal circumstances, the two largest demands on household labor were agriculture and warfare, and the walls' cost should be viewed against the background of these two activities. For agricultural labor, I employ Rosenstein's model for Republican families. While I have elsewhere raised concerns that Rosenstein's model may understate somewhat the labor costs of agriculture and therefore overstate available peasant labor, in fact, this is not without benefit to present purposes: if this criticism is valid, then using his calculations would overemphasize available household labor and serve, as with choices taken in the cost analysis, to check the overall hypothesis of the walls' significance.

Table 4.6 reproduces Rosenstein's figures for surplus labor available to Roman peasant households for both larger twenty-*iugera* and smaller seven-*iugera* holdings.[131] The latter size was reputedly the viritane distribution made after the conquest of Veii. Since Rosenstein considers seven-*iugera* farms insufficient for a family's needs, he includes in the figures for smaller farms the costs of working additional land through tenancy. Both household figures represent a diet of wheat, legumes, and a small garden. In order to maximize available labor, I count all family members on a "heavy" schedule based upon a working year of 320 days, Rosenstein's upper limit.

Calculating the average annual cost of military service in PD for the Early Republic presents difficulty since warfare likely remained irregular, and our sources are unhelpful. Padilla Peralta suggests a figure of 100 PD/year for the early fourth century. This is probably on the right order of magnitude, although for seven-*iugera* farms this would cause two of three family

130. For the methodology, see Padilla Peralta 2014.

131. Rosenstein 2004: 66–81, esp. 71; I exclude the cost of maintaining oxen.

Table 4.6. Disposable labor in person-days available to Roman households after meeting calorie requirements with wheat, legumes, and a small garden

	Family A: father, mother, two adult sons, daughter	Family B: father, mother, adult son, daughter	Family C: father, mother, daughter
Small farm (7 *iugera*) plus sharecropping	319	133	91
Large farm (20 *iugera*)	746	533	352

Source: Data from Rosenstein (2004).

structures modeled here to fall below agricultural requirements, and thus to fail, on a consistent basis. We may assume that some of the cost of military campaigning was externalized through raiding enemy fields and flocks, something commonly referred to in the sources. (Unlike military raiding, a corvée was met entirely by worker's households.) Thus, I use a lower figure of 60 days, or about two months of military service per eligible individual, a figure that fits within the capacity of all three smallholder family configurations, but leaves only a small margin of disposable labor. Let us assume that family members eligible for military service were also liable for a labor tax. The disposable labor (L) leftover to a Roman Republican family after accounting for war making, building, and farming can be expressed as a function of time (a):

$$L(a) = Sa - ((D_b + D_w a) \times m)$$

where a represents the extent of the wall-building project in years; S is the surplus of days of labor above agricultural requirements; D_b is the *per capita* cost of building, or labor for building the walls in days; D_w is the cost of war, or average days of annual military service; and m is the number of family members eligible for military service. What interests us is the length of time (a) at which a hypothetical household's disposable labor becomes positive ($L \geq 0$), as this represents the minimum years necessary to absorb the cost of the Republican walls while still satisfying the demands of agricultural production (see table 4.7).

Table 4.7. Years (*a*) at which a seven-*iugera* estate can absorb the cost of building the Republican walls ($D_w = 0$ in parentheses)

Total population (thousands)	Family A	Family B	Family C
75	5.3 (2.3)	37.8 (3.7)	7.9 (2.7)
100	4.0 (1.7)	28.3 (2.8)	5.9 (2.0)
125	3.2 (1.4)	22.6 (2.2)	4.7 (1.6)
150	2.7 (1.2)	18.9 (1.8)	4.0 (1.4)

Table 4.8. Years (*a*) at which a twenty-*iugera* estate can absorb the cost of building the Republican walls ($D_w = 0$ in parentheses)

Total population (thousands)	Family A	Family B	Family C
75	1.3 (1.0)	1.2 (0.9)	0.8 (0.7)
100	1.0 (0.7)	0.9 (0.7)	0.6 (0.5)
125	0.8 (0.6)	0.7 (0.6)	0.5 (0.4)
150	0.7 (0.5)	0.6 (0.5)	0.4 (0.3)

For the sake of comparison, table 4.8 models various scenarios for larger estates.

This extrapolation suggests that small farms risked failure if called upon to build the Republican walls in about four to five years, unless we are prepared to accept scenarios in which Rome's population was accurately reported by the fourth-century census return, with all that would imply. If the walls were built in fewer than four years, only large families could absorb the labor costs, even in scenarios of high population. A four-person household (Family B) with seven *iugera* of land would have found the walls' cost devastating no matter the project's duration. If we remove warfare entirely ($D_w = 0$), then the chances of success increase, although the Roman state would still have needed to spread the walls' cost over multiple years. Of course, the complete absence of warfare for a prolonged time in this period is historically unlikely, and I consider the possibility only because of the annalistic tradition that a period of anarchy followed shortly after the decision to build the new circuit walls. By contrast, most large farms could absorb the walls' costs with little problem. If the project lasted even two years, all population scenarios would allow for twenty-*iugera* farms to clear the cost entirely within the disposable labor annually available to them: the amortized cost of the building project would have mattered little to these larger estate's economic success.

4.8. Conclusions

Equipped with a notion of both the cost of the Republican circuit walls and how the Roman state met that cost, we are now in the position to affirm that the project was of a magnitude to disrupt the Roman economy if the time of its construction was sufficiently compressed. A threshold emerges of about five years, with any shorter timeframe causing labor shortages on many seven-*iugera* farms. It is worth repeating that no issues other than labor prevented the building project from proceeding quickly once the requisite material had been quarried and brought to the city. The model presented here also reveals the construction project's potential to provoke debt: when we compare the walls' effects on seven- and twenty-*iugera* farms, a significant advantage fell to the owners of large estates, who could absorb building costs in most scenarios reconstructed here, even in a compressed timeframe. Thus, we might imagine the walls' cost causing families with smaller holdings significant shortages of labor, while a small class of elites with larger farms retained a surplus. The project thus was likely to have exacerbated extant problems of economic inequality.

Much remains hypothetical in the face of several unknowns, especially total population and the project's duration. However, we are left to weigh the scenario described here against other possibilities. The last chapter stressed the walls' isolation in terms of the Roman state's general productivity in the decades following the Gallic sack. The annalists' explanation based upon the massive effort of rebuilding Rome after the sack does not match the archaeological record, while the sources present no other obvious source of economic stress. In this case, I suggest the following scenario: the psychological effects of the sack pushed the Roman state to update the city's Archaic defenses with a costly new building project. The burden of the building project's great costs fell directly upon the citizen body. This disrupted Rome's economic equilibrium and, ultimately, its political cohesion by straining the labor supply to the breaking point and wiping out gains made through the conquest of Veii. Rather than forming the end of a narrative of post-sack rebuilding as presented by Livy, the walls sufficed by themselves to explain the slow development of Rome's fourth-century economy.

5 THE *NOBILITAS* AND ECONOMIC INNOVATION

CENSORS, COINAGE, AND CONTRACTS

This chapter collects into a single discussion three topics not normally discussed together. The first reason for doing so is that censors, coinage, and contracts formed the essential instruments of urban production in Mid-Republican Rome. The creation and maintenance of public infrastructure were the purview of the censor, who arranged such activity by contracts, which expressed costs in monetary terms. Second, the developments of these separate but related topics display a notable if underappreciated degree of chronological overlap: the attachment of the censorship to the city's architecture, the use at Rome of coinage, and the use of contracts for major state expenditures all appeared, or became regular practice, around 300 BCE. The timing is significant as this was a moment of extraordinary change for the political structure of the Republican state. Over the course of the later fourth century, a new Roman ruling order emerged whose prestige was derived from membership in the senate, and whose ranks now included both patrician and plebeian elites.[1] Thus, this chapter turns to detail three developments in the organization of urban production, as well as the broader political context of these economic institutions.

Without a doubt, the rise of the new aristocracy, whom Romans called the *nobilitas*, was linked in a direct manner to major physical changes in the city. With the admission of the plebs to offices previously monopolized by patricians, political competition increased, and this put pressure on elites to translate accomplishments into durable political power. It is well recognized, for example, that

1. Hölkeskamp 1987.

votive temples were expedient to such aims, as they allowed for the perpetuation of the *gloria* of military success through visible and lasting monuments, and the period of the *nobilitas'* emergence saw a significant quantitative increase in temple building.[2] While such temples have received much interest, they form only part of a more substantial state investment in large-scale infrastructure beginning in this period.

What I want to draw attention to are the economic implications of this large-scale investment in Rome's architecture. In particular, any trace of the previously observed connection between monumental construction and plebeian debt disappears. This difference is well illustrated by the career of the most brilliant interpreter of the period's dynamic political landscape, Appius Claudius Caecus.[3] Appius oversaw a broad slate of social, political, legal, and religious reforms during his censorship in 312 BCE. Among his initiatives were the construction of Rome's first aqueduct and highway, both highly ambitious and expensive building projects. In his censorial activity, Appius was said to have drawn support from an urban sector of Rome's population called the "faction of the forum" (*factio forensis*), and modern analysis of Appius' political agenda has often viewed him as populist. Loreto goes so far as to call the censor an "authentic Roosevelt of the fourth century BCE" intent on raising employment through public works.[4] While we might argue that Keynesian economics, not to mention the very concept of employment, seem foreign to the Mid-Republican economy, even the possibility that large-scale construction might be seen as benefitting the city's broader population represents a significant shift. As detailed by the previous chapter, in the earlier part of the fourth century large-scale public building caused social unrest and economic collapse, in sharp contrast to building's socioeconomic impact by the fourth century's close. Indeed, while the sources presented Appius' building projects within a narrative of intense conflict, that conflict was portrayed as purely political and located between factions of the aristocracy itself. Appius was said to have fought with other senators over the projects' outsized expense, but never seriously to have constrained the plebs' economic abilities.

The different socioeconomic effects of building between the early and late fourth century imply a radical change over the interim in how Romans organized such productive activity. Frictions were partly eased by incoming wealth from increasingly successful warfare in Italy. However, this chapter points to

2. Pietilä-Castrén 1987; Ziolkowski 1992; Aberson 1994; Orlin 1997.

3. See Humm 2005.

4. Loreto 1993: 85.

fundamental institutional developments in the ways in which such income moved through the Roman economy. In this sense, the detailed study of the censorship, coinage, and contracting contribute to a more profound history of the emergence of a new mode of organizing state production in opposition to Rome's earlier reliance on forced labor. The period around 300 BCE thus becomes critical as the historical context in which important structures of the Republican economy emerged.

5.1. Urban Development, 350 to 318 BCE

Appius' censorial works represented the application of state funds to urban infrastructure on an enormous scale. The magnitude becomes apparent when Appius' projects are compared to the record of limited expenditure on public building at Rome in the preceding decades. We have so far seen a generally limited trend of public building at Rome for the early fourth century with the notable exception of the circuit walls. After that project, public construction was rarely attested through the middle of the century. It is possible, although one can only speculate, that the Roman state avoided large-scale building using dependent labor as such activity had become a politically divisive issue in the aftermath of the crisis precipitated by the walls' construction.

The one project reported by the sources for the entire decade of the 340s was L. Furius Camillus' temple to Juno Moneta (A14), vowed in 345 BCE and dedicated on the Capitoline the next year. Very much about this temple is debated, from the source of the epithet Moneta, to the structure's relationship to the later Republican mint, to its location and possible archaeological remains.[5] Tucci makes the case for identifying the temple with the remains of a small tuff podium in the Aracoeli gardens.[6] The sources note that Furius' temple was built on the site of an earlier *domus*, although there are conflicting reports as to whether that house belonged to M. Manlius or to Titus Tatius. The podium in the Aracoeli gardens, seen in figure 5.1, was built of two types of tuff with blocks of *tufo rosso delle scorie nere* superimposed irregularly on blocks of *tufo del Palatino*. If visible in the finished monument, the use of two stones perhaps gave rise to later stories that the temple replaced an earlier structure. The unsystematic disposition of stones might also suggest the temple's construction reused building materials,

5. Meadows and Williams 2001.

6. Tucci 2005; see also Ziolkowski 1992: 71–73.

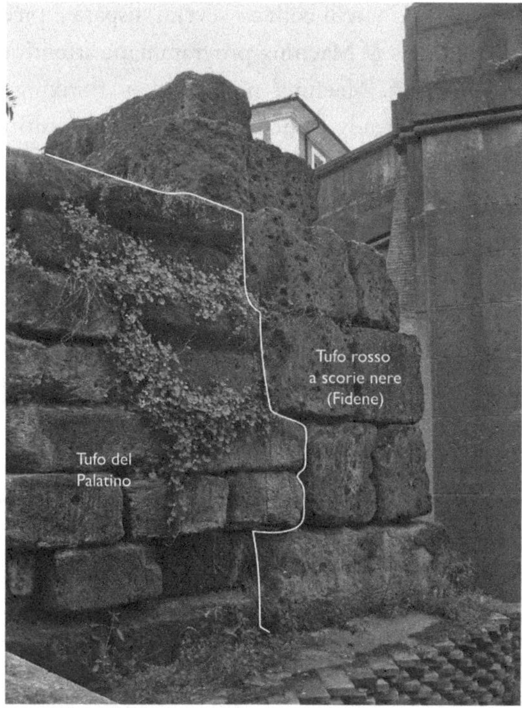

FIGURE 5.1 Podium in the Aracoeli Gardens (Capitoline) identified with Temple of Juno Moneta showing use of different stones.
Photo © S. Bernard.

and the discovery of earlier terracottas in the Aracoeli gardens supports the idea of a previous monumental structure on the site.[7] Repurposing or reuse would emphasize the minimal cost that the fourth-century structure entailed, but in any case the small temple built in a short timespan was unlikely to have had much economic impact. A similarly minimalist view can be taken towards other works in the ensuing decades such as the wooden starting gates for the circus built in 329 BCE (A16). As with the earlier fourth century, some construction or repair may go unmentioned by our sources but does not alter the general trend of limited urban construction.[8]

The first sign of a change in terms of state interest and expenditure on building came with a slate of projects overseen by C. Maenius, consul in 338

7. Ziolkowski 1992: 72.

8. Panella, Zeggio, and Ferrandes 2014: 179–87 note construction in the Velia during this period.

BCE and censor in 318.[9] Coarelli collects several disparate pieces of evidence to reconstruct the outlines of Maenius' programmatic attention to the northwest sector of the Forum. Maenius' novel way of thinking about Roman monumental space was already evident during his consulship in 338, when he celebrated a naval victory over the Latins at Antium by decorating the speaker's platform of the *comitium* with prows taken from enemy ships (A15). Besides giving their name to the monument, these *rostra* marked a turn from the dedication of war spoils as votives towards an interest in relating military success to political activity.[10] Maenius' consular accomplishments were also commemorated with equestrian statues of himself and his colleague near the *comitium* and a *columna Maenia* (A18) surmounted by a statue of him in the same area.

During his censorship, Maenius built a number of additional monuments in the same area of the Forum, near where he may have owned a house. He built projecting wooden balconies or bleachers called the *maeniana* for viewing spectacles in the Forum (A19), perhaps attached to his *domus*. Moneychangers' stalls, *tabernae argentariae* (A20), were first reported in the Forum in 308 BCE, by which point they had replaced older butcher stalls (*tabernae lanienae*). As later sources related these *tabernae argentariae* to the *maeniana*, Coarelli attributes their construction to Maenius in 318 BCE.[11] Noting Maenius' repeated contributions to this particular area of the Forum (*rostra*, equestrian statue, column, *tabernae argentariae, maeniana*) and the likelihood that he owned property there, Coarelli suggests that the censor was behind a fourth-century paving of the *comitium* in slabs of *tufo giallo* (A21).[12] Maenius' innovation is widely visible: in facilitating the viewing of games in the Forum, or in allowing space for monetized exchange, his monuments gave architectural formality to many functions at Rome for the first time.

Maenius' building projects represented important precedents for Appius. For one, Maenius was the first known censor to build multiple structures rather than a single work. For another, Maenius seems to have acted singlehandedly, and his censorial colleague Papirius Crassus' role in these projects, if he had one, was never mentioned. By contrast, earlier censorial construction was recorded as a collegial activity undertaken by both censors. Perhaps related to

9. Suohlati 1963: 216–20; Coarelli 1992: 39–53.

10. Hölscher 1994: 20.

11. Coarelli 1992: 145–46.

12. Coarelli 1992: 39–53. His reconstruction mostly convinces, although Steinby (2012a: 30–31) notes that the *atrium Maenium* was unlikely to have been public if Cato needed to purchase it during his censorship.

this, Maenius' name was associated, if not applied, to the *columna maenia* and the *maeniana*, as would later be the case with Appius' road, the Via Appia.[13]

5.2. The Ovinian Law and the Censorial *Cura Urbis*

The consistency with which two consecutive censors, Maenius and Appius, devoted attention to public monuments also signaled the beginning of that magistracy's regular oversight of urban infrastructure, the censorial *cura urbis*.[14] Rome's public monuments would become a fundamental concern for the censors. By the Late Republic, the association was such that public building contracts were sometimes called "censorial laws" (*leges censoriae*) even when overseen by other magistrates. Maenius and Appius stand at the beginning of this connection. This is not to say that earlier censors had not attended to urban construction, but such attention featured with less consistency (table 5.1).

The early origins of the censor's responsibility over the city's public monuments is obscure. Mommsen thought that the duty evolved from the censor's assessment of public and private property, including the land upon which *monumenta publica* were built. This is not impossible but the idea relies mostly on those tendentious accounts of Romulus' political actions.[15] It may simply be noted that the regular attention to the *cura urbis* starting with Maenius and Appius represented a significant change in the censors' interest in public construction. This shift also situated itself within a larger transformation of the censorial office at that time as indicated by the frequency of the office. After Appius' term, censors were elected with regularity every three to five, or at most seven, years into the third century and beyond.[16] In 319 BCE, the year prior to Maenius taking office, the death or resignation of one censor necessitated the re-composition of the college the following year.[17] However, prior to 319, the censorial *lustrum* was held only three times since 363, and the last certain census before 319 was in 332.

Noting the shift in the censorship's frequency, Cornell argues that a landmark legislation, the Ovinian law granting the censor the power to remove or enroll senators through a procedure known as the *lectio senatus*, was passed

13. Steinby 2012a: 30–36, noting also the Curia Hostilia.

14. Kunkel and Wittmann 1995: 397 n. 22.

15. Mommsen *StR* II^3 451 n. 5; followed by Suohlati 1963: 65.

16. 307, 304, 300, 294, 287, 283, 280, 275, 272, 269, 265, 258, 253 BCE, etc.; cf. Suohlati 1963.

17. Broughton *MRR* I 153–54.

Table 5.1. Censorial building projects from the beginning of the Republic to the end of the Second Punic War.*

Year	Censors	Project
435	C. Furius Pacilius, M. Geganius Macerinus	Villa Publica
378	Sp. Servilius Priscus, Q. Cloelius Siculus	Circuit walls (A6)
318	C. Maenius, L. Papirius Crassus	*Maeniana, tabernae argentariae, comitium* pavement (A15, 17–20)
312	Appius Claudius Caecus, C. Plautius Venox	Aqua Appia; Via Appia (A21–22)
307	M. Valerius Maximus Corvinus, C. Iunius Bubulcus Brutus	*locatio* of Temple of Salus (dedicated in 302) (A25); Via Valeria? (A23)
272	L. Papirius Praetextatus, M'. Curius Dentatus	Initiation of Anio Vetus (A44)
265	C. Marcius Rutilus Censorinus, Cn. Cornelius Blasius	Statue of Marsyas in Forum?**
241	C. Aurelius Cotta, M. Fabius Buteo	Via Aurelia? (A58)†
220	L. Aemilius Papus, C. Flaminius	Via Flaminia (A65); Circus Flaminius (A66)‡
209	P. Sempronius Tuditanus, M. Cornelius Cethegus	*locatio* of Temple of Fortuna Primigenia? (A89)§
204	M. Livius Salinator, C. Claudius Nero	*locatio* of Temple of Magna Mater (A97); *sarta tecta; via circa foros publicos* (A82); Salinator only: *locatio* of Temple of Iuventas (A98)

* This excludes the Compitum Fabricium attributed by Steinby (2012a: 86) to the censors of 275, but the evidence cited is thin.

** Cf. *LTUR* IV s.v. "Statua: Marsyas" 364–65 (F. Coarelli).

† Following Coarelli's dating of the Pons Aemilius to the third century (1988a: 139–47), I assign this road an early date and connect it either with C. Aurelius Cotta, censor 241 (Wiseman 1970: 133–34) or C. Aurelius Cotta, consul 200 (Fentress 1984). I prefer to follow Wiseman in relating the road to the foundations of Fregenae and Alsium in 245 (Vell. 1.14; Carnabuci 1992: 32–34, 44–47). Fentress focuses on Pisa as a staging ground for Ligurian campaigning from 195 onward, but the Viae Appia and Valeria followed, rather than preceded, campaigns; admittedly, the nature of Roman imperialism had changed in the interim, and her thesis cannot be excluded.

‡ Liv. *Per.* 20 making these projects censorial is more credible than Paul. Fest. 79 L, who makes Flaminius consul.

§ Confusion surrounds this temple: Liv. 34.53.5–6 states that the temple dedicated in 194 was vowed by P. Sempronius Sophus (consul 204) and *locavit* by *idem* as censor in the following decade. No man of that name held either office in that interval. Perhaps the temple related to P. Sempronius Tuditanus (censor 209), who campaigned as praetor in 213.

sometime prior to Maenius' censorship. Despite its apparently dramatic effect in formalizing the composition of the Republican senate, this law comes down to us only in an antiquarian lemma in Festus (290 L s.v. *praeteriti senatores*), and the tribune Ovinius responsible for its passage is otherwise unknown. After the establishment of a fixed senatorial body, it would have been necessary to employ some mechanism at regular intervals to make up for vacancies caused by the death of standing senators. The censorial *lectio* would have been just such a mechanism, and the growing regularity of the censorship after 319 BCE makes Cornell's argument attractive.[18]

Because the *nobilitas* of the late fourth century derived authority from senatorial membership, and no longer exclusively from patrician birth, the Ovinian law served an all-important purpose of defining the new aristocratic order. The granting of such power to the censors must have endowed the office with a newfound prestige. Steinby concludes from the fact that Appius held the censorship at a relatively young age, and unusually prior to his first consulship, that the senate played a larger role in guiding the actions of the young censor than the sources suggest.[19] But this is not necessarily the case: Appius entered the office at a moment of transition when the censor, prior to that point not an especially powerful magistrate, was starting to become a more regular, and also more prestigious, member of the Republican state.

There is no reason to think that the city's infrastructural needs directly motivated the passage of the Ovinian law and the consequent transformation of the censorship. The law was a *plebiscitum*, and Cornell suggests that it originated from the power struggle between patricians and plebeians in the later decades of the fourth century.[20] In this case, the law's passage emphasizes the effects that the political dynamics of the period had on the city's form, as we cannot fail to recognize the impact that the law would have had on the censors' *cura urbis*. Intentional or not, the attachment of the city's burgeoning physical space to a regularly appointed official who was not otherwise occupied with warfare will have eased a need for more constant attention to urban

18. Cornell 2000b. Hölkeskamp 1987: 142 n. 15; Humm 2005: 191–95 consider whether the first *lectio* was an innovation of Appius himself, but they must dismiss the claim of Diod. Sic. 20.36.5 that Appius performed his *lectio* "contrary to precedent," while Liv. 9.46.11 is explicit that Appius' *lectio*'s primacy stemmed from its admission of *libertini*.

19. Steinby 2012: 34.

20. Cornell 2000b. Kunkel and Wittmann (1995: 397) point to changing warfare and the need for a more regular census.

infrastructure. It must also have been at this time that the censors became occupied not only with adding to Rome's infrastructure, but with its regular upkeep. This was the task of *sarta tecta*, which Polybius included with new construction as Rome's costliest domestic expense.[21] Repair following catastrophic events like fires sometimes prompted the creation of extraordinary magistrates, but regular upkeep was first explicitly mentioned in 204 BCE when the censors were said to have pursued urban maintenance "more keenly and with greatest credibility" (Liv. 29.37.2: *acriter et cum summa fide*). This comparative praise implies that the practice was by then standard enough to merit only exceptional notice.

Thus, starting in the later fourth century, the Republican state tasked an elected magistrate on a regular basis with the repair of existing public monuments and the creation of new ones, if deemed necessary. In complement to this, the aedile first appeared in the capacity of *curator urbis* at the same time. The first reference to aediles overseeing infrastructure came during the rebuilding effort after the *incendium Gallicum*, but doubts have been raised as to the historicity of that entire episode in the last chapter. The next project attributed to an aedile was Cn. Flavius' *aedicula* of Concord vowed in 304 BCE (A24) followed by a more programmatic effort in 296 BCE, when the aediles Cn. and Q. Ogulnius refurbished the Capitolium, placed a statue of the wolf and twins in the Forum, and paved the Via Appia immediately beyond the city walls (A31). Notably, these aedileships related to the censor Appius: Flavius was his *scriba* and his political follower, while the Ogulnii returned to the construction of his road.

5.3. Appius Claudius Caecus' *Cura Urbis*

Appius began construction on the road (A21) and aqueduct (A22), universally ascribed to his censorship, in 312 BCE. To oversee the ongoing construction, Appius maintained his censorship, perhaps as long as 308 but well beyond the typical eighteen-month term.[22] The plainest description of the road and aqueduct appears in Appius' elogium, included among the gallery of *summi viri* in the Forum of Augustus and known from a better-preserved copy found at

21. 6.13.3; for fuller definition of *sarta tecta* see Fest. 254L s.v. *produit* and esp. Cic. *ad Fam.* 13.11.1, "to safeguard the good order of public buildings and places," *sarta tecta aedium sacrarum locorumque publicorum tueri*.

22. For the chronology, see Garzetti 1947: 190–95; Ferenczy 1967 34–35; Oakley 1997–2005 III. 378–79.

Arezzo. The text, which may derive from information nearly contemporary to Appius' career, concluded with a list of all of Appius' building projects: "In his censorship, he paved the Via Appia and brought water to the city, and he built a temple to Bellona."[23] Reference to the construction of *monumenta publica*, a not unparalleled but uncommon feature in epigraphic *elogia*, served to underscore Appius' reputation as a builder and the importance of his buildings to his career.

Regarding the censor's building projects, the sources contain a number of problems of detail that have occupied previous scholarship. There is, for example, the role of Appius' colleague, C. Plautius Venox, on whom the main ancient accounts part ways dramatically.[24] Appius' relationship to Plautius was either combative to the point of forcing the latter's abdication (Livy), or collegial such that Plautius acted under Appius' influence (Diodorus). Debate is even divided on the etymology of Plautius' cognomen "Venox." While Frontinus explicitly assigned its origin to Plautius' discovery of the "sources" (*venae*) of the aqueduct, it has been pointed out that Plautius' father also reputedly held the same cognomen, and an Oscan name *Venox* appeared already in the fifth century BCE from Capua.[25]

More generally, what runs through debates over this and other points of detail is the degree to which Appius' public works projects are interpreted as unusually great accomplishments. If the road and aqueduct entailed an unprecedented undertaking, then scholars are more willing to think that Appius relied on similarly unusual measures and support. An evaluation of the magnitude of the building program's cost thus becomes valuable to the overall historical interpretation. If we were better possessed of physical evidence for either the aqueduct or the earliest Via Appia, we might form an energetics model of Appius' building program as was done with the circuit walls in chapter 4. While the highly fragmentary archaeological evidence makes the reconstruction of either monument's building process difficult, it remains

23. The source has been thought to be a *clipeus* recording Appius' accomplishments hung in the Temple of Bellona (A35) following or even during his life. Massa-Pairault (2001: 97) suggests the *elogium* derived from a sarcophagus inscription. Humm (2005: 43–49) favors the priority of Frontinus, who gives Appius the cognomen Crassus (*de Aq.* 5.1), over the *elogium*, which has Caecus; however, the difference is probably scribal error, as see Rodgers 2004: 144.

24. *RE* XXI.1 22–23 "Plautus 32: C. Plautius Venox" (F. Münzer). Modern scholarship is similarly divided between friendly (Suolahti 1963: 29; Oakley 1997–2005 III.377) and inimical (Cassola 1962: 138; MacBain 1980: 371).

25. Raaflaub, Richards, and Samons 1992: 38; cf. *Imag. Ital.* I Campania / Capua 35.

possible to suggest some aspects of the organization and labor behind the two buildings' construction.

5.4. Building the Road and Aqueduct

There has been little study of the economics of the Via Appia's construction by contrast to the considerable amount written on the road's topography.[26] Appius' highway from Rome to Capua, a distance of 212 km, replaced an earlier connection between Rome and Latium.[27] The route was distinguished by a more permanently engineered course, recognizable above all in a long rectilinear section, the *via recta*, extending 84 km from the Almo stream just beyond Rome's walls to Terracina. The road was also famous for its interregional connection beyond Capua, and the link it provided between the city and, eventually, the Adriatic coast. This raises an important point: while initiated by Appius, the road across the peninsula took decades to finish, and there is ample record of continuing work. In 296 BCE, the aediles paved the road just outside the walls with squared-stone slabs (Liv. 10.23.11–12); in 294, the aediles continued the pavement to Bovillae with basalt pavers (Liv. 10.47.4). These projects suggest that the earliest road was bedded on packed earth and gravel, and this finds archaeological support, more on which below. The road's construction continued into the middle of the third century. A milestone found along the route in the Pontine area bears the names of the aediles P. Claudius, son of the censor Appius, and C. Furius, consuls of 249 and 251 BCE respectively, and attests to continuing work on the route over the subsequent decades (*CIL* I² 21).[28] The road's full extension to Brundisium was likely only accomplished with the establishment of a Latin colony at the Adriatic port in 244.

Still, despite the continuation of work after his censorship and even after his lifetime, there is no reason to deny Appius' involvement in the

26. Topography: Quilici Gigli 1990; Quilici 1997; Della Portella 2003; Quilici 2004; Spera and Mineo 2004; Manacorda and Santangeli Valenzani 2011. Humm (1996) provides an historical outlook; Laurence (1999) examines cultural issues; *LTUR* V s.v. "Via Appia" 130–33 (J. Patterson) provides a useful overview.

27. For the earlier route, see Cama 2011.

28. Coarelli 1988b: 37.

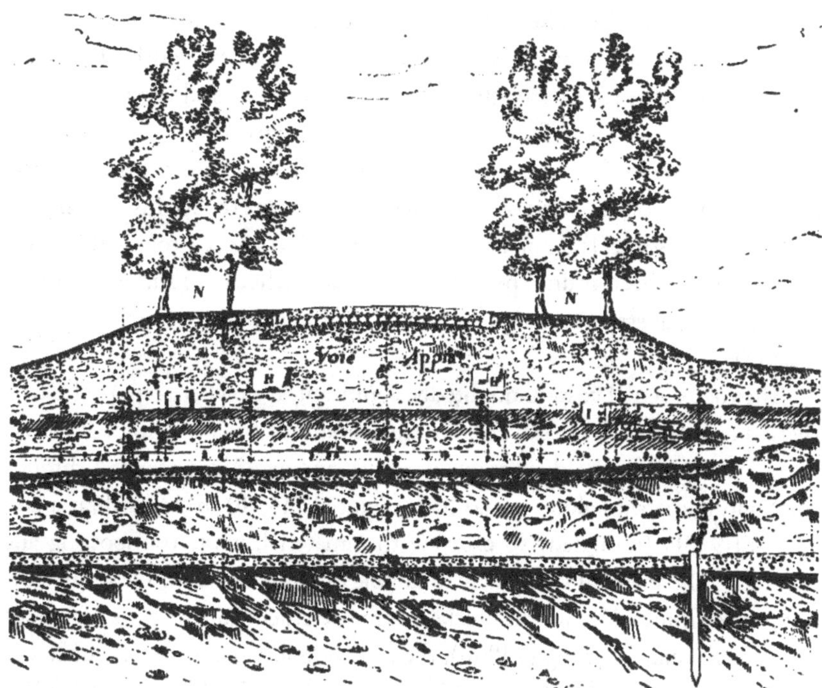

FIGURE 5.2 De Prony's sectional drawing of the Via Appia through the Pontine Marshes showing the construction of the original roadbed.
Image reproduced with permission from Humm 1996 based on De Prony 1824: fig. 14.

road's original form as far as Capua, nor his hand in building the innovative *via recta*.[29] Quilici demonstrates that the technological basis of the *via recta* divided into three sections: the 13 km of road through the flat plain southeast of the city, then the 28 km section crossing the crater of the Alban hills, and the final 43 km through the Pontine marshes, where the road was raised from the marsh floor on an earthen mound. The road did not run in a precisely straight line for the entirety, but turned very slightly (approximately 5 degrees) at Ariccia atop the ridge of the Alban crater. This turn suggests that the construction involved the joining of at least two different surveying and building projects at that point. The physical configuration of the original roadbed as it crossed the *ager Pontinus* can be determined from sectional excavations of the roadbed northwest of Terracina published in 1823 by de Prony and shown in figure 5.2, in which he found a simple elevated roadbed

29. Pekary's (1968) argument for a second-century date is refuted by Wiseman 1970: 141–43; see Coarelli 1988b; Humm 1996.

situated on virgin soil raised 1.4 m from the marsh floor and contained between curbs of two courses of squared-stone blocks. The width of the artificial mound beneath the roadbed was 10.5 at its base, and the road surface itself was 6.6 m wide.[30] Some road cuttings and artificial substructures of the route between Terracina and Fondi, and near Itri to the south, have also been attributed on the basis of construction technique to Appius' initial project.[31] Beneath some Trajanic basalt pavers near Terracina, a roadbed in limestone slabs has been found, perhaps part of the earlier road surface, while in other places, substructures supporting the road were built in rough polygonal masonry.[32]

The road's actual cost, undoubtedly significant, is nowhere reported, nor is there direct evidence for the composition or size of the labor force involved. Extrapolating from the dimensions in de Prony, the 43 km roadbed through the Pontine marshes alone would have required 514,710 m^3 of earth at a cost of 144,119 PD (unskilled) to excavate that material, while transporting and mounding the material were likely to double or triple this cost. De Prony does not provide dimensions for the blocks that formed the roadbed's curb, but if each was four Roman feet long (1.18 m), then providing two courses on either side of the entire 84 km *via recta* would have required 284,746 blocks of stone. The labor cost alone to quarry and dress that much material would have been on the order of 569,492 PD (skilled).[33] We do not know the provenance of the stone used in the road's curbs, and we cannot calculate its transport costs, but material must have been brought overland. While a high artificial roadbed was necessary to raise the road out of the Pontine marshes, the stretches over Monte Albano or above Terracina, where substructures in dressed stone were built, presented their own set of costs. In sum, the cost for Appius' road seems measurable in millions of PD and therefore of a similar level of magnitude to that for the Republican walls.

Once the road began to be paved in the early third century BCE, the cost would have grown considerably, as inscriptions from later periods attest. Hadrianic repair of 15.75 miles of the Via Appia near Beneventum cost HS 1,726,100, or HS 20.75 per Roman foot.[34] The rate-cost, as Duncan-Jones observes, is similar to that reported by several other documents and may

30. De Prony 1823: tb. 14; Quilici 1990; Humm 1996: 706–7.

31. Humm 1996: 708–9.

32. Lugli 1926: 1–2, 199, 204–5.

33. For simplicity this assumes stone of similar hardness to *tufo giallo*, although local *lapis Albanus* was significantly harder, potentially increasing labor costs.

34. *CIL* IX 6075 = *ILS* 5875; Duncan-Jones 1982: 124–25.

represent a rough standard cost for roadwork in the Empire. Applying this rate to the entire 212 km route from Rome to Capua produces an astronomical sum of HS 15,000,000 for paving alone. If an unskilled daily wage was on the order of HS 3, the cost of paving the entire road works out to 5,000,000 PD, making it again not inappropriate to compare the project's costs (though not its social consequences) with those of the circuit walls.

We can say a few things about the character of the workforce that met these costs. Since the polygonal masonry technique of the substructures above Terracina was not found at Rome, but rather in contemporary structures in Latium, it may be that some skilled labor came from workers from that region who were more familiar than urban masons with the limestone-based masonry techniques of the region. There was also a potential relationship between the labor force and the (slave?) labor attached to colonists whom Rome sent to recently founded sites along the route at Terracina-Anxur (329 BCE), or in the general territory of the route at Suessa Aurunca and Pontia (313 BCE). It is difficult to model the Roman economy's absorption of such costs, since the demographic picture becomes complicated by the extension of Roman citizenship to Campanians in 338 BCE, as well as by mass enslavements reported during the Samnite wars.

To the road's costs were added those of the aqueduct, initiated at the same time. Frontinus provided the clearest description of its course:

> The Appia begins in the *ager Lucullanus* between the seventh and eighth mile of the Via Praenestina, along a side path 780 paces to its left. Its flow from its source to the *Salinae* by the *porta Trigemina* measures 11,190 paces [ca. 16.5 km] in length. Of this course, the channel is underground for 11,130 paces, and carried on arches above ground for sixty paces close to the *porta Capena*.[35]

Outside the city, Frontinus noted that the channel was exceptionally deep. While this made it impervious to illegal siphoning, it has largely frustrated the modern search for the channel's remains.[36] Confirmation of its depth comes

---

35. *De Aq.* 5.4–5, *concipitur Appia in agro Lucullano via Praenestina inter miliarium septimum et octavum, deverticulo sinistrosus passuum septingentorum octoginta. ductus eius habet longitudinem a capite usque ad Salinas, qui locus est ad portam Trigeminam, passuum undecim milium centum nonaginta. <ex eo rivus est> sub<t>er<raneus pas>suum undecim milium centum triginta, supra terram substructio et arcuatura proximum portam Capenam passuum sexaginta.*

36. Cf. Front. *De Aq.* 65.7

from the recent discovery of nearly 50 m of the *specus* at the sixth mile of the Via Praenestina, found 21 m below ground.[37] The general location of the water's source was the area between the Via Praenestina and the Anio river.[38] The terminus of the aqueduct in the *forum boarium* by the *porta Trigemina*, at the foot of the Aventine, has left no archaeological trace, while the precise location of the *porta Trigemina* remains disputed.[39] According to Frontinus, the conduit crossed the east end of the circus valley between the Caelian and the Aventine on arches. This is near the *porta Capena* where the Via Appia also met the city walls, although no arches have ever been found. Because of the probable depth of the initial source, the arches would have been low.[40] From the aqueduct's final stretch around the Aventine, three associated sections of the *specus* have been identified. Discovered near the corner of viale Giotto and via di Santa Balbina, the longest section ran for 103.6 m and was cut into the living rock of the Aventine, then lined with blocks of *tufo del Palatino*. The *specus* had shelves on each side and was covered with a low-rising vaulted roof. Another section where viale Giotto meets via di San Saba was closed instead with slabs of *tufo del Palatino* built *a cappuccina*.[41] This latter vaulting technique is similar to that found in a long stretch of Mid-Republican aqueduct on the Caelian, perhaps a branch of the Anio Vetus, which also featured an ashlar-masonry tank and a repair in wood slabs.[42] The Appia's outflow lacked a tank or reservoir. Because of the low elevation of its source, the aqueduct was incapable of serving higher elevation areas of the city, serving instead essentially as an additional spring with high quality water for those living in the regions adjacent to the *forum boarium*.[43]

While the physical evidence for the aqueduct's earliest phase is sparse and not consistent enough to allow for cost analysis, its construction was undoubtedly expensive. The unusually high cost of hydraulic infrastructure in

---

37. Reported in La Reppublica April 16, 2017: Paolo Boccacci, "Roma, scoperta alla Prenestina: riaffora venti metri sotto terra l'acquedotto Appio." The concrete vault suggests that this section was rebuilt during the Empire.

38. Rodgers 2004: 146.

39. Coarelli 1991.

40. Ashby (1935: 53–54) doubts Frontinus, but see Rodgers 2004: 148.

41. Ashby 1935: 49–54; Van Deman 1973: 23–38.

42. The Caelian aqueduct was presented by Paola Palazzo and Simona Morretta at a conference held at the University of Rome La Sapienza on April 5, 2017 and will be published in the conference proceedings.

43. Front. *De Aq.* 18.7, 22.1.

general often caught the attention of ancient sources.[44] The highest known cost for any Republican project was HS 180 million allocated by the senate to the project to build the Aqua Marcia and repair the Appia and Anio Vetus in 144 BCE.[45] An overhaul of the city's drainage system cost 1,000 talents, some 6 million denarii, in the second century BCE, likely under Cato's censorship in 184. This was equivalent to the annual pay of ten legions at around the same time.[46] A modestly sized aqueduct on an estate near Antium cost 130,000 *asses* in 170 BCE.[47] Pliny called the Aqua Claudia, with its elevated course, the most expensive of all, citing an astonishing cost of HS 350 million.[48] A large part of the cost of these later aqueducts came from building above-ground conduits carried on arches. Since it was largely underground, the Appia may have been comparatively less expensive, but tunneling projects were no less impressive works in labor terms. According to Suetonius, the emperor Claudius retained 30,000 laborers without break for eleven years in an ultimately unsuccessful attempt to drain the Fucine Lake through a channel only three miles long, or slightly more than a quarter of the length of the Appia. Reckoning with a relatively full 300-day working year, since Claudius' workforce reputedly worked "without intermission," this represented a cost for hydraulic tunneling work of 33,000 PD per Roman foot.

As with the road, no evidence speaks directly to the nature or status of the aqueduct's workforce. Its novelty no doubt required specialists in hydraulic engineering. Comparative evidence also suggests that its execution required the mass mobilization of unskilled labor. Supplying such labor to underground hydraulic works very often necessitated solutions beyond the normal labor market. In this context were labor corvées allegedly employed to build Tarquin's *cloaca*, convict labor assigned to Nero's canal project between Ostia and Misenum, or the use of soldiers to tunnel an aqueduct at Saldae in Imperial North Africa.[49]

---

44. Dion. Hal. 3.67 = *FRH* 6 C. Acilius F6.

45. Front. *De Aq.* 7.4 = *FRH* 70 Fenestella F12. Problematically, there is no way to parse new construction from that of repair; for an attempt to translate this into labor cost, see Padilla Peralta 2014: 66–69.

46. *FRH* 7 C. Acilius F6 = Dion. Hal. 3.67.5; for legionary pay, see Frank 1933: 76; Kay 2014: 26.

47. Liv. 43.4.8.

48. *HN* 36.122.

49. Tarquin's *cloaca*: Liv. 1.59.9; Nero's prisoners: Suet. *Ner.* 31 with Millar 1984; soldiers at Saldae: *ILS* 5795 with Cuomo 2011.

The cost of both road and aqueduct also included the expense, impossible to quantify, of a high degree of technological innovation. Humm gives an extended interpretation of the two projects as adaptations of Greek urban technologies within what he views as the censor's general Hellenistic agenda.[50] Upon close scrutiny, however, much of the evidence for Appius' supposed Hellenism is ambiguous at best. For example, the unusual application of Appius' *praenomen* to the road (e.g., the Via Appia, rather than Claudia) has been held to imitate Alexander's and his successor's founding of cities bearing their names, but none of the censor's names was ever applied to the aqueduct, and we have already discussed Maenius' precedent.[51] Another supposedly Hellenizing aspect appears in a famous puzzle in Suetonius' description of a diademed statue at Forum Appi of a certain "Claudius Drusus [*sic*] who attempted to seize Italy through his clients." The cognomen Drusus is a textual error, but if "Caecus" was originally intended, a diademed Appius Claudius Caecus would then be a sign of the censor's adoption of a token of Hellenistic kingship and another example of his imitation of Alexander and his successors. However, Wiseman conclusively refutes the identification of this statue as Appius Claudius Caecus, while also noting that the diadem did not hold connotations of kingship, Hellenistic or otherwise, in fourth-century Rome.[52] It is worth noting that both alleged examples of Appius' Hellenism, the name of the road and the diademed statue at Forum Appi, ultimately stem from the work of Mommsen, who used such interpretations to support his now-abandoned belief that the censor was a tyrannical demagogue in the style of the Gracchi or Caesar.[53]

Some aspects of Appius' career show contacts with intellectual currents in his contemporary Greek culture; however, the idea of Appius' nascent Hellenism seems somewhat artificial in a society which formed cultural connections with the Greek world centuries prior. Meanwhile, the technological background of the censor's two major construction projects were very different from contemporary Hellenistic urban theory. The contrast was noted by multiple ancient authors who attributed to Greeks the original

50. Humm 2005: 484–97.

51. *Contra* Steinby 2012a: 34–36, who goes so far as to wonder if the practice was by that point constitutional, but surely this was convention, as cf. Paul Fest. 74 L.

52. Wiseman 1994: 40–42 on Suet. *Tib.* 2.2; the idea still finds followers: Massa-Pairault 2001: 106–7; Humm 2005: 485–89.

53. For the intellectual history of Mommsen's interpretation, see MacBain 1980: 357–58.

science of city planning, while roads and aqueducts were considered characteristically Roman.[54]

In technological terms, the aqueduct's innovativeness related first and foremost to the specific environmental and technological context of Central Italy. The natural karstic landscape of this region, where significant water resources were often trapped beneath a layer of tuff, prompted hydraulic tunneling from an early date.[55] Etruscan engineers used artificial channels (*cuniculi*) to irrigate settlements or drain water from arable land. Tarquin's *cloaca*, which served to drain the forum, belonged to this ecological background, and the story of a project to drain the crater of the Alban mount in response to an oracle during the siege of Veii has also been interpreted as a precursor to Appius' aqueduct.[56] In this sense, Appius' aqueduct can be seen as a path-dependent innovation based on experimentation at and around Rome itself, rather than as the importation of Greek technology. While some Etruscan *cuniculi* reach over 5 km in length, the majority were smaller, and this background does not diminish the novel scale of Appius' project.[57]

The road finds little technological parallel in the Hellenistic East. While orthogonal street patterns within Hellenistic cities were common and associated with famous Hellenistic architects like Deinocrates or Hippodamus, less common was the corollary attempt to connect settlements with straight lines of communication or to extend intra-urban grid plans across wider landscapes.[58] Alexandria is paradigmatic in this regard. In contrast to its famously wide boulevards laid out by Deinocrates, the Hellenistic metropolis lacked a paved road extending beyond its city limits, and the roads connecting the city with the Delta and beyond were notoriously difficult to track.[59] Meanwhile, Romans' fascination with surveying landscapes was well documented from the Mid-Republic onward.[60] Humm connects the remarkable straight course of the *via recta* to Pythagorean mathematical theory.[61]

54. Strabo 5.3.8; Dion. Hal. 3.67.5; Front. *De Aq.* 1.16.

55. Walsh 2013: 78–79.

56. Coarelli 1991.

57. Ward Perkins 1962; Judson and Kahane 1963; Barker and Rasmussen 1998: 197.

58. Cf. Boyd and Jameson 1981.

59. On routes around Alexandria, see Bernard 2009.

60. On Roman conceptions of space, see Nicolet 1988; Purcell 1990. Early centuriation figures into this discussion, but cf. Pelgrom 2008: 358–67 for interpretational problems.

61. Humm 2005: 491–93 with earlier literature.

However, Romans were capable of sighting and leading straight survey lines across terrain with a high degree of accuracy using only a *groma* and without any complex mathematics.[62] Indeed, there are reasons to think that the Via Appia was created as a straight line extended out from a single point, rather than as a hypotenuse derived via Pythagorean mathematics from a larger constellation of points. Quilici's aforementioned discovery of the slight alteration of approximately 5 degrees in the *via recta*'s course at Ariccia suggests that the road was made as two lines extended out as vectors in linear fashion and joined at that point. Also arguing against the creation of the road from a constellation of points is the fact that the overall colonial centuriation in the Pontine in some places followed different orientations.[63] The larger aim here is not to deny intellectual and technological contacts between Mid-Republican Rome and the wider Mediterranean world, but the road and aqueduct must also be understood within their Roman context.

5.5. Economic Change and the Mid-Republican Aristocracy

The great scale and novelty of Appius' public works support those accounts that emphasize the political friction arising from the costs of constructing the monuments. Road and aqueduct were radical departures for Roman public architecture both economically and physically, and political opposition to the censor's program seems therefore plausible if not expected. By the same token, however, it is hard to think that Appius oversaw such an ambitious building program without any support, as some sources suggest.[64] Diodorus must exaggerate the rift between censor and senate when he stated that, for the road and aqueduct, Appius "spent the entirety of the public revenue without a senatorial decree" (20.36.2), and he also misunderstood Mid-Republican financial procedure. In later periods the Republican censor's financial capacities extended as far as his use of "designated funds" (*pecunia adtributa*) set aside for his office explicitly by *senatus consultum*, and it is difficult to think that Appius spent beyond what the senate granted to him.[65]

62. Schiöler 1994.

63. Chouquer, Clavel-Lévêque, Favory, and Vallat 1987; Cancellieri 1990.

64. Steinby (2012a: 34) goes too far in the other direction by reviving the thesis that he was a mouthpiece for a senatorial faction.

65. Cf. Liv. 44.16.9 on senatorial approval; Suolahti 1963: 63–64; Walbank 1957–79: I.678–79.

Instead, it seems better to think that the costly building projects were contested between different elements within the elite, with Appius' road and aqueduct, like all of his innovative censorial activities, finding both opposition and support within the broader political and social struggle that surrounded his censorship. Who then were Appius' political supporters, and what did they want? The question of the censor's political base is longstanding, and its answer will take us directly to the relationship of economic change and politics in this period. I begin with Livy's much-discussed account of the career of Cn. Flavius, Appius' former *scriba* who continued the censor's political agenda in 304 BCE by seeking further tribal reforms:

> The "forum faction" (*factio forensis*) had voted Flavius aedile. Their power was born in the censorship of Appius, who first defiled the senate with the inclusion of sons of freedmen (*libertini*), and afterwards when no one accepted the senate he composed as valid, and he did not gain the urban political power that he had sought in the curia, he corrupted both forum and campus by distributing the *humiles* in all the voting tribes. So great was the anger during the election of Flavius that most of the *nobilitas* took off their gold rings and jewelry. From that time forward, the citizens of Rome divided into two parties: on one side the virtuous *populus*, patron and supporter of all good men (*cultor bonorum*), and on the other the faction of the forum, until the censorship of Q. Fabius and P. Decius. And Fabius, both to preserve order, and lest the *comitia* fall into the hands of the *humillimi*, separated out the "forum crowd" (*turba forensis*) and cast them into four tribes, which he called "urban."[66]

While this passage shows influences of Late Republican politics, other details appear in parallel accounts explicitly drawn from earlier annalists (*annales antiquissimi*), so that at least some aspects of this episode as Livy depicted

66. 9.46.10–14: *ceterum Flavium dixerat aedilem forensis factio, Ap. Claudi censura vires nacta, qui senatum primus libertinorum filiis lectis inquinaverat et, posteaquam eam lectionem nemo ratam habuit nec in curia adeptus erat quas petierat opes urbanas, humilibus per omnes tribus divisis forum et campum corrupit. tantumque Flavi comitia indignitatis habuerunt, ut plerique nobilium anulos aureos et phaleras deponerent. ex eo tempore in duas partes discessit civitas; aliud integer populus fautor et cultor bonorum, aliud forensis factio tendebat, donec Q. Fabius et P. Decius censores facti, et Fabius simul concordiae causa, simul ne humillimorum in manu comitia essent, omnem forensem turbam excretam in quattuor tribus coniecit urbanasque eas appellavit.* There is no convincing reason to amend *opes urbanas* to *urbanis humilibus* following Gronovius but none of the extant manuscripts.

it likely predate Gracchan-period or later Roman historians' elaboration.[67] Even so, untangling the identity of these sociopolitical groups within the context of fourth-century Roman politics is a complex task. Livy singled out a *turba* or *factio forensis*, who comprised two different but somehow related groups: *libertini* and *humiles* or *humillimi*. The *libertini* are identifiable as sons of freedmen whom the censor attempted to enroll in the senate.[68] The *humiles* targeted by Appius and Flavius' tribal reforms are more elusive, and in contrast to Livy's vague adjective *humiles* (on which, see below), Plutarch and the author of the *de viris illustribus* suggest that the tribal reforms primarily affected freedmen.[69] Oakley succinctly reviews the debate on the identification of these various sociopolitical groupings and sketches two contrasting interpretations.[70] One school of thought suggests that Appius sought to enroll urban inhabitants into the existing rural tribes. This has the merit of explaining how the censor generated a political following (*factio*) in the city, but must set aside the identification of these figures as freedmen by Plutarch and the author of the *de viris illustribus*. Oakley stresses that the enrollment of urban residents into rural tribes means that Appius attempted a radical reform not only of the tribal membership, but of the entire structure of the tribal voting system, which had until that point been established territorially in relation to Roman expansion. Because of this, Oakley leans towards an alternative interpretation, unifying the evidence of Plutarch and the *de viris illustribus* with Livy by equating the *humiles* with freedmen: Appius' reform, in his view, allowed sons of freedmen living in the country to register in the tribe of their areas of residency. As Oakley admits, this accounts less well for the idea that Appius sought to obtain urban political support, although he offers some potential ways around this.

There is, however, another problem with the second interpretation preferred by Oakley: if Appius did attempt to register freedmen living in the country in their respective rural tribes, then Fabius Maximus' decision to include these same (rural) freedmen in the urban tribes would have represented the point of radical separation in the tribal system from its initial territorial basis. However, the tradition makes Fabius Maximus an arch-conservative,

67. Humm 2005: 232–35; Oakley 1997–2005 III.603–7.

68. Humm (2005: 219–26) raises the possibility that these *libertini* were newly enfranchised Roman citizens with Italian, not necessarily servile, origins. I find the idea of wealthy freedmen unproblematic for the period.

69. Plut. *Publ.* 7.5; Ps-Aur. Victor *de vir. illust.* 32.2.

70. Oakley 1997–2005 III.629–35; also Humm 2005: 229–66.

while the reformer role belongs clearly to Appius. It is thus preferable to take the view that Appius attempted radical change, while Fabius Maximus acted conservatively to restore the "corrupted" residential basis of the tribal voting system by creating urban tribes for citizens domiciled in the city. This, of course, requires us to reject Plutarch and the *de viris illustribus*, but these sources' contradictory evidence need not be compelling. Nobody would, for example, attempt to uphold the veracity of a third, patently absurd version of events reported by Diodorus Siculus, in which Appius allowed Romans to register in whatever tribe and census class they wished.[71]

The interpretation that Appius tried to register city-dwelling *humiles* in the existing rural tribes has the merit of aligning with a particular urban orientation elsewhere applied to Appius' political followers. Not only did Appius seek *opes urbanas* in 312 BCE in the passage cited above, but on entering the consulship in 307 he allegedly "remained at Rome in order to increase his political power through urban political skills" (*urbanis artibus*).[72] Finally, beyond the context of these details drawn from Livy's account, Appius' aqueduct held utility largely to urban residents. Since the structure emptied at the foot of the Aventine and was otherwise too deep to be of much use for suburban estates, it provided fresh water to the population in the city itself.[73] Thus, one aspect unifying the *libertini* and *humiles* targeted by Appius' political reforms seems to have been topographical: these were political elements affiliated with the city, presumably for residential or commercial ties.

Livy qualified this urban group as *humiles*, but the adjective does not necessarily describe an urban resident. *Humilis* has a wide range of meaning, and Livy and other authors generally used it in two ways, to denote either economic or social lowness.[74] In Livy's reference to the *humiles* targeted by Cn. Flavius' reforms, the choice between the two meanings seems clear because some of Appius' supporters must have been wealthy.[75] As Appius' *lectio* was rejected by other senators on moral and not technical grounds, some of these *libertini* possessed sufficient wealth to make them eligible for the senate.

---

71. Diod. Sic. 20.36.4.

72. Liv. 9.42.4: *Romae mansit ut urbanis artibus opes augeret*; see Humm 2005: 257, 508–10.

73. Whether or not the Aventine was plebeian, as Mignone 2016 doubts, does not affect the urban utility of the aqueduct.

74. Extensive philological investigation by Humm (2005: 248–51); cf. *TLL* VI.3 Fasc. XVII s.v. "humilis" defn. II.A.1.a.

75. Staveley 1959: 413: "necessarily wealthy."

Humilis applied more to these figures' social than purely economic standing. Indeed, this seems to be how Livy used the word a few chapters previously to describe the aedile Cn. Flavius "born to humble circumstances, his father having been the son of a freedman" (9.46.1: *patre libertino humili fortuna ortus*). As an elected magistrate, Flavius was not poor, but in the eyes of his opponents his *humilis* background did not match his political authority.

If some of Appius' supporters were wealthy but did not yet possess significant social capital, where did their wealth come from? The question leads us to confront more directly the topic of the relationship between political and economic change in this period. An argument for seeing Appius' political supporters as in some sense defined by their economic activity was first proposed by Staveley, who held that Appius was part of a nascent Roman political party formed in the 330s BCE with strong mercantilist interests in Campania. His thesis fit Appius' road into the general ideology of his other censorial initiatives, as the route between Rome and Capua was interpreted as having facilitated commerce between both regions. Appius' censorship was thus, in Staveley's view, a coordinated attempt to change the balance of the Roman economy from "an essentially agricultural community into one in which agriculture and commerce played at least an equal part."[76] This idea is worth pursuing, but Staveley's presentation has some faults. First of all, the road served many purposes, with the need to transport Roman armies to the theater of war to the south forming an especially pressing concern during Appius' censorship. Trade seems more likely an effect of the road's construction than its primary motivation. Furthermore, while there are signs of increased market-oriented production in this period, as discussed shortly, the evidence supports exchange around Italy and between Italy and the Mediterranean, not strictly between Rome and Campania. Finally, the evidence for Appius' political inheritance of a party formed in the 330s around Campanian commercial interests and lead by rich plebeians like P. Decius Mus or Q. Publilius Philo is tenuous. Appius' supposed pro-plebeian stance fails to account, for example, for his support at a later date for an all-patrician consulship in alliance with Fabius Maximus, who was one of the supposed leaders of the party opposing him. This political fluidity is one of the chief reasons why modern scholarship largely abandons Staveley's method of *Gruppierungsrekonstruktion*.[77]

76. Staveley 1959: 419.

77. Liv. 10.15; MacBain 1980: 370–71; Hölkeskamp 1987: 41–61.

On the other hand, Staveley's idea that Appius may have been responding to changes in the Roman economy finds support in an increasing corpus of archaeological evidence for Roman involvement in commercially oriented production around the time of the censorship.[78] The study of Italian ceramics, particularly black gloss fine-wares and Campanian amphorae, now confirms beyond a doubt that Roman elites were by the first half of the third century involved in export production and trade around the peninsula and beyond.[79] Black gloss wares from the workshop of the *petites estampilles* were produced at and around Rome by the late fourth and early third century and exported to Gaul and North Africa.[80] Stamps of Roman producers including patrician *gentes* like the Valerii or Aemilii on Campanian Magna Graecia-Sicily (MGS) or Greco-Italic amphorae from the first half of the third century confirm the notion that elite families started to include members engaged at this time in foreign trade.[81] Remarkable confirmation of the involvement of the highest echelons of Roman society comes from one such amphora with a *titulus* bearing the signature of *M. VAL. COS*, to be identified with one of several consular Marci Valerii of the later third or early second century.[82] Such evidence would affirm the intuition of Gabba that the third century saw an increase of trade originating from the Italian peninsula and increasingly controlled by the Roman elite.[83] Since MGS amphorae served as containers for the transport of agricultural products such as wine or oil, whose cultivation was closely related to slave labor and economies of scale, this material indicates the turn of some Roman elites to more intensive market-oriented agriculture. Thus, Staveley's opposition between commerce and agriculture is mistaken as the evidence speaks not to the rise of commerce independent of landowning, but instead to the rise of commercial agriculture and the trade of agricultural products. In sum, I raise the possibility that new forms of wealth created through innovative modes of production and trade may have been the issue of political contention at the time of Appius' censorship and in the period that followed.

---

78. *Contra* MacBain 1980: 358–59.

79. Summary discussions in Morel 2007: 500–1; Panella 2014.

80. Morel 1969; Stanco 2009.

81. Van der Mersch 2001.

82. Olcese and Capelli 2016: 125.

83. Gabba 1981.

Thus, the censor seems to have made a sort of first attempt to integrate those reliant on new ways of producing wealth into the framework of Republican politics. The *libertini* will have been Romans whose wealth was gained outside of traditional aristocratic forms of dependency or clientship. The distribution of Roman ceramics across the western Mediterranean confirms that there was an extensive market available and wealth to be made in commercial activity. Not only elite landowners but merchants and other commercial agents, figures whom Fabius could enroll in the urban tribes, would have found opportunity in this environment, and these figures will have made up the collective *factio forensis*.

However, it also seems to have remained ideologically important for Roman elites in this period to generate wealth through socially appropriate channels, and this observation may explain why Appius' attempt to include some of these figures in the senate or in the rural tribes was contested by other senators as *morally* unacceptable. By offering a path to senatorial status for figures without equivalent social standing, trade and markets potentially expanded and thus threatened the dominant aristocratic order; moral censure of such rapidly accumulated wealth is well attested throughout history.[84] That is, the hypothesis of elite attachments to contrasting forms of wealth production at a moment of economic change conveniently offers an explanation for both support and opposition to Appius' political program. When, in 221 BCE, Q. Caecilius Metellus delivered a funeral *laudatio* for his father, the consul of 251 and 247 BCE, he praised the fact that his father "found great wealth in the proper way."[85] Specifically, Caecilius' referred to wealth earned *<u>bono</u> modo*, the qualification anticipating Livy's description of those opposing Appius' *factio forensis* as *fautor et cultor <u>bonorum</u>*. It should not be forgotten that the *nobilitas* emerged within a competitive context in which ideology, including economic ideology, formed an important means of accessing and maintaining political power. [86] The struggle over the relationship between different forms of wealth and political prestige continued at least to the Second Punic war, when the infamous *lex Claudia* in 218 BCE restricted senatorial participation in agricultural markets by limiting their ownership of large seagoing vessels, but archaeology leaves little doubt that, by the early

84. Parry and Bloch 1989.

85. Plin. *NH* 7.139–40 = *ORF*^{3} no. 6, fr. 2; for the authenticity of this sentiment, see Gabba 1981.

86. For theorization of such social friction between ideologies of market- and non-market economic activities, see Parry and Bloch 1989 on transactional orders. For more expansive application of the theoretical background to Rome, see Bernard *forthcoming* b.

third century, some Roman elites were already taking part in such forms of trade and wealth production.[87]

5.6. The Contested Meaning of Wealth among the *Nobilitas*

Thus, starting from the time of Appius and continuing through the next century, various factions within the Roman elite depended on different understandings of the definition of wealth and its ability to support political power. While not directly tied to the expansion and maintenance of urban fabric, this development led to structural changes in the organization of production, which included the city's building industry. Ultimately, I want to situate the initial production of Roman coinage, so important to the financing of public construction, within this context of different political attitudes towards wealth. To do so, I start first by looking at the role of metal within the struggle over aristocratic power outlined in the previous section. Metal's important role in the changing definition of aristocratic power can already be detected during Cn. Flavius' tribal reforms discussed in the previous section, when members of the senatorial *nobilitas* reacted to Flavius by removing their gold rings. Their action reveals the use by certain senators of precious metal not as a medium of exchanging wealth, but as a sign or token of aristocratic rank.[88]

The idea that metal functioned both as indication of elite rank and, eventually, as coinage in this period is important, because it demonstrates metallic wealth's ability to support aristocratic power on both sides of the struggle detailed above: metallic rings spoke to the conservative Roman senators' prestige and moral opprobrium against the *humiles*, while metal as coinage could, of course, readily facilitate the commerce and trade that supported newly wealthy Republican elites. These opposing ways of understanding metal's relationship to wealth and aristocratic power emerge clearly in a passage from the end of the Livy's first decade recording the triumphs of L. Papirius Cursor and Sp. Carvilius Maximus in 293 BCE (10.46). The meticulous detail of Livy's description, as well as the style and language with which each generals' spoils was described is a new feature in the *Ab urbe*

87. Liv. 21.63.3–4; Elster 2003: 187–90. My reading of this law follows Tchernia 2007; see otherwise Feig Vishnia 1987; Bringmann 2003.

88. Removing rings was a sign of mourning, as cf. Liv. 9.7.8; a gold ring from around this date with an aristocrat's name on it is known from Capua: *Imag.Ital.* Capua 47 I: 468.

condita, while similar descriptions appear commonly in the third decade, and this has suggested to scholars that Livy or his source drew for the first time from more detailed documentation of consular triumphs.[89] Livy's account strongly contrasted the two magistrates. Papirius was the son of the illustrious consul of the same name, and his political authority was strongly enforced by family tradition. He dedicated a temple to Quirinus that was likely vowed by his father, the glory of his spoils was compared to those captured by his father a generation previously, and even some of the captives in his triumphal parade were said to retain the fame of their ancestors. Meanwhile, Carvilius, born of equestrian rank and the first of his *gens* to reach the consulship, remained one of the great examples of *novi homines* from the Mid-Republic.[90]

The disparity between the two consuls' understandings of wealth emerges most clearly in Livy's discussion of what each consul did with the spoils of conquest. Papirius deposited all his metallic spoils, 2,533,000 *asses* of bronze and 1,830 pounds of silver, in the *aerarium*, and gave nothing to the soldiers. His wealth brought prestige to him and the state merely by sitting in the *aerarium*. Papirius also captured an enormous amount of arms and armor with which he decorated his new temple, the Forum, and even the fora and temples of colonies.[91] By contrast, Carvilius distributed cash to each soldier according to rank, after meeting the cost of his new temple and depositing an equivalent of 380,000 pieces of *aes grave* into the *aerarium*. According to Pliny, Carvilius melted down the arms and armor he captured in order to remake them into a colossal statue of Jupiter on the Capitoline. "From the leftover filings" (*e reliquis limae*, the level of detail is unparalleled) he also made a statue of himself.[92]

Both men thus took different views of the metallic income of military conquest and its relationship to political power. Papirius' power was traditional because it was inherited and communal, and he could thus rely on the symbolic, rather than material, value of his spoils. By contrast, Carvilius' metal was exchanged more tangibly for political prestige. Livy also explicitly noted that part of Carvilius' income came from allowing the wealthiest citizens

89. Oakley 1997–2005 IV 444–45.

90. Cf. Vell. Pat. 2.128.2 with Syme 1956: 262.

91. Papirius' display of armor may again have been family custom, as cf. Liv. 8.28.9–10 = *FRH* 1. Q. Fabius Pictor F17; Rawson 1990: 161.

92. Plin. *NH* 34.43; his attribution of the victory at Aquilonia to Carvilius, not Papirius, confirms that Livy is not Pliny's source.

of Troilus, which Carvilius sacked, to leave unharmed in exchange for great sums of money (*grande pecunia*). That is, Carvilius treated aristocratic prestige as fungible. Notably, both Papirius and Carvilius continued their prominent careers and both held the consulship together again in 272 BCE. By that measure, each man's actions, while oppositional, effectively sustained political authority at this moment in time. This suggests that by the first half of the third century BCE aristocrats were able to derive power from multiple ways of conceptualizing military income, a scenario that represents something of a development from the time of Appius' failed attempt to incorporate *libertini* into the senate in 312 BCE.

5.7. Metal and Money before Coinage

It thus becomes possible to recognize at Rome around 300 BCE competing elite ideologies of wealth's relationship to political power, extending tensions emerging during Appius' censorship in 312 BCE. Both triumphators of 293 operated in a Roman society in which metal's function as wealth was undergoing dynamic change leading up to the first use of coinage at Rome in the early third century BCE; the date and specifics of Roman monetization are detailed in the following section. Rome's early monetary history, however, extends well before the appearance of the first Roman coins.[93] The Twelve Tables refer to a bronze unit of account, while some fifth-century Roman laws reportedly assessed fines in bronze *asses*.[94] When prior to the fifth century the monetary use of bronze first began at Rome is obscure and debated. Our later sources connected important developments in monetization with the populist agenda of King Servius. Considering Servius' supposed *humilis* background, the choice to assign an innovation closely related to trade to this particular monarch may not be coincidental, even if the association finds little material support.[95]

93. The bibliography on early Roman money is considerable; see Crawford 1985: 32; Cornell 1995: 397; Kroll 2008: 37; for bronze in Iron Age Italy, see Catalli 2001: 13–23.

94. E.g. XII Tab. tb. 1.14, 8.3–4, etc.

95. Bernard *forthcoming* c; Plin. 33.42–43: *Servius rex primus signavit aes; antea rudi usos Romae Timaeus tradit*; for other sources, see Thomsen 1980: 25–28. Cf. Baron 2013: 49–50 for the question of whether or not Pliny's entire sentence goes back to Timaeus. Val. Max. 3.4 lists Servius among *humili loco nati*. The work of Pellegrini and Macellari 2002 makes the much-debated connection between *ramo secco* bronzes and the period of Servius untenable; see Orlandini 1965–67; Breglia 1965–67: 271; Peruzzi 1985: 225; Crawford 1985: 5–6 n. 4.

Metal's role in the Roman economy rapidly took on complexity in the mid-fourth century, immediately prior to Rome's earliest coinage. One piece of evidence in this regard appears in a cluster of legislation seeking to control or curtail usury between 357 and 342 BCE. The Twelve Tables may already have stipulated that usury not rise above "interest of a twelfth part" *unciarium fenus*, an enigmatic phrase, which, as Zehnacker argues, relates to interest on short-term loans of capital typical of a predominately agricultural economy. Interest may have initially been reckoned monthly, hence "twelfth part" or *unciarium*, because early loans were essentially agricultural; they did not extend for a long period and were intended to see peasants through to the next harvest, when debts could be repaid. Zehnacker suggests that behind usury legislation in the mid-fourth century was the need to address increasing application of such lending practices originally formulated for an agricultural economy to exchanges of non-agricultural wealth and longer-term credit.[96]

If it is true that lending became less strictly tied to agriculture in the mid-fourth century, then liquidity would have started to be a rising concern as exchanges began to involve a more complex array of forms of property, in turn indicating the increasing importance of non-agricultural production and wealth in the wider Roman economy. Accordingly, Zehnacker's intuition finds support from what appears to have been a liquidity crisis in 352 BCE. Under that year, Livy described a radical move by the consuls to create a five-man banking commission, the *quinqueviri mensarii*, who were responsible for resolving debts (7.21.5–8: *solutio aeris alieni*) by purchasing outstanding private debt with public funds. These *mensarii* addressed outstanding loans that were difficult to settle because of debtors' sluggishness (*inertia debitorum*), rather than lack of resources. That is, Livy's *mensarii* faced an issue of liquidity, rather than insolvency, and they achieved positive results by fairly assessing various forms of property (*aestimatio aequiis rerum pretiis*).[97] As with the period of Appius' censorship some generations prior, the central issue was arguably not the lack of wealth, but rather the valuation of particular and perhaps novel forms of wealth within the existing political and economic system.

96. Zehnacker 1980; Tac. *Ann.* 6.16 ascribes the code to the Twelve Tables, but this may be anachronism, as cf. *RS* vol. II 686–87.

97. Although problems caused by transfers of title during the next censorship suggest that this solution to debt remained less than ideal, cf. Liv. 7.22.6.

Livy's characterization of the debtors as essentially lazy reveals the moralizing tone with which late Republican authors regularly spoke about problems of debt. Nicolet attacks the entire episode as overly Hellenizing and as reduplicating another fiscal crisis in 216 BCE, when a panel of *mensarii* was also established.[98] However, Hellenistic *trapezites*, the etymological equivalent of *mensarii*, are never found similarly employed in resolving credit issues using public funds, while the later Republican *mensarii* were tasked with refilling a depleted *aerarium*, not making payments from it.[99] The critiques are thus not particularly strong, and in the unusualness of the actions of these fourth-century *mensarii*, and in their ultimate failure, it is instead possible to see the memory of an early experiment by the Roman state to solve increasingly problematic liquidity as the economic activities in which Republican elites engaged had begun to change.

Another sign of innovation in the realm of exchange in the fourth century were the moneychangers' stalls (*tabernae argentariae,* A19) first attested in 308 BCE on the north side of the Forum. Possibly assigned to the censorship of C. Maenius for reasons discussed above, these stalls predated all but the very earliest emissions of Roman coinage, and none of those early coin issues circulated in the city. This potential anachronism has raised the question of what these *argentarii* were doing in the forum prior to the circulation of coinage in the city. Andreau sees these figures as moneychangers working in part to assay the value of non-Roman coinage and facilitate its exchange for other goods.[100] The numismatic evidence in support of Andreau's claim is not straightforward, as only a limited quantity of late fourth century coins, mostly bronze, are found at Rome from the Greek cities of south Italy.[101] But it may not be necessary to see these *argentarii* initially fulfilling any rigidly defined role. Indeed, in 308 BCE, they first appeared in the record in relation to their receipt of silver and gold Samnite armor. Rather than a strictly coin-based role, the *argentarii* may speak to the growing importance of metallic wealth in exchanges in the Mid-Republican economy.

98. Nicolet 1963: 421; *contra* Storchi Marino 1993; Woytek 2014.

99. Bogaert 1968; also Andreau 1987: 222–24; interestingly, Plautus refers to *trapezites* as *tarpessita* or *tarpezita*, rather than *mensarii*.

100. Andreau 1987: 344–48; 1999: 30–31; Parise 1990: 397; Coarelli 2013: 37; *contra* Crawford 1985: 17.

101. Burnett and Molinari 2015: 92; also Reece 1982; Frey–Kupper 1995; Molinari 1995.

5.8. Coinage

Roman coins appeared within this cluster of innovations relating to economic exchange and liquidity at Mid-Republican Rome.[102] After some isolated small-denomination bronze issues with Roman legends struck probably in Naples around 325 BCE, the first "Roman" coinage appeared several decades later and took three distinct forms.[103] The first branch was silver and bronze coinage struck on the metrological standards of Campania and South Italy, the so-called Romano-Campanian coinage (figure 5.3). The earliest issue of this sort was a struck silver didrachm (*RRC* 13/1) displaying a bearded head wearing a Corinthian helmet on the obverse, and a horse's head above a plinth with the incuse legend *ROMANO(rum)* on the reverse. Along with hoard evidence discussed below, there are several reasons for seeing this coin as separate and earlier than other Roman silver didrachms. It was struck on a typically thicker flange, while an unusually high ratio of obverse to reverse dies suggests it was minted in improvised circumstances. So far as we know, it never circulated to Rome and was likely produced elsewhere, perhaps again in Naples. The didrachm was accompanied by a related fractional issue with similar iconography (*RRC* 13/2).[104] After a gap of some years, the Mars/Horsehead didrachm was followed by six further issues of Romano-Campanian silver didrachms. The seriation of these issues is established based on their reducing weight, from 7.3 g of silver (*RRC* 13/1) to 6.8 g. Their production continued on a comparatively small scale and unevenly into the period after the First Punic War.[105] Concurrent with this struck silver, Rome produced cast

102. For more expansive discussion of the start of Roman coinage, see Bernard *forthcoming* c. A massive scholarship includes Thomsen 1961; Mitchell 1966; Crawford *RRC*; Burnett 1977; Crawford 1985; Pedroni 1993; and contributions to *La monetazione romano-campana. Atti del X convegno del centro internazionale di studi numismatici* (1998). Reviews of literature in Hollstein 1998–99; Vitale 1999; Burnett 2012.

103. These Neapolitan Roman bronzes are obscure; their legends change from Greek (*POMAIΩN*) to Latin (*ROMANO*), suggesting development, and perhaps a larger series. Cornell 1995: 394 sees them as a commemorative issue to celebrate the *foedus aequum* with Naples in 326 BCE, but this would not account for multiple units. Vagi 2014: 79 suggests "everyday use by the Roman population of Naples."

104. The incorporation of multiple denominations makes difficult arguments attributing this strike to a single-purpose payments rather than to broader economic purposes. Humm 2005: 174–5 relates *RRC* 13/1 to the 450 *denarii nummi* paid by the Capuans to Rome annually after the concession of citizenship to the Campanian *equites*, but this does not account for the simultaneous production of a fractional unit. Coarelli (2013: 35–37) offers an imaginative dating of the early coins using obliquely attested historical events.

105. Burnett and McCabe 2016 identify the shift to *ROMA* legends on the later issues to the last years of the war.

FIGURE 5.3 Romano-Campanian silver didrachms, c. 300–220 BCE. Coins identified by the catalog numbers in RRC and depicted at 1:2 scale.
Images from Classical Numismatic Group, www.cngcoins.com.

currency bars and bronze coins (*aes grave*, cf. fig. 6.2). For reasons discussed in the next chapter, these cast coins and the Romano-Campanian coins seem to have been intended for different monetary purposes and unrelated to each other for at least the first half of the third century.

While the relative arrangement of these various branches of Rome's predenarius coinage is mostly secure, the absolute chronology remains debated. The literary tradition best represented by a much-discussed passage in the Elder Pliny placed the start of Rome's bronze coinage during the monarchic period and the start of silver coinage in 269 BCE, but both assertions do not accord with archaeological finds. Instead, modern scholarship dates the first cast bronze coins and bars to the years before the First Punic War and the first silver didrachm (*RRC* 13/1) slightly earlier and variously from the 330s to the 280s BCE.[106] Burnett's study of coin hoards containing early Romano-Campanian silver coins set the current orthodoxy for a start just before 300.[107] In particular, in the earliest hoards containing *RRC* 13/1, a relationship emerges between that coin and the latest didrachms of Tarentum's

106. Bronze: Jaia and Molinari 2011; a Pyrrhic war date for the bars is possible and depends upon the association of the sow on *RRC* 9 with an episode described by Aelian *NA* 1.38; silver: Burnett and Crawford 2014: 237 n. 11.

107. Burnett 1977; see also Mitchell 1967.

Period 5 didrachms and the earliest of Period 6, based on the Tarentine chronology established by Evans.[108] Crawford accepted Burnett's early dating and suggested a possible historical explanation. Observing that *RRC* 13/1 was an isolated issue, he suggested that the coinage was motivated by a similarly isolated exigency: the construction of the Via Appia (A21). He supported this by pointing to the distribution of hoards containing *RRC* 13/1 along the route of Appius' road in Campania.[109]

This potential link between large-scale construction and Rome's initial impetus to coin money lends great importance to this thesis in the present discussion. However, a full and updated account of the evidence makes the connection unlikely. To demonstrate this, let us first consider the date of the earliest silver didrachm more fully, and then turn to consider the coin's utility. The best evidence for a date is archaeological and numismatic. Less helpful is the coin's iconography, which allows for a very wide range of interpretation. Connections have been made, for example, between the bearded figure on the coin's obverse and Metapontine coinage, or between the horsehead on the reverse and Punic coins from Sicily. The bearded figure is normally interpreted as Mars, but has also been identified as Quirinus. And the combination of Mars and a horse head has been taken to indicate the censorial *ara Martis*, the Campus Martius, the *October Equus*, or the Roman cavalry.[110]

Numismatics and archaeology provide firmer, if still not absolute, chronological data. One issue with Burnett's chronology is the long gap of time, perhaps twenty or thirty years, implied between the minting of the first and second silver didrachms.[111] When Burnett first studied the hoards containing these strikes, it seemed indisputable that *RRC* 13/1 circulated with an older generation of South Italian coins than other Roman issues, especially because *RRC* 13/1 had not yet been discovered in any hoard alongside the next Roman didrachm, *RRC* 15/1. New evidence, however, modifies this view of the isolation of the strike. In the excavation of a villa at San Martino in Pensilis

108. This is supported by newly found hoards, such as that from Baselice; cf. Fischer-Bossert 1999: 347 n. 96.

109. Crawford 1985: 29; followed by Belloni 1993: 39; Cornell 1995: 396; Laurence 1999: 15–16.

110. For links with Metapontum and Punic Sicily, see Thomsen 1957–61 III. 92–95. For Quirinus, Hollstein 1998–99: 152–55. For a relationship with the censors, see Coarelli 2013: 34–35; with the *October Equus*, Breglia 1952: 31; with the cavalry and the *transvectio equitum*, see Humm 2005: 174–75.

111. Thus, see Mattingly 2004.

in Molise, not far from Larinum, a large hoard was discovered containing 163 total coins with eight Roman didrachms including, for the first documented instance, both the first and second silver didrachms in a single context. The five examples of *RRC* 15/1 were in excellent condition and some shared dies. By contrast, the three examples of *RRC* 13/1 were worn. Burnett rightly suggests that this implies a gap in time between the two issues, but the appearance of both Roman silver coins makes the first didrachm somewhat less isolated.[112] The San Martino hoard also provides good evidence to downdate *RRC* 15/1, as both the condition and die links of the five examples suggest they did not circulate for long before the hoard was deposited, probably around 250 BCE.[113] Since the San Martino hoard shows that the first two strikes were not entirely isolated, the consequent down-dating of the second issue to perhaps c. 260 and the early years of the First Punic War might argue for shifting the first issue (*RRC* 13/1) somewhat later as well, and closer to the years around 300 BCE.

Another important advance has been the revision of the chronology of southern Italy coinages upon which the relative chronology of Romano-Campanian silver depends, and particularly Fischer-Bossert's study of Tarentum's silver didrachms, which intends to replace the schema established by Evans in the early twentieth century. While Evans established his chronology mostly relying on stylistic changes, Fischer-Bossert incorporates the archaeological evidence of hoards, as well as a die-link study of several thousand coins. On this basis he down-dates by some fifty years those Tarentine coins belonging to the transition from Evans' Period 5 to Period 6 to c. 280. Since, as mentioned, hoards relate this transition to Rome's first didrachm, Fischer-Bossert argues that the Roman coins belong to a similar period.

In sum, while no new information provides a much-desired absolute date, the updated framework of relative dates tends to pull early Roman silver coinage further into the third century, away from the date of the Appian road's construction in 312 BCE.[114] This evidence also undermines a geographical

---

112. *Contra* Coarelli 2013: 39–40, whose attempt to relate *RRC* 15/1 to a supposed embassy to Delphi in 292 BCE ignores the shared die links exhibited by the examples in the S. Martino in Pensilis hoard, which confirm a date closer to that hoard's closing several decades later. Furthermore, Apollo appeared already on *RRC* 1/1, while his cult existed at Rome since the fifth century at least: there is no reason to sustain a specific historical connection between the god's appearance on *RRC* 15/1 and an event in the 290s.

113. Burnett 2006.

114. Persistent arguments for a fourth-century date do not consider the evidence discussed above: Humm 2005: 174–75; Coarelli 2013: 34–44; Vagi 2014.

connection between the coin and the censor's road. An updated distribution map of hoards containing *RRC* 13/1 shows a broader circulation than once thought, reaching as far north as the area of Pisa, while stray examples have been found in Sicily and even Spain.[115] Meanwhile, hoards containing the coin crossed the entire Via Appia, not only along Appius' route to Capua, but all the way to the area of Brundisium, where the road's extension reached after 244 BCE. If anything, rather than suggesting a relationship between Roman coinage and Appius' initial work on the road, the updated pattern of circulation shown in figure 5.4 argues for the road's importance in facilitating exchange between Rome and the Adriatic coast in the decades after its initial construction.

The connection between Appius' road and the earliest Roman didrachm is not only problematic on chronological and geographical grounds, but there is also the question of the coin's utility. Explaining coinage as strictly a means of paying for roadwork belongs to the traditional approach, which has sought to understand Rome's initial production of coinage by locating specific, outsized costs that would have spurred the Roman mint into action.[116] However, the structure of this complex coinage produced in several separate metals, techniques, and on different weight standards militates against any single impetus behind its creation.[117] Moreover, the sporadic initial nature of Roman coinage does not match any particular large state expenditure. Military campaigning was nonstop in this period, and it would be hard to imagine Rome striking coins to pay soldiers, but then ceasing to do so for a decade or more while warfare continued. The same can be said about Rome's construction industry, which remained active for decades after Appius' censorship. If campaigning or building motivated Rome's turn to coined money, it would be hard to understand why such activities did not result in more consistent coin production than the evidence suggests. Answering the question of why Rome first minted coinage thus eludes the search for a singular historical cause. In light of the context delineated up to this point, it seems better to understand the appearance of Roman coinage in socially embedded terms, as part of an ongoing and contested shift in the forms and interpretations of

115. Examples from Ponte Gini di Orentano near Pisa in Burnett and Molinari 2015: 54; for Spain, see Noguera 2012.

116. For the following, see expansively Bernard *forthcoming* c. Scholarship is increasingly accommodating to non-fiscal explanations for Roman coinage: Burnett 2012; Burnett and Crawford 2014; Woytek 2014; Burnett and Molinari 2015.

117. Von Reden 2010: 50.

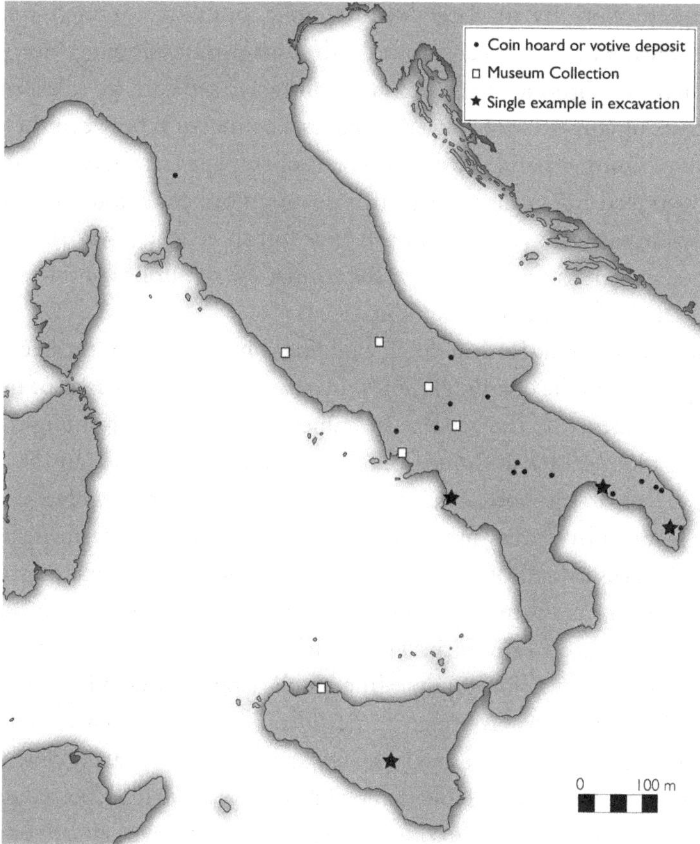

FIGURE 5.4 Distribution map of *RRC* 13/1, Rome's first silver didrachm. Compiled from data in Vitale 1998 and Burnett and Molinari 2015. Not shown: an example from La Palma in Spain (Noguera 2012).
Map © S. Bernard.

wealth, particularly metallic wealth. Coinage may have been adopted in part as a political instrument, an embodiment of the market-based exchanges that gave authority to a new group of Roman elites, as such wealth became increasingly recognized within the Republican political system in the decades following Appius' censorship.

5.9. Contracts

This history of Roman monetization leads to another topic with direct implications for the Mid-Republican *urbs*, and that is the reliance of the Republican state on contracts for organizing large-scale productive activities like construction. By the later Mid-Republic, building contracts were the normal means by which censors and other magistrates arranged for public construction. Without exception, such contracts used coinage to express the large costs of construction, and this makes a connection between the development of contracts and the development of coinage attractive. Meanwhile, we have traced how censors began to devote more consistent attention to the city's urban infrastructure in the later fourth century. Was this the period, then, when the censors first made regular use of public contracts for the organization of public construction?

The earliest extant Roman public building contracts date to the late second century BCE, and the question is how much earlier the practice may be inferred from this evidence.[118] The conceptual framework at least for forming contractual obligations existed at Rome from an early point. While the early history of leasing in Roman law is obscure, De Ligt makes the case that signs of its existence appear by the fifth century in the form of temporary sale. An enigmatic passage in Festus suggests that Roman antiquarians were aware of texts referring to early censorial contracts (*locationes censorum*) as "sales" (*venditiones*). To explain this, Festus or his source, likely Verrius Flaccus, imagined that the censors were originally responsible for selling produce from public land. However, it is more likely that Verrius or Festus was confused by the difference between *venditio* and *locatio* in his own time, whereas sale and lease may have been conceptually closer in the fifth century.[119] The Twelve Table's famous clause relating to the repeated attempt of a father to "sell" his son (*venditio filii*) suggests that the vocabulary of selling was by the fifth century applied to transactions that were not permanent, since otherwise a father would have had no opportunity to "sell" his son more than once.[120]

Of course, it is one thing to confirm that contracting was possible in the Early Republic and another to insist that magistrates regularly used large-scale contracts to arrange for public works. To judge from the narratives of wartime contracting in Polybius or Livy, state contracting was fully formed by the Second Punic War and dominated the arrangement of public needs. As for the earlier period, Badian influentially saw no reason to doubt that the

118. Two Sullan contracts from Rome (*CIL* I^2 808, 809), and the *lex parieti faciundo* from Puteoli. See also Front. *De Aq.* 96.

119. Fest. 516 L: *vend<itiones>... dicebantur censorum locationes; quod vel<ut fr>uctus locorum publicorum venibant.*

120. XII Tab. IV.2; De Ligt 2000; cf. Du Plessis 2012: 10–12.

censors used similar arrangements since the fifth century.[121] However, upon closer inspection the evidence he cites is unconvincing. His earliest instantiation is the construction of the Villa Publica in the Campus Martius 435, which Livy said that the censors "approved" (4.22.7: *probaverunt*). However, the Villa was not much more than publically designated land at that point, and its establishment likely involved little actual construction or expense.[122] The second example is Camillus' Temple of Juno Regina on the Aventine (A2), again based on Livy (5.23.7: *in Aventino locavit*), but chapter 3 raised reasons to doubt the details, if not the entirety, of the record of Camillus' work in the city.[123] The third example is the circuit wall of 378 BCE (A6), but here contractual obligation appears alongside reference to forced labor, and Livy's confusion in this passage concerning the walls' labor force has been discussed at length in the last chapter.

Meanwhile, in tracing the early history of contracts, legal scholarship focuses tightly on the formation of *locatio-conductio* contracts and is sometimes reluctant to push that institution before the earliest detailed discussion by jurists of the early second century.[124] Less formal *stipulatio* contracts were applied by that date to small building projects in private contexts such as, for example, on Cato's rural estate (*De Agr.* 14), but these sorts of arrangements seem too casual to suit the needs of large-scale, complex public construction in the capital.[125] If the lens is widened, however, to include state contracting more generally, there is fuller evidence than acknowledged from the mid-third century. In particular, the auxiliary process of *probatio* through which magistrates approved work arranged by contract appears on both coins and inscriptions of the third century BCE.[126] Two Latin inscriptions from Italy dating prior to the Second Punic War, one from Velletri, the other from Ostia, mention either *locatio* or the auxiliary institution of *probatio* in the probable

121. Badian 1983: 15–16; Anderson 1997: 79–80; also Strong 1968; Milazzo 1993: 55–63; Du Plessis 2004: 290.

122. Richardson 1976a.

123. The word *locatio* itself may have held a different meaning in the early period, Ziolkowski 1992: 203–8.

124. Mayer-Maly 1956: 15–16; Fiori 1999: 18–19; Du Plessis 2012: 9–10.

125. Taylor 2003: 16–17.

126. The word *probum* appears on mid-third century coins from Suessa Aurunca (*HN* Italy 448) and perhaps Beneventum (*HN* Italy 440).

context of public construction.[127] Neither of these inscriptions can be precisely dated, but we may now add several third-century inscriptions on the recently discovered bronze rams from warships sunk around Egadi, presumably during the final battle of the First Punic war in 241 BCE.[128] In these inscriptions, quaestors "approved" the quality of the rams that were presumably manufactured by private contractors for the state's warships and thus performed the function of *probatio* to conclude the contractual arrangement.[129]

Pushing the development of public *locatio-conductio* contracting back into the mid-third century presents a potential chronological overlap between the evolution of contracts and the period in which coinage was slowly emerging in the Roman economy. As noted, coinage was strongly related to later censorial contracts, which expressed payment amounts and values in terms of money with little exception. The ability to express value in monetary terms seems particularly useful for Republican building contracts for reasons of political context. There are essentially three ways of structuring building contracts for monumental construction, each relating to the conceptual division of the project: payment could be made for a set amount of time, for an agreed upon portion of an entire project, or for an entire project at once.[130] So far as we can see them, Republican building contracts tended to record agreements in the last category. This does not mean that contractual obligations were not used to arrange smaller component tasks or even daily wages. However, since the extant record is by and large a product of the initial step of the building process, and the state typically let contracts for entire buildings, or large portions of buildings, Republican contracts often recorded very large sums of money. Exceptional evidence often proves this rule. The exhaustively detailed Republican building contract from Puteoli, the *lex parieti faciendo* (*CIL* X 1781), which gave meticulously specific instructions for the structure to be built, listed only a single price for the entire project payable in installments as work was completed and approved. By comparison, Greek building inscriptions from Epidaurus or Athens recorded long lists of contractual arrangements for a variety of subsidiary tasks, each with their own

127. *CIL* I^2 22 and 24; on the latter, see Panciera 2006. Also see a possibly early inscription attesting wall building from Lucera (*CIL* IX 800 = *CIL* I^2 1710) discussed by Gregori and Nonnis 2013: 495.

128. Noted by Padilla Peralta 2014: 40–41; see Prag 2014a.

129. The role here of the quaestor, not an aedile or censor, overseeing public contracts is unusual but not inexplicable, as see Prag 2014b: 200–201.

130. Woodward 1995: 35.

price, sometimes listing contractual costs valued as low as a few obols.[131] Even Republican contracts recording construction by measure, rather than for whole structures, tended to give large components of a monument, and thus large costs. The Sullan-era contract for repair work on the Via Caecilia broke work into sections, but at costs of HS 150,000 to as high as HS 600,000.[132]

The political nature of building at Mid-Republican Rome may have played a part in shaping the state's tendency towards such lump-sum arrangements. The interest of a politically competitive *nobilitas* in gaining credit for "building" public monuments meant that the initiators of Rome's public buildings were political elites with no certain knowledge of building practice, and they were bound to be less interested in the details and particular costs involved. Sources hardly ever attested to an elected magistrate's interest in the actual form of a building.[133] Presumably, details of construction were left to those *negotiatores* or *conductores* who purchased contracts and took up responsibility for building work. Related to this was the limited term of appointment for most magistrates responsible for leasing contracts: the censor's 18-months may not have sufficed to attend to a building's construction beyond the arrangement of the lump-sum initial expense. It may be partly for this reason that more regularly-elected officials such as aediles became involved in state-contracts over time.

5.10. Conclusions

I have focused here on the temporal and structural relationship of several practices relating to the organization of production in the Mid-Republican Roman economy: the attention of the censors and other magistrates to urban infrastructure, the state's use of coinage, and the habit of arranging for large-scale expenditures like public building using contracts. There are reasons to think that these practices to some extent facilitated each other, and that they became regular parts of the economy over the same general period of time. Once the relationship between these practices is acknowledged, their rise may be seen as related to a larger institutional transformation as Rome's

131. Cf. Burford 1969.

132. *CIL* I² 808 with Guidobaldi 1999.

133. Exceptions: the debate between M. Claudius Marcellus and the pontiffs concerning the Temple of Honos and Virtus, Liv. 27.25.7–9; Q. Fulvius Flaccus' attempt to obtain marble tiles for the Temple of Fortuna Equestris, Liv. 42.3.

economy shifted from an reliance on forced labor seen in the early fourth century to more market-based strategies using coinage and censorially overseen contracts by the third century.

The economic changes described in this chapter have been portrayed as taking place in close connection with coeval political development, as both the direct and, often, indirect result of the evolving sociopolitical priorities of the Roman ruling class. The market as an organizing principle for Rome's third century urban economy was therefore not a matter of vague and progressive modernization, but was symptomatic of the particular development of the Mid-Republican political economy. Competing economic ideologies among the new nobility held importance as power was increasingly consolidated in the hands of a sector of the *nobilitas* whose wealth was based upon market exchange, as is evident not only from the literary record but from archaeological evidence. In the fourth and third centuries, the end of the patrician domination and the contested expansion in the number of elites with a stake in Roman politics demanded new economic structures as well.

6 THE LABOR SUPPLY OF MID-REPUBLICAN ROME

Starting around 300 BCE, Rome's building industry began to display considerable energy. Within the thirty years between the Roman victory at Sentinum in 295 and the opening of hostilities with Carthage in 264, we know of no fewer than sixteen public structures finished or started. Considering the particularly fragmentary state of the sources for the same period, this figure likely reflects a much more significant trend.[1] Starting in the early third century, then, sustained building activity at Rome began to create stable high demand for labor in the city. Demand created by such activity will have pulled workers to the city, and it is this demographic expansion and its effects that this chapter sets out to describe. Such demand will have affected urban production more broadly, since the increasing non-agricultural sector of the economy required not only builders, but a wide array of related craftsmen, merchants, and retailers to support the rising urban population's daily needs. At the same time, the economic developments that began in the time of Appius Claudius Caecus continued to liquefy wealth and move it across the spectrum of Roman society. A close relationship between liquidity, urban production including building, and population movement is readily observed in other historical periods.[2] Of course, the situation at Mid-Republican Rome was distinguished above all for the presence of slavery at the core of the Roman productive economy, and this makes it important to note that the third

---

1. Cornell in *CAH* VII.2^2: 405; for the period's sources, see Torelli 1978.

2. An instructive parallel comes from modern states in the Arabian Peninsula where public investment in construction has attracted immigrant builders and related service industry workers to the extent that 88% of the population of the United Arab Emirates, for example, were foreign nationals by 2007; this flow of migrants was temporarily halted by the financial (liquidity) crisis of 2008. See De Bel-Air 2015.

century not only represented a crucial period for the development of Rome's urban labor supply, but was also formative for the Roman slave economy.

6.1. Slavery and the Structure of Roman Labor

The dynamics by which the Mid-Republican labor supply met increasing demand are bound up with the question of the Roman slave economy. Indeed, one of the central debates concerning the nature of the Roman economy is the impact of slavery on the supply of free labor. In the view of Marxist scholarship of the last century, the dominance of the slave mode of production rendered all labor cheap, marginalizing free wage labor entirely. Finley in particular suggested that the denigrating opinions of some ancient authors toward wage earning were broadly representative of Roman elites who controlled a productive economy in which free wage labor was insignificant.[3] Accordingly, wages were conventional and low, and wage earning held little social or economic importance.

Recently, however, there have been significant challenges to this view. For one thing, Lis and Soly point out that a significant strain of ancient thought valued the "worthy efforts" of manual labor among the free and even aristocratic class.[4] For another, it is clear that something resembling wage labor existed in a number of decidedly non-capitalist economies from Mycenaean Greece to Neo-Assyrian Babylon, and the general thesis that wages were absent in such economies seems wrong.[5] Where Roman real incomes may be observed, such evidence does not indicate that wages were economically unimportant, but may have even offered a measure of income above subsistence.[6] For the Empire, Scheidel and Friesen suggest the existence of a "middling" economic stratum of Roman households, who possessed only modest disposable income, but whose aggregate wealth rivaled that of the entire elite.[7] In their view, Roman wage-earners collectively controlled a share of the Roman economy equivalent to the rich, and it is therefore hard to argue

---

3. Finley 1999: 41–42, 68–69 and *passim*; for him, negative opinions toward wage labor such as Cic. *de Off.* 1.150–1 were typical.

4. Lis and Soly 2012.

5. See "hirelings" at Mycenaean Pylos: Nakassis 2012; Jursa 2015 for Babylon. Recent Marxian discussion of the slave mode of production acknowledges hired labor to a greater extent, cf. Banaji 2010, ch. 4.

6. Mrozek 1989; Cuvigny 1996; Jongman 2007: 600–2; Allen 2009; Rathbone 2009.

7. Scheidel and Friesen 2009.

for the complete marginalization of wage-earners. Temin not only sees free wage-earners as prevalent in the Roman Imperial economy, but he argues that a broad labor market existed that integrated both free and unfree labor: the frequentness of manumission in Roman slavery distinctively incentivized the labor of slaves, who functioned as if under a long-term contract.[8] This assimilation of slavery to a sort of long-term contract perhaps underestimates the exploitation inherent in the Roman slave system, and it may be doubted whether any "speaking tool," as Varro referred to slaves, had much say over where he worked or what work he did.[9] Moreover, Roman manumission has been shown to be capricious and random and may therefore not have so readily served as an automatic reward for good work, while freed slaves often remained economically and socially tied to their ex-masters.[10] However, the idea that free labor had a significant presence in some areas of the Roman world, and particularly in Rome itself, remains attractive. Clearly, we need to build new models of thinking about Roman production that incorporate workers of various statuses.

This scholarly debate has mostly ignored the Mid-Republic. However, the period around 300 BCE seems to hold particular importance to the developing relationship between free and slave labor that characterized the later Roman world.[11] Slavery and manumission existed by the Early Republic, when both *servi* and *liberti* featured in the Twelve Tables.[12] But slavery's importance must have increased in the late fourth century as forced free labor's prominence began to decline in both public and private contexts. In 291 BCE, L. Postumius Megellus was prosecuted and fined for having used soldiers under his command to clear land on his estate during his consulship in 293 BCE.[13] In the private sphere, the legal curtailment of *nexum* in either 326 or 313 BCE—our sources do not agree on the date—likewise seems to have had a significant effect.[14] Afterward, the presence of corvée or debt bondage in Rome and Roman Italy seems trivial through the end of the empire, and such

---

8. Temin 2004; 2013: 114–38.

9. Varr. *R.R.* 1.17: *genus vocale instrumenti*.

10. Mouritsen 2011: 206–47.

11. The period's importance is noted by Finley 1998: 82–85; 1999: 69.

12. For the consolidation of the Roman slave economy at this time, see De Martino 1974.

13. Gabrielli 2003b.

14. Cornell 1995: 333; unfortunately, the wording of the *Lex Poetelia* as sources report it is imprecise, as cf. Hölkeskamp 1987: 160 n. 137.

events appear to signal a larger shift in Roman production concomitant with the growth of the slave economy in the fourth century BCE.[15]

Since this chapter began by observing the stabilization of high demand at Rome at around the same date as this apparent decline in the use of forced free labor, we are therefore led to ask what forms of labor met rising urban demand. Put simply, the answer seems to be that a combination of slave and free wage labor already existed at Rome by this point. The wars of the third century brought an extraordinary number of slaves into the hands of Roman masters and helped to install slaveholding at the center of the Roman productive economy. At the same time we discern the emergence of various institutions related to the need to support wage earning in the city. In what direct evidence exists for the status of urban workers in Rome and Latium in this period, *servi, liberti*, and *ingenui* of various backgrounds are found working side by side.

It is the character of the supply of workers to urban production that this chapter describes. Discussion takes into account the building industry, one of the largest single sources of urban demand for labor, as well as other productive activities located in the city. The argument is structured as follows: Rome underwent significant demographic expansion starting in the early third century, and it is reasonable to think that most of this immigration in some way responded to urban demand for work. Unfree labor was pushed to the city through slavery. But there are also reasons to think that free labor was pulled to Rome, mostly from Italy, by the opportunity of a nascent urban labor market. The model of mobile artisans of mixed personal status finds support, in the chapter's final section, in the epigraphic evidence for non-agricultural production.

This argument must operate without direct evidence for wages and prices, about which we know next to nothing for the period; one suspects this lack of evidence has discouraged recent, more quantitative research on Roman incomes from considering the Mid-Republican economy at all. However, we do know in very basic terms what a labor market looks like. Generally, a labor market operates to match the supply of workers with demand for work. In order to participate in a market, a worker must be free to some extent to choose both the location of his work and his occupation. The existence and extent of a market for labor is thus demonstrated by a worker's geographic and professional mobility—how far he travels to find a job, and how readily

15. Gabba 1981: 542; 1990: 10–11; Scheidel forthcoming.

he can change jobs in response to changing demand—and by the ability for employers to set different levels of compensation for work, usually in the form of a wage, or, in the case of independent artisans, we might think of a market price on the products of work. Thus, we may learn a great deal about the organization of production by assessing the evidence for a worker's mobility and for the potential for wages, even absent direct evidence for incomes.

A more concrete illustration of these labor market conditions appears in the biography of Plautus transmitted by Aulus Gellius and attributed to Varro:

> But Varro and other writers recorded that indeed he wrote the Saturio, the Addictus, and a third comedy, whose name eludes me at the moment, in a bakery when, with all the money he had made in his work as a stagehand lost in commercial ventures, he returned to Rome penniless and, because he needed to earn a living, hired himself to a baker to push the mills called "hand-mills."[16]

In this story, Plautus satisfied all the requirements of a labor market: he came to Rome for work, left again to pursue commercial opportunities, and switched professions in response to both demand and his desire for compensation. Of course, the playwright's actions here bear resemblance to one of his dramatic plots, and this passage cannot be taken on its own as historical evidence. However, I hope to demonstrate that the underlying conditions of work and labor mobility should be taken seriously for Mid-Republican Rome starting in the third century BCE.

6.2. Evidence for Urban Growth

Scholars have already suspected that the third century BCE was a period of significant expansion for Rome's urban population.[17] Our only potential quantitative data come in the form of census returns. While such figures display a significant (75%) increase between the time of Alexander the Great

16. Gell. *NA* 3.3.14: *Sed enim Saturionem et Addictum et tertiam quandam, cuius nunc mihi nomen non subpetit, in pistrino eum scripsisse Varro et plerique alii memoriae tradiderunt, cum pecunia omni, quam in operis artificum scaenicorum pepererat, in mercatibus perdita inops Romam redisset et ob quaerendum victum ad circumagendas molas, quae "trusatiles" appellantur, operam pistori locasset.*

17. Frank 1933: 37–42; Starr 1980: 11–23; Cornell 2000a: 46–47 attributes growth to slavery; Panella 2010: 62 n. 2.

(336–323 BCE) and the next known census in 293 BCE, the accuracy of these figures is highly disputed, as are all early census figures.[18] Moreover, even if we could somehow assure the reliability of these figures, it is not clear how, if at all, the population counted by the census related to the urban workforce. Thus, it seems better to point to other indices of population growth, which, while less exacting, remain suggestive. For example, observing the close proximity in time between the construction of Rome's first two aqueducts, some suggest that this reflected an increase in the need for fresh water by urban residents and thus rapid population growth.[19] Construction on the Appia (A22) started in 312 BCE, while work on the Anio Vetus began in 272 BCE (A44). The latter aqueduct in particular was built using highly innovative constitutional and financial procedures—it is the only known censorial work expressly built from a general's war spoils (*manubiae*). This innovation may indicate a sense of urgency and state-level recognition of pressing urban demand for fresh water.[20]

These new sources of fresh water allowed for more dense urban settlement, some signs of which appear in both textual and archaeological evidence. The shift at Rome in the time of the Pyrrhic War from the use of shingles to tiles for roofing houses, for example, may speak to the desire to guard against the threat of fire in increasingly dense residential settlement.[21] There is also some evidence to indicate that multi-story housing existed at Rome by this period. Livy's prodigy list of 218 BCE included a story of a cow climbing up and falling off the third floor of a building in the *forum boarium*.[22] The location, by the terminus of the Aqua Appia and thus convenient to the urban water supply, makes sense, and Palmer points out that a violent fire reported in the same area of the city in 213 BCE may also indicate a certain density of housing.[23] By the later second century at the latest, legislation regulating multi-story buildings speaks to increasing vertical construction.[24] Not all of the textual

18. See above, pp. 103–6.

19. Brunt 1971: 384; Panella 2010: 62 n. 2.

20. For the unusualness of the Anio Vetus' building process, see Aberson 1994: 193–98. For the idea of senatorial coordination, see Steinby 2012a: 39.

21. Plin. *NH* 16.36; Robinson 1992: 29; see above p. 34.

22. Liv. 21.62.3. Yavetz 1958: 506; Robinson 1992: 28; De Ligt 2012: 219; Kay 2014: 308.

23. Palmer 1976–77: 140.

24. Suet. *Div. Aug.* 89.2; see Cic. Off. 3.66, Val. Max. 8.2.1 for a second-century house on the Caelian.

evidence points in the direction of multi-story housing by the Mid-Republic, however. Separate legislation from the Mid-Republic apparently limited the thickness of buildings' walls to one and a half feet (c. 44 cm), and Vitruvius says that only buildings of fired brick or ashlar, neither of which was regularly employed for elevation courses of Mid-Republican domestic urban architecture, could support more than two stories with walls of such dimensions (*De Arch.* 2.8.17).[25]

What slender physical evidence exists for Mid-Republican residential architecture is also somewhat ambiguous as it relates to the idea of multi-story *insulae* in the city at this date. Several large *domus* excavated along the Via Sacra and in the *argiletum* indicate the persistence of large horizontally planned housing, rather than multi-story building blocks.[26] Because of these sites' close proximity to the Forum, it is possible that this evidence simply speaks to the continuity of large, elite housing in areas where wealthy residences were found already in the Archaic period.[27] However, the recent discovery of a second-century atrium-style house beneath the church of Santi Sergio e Bacco in the subura shows that horizontally planned houses were by no means restricted in the Republic to the Forum valley.[28]

While the evidence for the expansion of housing upwards is mixed, Rome's inhabited area in the third and second centuries does seem to have been spreading horizontally. Some areas of the city see new signs of inhabitation. Several ashlar-masonry structures of uncertain function represent spreading occupation, or possibly reoccupation, in this period on the Esquiline.[29] Movement into this area of the city may have been directly facilitated by the

25. Cf. Plin. *HN* 35.173.

26. On the atrium house in early Italy, see Jolivet 2011; Via Sacra: Carandini and Carafa 1995; Papi and Carandini 1999; *argiletum*: Delfino 2014: 120–23. It should be noted that the reconstruction of both Via Sacra houses in the earlier phases rests on highly fragmentary evidence.

27. The presence of elite houses probably characterized the general area. Cifani (2008: 130–36) notes two more possible Archaic *domus* beside the Sepulcretum and in the Carinae.

28. Andrews 2014. Three more Mid-Republican houses whose full plans are irrecoverable are (i) beneath San Pietro in Vincoli (Colini and Matthiae 1966: 11–15), (ii) a house with ashlar walls near the Meta Sudans (Schingo 1996: 154); and (iii) a multi-story house installed in the second century against the walls on the Quirinal at Salita del Grillo (Specchio 2011).

29. These include a circular building 15 m. in diameter on the Oppian; an adjacent small (c. 4–5 m long) rectangular shrine (Astolfi, Cordischi, and Attilia 1989–90; Cordischi 1993; Coarelli 2001; Cifani 2008: 74; Marroni 2010, 54–56); a terrace wall of *tufo giallo* along via Giovanni Lanza (Ferri 2002: 124); and traces of the Mid-Republican sanctuary of Juno Lucina (Andrews 2015: 49–50).

Anio Vetus, whose terminus was situated in the area of the *porta Esquilina*.[30] Burial also restarted in the mid-fourth century in the Esquiline necropolis, where there had been no burial for over a century.[31] Elsewhere, the earliest significant signs of settlement on the Caelian appear at around this same date, represented by the fourth-century circuit wall (A6), by an early third-century chamber tomb found in the area of the Ospedale di S. Giovanni, and by a substantial section of a Mid-Republican aqueduct, perhaps a branch of the Anio Vetus.[32] Another new zone for burial appeared at this time along the first extramural stretch of the Via Appia and included the fourth-century tomb of the Cornelii Scapulae, and the grand tomb of the Cornelii Scipiones, established in the early third century, as well as another unidentified Mid-Republican chamber tomb immediately adjacent to that of the Scipiones.[33]

Such urban expansion is reasonably taken as an indicator of increasing population density, and in this case is complementary to a distinct shift in settlement outside the city, in the third century *suburbium*, which seems to have responded to greater urban demand. Around c. 350–250 BCE, several dozen large farmstead or "villa" sites appear around the city, while the few earlier farmsteads seem to have been remodeled at this same time to accommodate increased production. Volpe notes that several such sites contained rows of irrigation ditches to support the cultivation of vines. Amphorae are relatively rare in contexts in the city at this date, and she suggests that these vineyards transported wine in perishable containers to urban consumers.[34] Viticulture was not the only production that saw intensification in the *suburbium* at this date: a Mid-Republican building found near the Auditorium villa on the Via Flaminia contained over 250 loom weights in a single room and may have functioned as a large textile production center.[35] In any case, archaeology now makes it indisputable that some degree of intensive, market-oriented

30. Andrews and Bernard 2017.

31. Colonna 1977.

32. Wall: Bernard 2012: 18; Caelian tomb: Scrinari 1969; *RMR* 245–46 (La Rocca); for the aqueduct, see above p. 132.

33. On the tomb of the Cornelii Scapulae, see Blanck 1966–67; Pisani Sartorio and Quilici Gigli 1987–88; the earliest burial in the Tomb of the Scipios belongs to L. Cornelius Scipio Barbatus, consul 298 BCE. For the unidentified tomb, see Volpe et al. 2014: 175–76.

34. Volpe 2009; 2012. This point is debated, as Panella (2010: 67) posits the possible existence of a Republican *mons testacceum*. Greco-Italic amphorae appear in limited quantity at Rome (Ferrandes 2016) and around Ostia (Olcese and Coletti 2016); R. Volpe suggests to me that this material might indicate limited urban consumption of particularly prized vintages.

35. Ricci 2002.

production began in Rome's hinterland already by the third century, and even earlier at some sites.[36]

6.3. Accounting for Urban Growth

Who were the new Romans who accounted for expanded settlement in the city and demand for production in the *suburbium*, and why did they move to Rome? As with any pre-modern city, we may assume that most urban growth was due to immigration. The Mid-Republican city's mortality regime can only be inferred from comparison with other periods and urban contexts, and, in general, pre-modern cities exhibited low to negative net natural population growth. The earliest evidence allowing any direct understanding of mortality at Rome are a number of *ollae* inscribed with burial dates and found near San Cesareo and likely dating to the late second century; the inscribed burial dates on these urns suggest the urban population displayed seasonal morbidity, perhaps suggestive of malaria.[37] In terms of bioarchaeological material, the recent excavation of a necropolis at Castellaccio Europarco on the Via Laurentina in the *suburbium* included seventeen burials dated to the fourth- and third centuries, nine of which contained adult individuals. Urban burial evidence remains sparse, but more material may eventually contribute more to this picture.[38] Still, as no strikingly unusual fertility or disease-resistant factors can be identified, it would be hard to argue that third-century Rome saw significant or even positive natural growth that would have been unusual for a pre-modern city. In fact, as Rome became increasingly densely occupied, it may have exhibited higher death rates.[39] This being the case, the demographic expansion of an urban center like Rome was owed to the influx of migrants who were pushed or pulled to the city, and we may usefully divide a discussion of these new Romans between the voluntary or involuntary nature of their movement to the capital.

---

36. Panella 2010: 59–66.

37. Shaw 2006; Hin 2013: 103; Lo Cascio 2016: 25.

38. Castellaccio necropolis: Buccellato, Catalano, and Pantano 2007; Killgrove 2013. Newly discovered Mid-Republican material at a necropolis near Ostia (Olcese and Coletti 2016: 80), and from the Esquiline necropolis (Barbera et al. 2005; Menghi, Pales, and Di Bernardini 2006).

39. Hin 2013: 221–28; Lo Cascio 2016 question the applicability to Rome of the so-called urban graveyard effect, promoted by Scheidel 2003.

6.3.1. Forced Transfers: Slaves to Rome

The most obvious evidence for the incorporation of new population into the Roman economy comes in the record of mass enslavements following military conquest. Slavery is the best known "push" factor relating to Roman mobility.[40] There is no denying that tens if not hundreds of thousands of captives were enslaved by Romans in this period, and some if not many of these slaves were brought to the city. Still, I think we must question whether the supply of slaves from conquest will have entirely satisfied urban demand for labor. First the figures: in the span of five years during the Third Samnite Wars, from 297–293 BCE, some 60,000 new slaves were captured by Rome.[41] Livy is our best source for these mass enslavements, and we lack consistent figures after 293 BCE, when his text no longer survives. However, sporadic notices confirm that large-scale enslavement continued, and during the first Punic War reports of 25,000 or more slaves sold following individual conquests are not unusual. Noting the overlap between the enslavements of the Third Samnite War and the sudden increase in reported temple dedications in the same period, several scholars have raised the possibility that these new slaves were in large part responsible for building public monuments in Rome.[42]

However, the city was not the only destination for war captives. Since, as we have seen, intensive agricultural production in Rome's *suburbium* had a substantial presence in the Mid-Republic, it seems prudent to think that some considerable portion of captured slaves went to intensifying suburban land tenure. Beyond the city's hinterland, Roman attention to the organization of captured territory and the supply of slave labor on that territory likewise seems high.[43] As Prachner points out, the ease with which Romans sold large numbers of war slaves in this period suggests that an extensive and fully formed slave trade already existed.[44] While this does not preclude the

---

40. Welwei 2000; Scheidel 2005.

41. Harris 1979: 59; Welwei 2000: 159–60.

42. Harris 1979: 59; Welwei 2000: 54; Padilla Peralta (2014: 44) extends the argument to public slaves like those entrusted by Appius Claudius Caecus with the cult of Hercules at the Ara Maxima.

43. Particularly true during the conquest of Sabinum and Picenum in the early third century, which Gabba (1981: 542–43) and Panella (2010: 74) rightly see as just as consequential as developments in landholding in the second century BCE. Cf. Dio 8.37.1 on Dentatus' desire to supply conquered slaves to the *ager Gallicus*.

44. In Welwei 2000: 54–55 n. 113; Welwei rightly emphasizes the importance of piracy and raiding alongside conquest in supplying slaves at this date.

use of slaves in urban production, it does mean that demand for slave labor was multifocal.

There are also reasons to think that the supply of slaves to production, agricultural and urban, was more complex than a simple narrative of conquest and mass enslavement. We may compare, for example, the labor force at the Latin city of Praeneste, which contained a significant bronze-working industry in the fourth century. A number of bronze strigils produced at Praeneste in that period bear stamps naming either workshop owners or perhaps craftsmen. The names are overwhelmingly Greek and indicate the strong presence of Greek artisans in Praeneste's productive economy.[45] A similar background applies to the artisan who signed an engraved third-century Praenestine mirror, *Vibius Pilipus cailavit*. Vibius Pilipus' name suggests a Campanian origin, and his gentilicium is equivalent to the Greek φίλιππος.[46] Bronze workers in this important fourth-century urban center close to Rome were to a significant degree migrants, predominately from Greece. None of these inscriptions records a status, but in the likely event that at least some of these workers were servile, it is noteworthy that no significant campaign by Praeneste against any Greek-speaking cities of Campania or south Italy is known in this period. Instead, Praeneste's labor supply came to Latium not directly through conquest, but more likely through a secondary slave trade. Moreover, this emphasizes the unsurprising fact that demand for slaves in Italy was by no means centered on the city of Rome itself, and it is likely that some slaves sold after conquest were purchased by non-Romans.

The complexity of the slave trade in Mid-Republican Central Italy makes it difficult to draw a direct correlation between quantitative increases in attested mass enslavements and temple dedications during the Third Samnite war, even if slaves acquired through conquest did to some degree contribute to the production of urban architecture. The relationship of conquest to urban building labor becomes even more complicated if we investigate the general appropriateness of slave labor for this productive activity by looking more closely at the structure of demand for building labor in particular. Energetics analysis would be helpful, but the state of the evidence, with little evidence from which to reconstruct the superstructure of public buildings at Rome before the later second century, makes such an approach too speculative to be useful. What we can say is that the building boom in third century Rome

45. See the catalog in Jolivet 1995.

46. *RMR* 290–92; Bourdin 2012: 553.

involved the construction of a great many temples and other monuments of significant architectural complexity. Particularly when Roman masons began to build superstructures in stone, a technological development which we cannot precisely place but which certainly occurred in the Mid-Republic, demand for skilled labor in particular will have increased dramatically.[47] The production, for example, of a single Ionic capital will have taken on the order of 400 hours of skilled labor.[48]

It is thus necessary to think about how Roman slavery in this period mapped onto potentially rising demand for *skilled* labor in the city. Sources note two instances in which skilled labor was explicitly included in relation to post-conquest enslavement, but problematically and perhaps instructively neither episode finds such labor contributing to urban production. First, in Livy's account of the aftermath of the capitulation of Capua in 211 BCE, Rome punished the city by executing 70 of the city's ruling elite and allowing 300 others to die in the custody of the Latin allies. The remaining Capuan citizens were put up for sale as slaves. However, Livy then goes on to say that, "in order to repopulate the city, a crowd of resident aliens, freedmen, traders, and craftsmen was retained," *urbi frequentandae multitudo incolarum libertinorumque et institorum opificumque retenta* (26.16.6–8).[49] Since Rome's actions intended to punish in brutal fashion those Capuan citizens who had participated in the city's disloyalty toward Rome, the (non-citizen) working class of Capua was not enslaved. In the second case, after the capture of New Carthage in 209 BCE, Polybius reported that skilled workers (*cheirotechnai*) were enslaved, but not in their respective crafts. Instead, these slaves became rowers in the fleet, with the promise of manumission if they performed that task diligently (10.17.9).[50] As attestation for the enslavement of skilled craft workers, both episodes call into question the direct relationship between military enslavement and urban production at Rome.

Mass enslavement may have contributed instead mostly to the supply of unskilled labor. Comparative evidence suggests that the large-scale employment of unskilled servile labor to public works projects was not regular ancient practice. Slaves were absent among the unskilled workers listed in the

47. Davies 2012, discussed below at p. 202.

48. Pegoretti 1869: 397, rounding down to allow for the use of tuff. For modern data, see Barker and Russell 2012: 93.

49. For context, see Fronda 2010: 151–53; Livy's characterization gains support from an inscription from Sena Gallica (*CIL* XI.6211) relating *incolae* to *opifices.*

50. Cf. Liv. 26.47.1: *opifices*.

accounts of the Erechtheon building program at Athens, something which troubled Finley.[51] Epstein argues that the Athenian situation reflected the unwillingness of slave owners to maintain workers full-time for the sporadic and uneven demand that unskilled building labor required. The argument makes sense, and it is likely not coincidental that large slave gangs are attested in the Roman building industry only in the context of repair and maintenance, activities for which demand was more predictable and consistent than for *ex novo* construction.[52] As mentioned, unskilled work in building and other productive activities in the Imperial city is often held to have been an important source of casual employment for free urban residents.[53]

The discordance of skill levels of war slaves and building workforces once more problematizes the direct correlation between Roman conquest and mass enslavements and the demands of urban production. I have focused on construction because of its visibility, but evidence discussed later in this chapter suggests that other urban productive activities likewise depended on workers of varying statuses. Again, this is not to deny the use of slave labor by Roman employers in urban production in the third century, and some attested workers in third-century Rome were identifiably servile. However, since the supply of labor was not strictly related to a surplus of war captives flowing into the Roman productive economy, it is more likely that employers were presented with workers of various statuses brought to Rome either by an organized slave trade, or for other reasons to which we now turn.

6.3.2. Free Transfers: The Urban Labor Markets of Rome and Republican Italy

Having seen the limitations of involuntary migration through slavery as it applied to urban demand for labor, I now consider whether and to what extent free labor was "pulled" to third-century Rome by the opportunities for work. Thirty years ago, the idea of individually mobile Roman workers

---

51. Finley (1999: 74–75) gives three unconvincing explanations: 1. Piety in the case of temple building attracted free labor. 2. State-investment allowed for wages—of course, we find state investment elsewhere where we also find *servi publici*. 3. The need for skilled labor drew free artisans, not slaves, while he seems to think that slaves made up unskilled workforces; this seems backwards.

52. Examples include Crassus' 500 builders used to repair and resell houses (Plut. *Crass.* 2.4), and the *familiae publicae* who maintained Rome's aqueducts (Front *De Aq.* 119, 124; epigraphic evidence in Bruun 1991).

53. See above, p. 16.

would have seemed more radical, but the last few decades have repeatedly emphasized the typicality of mobility in Roman Italy.[54] Some recent bioarchaeological work claims to identify non-Roman individuals in burials in the Roman *suburbium*.[55] It is sometimes still suggested, however, that the majority of Roman migration, even among free populations, was compulsory: if Romans did not move as slaves, they moved because of state-sponsored migration policies such as colonization or land redistribution programs.[56] While these are highly visible forms of mobility in the historical record, the programmatic way in which our sources' depict state-directed Roman colonization in this period has been rightly questioned. More than that, even if we uphold parts of the Republican colonial narrative, we still find sources regularly reporting Rome's need to supplement colonies, which had trouble retaining *coloni* who left of their own accord.[57] Thus, migration under the direct control of the Republican state, even if important, can only have been one aspect of a larger and more dynamic background of movement in Republican Italy.

In terms of human mobility in early Rome, elite movement is discerned from the literary record of aristocrats from elsewhere in Italy moving to Rome or owning property there, such as Lucumo, Attius Clausus, and Vitruvius Vaccus. Similar movement appears in epigraphic and archaeological evidence, such as dozens of *tesserae hospitales* with Latin and Etruscan names found in Rome, Italy, and as far as away as Carthage.[58] The Republican state seems to have posed no serious legal or institutional obstacles to mobility.[59] Instead, social networks between aristocrats from different communities seem to have

54. For earlier opinion of minimal mobility, see Brunt 1971: 161–62. Hopkins 1978: 57 already recognized that Republican Italy's economic development entailed large-scale migration. Rome's massive population is inexplicable without considerable migration, as see Morley 1996: 46. For general discussion see De Ligt and Tacoma 2016; Tacoma 2016; for Republican Italy, see Bourdin 2012.

55. Killgrove (2013) identifies an individual from the Castellaccio necropolis as non-Roman and possibly non-Indo European on the basis of isotope analysis and skeletal morphology. Caution is demanded for this approach, as see Bruun 2010.

56. Scheidel 2004: 20; however, see Hin 2013: 215–6.

57. E.g., Liv. 39.3.4–6, 41.8; cf. Broadhead 2001; for revisionist views on Mid-Republican colonization, see Bispham 2006; Pelgrom and Stek 2014.

58. Ampolo 1976–77; Bourdin 2012: 519–89. On *tesserae hospitales*, see Maggiani 2006; Luschi 2008.

59. Broadhead 2001.

Table 6.1. Mid-Republican Latin authors of non-Roman origin*

Author	Origin	Status
Livius Andronicus (fl. 240)	Tarentum	*libertus*
Q. Ennius (239–164)	Rudiae (Apulia)	*ingenuus*
M. Pacuvius (220–c. 130)	Brundisium (Apulia)	*ingenuus*
T. Maccius Plautus (c. 250–184)	Sarsina (Umbria)	*ingenuus*
Caecilius Statius (fl. 180)	Mediolanum	*libertus*
Terence (c. 200–159)	Carthage	*servus*
Accius (170–c. 90)	Pisaurum	*libertinus*

* Table compiled from Conte 1994.

taken on a formality of their own, expressed through relationships of *vicinitas* or *hospitium*.[60]

When it comes to those non-elite individuals who constituted Rome's productive labor supply, I suspect the latter group was no less mobile than the aristocratic class. To support this I start with one group of Mid-Republican "workers" who will be well known, although not necessarily from this perspective. From the mid-third century onward, Latin literature emerged at Rome through the efforts of a number of authors who moved from elsewhere in Italy to the capital, where they found support with various urban patrons (table 6.1).[61] In general, Latin literature in its infancy depended upon immigrants of diverse status, some slave but others free. So far as our literary sources portray them, those involved in building trades in Republican Latium also appear mobile. There are accounts in the sources of architects traveling between Greece and Rome in the mid-second century BCE, figures such as Hermodorus of Salamis at Rome, or Cossutius at Athens and Antioch.[62] These two figures were both free individuals, but by the early first century BCE, inscriptions record Central Italian *architecti* of all statuses, *servi, ingenui,* and *liberti*.[63] The Elder Pliny names several mobile artisans in Central Italy from an earlier date. This includes Vulca from Veii, who was said to have been summoned by the Tarquins to contribute sculptural terracottas to the temple

60. Lomas 2012.

61. Two noteworthy exceptions are Naevius, a Campanian *civis Romanus*, and the early historiographers who were largely Roman citizens from major *gentes*.

62. Bernard 2010: 51.

63. Slave: *CIL* X 4587; free-born: *CIL* I^2 1916; freedman: *CIL* I^2 1734.

of Jupiter Optimus Maximus.[64] Pliny may have seen the Greek signatures of Damophilus and Gorgasus on the walls of the Temple of Ceres. Marcus Plautius, who was given citizenship for decorating the Temple of Juno at Ardea in the Early Republican period, was originally from Asia Minor. Even the poet Pacuvius from Brundisium seems to have been involved in decorating temples at Rome.[65]

Along with these stories of migratory temple painters, Pliny also recorded another mobile craftsman at Rome named Helico the Helvetian:

> They say that the Gauls, confined at that time by the impassable mass of the Alps, first found reason to pour themselves down into Italy because Helico, a citizen of the Helvetii, delayed in Rome on account of the Gauls' artisanal craft, upon his return brought back with him dried fig and raisin, and promises of oil and wine.[66]

Like Plautus' biography discussed above, the story of Helico presents almost certainly fictitious details, serving in this case to explain the Gallic invasion of Italy through ethnic difference and the enticement of Mediterranean goods. The story was possibly invented during the first century BCE, in the midst of the Cimbrian invasions, in which the Helvetii took part, or during Caesar's involvement in suppressing the Helvetii migrations shortly thereafter.[67] However, the notion that Gallic craftsmen and trade traveled to the towns of Italy over the Alps from an early point cannot be dismissed entirely. A clay bowl found at Mantua bears the Etruscan graffito *eluveitie*, or the ethnonym Helvetius.[68] Some level of circulation and contact, however indirect, with not only Italians but Romans is also suggested by the circulation of third-century coinage at the Gallic settlement of Monte Bibele in the Po Valley, where a hoard of South Italian silver didrachms includes five coins of Rome, while sporadic

64. Plin. *NH* 35.157. Hopkins (2016: 118–19) suggests Samian builders assisted in this temple's construction.

65. Plin. *NH* 35.154: Damophilus and Gorgasus; 35.115: Plautius; 35.19: Pacuvius; on all, see Moormann 2011: 16–27.

66. Plin. *NH* 12.5: *produnt Alpibus coercitas ut tum inexsuperabili munimento Gallias hanc primum habuisse causam superfundendi se Italiae, quod Helico ex Helvetiis civis earum fabrilem ob artem Romae commoratus ficum siccam et uvam oleique ac vini promissa remeans secum tulisset.*

67. Williams 2001: 108.

68. Vitali and Kaenel 2000; Bourdin 2012: 552–53.

finds also include various third-century Roman silver and bronze coins.[69] Behind the invented figure of Helico, the underlying idea of artisanal mobility around the Italian peninsula and beyond during the Mid-Republican period demands further attention.

6.4. Remuneration, Wages, and the Potential of the Labor Market

To support the picture gleaned from the literary evidence of the mobility of non-agricultural labor in Italy, both slave and free, I turn now to an approach focusing on the development of those institutional structures, which facilitated the labor market at Mid-Republican Rome. The idea that demand attracted individually mobile workers to Rome requires the possibility that these workers could be hired and paid. This will have entailed a wage or, in the case of independent craftsmen, some return on the sale of their products that was capable of being converted into commodities.[70] Remuneration need not have been cash, and kind wages are well attested in antiquity, but this only shifts the issue: unless they had direct access to agricultural land, urban employers will then have needed to acquire food to pay their labor. As stated earlier in this chapter, there is no evidence for wages at Rome in this period.[71] However, I point out in this section that we see significant third-century shifts in Roman money and in the formation at Rome of retail spaces, and both these trends suggest that wage payments were possible, if not regular, in the city by that point.

6.4.1. Coinage

The development of Roman bronze coinage in the third century BCE can be interpreted to reflect increasing demand for coins at least partly for urban markets in which we assume wage-earners were participating. As the previous

---

69. Amandry 2008; Burnett and Molinari 2015: 44–46.

70. The formation by this time of a third ingredient, the consensual contract, is addressed in the previous chapter.

71. Republican comedy is sometimes used to describe Roman society's monetization shortly after the Second Punic War. Kay (2014: 116–24) notes that Romans would have found repeated mention of banking and coinage odd without intimate familiarity with such practices, but Andreau (1987: 333) seems correct that such plays describe particular details of Greek financial practices.

chapter discussed in detail, Roman coinage appeared in the late fourth century when bronze and silver were first struck sporadically, probably at Naples, bearing the name of Rome. This Romano-Campanian coinage eventually stabilized by the time of the Pyrrhic War and was shortly thereafter paralleled by the production of cast-bronze coinage (*aes grave*) on a libral standard. Setting aside the difficult issues of this cast coinage's seriation and chronology, it will be enough here to note its volume. In *Roman Republican Coinage*, Crawford lists nine emissions of this libral bronze in a span of about fifty years, from c. 270–218 BCE, while there is also a great deal more unattributed *aes grave* from Central Italy from this period.[72] The weight of the libral *as* fluctuated, but the bronze *aes grave* continued down to the Second Punic War, when the weight standard underwent a series of more dramatic weight reductions related to pressures put on Rome's metal supply during the early phase of the war.[73]

Prior to the middle of the century at least, bronze cast coinage was a largely separate entity from the Romano-Campanian silver.[74] We see this separation most obviously in the way each coinage was produced, cast or struck, but they also had very different denominational structures. Remarkably, *aes grave* was regularly produced in seven denominations, all the way down to the *semuncia* or 1/24 of an *as* (figure 6.1). Some strikes also featured a *dupondius*, while one bronze issue of the later third century included a *quartuncia* or 1/48 fraction (*RRC* 38/8). By comparison, the early Romano-Campanian silver was struck in one or sometimes two denominations, with one or two related struck bronzes.[75] Third-century cast bronze was thus in a very real way small change. We do not know the value of these bronze fractions in real terms, but we might guess that the libral *as* itself was based on the equivalent of a day's ration. The Twelve Tables established that a creditor was liable to give a debt-bondsman in his custody a minimum daily *libra farris*, or a pound of wheat (327 g).[76] If this gives some sense of the value of the libral *as* in the Mid-Republic, then the coin was

72. For unattributed *aes grave*, see *HN*: 51.

73. Crawford 1985: 52–74; Burnett 2012: 309–10.

74. Burnett 1998: 35–66; arguments (Lo Cascio 1980–1 345–46; Marchetti 1993; Coarelli 2013) for earlier links between cast bronze and struck coins require chronological suppositions that are difficult to sustain.

75. Some later Romano-Campanian emissions include more fractional issues: e.g., *RRC* 26/1–4.

76. XII Tab. tb. 3.4; see Ampolo 1980: 24.

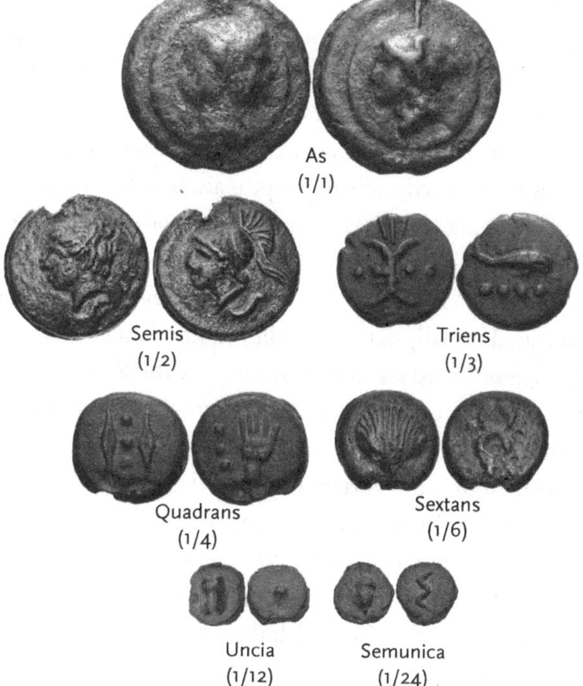

FIGURE 6.1 The denominational structure of the earliest *aes grave* coinage (*RRC* 14/1–7, c. 280 BCE). Coins depicted at 1:3 scale.
Images from Classical Numismatic Group, www.cngcoins.com.

not fiduciary, and may have represented its weight in wheat. Considering the very large size of the early *aes grave as*, it would make sense that it held a non-fiduciary value. In that case, a *semuncia* represented a wheat equivalent of only 13–14 g, and the cast-bronze coinage included denominations of a surprisingly low value, starting at a day's wheat wage and containing multiple fractions below that amount. Cast bronze was a flexible and liquid medium of exchange and appears intended for transactions equivalent to or smaller than a day's pay.

The separation of *aes grave* and silver also emerges in each metal's respective pattern of circulation. Hoards including Roman coinage are almost always exclusively silver or bronze through the third century, and this indicates unsurprisingly that the Romano-Campanian coinage and the heavy cast bronzes circulated independently.[77] In general, silver hoards appear widely

77. The first exception is Mandacini (*RRCH* 71) with a single *victoriatus*. The Morgantina hoard that dates the *denarius* is another case.

throughout the peninsula and in theaters of war such as Sardinia, Sicily, and eventually Spain.[78] By contrast, *aes grave* hoards of a third-century date concentrate most densely on Latium both inland and along the coast, and in six hoards known from Rome and its *suburbium* (figure 6.2).[79]

This distribution is particularly true of the earliest issues, the libral and supralibral series, which predominately appear around Rome and along the Latin coastline, while later *aes grave* has a somewhat broader circulation.[80] The only appearance of Romano-Campanian silver in a hoard from Rome itself is an unusual deposit from the Capitoline, which contains several Celtic coins and may have been deposited initially in the Po Valley rather than in the city.[81] A possible scattered quadrigatus hoard was found in a well by the Forum, but pre-denarius silver is otherwise rare in urban contexts.[82] Meanwhile, bronze was decidedly the metal of urban exchange in the city. From the several thousand coins found in excavation in and around the Forum, or in the dredging of the Tiber, no more than a dozen are silver coins of the third century BCE.[83]

These different patterns of circulation suggest that Rome participated during the third century in two different monetary zones. One (bronze) centered on Rome itself and Central Italy, while the other (silver) involved Italiote Greeks and the Western Mediterranean.[84] In practical terms, it makes sense that silver traveled further than bronze. Higher value silver coinage was easier to transport, while the early libral *asses* were impractical to carry in large quantities over long distances.[85] The earliest hoards of Roman silver in Spain contained local Spanish bronzes, something that aligns with episodes in the Second Punic War in which commanders seem to imply that local bronze was

---

78. Cf. maps in Vitale 1998.

79. *Aes grave* also appears in hoards of the second century, and particularly interesting are several Mazin-type hoards from inland Dalmatia; see Bertol and Farac 2012; Bilic 2015: 14–15.

80. Jaia and Molinari 2011; Williams 2011: 1110.

81. *RRCH* 60; Serafini 1943–45; Burnett and Molinari 2015; *RRC* 13/1 appears in museums in Rome, but only in privately assembled collections, and original provenance is unknown and need not be the city.

82. Burnett and Molinari 2015: 59.

83. Dondero 1950; Reece 1982: 119; Frey-Kupper 1995: Burnett and Molinari 2015: 59–60.

84. Burnett and Molinari 2015: 83.

85. By my calculation, a late-third century legion was owed 613,800 *denarii* a year, equivalent to 2,700 kg of silver or 331,500 kg of bronze.

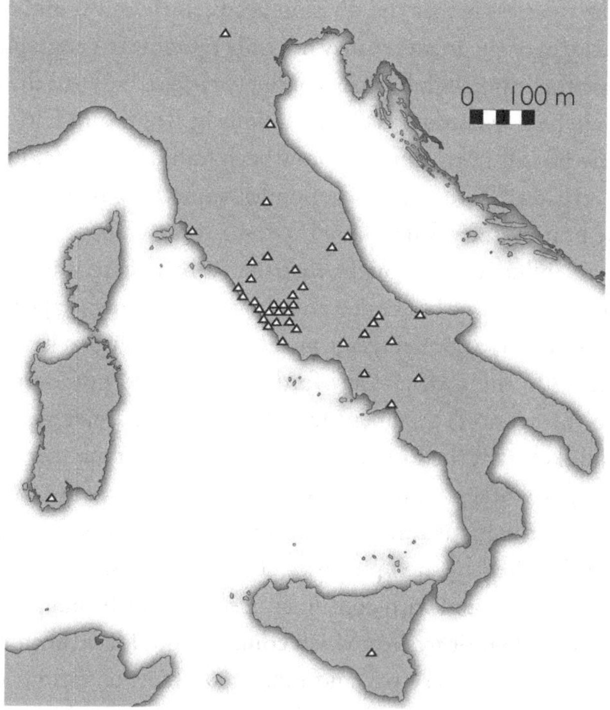

FIGURE 6.2 Distribution map of third-century hoards containing Roman *aes grave*. Hoards: 1–2. Tor Vaianica (Jaia and Molinari 2011). 3. Ardea (*RRCH* 20). 4. Ariccia (*RRCH* 13). 5. Genzano (*RRCH* 14). 6. Anzio (*RRCH* 18). 7. Tivoli (*RRCH* 27). 8. Pozzaglia (*RRCH* 43). 9. Portus (Spagnoli 2007). 10. Ostia (*RRCH* 15). 11–14. Rome, Monte Mario (*RRCH* 40, 41, 42; Molinari 2004). 15. Rome, Tiber (*RRCH* 44). 16. Rome, Via Tiberina (*RRCH* 81). 17. Santa Marinella (*RRCH* 21). 18. Cerveteri (*RRCH* 53). 19. Vico Matrino (*RRCH* 47). 20. Ferento (*RRCH* 39). 21. Amelia (*RRCH* 38). 22. Citta Ducale (*RRCH* 97). 23. Vetulonia (De Benetti and Catalli 2003–2006). 24. La Bruna (*RRCH* 16). 25. Castagneto (*RRCH* 51). 26. Tortoreto (*RRCH* 101). 27. Comacchio (*RRCH* 25). 28. Trento (*RRCH* 57). 29. San Germano (*RRCH* 45). 30. Isernia (*RRCH* 78). 31–32. Pietrabbondante (*RRCH* 24, 31). 33. Gildone (*RRCH* 26). 34. Termoli (*RRCH* 70). 35. Capua (*RRCH* 56). 36. Carife (*RRCH* 50). 37. Cava dei Tirreni (*RRCH* 52). 38. Sulcis (*RRCH* 46). 39. Piazza Armerina (*RRCH* 17).
Map © S. Bernard.

acceptable for paying troops.[86] The implication is that, while Roman soldiers in the field received and used bronze coinage, such bronze may have been supplied through local markets rather than brought from Rome.[87] What

86. E.g., Granada (*RRCH* 33); Cheste (*RRCH* 75); Mogente (*RRCH* 91); Tivissa (*RRCH* 94); several further hoards in Villaronga 1993. Cf. Scipio's request for supplies at Liv. 23.48.4.

87. Problematically, sources are ambiguous on the actual metal used to pay *stipendium*; cf. L. Cincius *apud* Gell. *NA* 16.4.2: *nummi argentei*; Varr. *De vita pop. Rom.* = Non. 853 L: *in*

I would like to stress is that the division between the silver and cast-bronze Roman coinages of the third century not only pertains to geography, but also to economic function, with bronze seemingly targeted toward the monetization of smaller-value commercial transactions in Rome and Latium. As several *aes grave* hoards in Latium have now been found at sanctuaries, Molinari suggests a relationship to temple economies, something that would also emphasize the non-military function of the cast-bronze coinage.[88]

Crawford influentially thought that the Roman state was unconcerned with consumer liquidity, but issued coins to pay for its own expenses.[89] Some have challenged this argument, but mostly for later periods of Roman coin production.[90] On the surface, Crawford's thesis would pose something of a problem to this section's argument for using bronze as evidence for labor: it would be unlikely that the Roman state cared in a direct manner that coinage was used to pay workers or to make small-scale purchases in urban markets. However, since the nature and distribution of Roman cast bronze makes it appear so well suited to such purposes, it seems necessary to ask how state concerns were integrated with consumer needs for small change. There were two chief state expenditures for which coinage would have been required in the Mid-Republic: military pay and public contracts of various sorts.[91] We have already seen how silver may have been more useful in this period for the army. The link between the state and monetized wages will have likely come in some manner from the need to pay for state contracting.

By the later third century, state contracts were myriad and came in all sizes. Contracts were let for smaller tasks: feeding the geese at the Temple of Juno Moneta, reddening the face of the cult statue in the Capitolium with cinnabar, leasing parade horses for festivals, or convening the centuriate assembly.[92] Where we can see them, larger contracts and particularly public building contracts tended to express value in very large sums of coin, as noted in the last chapter.[93]

---

nummis aeris. Polybius 6.39.12 relates a pay scale in both metals, but gives daily pay rather than monthly as was customary; see Boren 1983. Pay was probably made in both metals at different times and changed according to various factors. For the importance of bronze coinage to warfare in Italy more generally in the third century, see Termeer 2016.

88. Molinari 2004.

89. Crawford 1970.

90. Lo Cascio 1981; Howgego 1990.

91. Hollander 2007: 97–101 also includes the *annona* and magistrates' allowances. The former was not a concern for our period, while evidence for the latter is mostly later.

92. Geese: Plin. *NH* 10.51; Capitolium: Plin. *NH* 33.36; horses: Liv. 24.18.10; assemblies: Varr. *Ling.* 6.92.

93. See pp. 156–7.

But each contract let by the censor represented the aggregate of numerous costs arranged by contractors (*redemptores*). While subcontracting was not directly the state's concern, those *redemptores* purchasing such contracts were already by the later third century, and perhaps earlier, a significant part of the state economy and carried political influence.[94] Senators themselves seem to have been legally restricted from public contracting by some point in this period.[95] However, the involvement of contractors in vital state activities such as military supply gave them political power of their own, allowing them at times to extract concessions from the senate.[96] It is not unreasonable to think that pressures from urban contracting were indeed relevant to the production of early bronze coinage for transactions of variable value, some involving small change: hiring workers, purchasing and maintaining slaves, buying daily rations, purchasing raw materials, and so forth.

6.4.2. The Topography of Selling

If workers in third-century Rome had the ability to collect a wage in cash, and the nature and circulation of bronze coinage suggests that some did, the next question is how easily they could transform such wages into commodities. Some consumer needs for coinage such as urban rents and taxes at Rome are poorly attested in this and most periods. However, there is evidence for urban markets for food and other necessities. In the third century, several spaces related to monetized exchange appeared or developed significantly within the city's topography. Starting with the evolution of the city's *tabernae*, Livy held that *tabernae* already featured in the Forum in the sixth century (1.35.10).[97] By tradition, these butchers' shops (*tabernae lanienae*) were at some point transformed into bankers stalls (cf. Varr. *apud* Non. 853 L). When exactly this change occurred is not clear, as has been discussed elsewhere, but the transformation was complete by 308 BCE. In 210, fire broke out on the north side of the Forum where the *tabernae argentariae* were located. The old *tabernae* were destroyed and subsequently rebuilt as *tabernae novae* (A77). Already by that date, further *tabernae* were installed along the south side of the Forum as

94. Badian 1983: 16.

95. Prag 2016.

96. E.g., Liv. 23.48.5; 24.18.10.

97. Full discussion in Holleran 2012: 105–6; also Morel 1987; *LTUR* V s.v. "Tabernae circa Forum" (E. Papi) 12–13.

well, probably for both productive and commercial functions.[98] By 192 BCE if not earlier, there were also *tabernae* in the *forum boarium* (Liv. 35.40.3).

Contemporary to this development of Rome's *tabernae* come the earliest attestations of several commercial *fora* and the first *macellum*. The earliest references to the vegetable market, *forum holitorium*, at the northwestern edge of the *forum boarium*, relate to the dedication of a Temple of Janus there by C. Duilius in 260 BCE (A51). This was the first of a series of four temples built in a row over the next several decades, which would have served further to delimit the space. Varro described the *forum holitorium* as "the old *macellum* where there are plenty of vegetables" (*Ling.* 5.146: *hoc erat antiquum macellum ubi olerum copia*); the location along the Tiber bank at the northern end of the *forum boarium*, where the market received produce shipped downstream from the Tiber Valley and the *suburbium*, makes sense. Eventually, this market was complemented by the construction of the Republican *macellum* on the Forum's north side. Varro (*Ling.* 5.146–47) noted that a number of less permanent places of sale including a "delicacies market" (*forum cuppedinis*) and probably a fish market (*forum piscarium* or *piscatorium*) were at some point brought together in a single structure dedicated to the sale of "anything relating to human sustenance" (*quae ad victum pertinebant*). Since the father of C. Terentius Varro, consul in 216 BCE, reportedly had a stall in this *macellum*, De Ruyt dates its creation to the mid-third century.[99] Along with the *tabernae* in the same area, the *macellum* burned down in the fire of 210 BCE (A80). Part of the building phase subsequent to the fire has been excavated and may have held the same plan as the later *macellum* in the same area: a large open courtyard surrounded by stalls with a fountain or *tholos* in its center.[100] The *tholos* would indicate that the building specialized to some extent in the sale of meat and fish, expensive foodstuffs which were important status markers for aristocratic households.[101]

Along with permanent marketplaces, the city also contained periodic markets, *nundinae*, which connected suburban farmers to urban consumers looking to purchase agricultural produce with wages.[102] Such periodic markets

98. For the mixed function of *tabernae*, see Holleran 2012: 113–25.

99. De Ruyt 1983: 46–50; 2000; see Val. Max. 3.4.4; also Andreau 2012: 75; more agnostically, Holleran 2012: 162–63.

100. Tortorici 1991: 40–44.

101. De Ruyt 2007.

102. De Ligt 1993: 111–14.

in Rome were allegedly of great antiquity: they appear already in the Twelve Tables, while sources attributed their creation to King Servius.[103] In the first decades of the third century, however, legislation surrounding such markets indicates their changing importance to the urban economy.[104] In 287 BCE, a *Lex Hortensia de nundinis* was passed restricting the holding of *nundinae* on the same days as *comitia*.[105] While *nundinae* apparently remained *dies fasti*, allowing country dwellers coming to Rome for market days to attend to legal or commercial concerns, such days were from this date onward no longer available for political assemblies. Scholarship acknowledges two motives for this law.[106] On the one hand, the law limited the participation of rural residents in urban assemblies and may reveal elitist political motivations. On the other, this action reflected the changing priority of commercial and political affairs. In the earlier period, when many Roman elites lived within walking distance of Rome, it was expedient to set one day a week for political and legal affairs, and the market may have arisen originally around this activity.[107] By the Mid-Republic, periodic markets took on a greater necessity of their own, as they had come to serve a larger urban clientele. Buyers and sellers may thus have wanted to rid themselves of the distraction of political assemblies, and the law stands in this case as evidence for rising formalization in those market-based connections between urban consumers and suburban agriculture.

All told, workers earning a cash wage would have found multiple venues in which to commute those wages into daily needs at Rome by the eve of the Second Punic War. The result was the crystallization at Rome of a sort of topography of retail glimpsed most famously in the speech of the choragus from Plautus' *Curculio*, which describes where a Roman in the earliest years of the second century might find typical Roman characters, but also various things, services, or people for sale: pimps, profligate husbands, moneylenders, millers, and butchers:

> But until he comes outside, I will show you where you may easily find each person, lest anyone seeking to meet either a wicked or upright

103. Cassius Hemina *FRH* F18 (Peter *HRR* F14) = Macr. 1.16.33.

104. Knapp 1980: 36 on *nundinae* in third-century Italy.

105. Sources in Elster 2003: 125–27.

106. Michels 1967: 103–6 does not decide between the two explanations, although political motivation is favored by Hölkeskamp 1987: 169; De Ligt 1993: 112.

107. De Ligt (1993: 113) notes comparative evidence for similar arrangements.

> man, noble or ignoble, waste their time with excessive effort. Let him wanting to meet perjurers enter the *comitium*; who wants liars and braggarts search near the shrine of Cloacina, rich and prodigal husbands beneath the basilica; in the same place are usually worn-out whores and the men who engage them; those stocking up for dinner parties by the *forum piscatorium*; at the end of the Forum, good, wealthy men stroll about; in the middle by the sewer, mere pretenders. Gossips and badmouthers above the *lacus Curtius*, who boldly speak empty slander about each other and who have enough that might be truly said about them. Beneath the *tabernae veteres* are those who lend and borrow on interest; beside the Temple of Castor those to whom your loan unexpectedly goes badly. On the Vicus Tuscus are men who put themselves on sale; in the Velabrum, the baker, the butcher, the soothsayer: either those who themselves sell or who offer others things for retail. . . .[108]

This remarkable passage is the fullest contemporary description of the city of Rome in the Mid-Republic. Even if it does not give a comprehensive account of the city, the scene plays on a topography of buying and selling and a link between economic exchange and location. The implication is that the location of certain vendors (in the wide sense of that word) was recognizable and reliable by that date, and such reliability in turn speaks to stable urban demand. Especially the growth of infrastructure related to buying and selling food marks the greater detachment of the urban population from agricultural production, and the greater number of those in Rome who relied solely on wages and markets for their livelihood. It is not hard to draw a connection between these developments and other trends described above, particularly

108. Plaut. *Curc.* 466–84: *sed dum hic egreditur foras, / commonstrabo, quo in quemque hominem facile inveniatis loco, / ne nimio opere sumat operam si quem conventum velit, / vel vitiosum vel sine vitio, vel probum vel improbum. / qui periurum convenire volt hominem ito in comitium; / qui mendacem et gloriosum, apud Cloacinae sacrum, / ditis damnosos maritos sub basilica quaerito. / ibidem erunt scorta exoleta quique stipulari solent, / symbolarum collatores apud forum piscarium. / in foro infimo boni homines atque dites ambulant, / in medio propter canalem, ibi ostentatores meri; / confidentes garrulique et malevoli supera lacum, / qui alteri de nihilo audacter dicunt contumeliam / et qui ipsi sat habent quod in se possit vere dicier. / sub veteribus, ibi sunt qui dant quique accipiunt faenore. / pone aedem Castoris, ibi sunt subito quibus credas male. / in Tusco vico, ibi sunt homines qui ipsi sese venditant, / in Velabro vel pistorem vel lanium vel haruspicem / vel qui ipsi vorsant vel qui alii subversentur praebeant.* There are numerous textual problems, for which see Moore 1991. For the topography, see Sommella 2005.

the increasing urban population, and the concomitant rise of small-change coinage.

6.5. Patterns of Urban Production

Not only did a topography of selling take shape in Mid-Republican Rome, but whole districts of the city started to reflect the clustering of artisans involved in the same or related crafts. Such occupational clustering speaks to increasing specialization and professionalization and was a well-known feature of later Roman urbanism in the capital and elsewhere.[109] As Hawkins notes, the spatial clustering of work related to the way that craft industries were organized in the Roman world: with high horizontal specialization, but little evidence for factories, the assembly of complex products often required objects to be passed from workshop to workshop as artisans skilled in a particular component of a larger productive process contributed their individual effort to the creation of complex handiworks.[110] By at least the early second-century, lumbermen were found in the *forum boarium* at the foot of the Aventine, where a *porticus inter lignarios* was built in 192 BCE outside the *porta Trigemina* (A96). The area housed the later *vicus materarius* and the *vicus columnae lignae*, toponyms which further indicate the concentration of woodworking craftsmen. That this district was not merely a lumberyard for arriving timber, but was home to artisans, is confirmed by a passage of Terence's *Adelphoe*, written in the mid-second century, in which a figure is directed to visit a furniture workshop by the *porta Trigemina*.[111]

A second cluster was a potters' quarters on the city's eastern side. Kiln rings have been found in Mid-Republican contexts around the Forum or on the Palatine, suggesting that some degree of small-scale household production continued throughout the city.[112] But there is also evidence of the concentration of ceramic artisans in certain districts. One of the twenty-seven shrines of the Argeii listed by Varro was on the Oppian on a road running "among the potters" (*via. . . in figlinis*), and the list of the *sacraria Argeorum* is generally

109. Morel 1987; Goodman 2007; 2016.

110. Hawkins (2012); also Goodman 2016: 321.

111. Ter. *Adelph.* 582–84 with Gilula 1991; *contra* Frank 1936.

112. Kiln spacers noted in Mid-Republican contexts in the Argiletum by Di Giuseppe (2010: 306) and on the northeast Palatine by Ferrandes (2016: 95).

agreed to be at least fourth century in date, if not earlier.[113] Confirmation of this potters' district of the city at this early date comes from the discovery in the late nineteenth century of a large kiln containing Mid-Republican ceramics at the corner of via dello Statuto and via Merulana.[114]

In complement to the crystallization of a professional topography at Rome in this period is some evidence of individuals starting to identify themselves on the basis of their occupations, again speaking to increasing craft specialization. A recently published base of a fifth-century vase from the Palatine was inscribed *SEMP*[- - -]*OS FICOLOS FECED MED*.[115] The signing individual, perhaps Semprolos or Sempronius, named his occupation as potter (*ficolos*) on an object of his own dedication or possibly creation.[116] Within this same context may cautiously be mentioned the increasing attestation of *cognomina* related to craft production used by some Mid-Republican *gentes*. There is, for example, L. Sextius Lateranus, who was instrumental in opening the consulship to plebeians in 367 BCE, and several members of the *gens Servilia* are recorded with the *cognomen* Structus from the fifth century BCE.[117] For this early period, the historicity of occupational cognomina in particular has been challenged.[118] Since epigraphic evidence confirms that cognomina were in use at Rome by the late fourth century, we might give greater historical credence to the well-known story that C. Fabius painted frescoes on the walls of Temple of Salus (A25) in 304 BCE earning himself the cognomen Pictor ("painter"), which he then passed down to his descendants, including the first Roman historian.[119] C. Marcius Figulus ("potter") was consul in 162 and 156 BCE.[120] A P. Licinius Tegula ("roof tile") wrote a hymn performed publically in 200 BCE (Liv. 31.12.10). He is sometimes identified with the poet Licinius Imbrex ("gutter tile") cited by Aulus Gellius (*NA* 13.23.16). It is unknown what if any role Marcius' or Licinius' ancestors had in ceramic production.

---

113. *LTUR* I s.v. "Argei, sacraria" (Coarelli) 120–25; Maddoli 1971; Storchi Marino 1991–1992; Nagy 1993; Marroni 2010: 43–60, 217–27.

114. Lanciani 1877: 181–83.

115. Panella, Zeggio, and Ferrandes 2014: 178–79; Colonna 2016.

116. Colonna 2016 restores Semprolos and argues for dedication.

117. Sp. Servilius Structus; consul 478 BCE; C. Servilius Structus, consul 476 BCE; Sp. Servilius Structus consul trib. 368 BCE. For members of this branch, cf. *RE* II.A.2 s.v. "Servilius (Structus)" coll. 1809–10 (F. Münzer).

118. Bruun 2000: 51–54.

119. For early epigraphic cognomina, see Bruun 2000; for Pictor the painter, Cic. *Tusc.* 1.4; Val. Max. 8.14.6.

120. Di Giuseppe 2012: 87 for the Marcii Figuli.

6.6. Status and Mobility in Mid-Republican Urban Labor: The Epigraphic Evidence

The mixed status and mobile character of Mid-Republican Rome's labor supply may be further supported by looking more closely at the epigraphic record of artisan production. From c. 350 BCE onward, there was a remarkable proliferation of the epigraphic habit as it related to Italian *instrumentum domesticum*. Included in this trend are the stamped Praenestine strigils discussed above. In complement to those Praenestine bronze workers are three Roman artisans whose signatures appear on metal objects (table 6.2). Scholarly opinion places the Ficoroni Cista, on which there has been extensive study, in the fourth century. The date of the other objects cannot be specified with precision, although letter forms point to the period before the Second Punic War. All inscriptions identify the signatures of Roman workers. In two cases, we find a *nom parlante*, a not uncommon trope in which the object identifies itself and its maker with the verb *facere* plus the accusative *me* and the locative *Romai*, while the third object lists a Roman tribal affiliation.[121] Notably, at least two individuals have non-Roman, and specifically Italic, elements in their names. The names of Novius Plautius and Trebius Pomponius combine Oscan praenomina with Roman gentilicia. Novius' praenomen is Campanian, and he has been conjectured to be a freedman of the prominent fourth-century *gens Plautia*.[122] It is tempting to connect Trebius to Gaius Pomponius of the same *gens*, although a date of c. 300 BCE has been suggested for the sword on which Trebius' name is found, while the statuette of Gaius Pomponius must postdate the creation of the tribus Quirina in 241 BCE.[123]

Thus, most if not all of these Roman metal workers show indications of an origin in the broader region of Central Italy. The idea that these artisans or their families moved to Rome should not surprise us considering what

121. On such signatures, see Rouveret 1994: 229. The verb *facere* can indicate dedication in Archaic Latin, as see Colonna 2016: 100, but must indicate manufacture in the case of the Ficoroni cista and the San Vittore sword, where an object was "made" at Rome but not found there.

122. A significant literature includes Dohrn 1972: 45; Massa-Pairault 1985: 96; Rouveret 1994: 228–29; Terrenato 2014: 48.

123. A fourth possibility is C. Ovius whose signature appears on a bronze applique now in the Museo Nazionale at Rome, but of uncertain provenance, *CIL* I² 545. The inscription ends *O.VF*, which has been read as a tribal affiliation *Ouf(entina)* and would argue for Ovius' Roman citizenship, as see Taylor 2013: 55–56, but is almost certainly to be read as a patronymic, *Ov(i) f(ilius)*. See Nonnis 2012: 324.

Table 6.2 Metal workers from Mid-Republican Rome

Signature	Object	Reference
Novios Plautios med Romai fecid	Praenestine cista (Ficoroni cista)	*CIL* I^2 561
Tr(ebios) Pomponio(s) C(aii) [-]/[m]e fecet Roma[i]	Sword, from San Vittore del Lazio	Nicosia, Sacco, and Tondo 2013
*C(aii) Pomponi Quir(ina tribus) opos**	Statuette of Jupiter, from near Orvieto	*CIL* I^2 546

* This reading is affirmed by Vine 1993: 360.

we have otherwise discussed in terms of the potential individual mobility of craftsmen in Republican Italy. There is only a limited picture, however, of these metal workers' status. Gaius Pomponius was a free citizens as indicated by his tribal affiliations. Novius Plautius' status as a possible freedman, or even slave, is debated, although he did not specify in his own signature. Unfortunately, Trebius Pomponius' signature cannot be read precisely at the point where he named either his servile status or his filiation.

A second class of inscribed craft objects from this period reveals more about personal status: dozens of workers' signatures on pottery made either at Mid-Republican Rome or in Roman contexts. This category includes a number of signatures on black-gloss ware ceramics. Recent work emphasizes the diffused nature of the production of these pots.[124] Nonetheless, considering that at least some pots were made at Rome and others in Roman contexts such as in the Latin colonies, this material at least partly reflects Rome's urban production, and it is therefore important that signatures on black-gloss pots name both *servi* and *ingenui* workers.[125] Of the 149 signatures on third-century black gloss ware catalogued by Di Giuseppe, 129 do not specify status. The 20 that do specify status contain four different servile names and six, or maybe seven, free individuals.[126] Onomastic study suggests these individuals were of Italic, Greek, and Roman backgrounds.

124. Ferrandes 2007; Stanco 2009; Di Giuseppe 2012.

125. Morel 1988: 54–55.

126. Di Giuseppe 2012: 100–14; Kaeso Serponius' status is debated, as see below.

From Rome itself, our sample size of signatures on pottery is more limited, but suggests a similar mixture of origin and status. Individuals whose names suggest Italian backgrounds signed vases from the city already in the fifth century, although many early signatures may identify vessels' dedicants rather than potters.[127] Colonna argues that the aforementioned *figulos* who signed the Palatine vase, perhaps Semprolos, was of Etruscan origin, although his status is not specified.[128] A black-gloss phiale signed *K(aeso) Serponio(s) caleb(us) fece(t) vequo Esquileno C(aii) s(ervus?)* has occasioned much debate: was this potter working at Cales in a place known as the *vicus Esquilinus*, perhaps named after the Roman hill, or was he working among the potters in the Esquiline *figlinae* at Rome? If the latter, then he was an immigrant to the capital from Cales, as Di Giuseppe suggests.[129] Several inscribed clay objects, perhaps kiln wasters or firing supports, found together in the aforementioned kiln on the Esquiline, bear signatures naming *C.Sextios V(ibi) s(ervos)*. and *P.Sextios V(ibi) f(ilios)*.[130] In this case, a slave and a free individual of the *gens Sextia* appear to have worked side by side.

Thus, signatures from metal and ceramic objects produced in Mid-Republican Rome or in Roman contexts in Italy indicate that Roman artisans during this time were mobile and bore a mixture of personal statuses, with such variety of status sometimes evident within single workshops. These observations form an important context for considering the single epigraphic attestation of builders active in the city of Rome prior to the Second Punic War. In 1866, Pietro Rosa's excavations on the *clivus Palatinus* revealed an ashlar-masonry structure with an inscription cut across the face of two blocks (figure 6.3).[131]

The Latin inscription names two Greek individuals: *Pilocrate(s) / Diocle(s)*. Rosa and Hülsen believed the structure on which the inscription was found

---

127. See Colonna in Stibbe et al. 1980, esp. p. 69.

128. Colonna 2016: 102; Sempronius would also fit and the *gens Sempronia* is well attested at Rome in the fifth century.

129. Di Giuseppe 2012: 49–53. *Contra* Bispham 2006: 87; Pedroni 2001: 109–16; Coarelli 1995b: 177. Likewise, his status is debated: Mommsen (*CIL* I^2 416) restored *C.S.* as *Gaii servus*. For Di Giuseppe (2012: 51), he was free; unlikely is that he was a *nexus*, as argued by Pedroni 2001: 113.

130. *CIL* I^2 466–67; P. Sextius' name appears on other ceramic objects, as see *CIL* I^2 468. Coarelli (1996: 40–41) points to a connection with L. Sextius Lateranus, whose cognomen, as noted above, might suggest involvement in tile production.

131. *CIL* VI 36615; Tomei 1993; Cecamore 2002: 77.

FIGURE 6.3 Archival photograph of ashlar structure on the *clivus Palatinus* with the inscription of Pilocrates and Diocles (*CIL* VI 36615).
Photo reproduced by the concession of Ministero dei Beni e delle Attività Culturali e del Turismo – Parco Archeologico del Colosseo.

pertained to the Mid-Republican Temple of Jupiter Stator (A34), built somewhere in this area.[132] Instead, the structure was probably a drainage conduit of Mid-Republican date, perhaps from the third century.[133] Meanwhile, the location of the inscription across the interior face of blocks belonging to the structure's lower courses suggests, as Rosa already recognized, that the two names were inscribed during the building process, as this area of the building would have been more difficult to access once the structure was complete.[134] Following this, we appear to have the names of two builders active in Mid-Republican Rome: P(h)ilocrates and Diocles.[135]

---

132. The temple's location remains one of the great puzzles of Mid-Republican topography: *LTUR* V s.v. "Iuppiter Stator, Aedes" (J. Arce) 271; Coarelli 1983: 21–33; Ziolkowski 1992: 87–91; Tomei 1993; Cecamore 2002: 129–44; Wiseman 2004; Coarelli 2012: 106–8; Ziolkowski 2015.

133. Cecamore 2002: 75–77; the stone has been identified as *tufo giallo* but shows the characteristic foliation and module of *tufo del Palatino*, and this is suggestive of hydraulic works of a date prior to the mid-second century.

134. Rosa's report cited in Morganti and Tomei 1991: 570 n. 56.

135. The Greek case intended with the terminal *–e* is difficult to understand. I assume as all have done that we have two names, rather than one name and a patronymic with both names in the genitive.

Nothing indicates whether these Greek individuals were slave or free. What can be said is that, as with other evidence discussed thus far, their non-Roman backgrounds demonstrate that the urban labor supply in this period relied to some extent on a mobile population. Especially noteworthy is the evident bilingualism: both names, clearly Greek, were written in Latin, by either themselves or a lapicide. Whether these two individuals were bilingual, and had acquired such ability before coming to Rome, or whether they had by this point spent sufficient time with the local language in Rome, cannot be determined. However, interestingly enough, an extensive corpus shows that bilingualism or linguistic-ethnic variance was a regular feature in inscriptions pertaining to *fabri* employed in construction in the towns of Republican Italy. We find a possible Etruscan mason signing in Oscan at Pompeii,[136] Latin signatures of Greek craftsmen on architectural terracottas from Picenum,[137] a Greek artisan's name in Latin on a tile from Fregellae,[138] a Greek builder's signature in fresco from Herdonia,[139] a roof tile from Pietrabbondante with a (Samnite?) individual's signatures in both Latin and Oscan,[140] a Greek coroplast's name in Etruscan on a figural terracotta revetment from Arretium,[141] an architect possibly of Etruscan origin signing a mosaic in Latin at Paestum,[142] and a Roman architect signing a nymphaeum in Greek at Segni in Latium.[143] The last case has plausibly been attributed to Hellenistic aspirations on the part of the architect; however, the variation between onomastic background and local language in the numerous other examples, as with Philocrates and Diocles from the Palatine, suggests cultural and probably geographical mobility among these artisans. Though none of these builders possessed the renown of Hermodorus or Cossutius, the mobility exhibited by these two celebrity architects seems part of a far broader background of movement among the supply of skilled building labor.

---

136. *Imag.Ital.* Pompeii 40: *Atis Arruntiis*. The gentilicium Arruntius is Etruscan, as see Schulze 1991: 175.

137. *CIL* IX 6078.75: *Dionisios (et) Coloponios epoi(oun)*; also *CIL* XI 6709.16; the date of these is debated as see Nonnis 2012: 204.

138. Sironen 1997.

139. Manacorda 2006: *Pilipus Cepalo(nis?) faber Alexsand(er* or *rinus)*

140. *Imag.Ital.* Pentri/Terventum 25 with bibliography cited there.

141. Rix *ET* Ar. 7.1; Nonnis 2012: 322–23.

142. *AE* 1975.266; Torelli 1992: 94; Roselaar 2011.

143. Cifarelli 1995.

6.6. Conclusions

Several different approaches have suggested a set of similar characteristics to urban labor in Mid-Republican Rome. As far as can be observed, Rome's workforce in the fourth and third centuries comprised individuals of often non-Roman background and of variable statuses. Around 300 BCE, the practice of forced free labor declined; however, the idea that consequent urban demand for labor at Rome was met by slaves to the exclusion of free labor is untenable. Slaves fulfilled some of the demands for skilled labor in third-century Rome, although they may not have come to the city directly through ongoing wars of conquest. In addition, the presence of free-born workers is hard to deny. Wage labor's presence in third-century Rome finds support in both the development of monetary instruments, particularly bronze coinage, and in the expansion of infrastructure relating to the sort of buying and selling necessary to convert wages into commodities. There is no reason to uphold details about Helico the Helvetian, or from Plautus' biography, but the general ideas of labor whose mobility was based upon *ars fabrilis*, or of job switching at Rome, are entirely plausible for this period. The consequence of this discussion is to suggest that, already by the third century BCE and before the Second Punic War, Rome's urban labor supply showed some of the characteristics ascribed to the later city's economy.[144] This has the effect of emphasizing the long durée in our understanding of economic change: rather than stemming from any single moment or historical event, Rome's urban labor supply formed through a longer and complex transformation in the institutional structures of production.

144. For the Imperial labor supply, see Brunt 1966; 1980; Morley 1996; Holleran 2011; Tacoma 2016.

7 TECHNOLOGICAL CHANGE IN ROMAN STONEMASONRY BEFORE CONCRETE

The last chapter described the mixed nature of Mid-Republican Rome's labor supply, which incorporated free and slave workers already by the third century BCE. Another way to approach the topic of urban labor in Mid-Republican Rome is by looking at the development of building technology in the city. The relationship between Republican building technology and labor has been a productive theme especially in previous studies of reticulate masonry, *opus reticulatum*. Emerging in the second and first centuries BCE, this modular manner of facing concrete walls was lower skilled and more industrialized, and for those reasons the technique is seen as ideally suited to a situation in which (slave) labor was increasingly cheap and widely available.[1] The following discussion takes the general observation that Republican building techniques speak to the organization of the responsible workforce and extends it to earlier Roman architectural practices prior to the advent of concrete. The argument is that changes in the technologies of ashlar masonry at Mid-Republic Rome speak to evolving social relations of work, and particularly to the rise of a labor market in the city's building industry from 300 BCE onward.

Along with pursuing the relationship between technology and labor, this chapter has a second goal, and that is a desire to challenge the prevailing opinion that pre-concrete Mid-Republican architecture depended upon a largely static technological basis. Building technology of this earlier period barely features in standard accounts of the development of Roman architecture.[2] Instead,

1. Von Gerkan 1958; Coarelli 1977a; Carandini 1979; Torelli 1980; Rakob 1983; DeLaine 2001.

2. E.g. Brown 1961: 12–17; MacDonald 1982.

architectural production in the city is seen to have evolved rapidly during the Late Archaic period, when ashlar masonry was first introduced, but then to have stagnated for several centuries, remaining not significantly altered until the Late Republic. Any changes acknowledged in the interim were mostly on the level of style and form, such as the development of the *peripteros sine postico* or the appearance of the *fornix* or *porticus*.[3] This view would imply that a temple built ca. 450 BCE was constructed using the same techniques as a temple made two hundred years later, and third- and second-century building practices at Rome thus appear highly conservative.

It is, however, hard to believe that the significant investment in urban infrastructure at Mid-Republic Rome starting c. 300 BCE did not result in innovations. Indeed, the novelty and cost of Appius Claudius' building projects suggests an environment conducive to experimentation on a grand scale starting in the late fourth century. It might therefore be argued that the problem has largely been one of invisibility; however, there is extant material in significant quantity in the form of archaeologically excavated masonry structures built from the stones of Latium and Central Italy. Close inspection of this material shows building techniques developing over time in the hands of Roman stonemasons, with related implications for the economic structures of Rome's urban society.

7.1. Vitruvius *De Arch.* 2.7 on Republican Stonemasonry

The best ancient witness to the technical knowledge of Republican stonemasonry is Vitruvius' *De Architectura*. Vitruvius published his treatise during the early Augustan period, and his own experience as a builder under Caesar informed his work. There are also reasons for thinking that, at certain points, he transmitted much earlier information, and one such point is his discussion of Italian stonemasonry. In his second book, Vitruvius wrote at length *de copiis materiae*, "on the supplies of material resources," that supported building at Rome. After several chapters on cement components (2.4–6), the author devoted a chapter to those quarries providing Rome with material suitable for the rubble in *caementa* as well as for dimension stone. By Vitruvius' own time, *opus caementicium* was far more prevalent than ashlar masonry using volcanic tuff, so that the attention he paid to tuff ashlar masonry already suggests a somewhat outdated tradition of technological knowledge. Indeed,

3. Castagnoli 1974; Gros 1996.

Pliny the Elder would repeat much of Vitruvius' information on volcanic tuff in his *Historia Naturalis* about a century later, but he began by noting his discussion's limited practical utility, as volcanic tuff was "useless for buildings, owing to its fragility and softness" (36.48).

The idea that Vitruvius transmitted an earlier technical tradition in his discussion of tuff ashlar masonry gains strength from a closer examination of details in the pertinent chapter itself (2.7). The passage's contents are as follows: Vitruvius classified stones into different categories based upon their different physical properties, in particular hardness, and listed them from soft to hard. Soft stones were found close to the city in quarries at Rubra, Palla, Fidenae, and Alba. Stronger stone came from somewhat further away, but still in Latium: Tibur, Amiternum, and Soracte. The hardest stone he called *silex*, thought to describe basalt quarried outside the city.[4] Appended to his list were quarries in Umbria, Picenum, and the Veneto. While none of these latter stones was used in the capital, their mention serves to extend Vitruvius' interests as far as the borders of Italy, starting with Latium and including Etruria and the Adriatic coast.

Vitruvius showed explicit interest in how a stone's properties translated into architectural utility. In this focus, his discussion parted ways from earlier Greek treatises on stones such as that of Theophrastus, whose fourth-century *Peri Lithikou* was concerned with physical characteristics, but showed no interest in the function of stones as building materials. The next section of Vitruvius' chapter detailed how even softer stones could successfully sustain architectonic loads if masons employed them in strategic ways, such as restricting their use to covered areas in the building in order to shield them from the elements. Some stones were durable in some conditions, less so in others. Vitruvius claimed that travertine, for example, was susceptible to the elements but resistant to fire, qualities he related to Hellenistic elemental science, perhaps drawing from Lucretius.[5] Then, after digressing on the excellent quality of stone from Ferentinum, he drew his discussion to a close by returning to the topic of those quarries closest to the city (2.7.5):

> Because of their proximity, however, necessity compels the use of stone from quarries at Rubra and Palla, and those other quarries nearby the city, such that anyone wishing to complete his work without fault

4. Blake 1947: 39–41; Jackson and Marra 2006: 411.

5. Gros 2003: 104; cf. Lucr. 5.1091–1100.

> should proceed as follows: two years prior to the time when construction will start, let these stones be quarried not in the winter, but in the summer, and remain exposed in an open place. Then whatever material, affected by the elements, is injured in two years' time should be thrown into foundations. The remaining material, which shows no damage, its quality having been confirmed by nature, will be able to endure in structures above ground. Not only are these things to be observed in ashlar masonry, but also in structures built of concrete.

The concluding sentence in this passage implies that the utility of this practical information was first of all to ashlar masonry, but could also be applied to *opus caementicium*. That is, while applicable to concrete, such practices were generated for ashlar masonry and may therefore have developed prior to concrete's emergence in the second century BCE. Some noteworthy absences in his discussion of building stones point similarly to Vitruvius' contact with information of a similar date. For example, Vitruvius neglected to mention *lapis Gabinus*, the hard green tuff from Gabii, prized for its resistance to fire. The use of considerable quantities for the rear wall of Augustus' forum, begun in the late 40s BCE, confirms that the Gabine quarries were actively worked around Vitruvius' time, and there are several urban monuments of Gabine stone dating to the early first century.[6] Another notable absence in his discussion is marble. Elsewhere in his treatise, Vitruvius confirms that marble architecture was well known to him: indeed, the chapter following his discussion of building stones made reference to marble architecture at Rome (2.8), while Vitruvius elsewhere referred to an active marble trade in Asia Minor.[7] Elsewhere in his work, he went so far as to denigrate a Mid-Republican temple for being built of tuff not marble (7.*pr*.17). Not only was he aware of marble, but Vitruvius wrote at a time when large quantities of Luni marble were shipped to Rome for the building projects of Caesar and Augustus, and it is therefore striking to find such an important Italian building stone unmentioned in a passage otherwise so attentive to Italy's geological resources. Notably, however, the use of Luni marble at Rome was a relatively recent phenomenon, reputedly starting in the time of Caesar.[8] Roman builders relied on

---

6. Farr 2014; Strabo 5.3.10–11 does not mention the stone's fireproof qualities, but cf. Tac. *Ann.* 15.43.

7. 2.8.3: *nonnullis monumentis, quae circa urbem facta sunt e marmore*. For Vitruvius on the Greek marble trade, see 10.2.15 with Russell 2014: 13.

8. Plin. *HN* 36.48.

imported Greek marble for the city's earlier marble architecture, something that might help to make sense of Vitruvius' (earlier) source's exclusion of what was previously a non-Italian building stone.[9]

Those stones Vitruvius did focus on were decidedly rare in ashlar masonry at Rome at the time of his writing. This especially applied to stones from quarries *circa urbem*, which he noted as being of critical importance to urban construction. By the late first century BCE, the quarries he mentioned, the *lapidicinae Rubrae, Pallenses,* and *Fidenates,* no longer supplied large quantities of dimension stone to urban architecture. The reddish *tufo lionato* from quarries in the Anio Valley, likely Vitrivius' *lapidicinae Rubrae,* was still used to some extent. However, the *tufo rosso a scorie nere* from Fidene and especially the yellowish tuff, *tufo giallo,* from quarries at Grotta Oscura, Vitruvius' *lapidicinae Pallenses,* were not used in Late Republican ashlar construction.[10] Use of *tufo giallo* for ashlar masonry peaked in the fourth and third centuries BCE and continued into the mid-second century BCE. The sporadic appearance of blocks of the stone in buildings of the first century BCE relates not to primary quarrying but to reuse, as discussed below.

Several factors, then, begin to converge in suggesting an earlier, conceivably Mid-Republican source for Vitruvius' discussion of the stones for urban ashlar masonry. Indeed, a similar chronological context may be reflected in the chapter's geography, which followed expanding Roman imperialism in Italy step by step in the fourth and third centuries BCE. In order, Vitruvius started with quarries from sites in the Tiber Valley closest to Rome (Rubrae, Pallenses, Fidenates), moved to broader Latium (Albanae, Tiburtinae, Amiternae, Soractinae), then to Campania, Umbria, and finally the Adriatic coast (Picenum, Venetia). The map of Roman territorial control this passage portrayed appears to reflect the historical context of the Mid-Republican period.

7.2. Stonemasonry Technology and "Roman" Architecture

Before turning more closely to consider the particular historical context in which the information transmitted by Vitruvius 2.7 may have formed,

9. Bernard 2010.

10. For the identification of Vitruvius' *lapicidinae pallenses* with *tufo giallo della via Tiberina,* see Jackson and Marra 2006: 410–11 correcting Lugli 1957 I.253–57.

I should emphasize some technical aspects this passage contains. As noted, the paragraph characterized stones by provenance and particular physical properties within the context of architecture. Some areas further away from the city yielded stones with qualities of durability that were attractive to builders, while stones found closer to the city were more convenient but had physical deficiencies that needed to be addressed. The implication is that a Roman builder would have had available stones of different properties and provenances and would need to combine them appropriately in a final monument. The idea that certain stones could bear architectonic loads if confined to covered places (*locis tectis*) also suggests this: one presumes that such places were either under eaves, plastered over, or else somehow protected by revetments or other stones.[11]

The passage thus reflects a context in which multiple stones were strategically employed at the same time in single monuments according to their geological properties, as such properties were understood.[12] Jackson et al. demonstrate that such mixed stone use was common in Late Republican architecture at Rome. As they show, in a building complex like the Forum of Caesar, masons made "judicious" use of travertine and other stones with higher compressive strengths by employing such materials at load-bearing points in piers or arches, while less critical parts of the monument were built in softer tuffs.[13] Lugli documented similar strategic stone mixing in the typical employment of harder stones such as *tufo lionato* in the facing of *caementicium* vaults in the city's architecture, whereas *tufo del Palatino* and *tufo giallo* were used in the surfaces of less structurally important walls.[14]

While Republican masons worked judiciously with different types of tuff in buildings at Rome, this practice of incorporating multiple, geologically distinct stones into a single phase of construction was rare in Italian architecture of this period outside the city. More typically, different stones found in single structures related to chronologically discrete construction phases, and building in dimension stones relied predominately on local materials. Tellingly, exceptions to this rule belong to Roman contexts, such as the two

---

11. *Contra* Jackson et al. 2005: 504, the Latin phrase need not specifically relate to the use of plaster.

12. Such geologically strategic mixed stone should be differentiated from the aesthetically or economically driven practice of using limestone for a building's interior elements and marble for more visible components, as common in Greek architecture.

13. Jackson et al. 2005: 506.

14. 1957 I.408–9.

stones used to build the walls of the fourth-century *castrum* of Ostia. Likewise, Jaia connects the use of harder, non-local stone as a revetment for softer, local material in Mid-Republican public works at Lavinium to the city's status as a *municipium* and the Roman state's ability to provide material from beyond Lavinium's own territory.[15]

The judicious use of multiple stones forms an important, although underappreciated, technological component distinguishing Rome's architecture and its extension into Roman Republican urban contexts. The practice is readily related to the city's command of a more extensive supply chain than other towns and urban centers in Italy. That is, as Roman conquest brought more territory under control, the capital city began to draw from a wider range of stone resources than other communities, and this can be seen reflected in the city's stonemasonry. Already by the Early Republic, Rome was able to supplement urban quarries with stone sourced from its expanding hinterland. New petrochemical research confirms the use of *lapis Albanus* in the exterior walls of the early-fifth century podium beneath the twin temples at Sant' Omobono.[16] Also in the *forum boarium*, the Temple of Apollo Medicus was built in the mid-fifth century on a high podium of *tufo del Palatino* encased within an external wall of *tufo lionato* from Monteverde.[17] It is possible that temple podia were also protected with a coat of plaster, something which is preserved in Latin temple podia outside of Rome in this period but harder to trace, although not entirely absent, in the city's own archaeology.[18] However, the use in both instances of harder tuff used for these podia's exteriors, while softer material was reserved for the interior cores, nonetheless shows masons systematically deploying different stones as a sort of cladding in these structures.[19]

This use of lithified and less well-lithified tuffs in tandem at the Temple of Apollo Medicus or at Sant' Omobono was exceptional for its time, and the mixing of different tuffs was generally neither regular nor systematic in Early Republican architecture. In the Forum and on the Capitoline, we find

15. Jaia 2013: 479–81.

16. Farr, Marra, and Terrenato 2015.

17. Ciancio Rossetto 1997–98: 184. Earlier work tends to date the Monteverde tuff to a later date, as cf. Frank 1924: 29 (179 BCE) and Blake 1947: 30 (352 BCE).

18. Nielsen and Poulsen 1992: 78 for the Temple of the Castores.

19. Marchetti Longhi (1936: 107) observes that the use of plaster did not prevent Roman masons from mixing different types of tuff in a systematic manner.

late sixth- and early fifth-century BCE structures such as the Temple of the Castores or the Capitolium built exclusively from *tufo del Palatino*. The same was perhaps true for the earliest iteration of the Temple of Saturn, though the late sixth-century BCE phase is poorly known.[20] The structure in the Aracoeli gardens, likely the podium of the Temple of Juno Moneta (A14), shows a haphazard use of *tufo del Palatino* and *tufo rosso delle scorie nere* in its mid-fourth century podium. It is possible that this irregular attention to cladding in the fifth century was dictated by the fact that the Temples of Apollo and at Sant' Omobono sat in the *forum boarium*, directly in the floodplain of the Tiber, where a tradition of building temples on high podia may have evolved from greater attention to protect structures against water damage and regular flooding.[21]

7.3. The Development of the Technology of *Tufo Giallo*

This discussion of the strategic employment of different tuffs in ashlar masonry in the capital returns us to the question of the precise historical context of this practice's emergence. Since the technology of mixing tuffs relied on access to a variety of building stones from quarries beyond Rome, its development should relate to the expansion of Roman territorial control and the concomitant ability to extract stone from a wider area in Central Italy. This gives significance to the aforementioned overlap between the geographical progression of Vitruvius' description of building stones at 2.7.1 and the pace of Roman conquest in Italy in the fourth and third centuries BCE. This section further considers this period as the date of an emerging strategy of mixed-stone masonry at Rome by focusing on one of the key quarries in Vitruvius' discussion, the *lapidicinae Pallenses* of Grotta Oscura, the source of *tufo giallo della via Tiberina*.

The evolution of Roman masons' awareness of the friability of *tufo giallo* and its vulnerability to the elements is best observed by examining the archaeological evidence for that stone's use in Mid-Republican monuments. The Grotta Oscura quarries provided Roman masons with copious quantities of stone for two centuries, from at least the construction of the fourth-century circuit walls to the opening of tufo lionato quarries in the Anio Valley on a

20. See Cifani 2008: 109–10.

21. Ammerman and Filippi 2004; although note Diffendale et al. 2016: 12.

large scale for the Aqua Marcia's construction in 144 BCE.[22] This long reliance on *tufo giallo* has left a considerable mark in the archaeological record, and a series of dateable Roman monuments may be identified spanning a period of over two centuries.

The Republican circuit walls, as the earliest significant use of *tufo giallo* in Republican architecture, paid little attention to the stone's physical properties. A previous chapter argued that masons' marks on the walls' blocks related to the practice of proofing material for some period of time to remove quarry sap.[23] However, the walls' builders seem not to have transferred any related observations on the stone's porosity and friability to its use in the finished monument. The circuit did employ some amount of *tufo del Palatino* in phase with *tufo giallo* in building the double-walled *agger* on the Esquiline, although the pattern of use for each stone revealed no attempt to clad or otherwise protect one stone behind another. Instead, *tufo giallo* was employed for long stretches of the agger's exterior face, exposing it to the elements and to degradation.[24]

The next monument in chronological order to use *tufo giallo* was the earliest detectable iteration of the Temple of Portunus in the *forum boarium* beside the river port (A26). Colini's excavation beneath the still-standing Late Republican temple revealed parts of an earlier ashlar podium about 6 m (11 courses) high with a molded cornice, and a vaulted cryptoporticus, spanned by an arch over 5 m wide.[25] The high podium as well as the arched passageway were built entirely in *tufo giallo*. Diosono recently identifies the material of an associated fluted column drum and cornice fragment as *tufo giallo*, making this some of the earliest material evidence of stone columns in Rome's architecture.[26] The complex, loosely dated to the fourth century BCE, may have formed part of a larger construction effort, if it related to river embankment walls in *tufo giallo* described in the area by Lanciani.[27] The temple's podium thus employed *tufo giallo* for external or load-bearing sections in

---

22. Coarelli 1977a: 17–18.

23. Above, pp. 92–4.

24. For continuing degradation, see Bandini and Pennino 2008.

25. Colini and Buzzetti 1986; Adam 1994; Ruggiero 1991–92; Del Buono 2009; Diosono 2016.

26. Diosono 2016: 84–5; *contra* Del Buono 2009: 24; Ruggiero 1991–92: 254. Cifani (2017: 118–19) suggests the Capitolium featured stone columns and gives examples from Archaic Etruscan architecture; see also Nielsen and Poulsen 1992: 78; and note tuff column fragments reused in the second phase (late third century) of Largo Argentina temple A (A54): Coarelli 1981: 16–18.

27. Lanciani (1897: 62–63) associates these structure with the course of the Republican walls in the *forum boarium*; see Blake 1947: 125; Coarelli 1988a: 39–42; Bernard 2012: 24–25.

contradiction to Vitruvius' prescriptions, and in close proximity to the river where flooding would have been a pressing concern. Water damage may have been mitigated if the blocks were coated with plaster, as has been proposed.[28] However, the use of a *tufo giallo* for the colonnade is not well paralleled, and especially the cryptoporticus' *tufo giallo* voussoirs, subjecting the stone to significant and potentially dangerous compression, is a practice never attested again with blocks of that material.

Over the course of the third century BCE, masonry practices began to change. In 294 BCE, the Temple of Victory (A33) was finished on the Palatine with a podium exclusively built of *tufo giallo*. Davies argues that the temple's narrow intercolumniation and plan related to its innovative but tentative use of a stone entablature for the first time in Roman architecture. She argues that the temple's superstructure was made of *peperino*, as *tufo giallo* would have been too brittle to carry the weight.[29] No fragment of this or any stone superstructure from the period survives, but we might point to examples of roughly similar date of intricately carved architectural moldings in *peperino* in smaller monuments at Rome such as the so-called donative of Fulvius Flaccus at Sant' Omobono or the Doric frieze of the sarcophagus of Scipio Barbatus.[30] If the Temple of Victory did use a more lithified stone for its superstructure above a purely *tufo giallo* base, this would represent a major change in the strategic distribution of two tuffs in a single structure.

At Largo Argentina, where we may observe a good chronological progression of building techniques, the two earliest temples in the *area sacra*, Temples C and A, both employed *tufo giallo* to some extent in their earliest building phases. Temple C's (A29) large podium (30.5 × 17.1 m), dated to the early third century BCE, was built as thick ashlar walls around two voids, one representing the cella, the other representing the temple's porch (figure 7.1).[31] These voids were originally filled with earth and rubble so that the construction economically employed ashlar only where necessary to support walls or columns of the temple's elevation. A staircase with treads of Monteverde tuff

---

Ruggiero 1991–92: 265 argues for dating the Portunus complex to the late fourth century; Del Buono 2009: 24 allows for an earlier date.

28. Ruggiero 1991–92: 25; Diosono 2016: 86.

29. Davies 2012.

30. Cf. Diffendale 2016: the circular monument and the Flaccus inscription from Sant' Omobono are not necessarily related.

31. Date, Strazzulla 1981; Kajanto 1981; construction, Coarelli 1981.

FIGURE 7.1 The podium of Temple C in Largo Argentina, originally constructed in the early third century BCE.
Photo © S. Bernard.

along with Anio tuff provided access to the podium on the temple's front (eastern) side. The two stones were haphazardly used in the stairs likely resulting from later repair, and there is some evidence in this part of the structure of fire damage.

Temple C's podium walls were built of two different stones: the interior courses were of typical *tufo giallo,* identical in quality to that found in the circuit walls. The external façade of the podium, however, was of a different, more lithified tuff. External blocks were cut on a thinner module (0.42 m wide) than the typical 0.60 × 0.60 × 1.50 m standard of the internal blocks of *tufo giallo*. The geological identification of this external stone is established by Jackson and Marra as, in fact, *tufo* giallo, only from a different quarry within the same geological formation, probably from the area of Prima Porta. This is important, because it would potentially show masons seeking finer quality stone for the external courses of the temple's podium, picking up on practices seen in the fifth century in the Tiber port in other areas of the city's topography. It would also be the first documentable time that *tufo giallo* from Grotta Oscura was restricted to a structure's interior, as opposed to the circuit walls or the Temple of Portunus. By contrast, Jackson

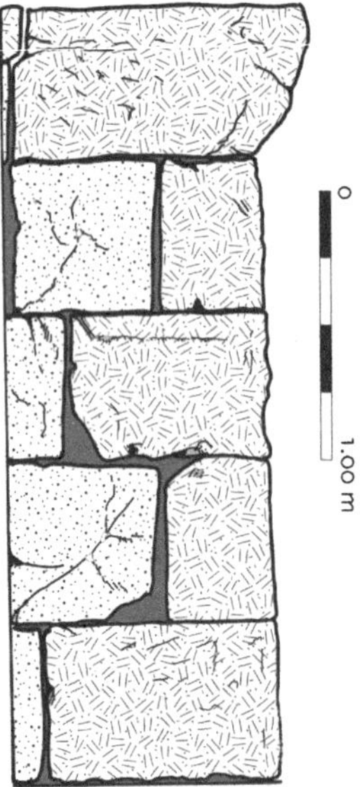

Harder tuff (Tufo giallo della via Tiberina from Prima Porta?)

Softer tuff (Tufo giallo della via Tiberina from the Grotta Oscura quarries)

FIGURE 7.2 Section drawing of north podium wall of Temple C at Largo Argentina showing use of different stones.
Drawing © S. Bernard.

and Marra argue that the exterior walls represent a later phase of the temple's podium, when repairs were made to the then-degraded *tufo giallo* of the interior walls.[32] However, such phasing, expressly rejected by Marchetti Longhi after his initial exploration of the structure, is difficult to sustain from an architectural standpoint.[33] The external blocks of the podium bond course by course into the Grotta Oscura tuff of the interior walls behind them, as seen in figures 7.2 and 7.3.[34] In other words, the exterior courses of harder stone were integral to the podium's whole construction, and it seems best to assign them to the same phase. This also makes sense in consideration of the fact that this exterior wall carried the earliest known *cyma reversa* molding in Roman

---

32. Jackson and Marra 2006: 427.

33. Marchetti Longhi 1932: 281–2, 287; cf. Coarelli 1981: 15.

34. The slightly trapezoidal cut of the interior blocks is not unusual, appearing for example in the circuit walls, and need not result from reworking.

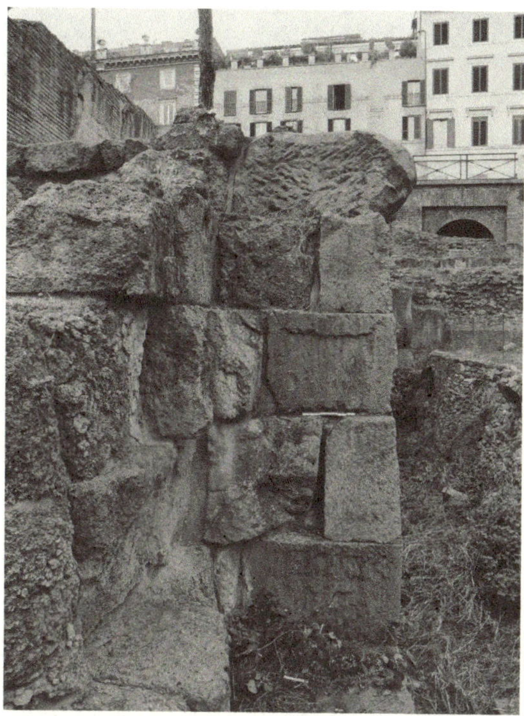

FIGURE 7.3 Section of north podium wall of Temple C at Largo Argentina showing use of different stones.
Photo © S. Bernard.

architecture: masons building this temple deliberately selected a harder material not only for its resistance, but also to carry a more complex architectural ornament.[35] The same economical practice seen in the two earth-filled voids in the podium, where material costs were reduced by limiting the use of stone to places where it was not necessary to support a superstructure, appears to have extended to the podium's walls with the harder, and thus more labor intensive to produce, *tufo giallo* reserved only for the structure's exterior-most courses.

We may compare the early awareness of the limitations of Grotta Oscura *tufo giallo* at Temple C to Temple A, the northernmost structure in the *area sacra* of Largo Argentina (A54). Beneath the hexastyle peripteral temple there are two earlier phases of the structure, both pertaining to a simple prostyle

35. The podium was plastered, as see Marchetti Longhi 1932: 298; for the molding, see Shoe Merritt 2000: 146.

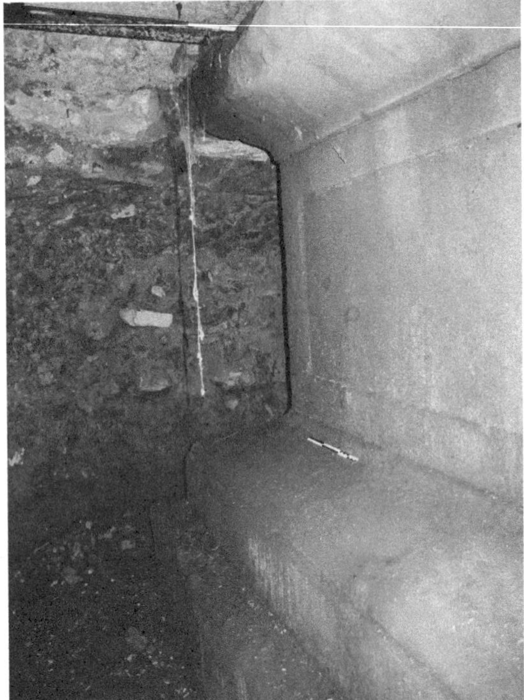

FIGURE 7.4 Molded podium wall of second phase of Temple A at Largo Argentina, late third century BCE.
Photo © S. Bernard.

cella raised on a small podium (9.5 × 16.0 m). The earliest phase of this temple is represented by two foundation courses of *tufo giallo* with a simple listello molding on the upper course.[36] Noting signs of burning on some of these blocks, Coarelli argues that this earliest temple, built slightly later than Temple C, was entirely destroyed in the third century and then quickly rebuilt in the same form, but this time with a podium of more lithified *tufo lionato* from Monteverde. This second temple's podium, 1.85 m tall, carried complex ornament with an inset fascia contained at both bottom and top by a cornice with *cyma reversa* moldings (figure 7.4). Again, *tufo giallo* seems to have been judged by this date insufficient to carry such ornament, with masons preferring different stones. Superimposed on this podium were two elevation courses of the cella made of *tufo rosso a scorie nere*. The close match between the cella walls of *tufo rosso* and those of the twin temples at Sant' Omobono in

36. Marchetti Longhi 1936: 87–91; Coarelli 1981: 16–17.

a phase dating to the rebuilding of those latter temples shortly after 212 BCE suggest that this second phase of Temple A may have been built at a similar date. The temple's second phase thus contained no fewer than three different stones, with those *tufo giallo* blocks now restricted entirely to below-ground foundations.

We catch glimpses at other sites of similar treatments of *tufo giallo* from roughly similar dates. Beneath the southernmost of the three Mid-Republican temples beneath the church of San Nicola in Carcere in the *forum holitorium*, excavations in the 1960s revealed a wall belonging to the podium of the earliest phase. This structure is extremely fragmentary but well documented by Crozzoli Aite, who identified this wall as part of the original Temple of Spes (A57) vowed towards the end of the First Punic War and destroyed by fire in 213 BCE. The podium wall was entirely *tufo giallo*, except for a few blocks of Monteverde *tufo lionato* on the easternmost (exterior) side.[37] The location of the more lithified Monteverde tuff may suggest another case where harder *tufo lionato* formed a cladding around softer *tufo giallo*. Similar construction also characterized the earliest phase of the adjacent Temple of Sospita, the central temple beneath the church of Santa Nicola in Carcere, vowed in 197 BCE and dedicated three years later (A88). The temple's high podium was mostly of *tufo giallo*, but may have had an exterior face of Monteverde tuff, with some blocks of *tufo del Palatino* atop the podium perhaps representing the lowermost course of the cella walls. The Temple of Pietas nearby, beneath the Theater of Marcellus, had exterior podium walls of Monteverde tuff with an architectural molding, while the podium itself sat above a platform of *tufo giallo*, representing the lowest stonemasonry of the temple (A106).[38] In all of these cases, while the evidence is very fragmentary, it would appear that different stones were used in conjunction, with *tufo giallo* generally confined to the lowest parts of each structure.[39]

As masons took greater stock of the potential limitations of *tufo giallo* in temple architecture, they also seem to have stopped using the stone for pavements, where it could be damaged by foot traffic. On the Palatine, the raised terrace in front of the Temple of Magna Mater in 191 BCE (A95) had supporting walls of *tufo giallo*, but the platform itself supported on these walls was paved with slabs of harder Monteverde tuff. Similarly, while the

37. Crozzoli Aite 1981: 58–61.

38. Vitti 2010: 552–53.

39. Crozzoli Aite 1981: 62–63.

fourth-century paving of the *comitium* (A20) was of *tufo giallo*, the third-century paving (A53) was of Monteverde tuff. On the Forum's other side, masons rebuilding the *domus Vestae* after a fire in the last quarter of the fourth century BCE (A13) still used *tufo giallo* for the foundation courses of most of the structure's interior walls, but the precinct was accessed by a staircase of *tufo del Palatino* treads.[40]

Tufo giallo also began to be avoided for architectural structures such as vaults or parts of a building liable to significant axial compression, representing a change from the practice seen in the cryptoporticus beside the early Temple of Portunus.[41] At some point two artillery arches were added to the circuit of the Republican walls, one near Largo Magnanapoli on the Quirinal and another at Piazza Albania on the Aventine, seen in figure 7.5. While these were inserted into the walls of *tufo giallo*, the arches themselves were built from blocks of *tufo lionato* from Monteverde. These artillery installations could date as early as the Second Punic War, when the city's fortifications were quickly updated with Hannibal's armies in the vicinity, but may be as late as Sulla's first march on Rome in 87 BCE, when Rome's walls were also repaired.[42] We can be more sure of the date of similar practices in the construction of the Aqua Marcia in 144 BCE, where the above-ground *specus*, built entirely of *tufo lionato* from Anio, was carried on arches with voussoirs of the same stone atop piers of *tufo giallo*.[43] Likewise, the Pons Mulvius, built in 109 BCE, restricted the use of *tufo giallo* to the core of the bridge's piers where it was clad in a mixture of Gabine tuff and travertine.[44]

---

40. The phasing of the *domus Vestae* in this period is highly complex. Fire in the sanctuary of Vesta is reported at Liv. *Per.* 19.14 after the conclusion of the First Punic War in 241 BCE. The fire is often dated to that year (cf. Scott 2009; Arvanitis 2010). A story circulated that the pontifex maximus L. Caecilius Metellus heroically saved the *sacra Vestae*, but was blinded in the act (Plin. *NH* 7.141). Caecilius was elsewhere said to be exceptionally healthy into his old age (Cic. *Sen.* 30, 61), and he was Pontifex Maximus until 221 BCE (cf. Val. Max. 8.13.2). Thus, one suspects the fire happened closer to 221 than 241. No signs of burning have been found, but a significant phase of *tufo giallo* and other tuff is associated with third-century ceramics (Scott 2009: 21). Scott associates this work with *opus incertum* walls, but this seems too early for that technique, and Arvanitis' dating is preferable (2010: 48–51).

41. Unfortunately, the stone used for the arches of a large viaduct associated by Gatti 1940 with the Via Aurelia of 241 is unknown; cf. D. Marchetti in *NSc* 1889: 363.

42. Coarelli 1995a: 32 for a Sullan date; Lugli 1957: 264 for an earlier date. Compare Liv. 22.8.6 and App. *BC* 1.66.303.

43. Van Deman 1973: 127.

44. Blake 1947: 134.

FIGURE 7.5 Republican walls in Piazza Albania (Aventine) showing later addition of artillery arch in *tufo lionato di Aniene,* late second or early first century BCE.
Photo © S. Bernard.

The technological development we are following should not necessarily be seen as linear, but nonetheless moved in a clearly discernable direction towards the confinement of *tufo giallo* to subterranean or interior and non-load bearing parts of Roman monuments. The earliest phase of the Basilica Fulvia (A107), initially built on the Forum's north side in 179 BCE, had walls and even column bases of *tufo giallo*, one of which can be seen in figure 7.6.[45] This reliance on *tufo giallo* continued an earlier practice in the same area of the Forum, as Carettoni found remains of previous structures consisting of pavement slabs of *tufo giallo* beneath the Basilica, perhaps parts of earlier *tabernae*.[46] At some date in the mid-second century, however, the Basilica's floor was raised slightly, and its central *aula* was now paved in travertine. The walls of this phase used *tufo lionato* from Anio, one of this material's earlier attestations at Rome.[47] Across the Forum, excavations beneath the floor of

45. Freyberger and Ertel 2016: 37–39.

46. Carettoni 1948: 111–28; Freyberger, Ertel, Lipps, and Bitterer 2007: 494–95; beneath this were fragmentary wooden structures.

47. Freyberger et al. (2007: 497) date the structure to 159 BCE; Bernard (2013b: 516) considers the censorship of L. Aemilius Paullus in 164, but the difference is slight.

FIGURE 7.6 Remains of first phase of Basilica Fulvia (179 BCE) on north side of Forum. Arrow indicates *tufo giallo* column base.
Photo © S. Bernard.

the Basilica Iulia revealed two parallel walls of *tufo giallo* defining a small room with a drain of the same material running through the center. These are interpreted as part of Tiberius Sempronius Gracchus' Basilica (A129), built on the Forum's south side in 169 BCE, on the site of an earlier property belonging to Scipio Africanus. Found along with the *tufo giallo* walls were travertine pavers, suggesting that the building was constructed with subterranean foundations in *tufo giallo* paved in more durable stone, identical to the second phase of the Basilica Fulvia.[48] Once marble was introduced at Rome, it was used along similar lines. In the round temple in the *forum boarium, tufo giallo* foundations rested beneath a stepped crepidoma in travertine and a superstructure in marble (figure 7.7).[49]

One of the very latest dateable monuments with significant amounts of *tufo giallo* shows the end result of this technological development. In the 70s BCE, along with the construction of the large structure on the eastern side

48. Carettoni and Fabbrini 1961.

49. Rakob and Heilmeyer 1973: 10–11.

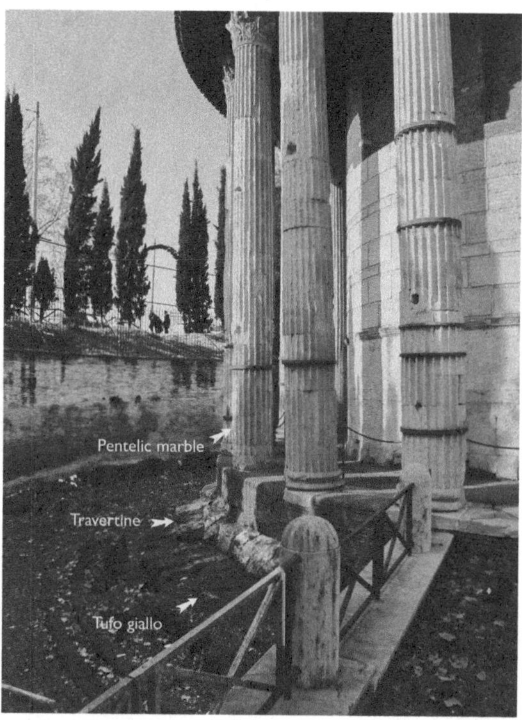

FIGURE 7.7 Round Temple (Hercules Victor or Invictus?) in *forum boarium* indicating different use of building materials, late second century BCE.
Photo © S. Bernard.

of the Capitoline conventionally called the Tabularium, the small temple to Veiovis at the foot of the hill was entirely rebuilt. *Tufo giallo* was used in the temple's construction, probably reused from the temple's earlier phase.[50] The rebuilt temple was raised on a podium of travertine, with cella walls of *tufo lionato* from Anio and *tufo giallo.* Anio tuff was used for piers in the walls, but also for the lowest blocks of corners, which were carved into engaged pilasters. The entire tuff elevation was then covered in plaster (figure 7.8). In this case, *tufo giallo* was not only restricted to non-load bearing spans of the wall's elevation where it was exposed to almost no architectonic stress, but it was raised off the ground and plastered so as to be entirely impervious to water or the elements.

The data in support of a trend towards the strategic use of *lapis pallens* as described by Vitruvius is summarized in table 7.1. Over time, blocks of *tufo*

50. Colini 1943: 50.

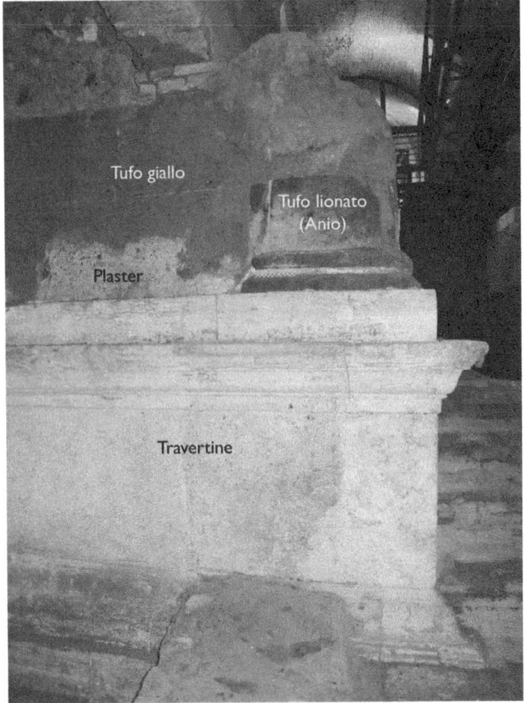

FIGURE 7.8 South wall of Temple of Veiovis at foot of Capitoline (79 BCE) showing different use of building materials.
Photo © S. Bernard.

giallo were increasingly confined to subterranean foundations or interior cores and moved away from load-bearing areas or axial compression. As the supply of more durable materials was increasingly established, masons began to use *tufo giallo* strategically in conjunction with other types of tuff and then travertine, marble, and plaster, before abandoning it as a dimension stone entirely.

7.5. Lifting Technology

The link between Vitruvius' description of ashlar technology and the archaeological evidence offers one way of tracing change in the technologies of Mid-Republican architecture, but other developments in the production of the city's architecture are also observable. In particular, the lifting technologies employed in creating stone monuments can be seen to change

Table 7.1 Roman Monuments Showing the Development of the Use of *Tufo Giallo*

Monument	Date	Use of *tufo giallo*
Circuit walls (A6)	378 BCE	Exposed above ground
Temple of Portunus, early phases (A26)	Fourth century	Exposed above ground, used for voussoirs
Comitium (A20)	318 BCE	Paving stone
Temple C, Largo Argentina, first phase (A29)	Early third century	Used for podium core, clad in harder variety of *tufo giallo*
Temple of Victory on the Palatine (A33)	294 BCE	Entire podium, possibly supporting superstructure in different stone?*
Temple A, Largo Argentina, first phase (A54)	Mid-third century	Used for podium's exterior walls
Temple of Spes, *forum holitorium*, first phase (A57)	247 BCE	Possibly restricted to the podium core
Rebuilding of precinct of Vesta after fire (A64)	c. 225 BCE **	Walls
Tabernae beneath Basilica Fulvia (A107)	209 BCE	Paving stone
Temple of Juno, *forum holitorium* (A88)	194 BCE	Possibly restricted to the podium core
Temple of Jupiter, Tiber Island (?) (A90)	194 BCE	Podium and foundations
Precinct of Magna Mater (A97)	191 BCE	Walls of *tufo giallo* supporting paved platform of Monteverde tuff
Temple of Pietas, *forum holitorium* (A106)	181 BCE	Molded podium wall of Monteverde tuff on top of *tufo giallo* platform
Basilica Fulvia, earliest phase (A107)	179 BCE	Paving stone and column bases
Basilica Sempronia (A129)	169 BCE	Foundation walls and subfloor drain; paved over with travertine
Basilica Fulvia, second phase	164 or 159 BCE	Paved over with travertine; elevation walls in Anio tuff

(*continued*)

Table 7.1 Continued

Monument	Date	Use of *tufo giallo*
Aqua Marcia	144 BCE	Non-load bearing parts of piers between arches of Anio tuff
Pons Mulvius	109 BCE	Core of piers, clad with Gabine tuff and travertine
Round temple in *forum boarium*	c. 100 BCE	Foundation only; elevation in marble and travertine
Reconstruction of Temple of Veiovis	78 BCE	Reused (?) blocks raised on travertine podium, restricted to non-load-bearing areas in conjunction with Anio tuff, and plastered.

* Cf. Davies 2012.

** For this date, see discussion above n. 40.

over this period. Rome's earliest stone architecture relied on the simple use of earthen ramps.[51] Evidence for this comes in the form of a correspondence found between the height of stone courses and layers of earthen fill detectable in some early temples, a sign that builders raised the ground level as they carried material for each successive course up to a rising monument's walls.[52]

Notably, ramps as well as other mechanisms for lifting architectural loads often reflect particular socioeconomic contexts. Ramps regularly featured in societies where labor was cheap; their use required higher volumes of labor, but lower ratios of skilled workers. Their appearance in Archaic Rome is not out of keeping with the traditions about forced labor under the kings, while they are found widely in command economies. Bronze Age societies in Egypt, Greece, and the Near East created megalithic structures with ramps and sleds, but without the assistance of cranes. In turn, through the use of windlasses or pulleys, cranes provided significant mechanical advantage, but their complexity also demanded greater skill. Lifting machines were credited

51. There is no study of lifting in Roman architecture equivalent to Coulton 1974 for the Greek world, although see important discussion in Cifani 2008: 240–43; also Bernard 2013a: 100–106.

52. Ioppolo 1989: 31 for Sant' Omobono; Cifani 2008: 241–42 notes similar evidence in the Capitolium and circuit walls.

to famous "inventors" such as Archimedes, the court engineer and relative of Hiero II of Syracuse, who was held in antiquity to have discovered the use of the compound pulley.[53] The context of such innovation in the hands of highly specialized engineers often contains hints of competition and markets, a background also perceivable in Vitruvius' discussion of contractors like Paconius who attempted (with mixed results) to devise a novel machine to transport a heavy load.[54]

For the potential socioeconomic ramifications, then, it is worth noting that the first positive evidence for the use of cranes to lift and place blocks in Roman monuments appears only in the Mid-Republic. Of course, it is not impossible that cranes were used earlier: the simplest manner of attaching a crane's rope to a heavy block was with the use of a rope-cradle formed simply by tying off a loop of rope around the load, as shown in figure 7.9. Once lifted and placed, the loop was removed or untied, and this left no permanent mark on the stone itself. Because rope cradles passed underneath a block on the ground, any load lifted in this manner had to be manually raised slightly or propped up somehow before it could be loaded onto a crane, so the use of a simple rope cradle implied an additional cost of manpower per block. Eventually more specialized mechanisms were employed to avoid this step. Typically, such mechanisms involved the insertion of some device into specifically made cuttings in the block. It is these cuttings, often still observable in finished architecture, that permit us to trace the different techniques of lifting involved in the assembly of Roman monuments.

The two primary devices in Republican architecture for attaching a block to a crane without simply lashing a rope around the block were iron lifting tongs or the lewis (figure 7.10). Other attachment techniques such as u-shaped cuttings for ropes, or protruding bosses, developed in Greek architecture and circulated in the Archaic period in Southern Italy and Sicily, but are not found at Rome.[55] Evidence for lifting tongs appears earliest at Rome and consists of small indentations, normally no more than 5–10 cm deep and slightly conical in profile, cut for the insertion of tong points into opposite faces of a block. As noted in chapter 3, the *tufo giallo* blocks of the Republican circuit walls are the earliest dateable blocks to display such cuttings. The corresponding

53. On the compound pulley, see Wilson 2008: 344.

54. *De Arch.* 10.2.11–13.

55. Coulton 1974: 8.

FIGURE 7.9 Restoration project on Athenian Acropolis showing modern use of a rope cradle to lift heavy blocks of stone.
Photo © S. Bernard.

iron tongs are well known from ancient representations,[56] as well as from Vitruvius, who describes "iron forceps (*ferrei forfices*) joined to a block with points fitting into holes in the stone."[57] As ancient depictions clarify, the tongs were formed as scissors suspended from an iron ring or lashed together and suspended from tackle, such that the loading of the weight forced and locked their tips into the block's holes as the load was raised.

The use of the lewis, attested by the sixth century BCE in Greek architecture, goes unmentioned by Vitruvius. The only ancient description is found in the later text of Heron of Alexandria, who described a specialized

56. Late Republican depictions include terracotta reliefs from the Via Cassia outside Rome and from Pratica di Mare; Felletti Maj 1977: 194–95.

57. *De Arch.* 10.2.2: *ad rechamum autem imum ferrei forfices religantur, quorum dentes in saxa forata accomodantur.* Heron of Alexandria (*Mechanics* 7 = Drachmann 1963: 104–5) does not mention *ferrei forfices*, but describes an implement called a "crab," consisting of hooks fit into holes and then lashed to the block with rope.

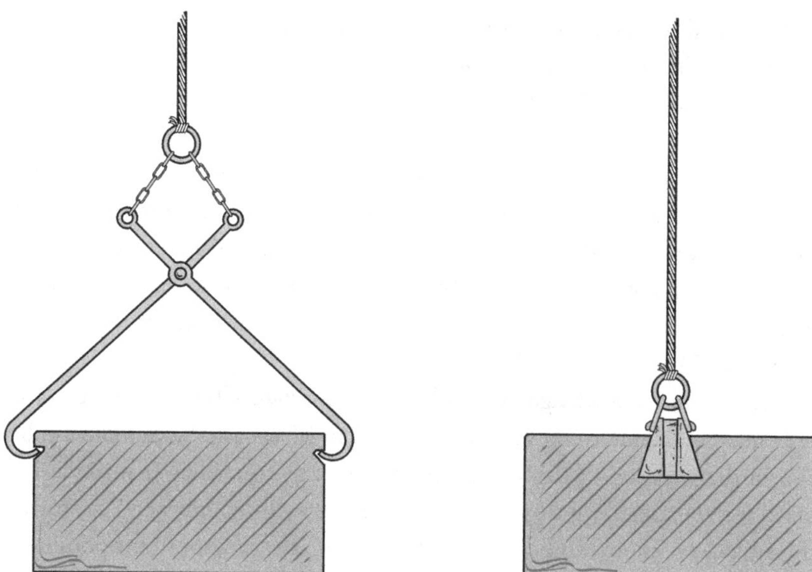

FIGURE 7.10 Two mechanisms for lifting heavy loads in Mid-Republican architecture. Left: lifting tong or *ferrei forfices*. Right: lewis.
Drawing © S. Bernard.

cutting in a stone's top face, rectangular in profile but with slanting sides producing a slight undercut, essentially forming a trapezoid. Into this cutting were inserted "two pegs of iron, whose ends are bent like the shape of the letter *gamma*" and a third straight iron peg between them. The description resembles a rare surviving example of a complete Roman lewis iron from Raetia, with its wedge-shaped base and a top hooked for receiving a rope or ring.[58] The two *gamma* irons along with the straight third iron were driven into the hole and then connected to the end of the rope. When the load was raised, Heron says, the "middle iron will not let go of the two irons with their curved ends inside the stone to hold it." In other words, the central iron locks the wedge-shaped irons to the sloped sides of the cut in the top of the stone.[59] This technique was convenient for several reasons. Lewis irons were more compact and required less metal than tongs. Since this device did not span a block like tongs, lewises could be used for loads of various shapes or

58. Aylward 2009.

59. Heron *Mechanica* 8 = Drachmann 1963: 105–6.

widths. And finally lewises could quickly be moved from one block to another once the crane rope was slack.

To the end of his description, Heron appended a word of caution that the irons be made from high quality metal, as material that was too hard or too soft was liable to fracture or bend, and this would lead to the device's failure.[60] Not only the material of the lewis, but that of the load itself, figured greatly into Roman masons' decision to use lewises on sites. In Imperial architecture, lewises were never employed to lift granite blocks as, despite that material's great weight, its large crystal structure made it more brittle and liable to fracture under the pressure of an engaged lewis.[61]

Thus, a close knowledge of the physical properties of building material not only mattered in choosing what stone to put in what part of a monument, but also in the selection of the appropriate technology to maneuver material into place. It is remarkable in this case that lewis holes at Rome appear on the tops of those blocks of more lithified *tufo giallo* that form the exterior of the podium of Temple C at Largo Argentina (A29) (figure 7.11). As discussed, it is likely that the two different types of *tufo giallo* employed in the interior and exterior walls of the building's podium represent the judicious selection of different stones within a single building phase. The use of a lewis can be seen as logical for blocks of the podium's exterior face because, as opposed to *ferrei forfices* holes on a block's lateral faces, cuttings for a lewis were concealed on the top of a block and left a smooth exterior surface. By contrast, Temple C's interior blocks of softer *tufo giallo* from Grotta Oscura show cuttings for the insertion of lifting tongs. Thus, this structure reveals evidence of particular lifting techniques being applied to different materials used in the same construction project.

Evidence for a lewis appears more regularly in Roman monuments with the use of marble in the mid-second century BCE, as lewis cuttings are regularly found on marble blocks, particularly column drums.[62] Material again dictated technological choices, as marble was hard enough to withstand the pressure of an engaged lewis, while its fine grain structure made it less liable to fracture than granite. The tuff used in the exterior of temple C was much harder than volcanic tuffs typically employed in the early third century.

60. Lancaster (1999: 436) suggests that Roman masons understood the maximum load of a lewis to be about 7.5 tons.

61. Aylward 2009; L. Lancaster pers. comm.

62. Bernard 2013a: 101.

FIGURE 7.11 Blocks from face of north podium wall of Temple C at Largo Argentina. Upper surfaces show cuttings of sockets for insertion of lewises.
Photo © S. Bernard.

For the most part Roman masons preferred to raise tuff blocks with lifting tongs, which they may have considered safer for the softer stone.[63]

Thus, Temple C would suggest that, already in the third century, different materials were treated differently in terms of the technology applied to them, and indeed further examples emerge in this regard. Chapter 3 noted that lifting-tong holes on *tufo giallo* blocks of the Republican circuit walls were irregularly distributed, both right-side-up and upside-down, likely reflecting the use of lifting engines to offload material at the Tiber port, while the actual placement of blocks into the walls was done using the *agger* as a ramp. In fact, the walls are not the only place where blocks of *tufo giallo* from Grotta Oscura display what we might call "upside-down" holes for lifting-tongs, or holes that are situated on the lower-half of a blocks long side. Such upside-down holes appear irregularly on blocks of the same material at temple C and

63. Lancaster (2005: 65–67) notes similar considerations in the construction of the Colosseum.

FIGURE 7.12 Interior (west) face of cella foundations of western temple at Sant' Omobono, late third century BCE. Blocks of *tufo rosso a scorie nere* show consistent holes for lifting tongs.
Photo © S. Bernard.

in the walls of the first phase of the Basilica Fulvia in the Forum (A107). We may compare this to the regular disposition of holes for lifting tongs on the upper margins of blocks used in walls of identical *tufo rosso a scorie nere* in two different structures: Largo Argentina temple B and the western temple at the *area sacra* of Sant' Omobono (figure 7.12). In sum, different stones reflect different approaches to on-site construction.

7.6. Technology and Demography

Having outlined two cases of technological change in Mid-Republican Roman architecture, I now turn to the socio-historical implications of such change. Clearly, close knowledge of a stone's physical properties was vital for the technologies and practices employed in using different building materials. It is likely that such knowledge circulated largely via masons' experience working with various building stones. Less likely is that the stock of knowledge among Mid-Republican Rome's builders developed through the dissemination of technical or theoretical texts. Pre-modern building as a whole is often seen as a largely experiential practice, with skills commonly gained through apprenticeship or learning-by-doing. More particularly, an almost anti-textual disposition among Roman builders emerges from the preface to Vitruvius' seventh book, in which the author discussed his literary antecedents, both Greek and Roman. Greek technical writing on architecture was by Vitruvius' time a well-established genre, having originated in fifth-century Athens and developed in Hellenistic Asia Minor. By comparison, Vitruvius claimed to have found almost nothing written on the architectural trade by Roman contemporaries. To his knowledge, the entirety of the corpus of Republican technical writers on architecture consisted of only three works: a volume by a Fuficius or Fufidius, perhaps Oscan in origin,[64] one book of Varro's *De novem disciplinis*, and two books by a P. Septimius. Fuficius and Septimius are unknown.[65] Varro is well known, but apparently his architectural writing was less influential for Vitruvius' own work than his etymological treatise *De lingua Latina*, which Vitruvius elsewhere lavished with praise.[66] Vitruvius explicitly expressed dismay that even the better-known Roman architects of the Republican period did not bother creating written accounts of their practice:

> Since our predecessors are also shown to have been great architects, no less than the Greeks, and even quite a few of our own contemporaries, but few of them published their techniques, I did not think that I could remain silent, but I should expound upon individual architectural topics in individual volumes in an orderly fashion.[67]

This passage contains a clear rhetorical conceit intended to burnish the author's work: since Romans were excellent builders, but their disinclination to publish their methods obscured their accomplishments in comparison to Greek architects, Vitruvius' literary project repaired a false cultural imbalance. But beyond this rhetoric, reasons to trust this summation of the extent of theoretical Roman architectural knowledge can be inferred from Vitruvius' own descriptions of Roman (as opposed to Greek) building techniques, which often seem more empirical than theoretical. This applies to Vitruvius' description of the practices of using tuffs local to Rome: while he explained variations in rocks with elemental science, ultimately he instructed masons to decide on the soundness of stone based on their observation of that stone's condition after leaving it outdoors for two years. The same approach runs through many

64. Cf. *Imag.Ital.* II.1079 for an Oscan Cerrinus Fufidius on a brick from Bovianum.

65. Septimius may have been Varro's quaestor, cf. Cam 1995 *comm. ad loc.*

66. *De Arch.* 9.*pr.* 17. Nothing of Varro's work on architecture survives, although fragments of other texts include close descriptions of monuments such as Lars Porsenna's tomb at Clusium (Plin. *NH* 36.19). Festus' lexicon contains much architectural information, mostly of an etymological nature and perhaps similar in style and substance to Varro's writing.

67. *De Arch.* 7.*pr.* 18: *cum ergo et antiqui nostri inveniantur non minus quam Graeci fuisse magni architecti et nostra memoria satis multi, et ex his pauci praecepta edidissent, non putavi silendum, sed disposite singulis voluminibus de singulis exponeremus.*

of the previous chapters on other Italian building materials, where space was given to theoretical or scientific explanations, but actual practices depended on firsthand experience. Famously, he advised that the best sand for concrete aggregate was distinguished by the crackling noise it made when rubbed in the hand and the fact that it did not leave color behind when shaken on a white cloth (2.4.1). Whatever the elemental or scientific basis, the ultimate test of this sand's utility was based upon experience and evaluation.

The point is that Republican architectural practice developed literally close to the ground as Roman masons gained an understanding of the physical properties of various building materials through repeated experience working with such materials. This carries historical and particularly demographic implications, since it is hard to imagine technical knowledge of a material's physical properties reaching Rome except by the movement of experienced masons from that material's source. This supposition of labor mobility, that specialized masons often accompanied supply chains of building materials, has been proposed for other types of building techniques and stones, particularly marble. The earliest known Corinthian marble temples in Rome, the round temple in the *forum boarium* and the Temple of Apollo *in circo* (see A119), have capitals whose ornament style is clearly patterned off of capitals from the Temple of Olympian Zeus at Athens started by Antiochus IV Epiphanes shortly after his accession in 175 BCE.[68] The marble from which the Roman temple's capitals were carved was quarried in Attica on Mt. Pentelikon from quarry pits that were utilized at Athens at the same time, and the correspondence in both material and style supports the idea that both masons and stone moved from Attica to Rome.[69] It is relevant to add that lifting technology, too, moved with masons and material: the same two marble temples in Rome have capitals divided laterally into two pieces, splitting the drum of the capital about where the volutes spring from the lower acanthus-leaf frieze. This practice of producing Corinthian capitals in two pieces seems initially to have been a response to the need to lift massive blocks of stone, and we first see it in enormous Corinthian capitals at Alexandria and, of course, in the Temple of Olympian Zeus at Athens. The need to split capitals into two blocks at Rome seems less obvious, as capitals from the Temple of Neptune *in circo* or the round temple were significantly smaller and lighter than their Hellenistic antecedents. Instead, the use of two blocks to build Corinthian capitals may

68. Delbrück 1907–12: II.43.

69. Bernard 2010; for Hellenistic quarries in Athens, see Bernard and Pike 2015.

have been adopted as part of the typical working practice of Attic masons involved in carving these Roman capitals.

I would suggest that a connection between material, technology, and the mobility of workers experienced in local materials also existed for the earlier phases of Republican masonry, when local volcanic tuffs from Central Italy formed the typical material for dimension stone. There is little direct evidence for those masons building architecture from tuff blocks at Rome. Indeed, the only extant builders' signature on a Mid-Republican tuff building records two Greek names across blocks of *tufo del Palatino*, as discussed in the last chapter. However, as the stonemasonry practices described above depended on the movement of information formed outside the city to the city's builders, the evidence remains suggestive.

The technological changes in Mid-Republican architecture detailed in the previous sections thus may indicate the centripetal movement of builders with their own local knowledge to Rome, something which would fit the general attraction of labor to Rome in this period, as described in the previous chapter. Thinking about how and why such skilled labor moved from Latium to Rome, we may first of all note that *tufo giallo*'s arrival at Rome in any quantity accompanied conquest and, very likely, the forced transfer of conquered populations, presumably as slaves. The contemporaneity of that material's large-scale use with the capture of the *ager Veientanus* suggests a strong relationship between imperial expansion, mass enslavement, and the exploitation of natural resources. As noted in this chapter, the earliest instances of *tufo giallo* in Roman architecture do not show a developed sense of the physical limitations of that stone compared to later monuments. In this regard, it is worth emphasizing the comparative absence of Grotta Oscura *tufo giallo* from Veii's own architecture: the labor force involved in supplying stone may not have possessed an intimate knowledge of its material properties.[70]

However, the connection between slavery and stonemasonry, which holds true for *tufo giallo*, is less easily found for other Mid-Republican building materials and technologies. Gaggiotti argues that the technique of *opus signinum* flooring, otherwise known as *pavimenta poenica*, was brought to Latium by Punic slaves forced to settle in the region after the Second Punic War.[71] However, since his publication the technique has been discovered in an

---

70. However, Schatzmann (2015) notes a road between the *tufo giallo* quarries and Veii perhaps relating to the transport of stone to the Etruscan city.

71. Gaggiotti 1988.

earlier Italian monument, a bath complex at the Latin colony of Fregellae.[72] More generally, in cases where information is forthcoming, a strict link between conquest and the appearance of one or another building stone in Mid-Republican architecture often seems less tenable. Instructive is the earliest use of marble at Rome, which appeared in the city during an important phase in the conquest of Greece. The Pentelic marble temple built by Q. Caecilius Metellus in 146 BCE, the first of its kind in Rome, was installed within a new porticus in the Campus Martius along with a number of Greek masterpieces, including Lysippus' celebrated Granicus group, taken to Rome as spoils from the Fourth Macedonian War. It is likely that Roman viewers were meant to connect the temple's Greek building material with the spoliated statues displayed within the structure. However, the architect who designed Metellus' marble temple was Hermodorus of Salamis, a Greek builder who was hired, not forced, to work on the project in Rome. In the years following Metellus' conquest, Hermodorus was employed by other Roman *triumphatores* to build more marble temples in Rome. Some of these Roman magistrates commissioning Greek-style temples from Greek marble never triumphed in Greece or commanded armies there, so that their construction of triumphal monuments in Attic marble was supported above all by the technological knowledge of the available skilled labor supply at Rome. Some labor working for Hermodorus' projects was probably slave, but the link between conquest, slavery and forced migration, and the urban skilled labor supply was not as straightforward as had potentially been the case following the sack of Veii.[73]

What is more, besides the arrival to Rome of *tufo giallo* after the sack of Veii and Attic marble after the Fourth Macedonian war, there are few signs of chronological convergence between territorial conquest and the urban use of stone from conquered territory. Table 7.2 lists the earliest known monuments of Republican building stones alongside the date of Rome's acquisition of the territory on which their respective quarries were located. In many instances, the use of a territory's material in Roman architecture followed a lag of decades or even centuries after that territory's conquest. In cases such as *lapis Gabinus* or travertine, building stones were used by communities near their respective quarries for a long time before they appeared in Rome's own architecture, and we may presume that the practice of using such stones was honed locally before material and information were then imported to the capital. Luni marble

72. Tsiolis 2013.

73. Bernard 2010.

Table 7.2. **Earliest Appearance of Building Materials in Mid-Republican Architecture**

Material	Earliest known public monument	Incorporation of quarry zones into Roman control
Tufo giallo (Grotta Oscura)	378 BCE (circuit walls) (A6)	396 BCE (Veii)
Tufo giallo (Prima Porta?)	c. 290 BCE (Largo Argentina temple C, exterior of podium wall) (A29)	396 BCE (Veii)
Tufo rosso a scorie nere	345 BCE (Temple of Juno Moneta) (A14)	435 BCE (Fidenae*)
Tufo lionato (Monteverde)	435 BCE (Temple of Apollo Medicus)**	396 BCE (Trans Tiberim)
Travertine	169 BCE (paving stones in Basilica Sempronia)† (A129)	338 BCE (Tibur)
Tufo lionato (Anio)	144 BCE (Aqua Marcia)‡	435 BCE (Fidenae or Ficulea?§)
Peperino di marino	c. 500 BCE (Sant' Omobono, perimeter wall of platform supporting twin temples)	Sixth century BCE (Alba)
Lapis Gabinus	109 BCE (Pons Mulvius)§§	Sixth century BCE (Gabii)
Tufo di Tuscolo	78 BCE ("Tabularium")	381 BCE (Tusculum)
Luni marble	40s BCE (Mamurra, cf. Plin. *HN* 36.48)	177 BCE (colony of Luni established)

* Barbina et al. 2009: 330–31.

** Notably, the assignment of this material to the first phase by Ciancio Rossetto 1997–98 puts its earliest use before Rome's control of the source; for *transtiberim* as foreign territory in the fifth century, see *RS* II.629 on XII *Tab.* III.7.

† More extensive use of travertine comes in the later second century, at which point it replaces tuff for architecture and other purposes including inscriptions.

‡ Blocks at the core of the round donative monument at Sant' Omobono are *tufo lionato*, perhaps from the Anio, but the Aqua Marcia is the earliest significant use.

§ Quilici 1974 documents extensive Anio quarries along the Via Tiburtina east of the city, roughly between Fidenae and Ficulea. Rome incorporated this territory by the fifth century at the latest.

§§ Farr 2014: 251 includes earlier examples, while the first large-scale exploitation belongs to the first century BCE.

had a long history of exploitation before its initial export of to Rome.[74] Thus, while conquest did in some instances lead to the supply of building material and probably also labor to Mid-Republican Rome, this connection did not apply to the majority of cases. In many cases stonemasons seem to have moved to Rome outside the immediate context of conquest. Such movement of labor and the related accumulation of technological knowledge supported the development of urban building technologies: thus, the rise of a strategic tuff masonry in Republican Rome's architecture forms a proxy for the attraction of specialized labor from the city's expanding imperial, but also economic, hinterland to the urban market.

The sum of this discussion of Mid-Republican Rome's architecture is to suggest a labor market consonant with that described by the previous chapter. The composition of the workforce was in some cases directly relatable to war and conquest, and in many other cases dependent on the centripetal pull of urban demand for workers, in this case skilled stonemasons, to the capital from outlying areas. As I cautioned in the last chapter as well, the existence of market demand for skilled stonemasons at Rome in this period need not imply that all such workers moved to Rome of their own volition. We should emphasize the role of contractors or architects like Hermodorus of Salamis in transferring specialized technical knowledge to Rome. The status of those laboring for these *redemptores* at Rome is very hard to detect, but likely included labor of various status, as in other urban productive industries discussed in the last chapter.

7.7. Conclusions

Roman ashlar masonry underwent important technological developments in the third and second centuries BCE. An increasingly consistent understanding emerged of how to use different stones in different parts of a monument so as to maximize each material's architectural effectiveness with regard to its physical properties. This practice was characteristic of Rome itself where it was supported by expanding territorial control, and such judicious combination of volcanic tuffs in single monuments appeared only rarely in contemporary construction in other towns of Italy. Moreover, since a block of stone's hardness and liability to fracture dictated the ways in which it was maneuvered, as masons became more attentive to each stones' properties,

74. Sassatelli 1977; Bonamici 1989; Dolci 1995: 362.

they also applied different lifting technologies to different stones, sometimes in the construction of a single monument.

Knowledge regarding the physical properties of the stones used at Rome was vital for the formation of these technologies, and its circulation to Rome depended on the movement of skilled masons, in addition to building materials. This means that the technologies described here carry the implication of urban labor migration. In some cases, skilled labor came to Rome directly as the result of conquest and slavery, but much of this movement seems better understood as dependent on the pull of masons to the capital's labor market. Read against the discussion of the last chapter, the technological changes detailed here provide further support for a scenario of high demand for builders or contractors and the expansion of Mid-Republican Rome's labor market.

8 CONCLUSION

Read together, the different themes of the preceding chapters present an account of change both in the economic structures of labor attached to urban production, particularly building, and in the social relations they implied. This book's narrative began with the moment most associated with urban transformation by the ancient sources, the Gallic sack of Rome in 390 BCE. According to the tradition best represented by Livy, the Gaul's complete destruction of the city entailed a subsequently major effort to rebuild Rome. The substantial cost implied in this construction project was held to have increased private debt to unsustainable levels, disrupting Rome's political and social balance and slowing the Roman economy for several decades. Some new archaeological evidence does attest to fire damage in the city center around the time of the sack, but the historiographical idea of a holocaustic *incendium Gallicum* necessary to Livy's narrative remains unsupportable. This minimalist view thus needs to be reconciled with other indicators of Rome's relatively limited economic capacities in the years following the sack. A reconstruction of the broader Roman productive economy in the early fourth century suggests that Rome's supply of labor was increasingly thinned, especially as Roman production expanded into the *ager Veientanus* following the conquest of Veii.

One particular building project stands out in this early fourth century context: the construction around 378 BCE of Rome's circuit walls, probably initiated in response to the Gallic threat, represented the largest single productive endeavor undertaken by the Mid-Republican state. An energetics model of the labor cost of the walls' construction contextualized within the broader flow of labor in the Mid-Republican economy suggests that this building project caused serious problems for many Roman households. The institutional framework through which the state achieved this project also mattered. There are reasons to think that the walls were built using forced citizen labor, making the unremunerated costs of the building project even more burdensome. In this model, the walls on their own form a plausible explanation for economic development in the early fourth century, and it is perhaps telling that the Roman state did not attempt another building project of similar magnitude for over half a century.

Once building at Rome on a grand scale resumed by the later fourth century, it had a notably different socioeconomic character. Unlike the walls, the road and aqueduct built by the censor Appius Claudius Caecus beginning in 312 BCE had no discernibly detrimental effect on citizen debt or political cohesion. This is despite the sources' great focus on the outsized costs of such projects, something that seems historically plausible considering their novelty and magnitude. The different social consequences of large-scale state building reflect the start of a period of significant change in the way in which the Roman state organized construction and other major productive activities. In particular, there is a meaningful coincidence to the emergence in the decades after 300 BCE of Roman coinage and evidence for state contracting. The increasingly close association of the censor, as well as the aediles, with the upkeep of the city's infrastructure at that same time represented a new way of organizing the state's investment in its costliest urban expenditure around contractual relationships. Meanwhile, several indications suggest that Romans were growing increasingly reluctant to turn to old forms of dependent citizen labor. Slaveholding and market-oriented labor were gaining prominence at the same time, and this was therefore a consequential moment of economic change in the Roman state's mode of production. We must also bear in mind that such change was not autonomous, but was propelled by the desires of an emerging segment of the ruling elite who depended upon wealth accrued through more market-oriented forms of production and exchange.

Supported by these institutional changes, there was an increase in the importance of both slave labor and a market for free wage labor in Rome's urban economy of the third century. This is noteworthy, as the urban building industry gained steam from c. 300 BCE onward, when we may detect sustained investment in public construction at Rome, and consequently sustained urban demand for building labor. While there is no direct evidence for wages or prices, consilient epigraphic, numismatic, and archaeological evidence suggests that the labor market played an increasingly important role in the organization of urban labor. Roman workers were mobile and were moving to the city, where they contributed to a phase of demographic expansion.

A similar picture of mobile artisans pushed and pulled to Rome's expanding building industry is visible in technological changes in Mid-Republican architecture. Rome's masons showed increasingly systematic awareness of the use of different building stones. Such recognition, visible in the tradition represented by Vitruvius' *De Architectura*, led to the strategic mixing of different stones in structures based upon their durability or hydraulic resistivity, as well as the proliferation of different lifting technologies adapted to various stones. These developments depended on the importation to Rome not only of particular stones from surrounding Latium, but of information carried by masons experienced with each stone's physical attributes. In some cases, the transfer of skilled labor took place as a direct result of conquest and imperial expansion, but in more cases the transfer of building stones (and masons) from Central Italy to Rome occurred centuries after the incorporation into Rome's imperial territory of their respective regions of origin and seems better explained by labor-market forces. This reinforces the picture of the circulation of mobile masons around Mid-Republican Latium sometimes but not necessarily in direct connection to the conquests and mass enslavements of Republican imperial expansion. This discussion of the attraction of Central Italian labor to Rome opens up questions of the demographic and economic effects of the capital's growth on the various communities from which it drew population and resources. The topic of the implications of Mid-Republican Rome's development on Italy merits further exploration.

An overarching theme of this study has been the progressive rise of market exchange within the city's economy during the Mid-Republican period, as Rome grew demographically and physically larger. The increasingly meaningful economic division between city and countryside implied the greater need to exchange the products of urban labor for those of agriculture, with monetization, contracting, and labor markets fitting into this trend. At the same time, it is important to acknowledge that these developments were not part of some sort of vague evolution or inevitable modernization process. Rather, this study has tied such changes to the particular and dynamic political economy of Mid-Republican Rome. As the patricio-plebeian *nobilitas* emerged, new ways of producing and exchanging wealth were incorporated into the prevailing social structure with significant effects. The important transition of the Roman economy from *nexum* to slavery in the later fourth century has been noticed before.[1] The chapters extend this observation to the urban situation by noting the very different ways in which the Roman state organized architectural production from one end of this period to the other.

1. Gabba 1990: 10–11; also Gabrielli 2003b: 254–5.

We have compared the compulsory labor involved in the building process behind the circuit walls of the early fourth century to the arrangement of construction projects during and after the censorship of Appius Claudius Caecus, from which point onward the Roman state, at least in Italy, no longer relied on corvée labor to any considerable degree through the High Empire.

An economist looking at this situation of economic change might be tempted to interpret it through the lens of relative prices: as the cost of Archaic modes of production became inefficient, this encouraged the emergence of new institutional structures.[2] That is, the political enfranchisement of the plebs starting in the fourth century made it harder to extract their labor through coercive means, while at the same time conquest and expansion increased the stock of slaves and made slaveholding cheaper. This leads to an important question for our overall understanding of the ancient economy: if debt and inequality caused by large-scale building projects in the early fourth century were creating inefficiencies in Rome's political cohesion at home and its military capacity abroad, did Romans understand coins, censorial contracts, and so forth as ways to remedy their situation? In other words, to what degree was observable change reflective of what might be called conscious economic policy directed by the Republican state? The issue seems fundamental, but is difficult to answer: hard enough as it is to reconstruct historical events in the period, it is probably impossible to access in any satisfactory manner how Mid-Republican Romans perceived economic behavior. Finley, of course, argued that ancients did not possess a technical or independent economic vocabulary.[3] To the contrary, in Appius' *factio forensis*, or in the debate over *quaestus* in Livy's account of the *Lex Claudia* restricting senatorial trade, we might discern that Romans writing in later periods at least conceived of some aspects of Mid-Republican history in economic terms.[4] However, it is important to view these episodes of social struggles over wealth and its creation in the Mid-Republic not independently, but as part of competitive politics. This suggests in turn that the dynamics of economic behavior were to a large degree embedded within matters of politics and status, and it is telling that consequential developments in the organization of Roman architectural

2. North 1990: 84.

3. Finley 1999: 17–21; similarly, Nicolet 1982; see now Andreau and Chankowski 2007; Viglietti 2017 suggests Romans understood price formation in complex ways in the Early Republic.

4. Tchernia 2007 makes a good argument that Livy's reference to *quaestus* belonged to the language of the original bill. For *quaestus*, see Andreau 2007.

production sometimes stemmed from apparently unrelated political measures. This characterizes the effects of the fourth-century *Lex Ovinia*, discussed in chapter 5. As best we can tell, this law's establishment of the regular censorial *lectio senatus* related to the need to draw and maintain the boundaries of the emerging senatorial aristocracy. That is, political, not economic or urban, concerns were the primary driving force. As I have argued, the more regular censorship which resulted will have facilitated the censor's oversight of urban infrastructure as may be gleaned in our record of the office, but this effect is best viewed as unrelated to the law's background and passage.

In this case, the question of motivation in Roman Republican economic change remains elusive, but the period emerges nonetheless as one of undeniable and broadly significant development for Rome's urban economy: the organization of urban production changed dramatically during the fourth and third centuries BCE. This is visible in the way Romans set about building monumental urban architecture, with all that complex process implied. Over the long run of the Mid-Republican period, Rome began to display several institutional aspects of the urban economy familiar from the city of the Late Republic and Empire. In many ways, the roots of that great capital should be recognized in the period when Romans first engaged in the conquest of Italy and the Mediterranean.

APPENDIX 1

COST ANALYSIS OF ASHLAR MASONRY IN VOLCANIC TUFF

Since most energetics analyses of Roman architecture have thus far focused on Imperial monuments of brick, mortar, and marble, it will be useful to set out the technical evidence for work rates involved in the production of *opus quadratum* in volcanic tuff as was typical of Mid-Republican Roman construction. This appendix also discusses labor figures for earthen construction techniques relevant to the building of the walls' *agger*.

I. EXTRACTION

There is no direct evidence for quarrying rates in the Republican period. At Plaut. *Capt.* 721–38, a slave is assigned to quarry "eight blocks in a day," but material and dimensions are unreported, making this of little help. For comparative costs of quarrying volcanic tuff, DeLaine mostly relies on Pegoretti, while Abrams draws from timed experiments using stone and metal tools. Beneficially, the primary building stone of the Mayan culture studied by Abrams is a welded pyroclastic tuff similar in composition and specific density to Central Italian tuff. Adjustments here include a 5-hour maximum workday for reasons discussed elsewhere, and the assumption of a 45% loss of material in the quarrying process.[1] According to DeLaine, one skilled quarryman and two unskilled laborers produce 0.75 m^3 of lithoidal tuff in a 5-hour day.[2] According to Abrams, one skilled quarryman and an unspecified number of unskilled laborers produce 1,500 kg of tuff with steel tools, and 1,000 kg of tuff with stone tools. Roman iron tools fall in the middle in terms of efficiency, so let us use a figure of 1,250 kg/day. Applying these two estimates to the standard-sized *tufo giallo* blocks in the wall (specific weight = 1,520 kg/m^3; typical block volume = 0.41 m^3; typical block weight = 623.20 kg) and

1. Abrams 1994: 46.

2. DeLaine 2001: 258, converting from 1.2 m^3 in an 8-hour day.

accommodating the loss of 45% of the quarried material, DeLaine's figures suggest that skilled quarrymen produce 1 block of *tufo giallo* in a 5-hour day (1 block/m-day = 0.75 m^3 of material at a rate of 0.75 m^3/PD). Thus, Abrams' figure provides almost the exact same result (1.09 blocks/PD = 1,149.45 kg of material at a rate of 1,250 kg/m-day). The convergence is especially welcome considering the estimates were formed through different methods.

Applying the same figures to *tufo del Palatino* (specific weight = 1,890 kg/m^3; typical block volume = 0.12 m^3; typical block weight = 226.80 kg), DeLaine's figures suggest a quarryman produces 3.41 blocks per day, each block needing 0.22 m^3 of material by volume, while Abrams' figures suggest 3.01 blocks per day, each block needing 415.80 kg of material by weight. The model ultimately follows DeLaine's suggestion that each quarry team consists of 1 skilled worker assisted by 2 unskilled laborers, but uses Abrams figures as they allow for somewhat less efficient quarrying tools than those used by Pegoretti's nineteenth-century quarrymen. In any case, the difference is negligible.

2. PROCESSING

The blocks of tuff destined for the wall went through limited post-quarry processing. The process of quarrying involved cutting out channels downward from the rock surface to the desired dimensions, then freeing the block from the rock surface with wedges, and therefore blocks came from the quarry already finished on five of six sides.[3] In order to achieve a roughly flat surface, the mason employed a hand-axe or a mallet and pointed chisel.[4] There is, unfortunately, wide variety in the estimations of cost for this stage of the process. Abrams' rates using steel tools extrapolate to a cost of 3.12 PD skilled labor for each block of *tufo giallo*, and 0.93 PD skilled labor for each block of *tufo del Palatino*.[5] Using Pegoretti's lower rate for rough finishing of volcanic tuff (4.33 man-hours/m^2 of surface) and extrapolating for a 12-hour day, a block of *tufo giallo* requires 1.0 PD, while a block of *tufo del Palatino* needed 0.43 PD.[6] The difference is hard to reconcile, and for the sake of the model I employ Pegoretti's lower costs to counteract the general hypothesis of the walls' effects. All this masonry work is considered skilled.

3. TRANSPORT

Transport costs break down into (a) the effort to bring material downriver to Rome, and (b) the movement of material from the port to various building sites. For the purposes

3. Cifani 2008: 237.

4. Säflund 1998: 118.

5. Abrams (1994: 48) assigns a cost to the basic facing of tuff blocks involving cutting five flat sides with stone tools of 1 m^3/11.60 PD, and with steel tools of 1 m^3/7.73 PD.

6. Pegoretti 1869: 539. Five sides of a *tufo giallo* block had a surface area of 2.81 m^2; five sides of a *tufo del Palatino* block had a surface area of 1.18 m^2.

of the model, I consider transport costs unskilled because, while specialized transporters are well known in the Empire, their skills were not related to building per se.[7]

a. Material was loaded onto boats at a cost of 0.1 PD skilled + 0.1 PD unskilled per cubic meter of stone.[8] Transport of *tufo giallo* from the Grotta Oscura quarries to Rome was accomplished by river; Strabo reports this practice for the import of stone from local quarries in his own time (5.3.11). Several moles found in the Tiber and dating from later periods in antiquity may have replaced earlier structures dating as far back as the fourth century. One such candidate is the Tor di Nona mole at the northern bend of the Tiber around the Campus Martius, as that structure includes Republican masonry.[9] It is also possible that rafts were unloaded by drawing them onto the sloping river bank.

   To calculate the requirements for shipping the requisite blocks of *tufo giallo* 30 km downstream[10] from quarries to offloading sites in the city, I summarize the extended discussion of Volpe: a typical wooden raft could carry a load of 12 tons amounting to about 18 blocks of *tufo giallo*.[11] Ostia's small boats needed to be hauled up river, but the downstream trip could be made by the current. The course of the Tiber from Grotta Oscura to Rome is navigable in all seasons and flows at a rate of 3.3 km/hr. Thus, one raft trip took 9 hours, or roughly one day, with another day to tow the boat back upstream. At a minimum, such boats needed 3-man crews, so that each loaded voyage (= 18 blocks or 54,955 boat trips) required 6 PD along with a yoke of oxen for the return trip.
b. The movement of material within Rome was complicated by the likelihood that blocks of tuff were brought to some intermediate staging area, where their quality was assayed for a significant period of time before their distribution to individual worksites. In later periods, the Campus Martius served as a staging ground for the movement of stone from the Tiber port to various building sites, particularly for marble.[12] In building the circuit walls, if the longest distance stone would travel from there was about 2 km, and the shortest trip about 0.5 km, the average distance each block traveled was 1.5 km. It is not certain that blocks were moved over that distance with the benefit of draught animals

7. For specialized transport labor, see Martin 2002: 161; Bernard 2013a: 113–14.

8. DeLaine 2001: 258.

9. Volpe 2014: 66; Le Gall 2005: 228–30.

10. This is the distance by river, while the overland route was shorter; Volpe 2014: 65.

11. Volpe (2014: 65) also considers the possibility of flat-bottom boats such as were used on the Tiber into the early twentieth century that could carry loads of up to 180 blocks; cf. Casson 1965: 32 n. 10.

12. Haselberger 1994; Maischberger 1997; Bernard 2013a: 111.

and wheeled vehicles, and sleds are attested for the movement, for example, of the statue of Magna Mater onto the Palatine.[13] However, wheeled vehicles are known at this date in Central Italy, and the use of draught animals appears, for example, in Diodorus' description of the building project of Dionysius I of Syracuse. Ox-carts also appear in later Roman depictions of building sites. The use of carts would reduce the total (human) labor cost. Roman sources suggest that the typical ox-pulled cart with one team of oxen was limited in its capacity to little more than 500 kg, which would entail that each cartload moved a single block of *tufo giallo* per trip.[14] The rate of travel for a heavily laden cart was slow, perhaps no more than 1.7 km/hour over level terrain. In that case, counting the return trip at twice the speed, the round trip for each block required a driver and an oxen team a total 1.5 hours per block of *tufo giallo*. Since this is less strenuous than moving the block by human effort alone, I use a 12-hour day = 0.13 PD per block. The fact that almost all of the journeys necessary to bring stone from port to building site involved some elevation gain implies that this calculation underrepresents the real cost.

Tufo del Palatino needed to be moved significantly shorter distances as it was quarried within the general confines of the city, and many quarries were situated along urban routes.[15] The longest trip from extraction to construction was on the order of the 1 km, for example, from the Vigna Quirini quarries to the Esquiline *agger*, or from the Santa Bibiana quarries to the Aventine.[16] Other quarry zones on the Palatine itself, or perhaps near Termini station, were located in close proximity to the walls themselves. I use a mean distance of 0.5 km trip for each load of two lighter blocks of *tufo del Palatino* at the same 1.7 km/hour loaded and 3 km/hour unloaded speed, thus giving a labor cost of about 0.5 hours per two blocks for a driver, or 0.02 PD per block and a yoke of oxen. In all cases, the model incorporates additional loading costs of 0.1 PD skilled + 0.1 PD unskilled per cubic meter of stone, per trip.

4. ASSEMBLY

Since the wall relied on dry ashlar masonry, the essential manpower cost was raising, maneuvering, and placing blocks into position. Along with the excavation of the walls'

---

13. Verg. *Georg.* 1.164; Bernard 2013a: 108.

14. DeLaine 1997: 108.

15. 2008: 234–35.

16. No archaic *tufo del Palatino* quarries are definitively identified in the city's southern extent; see Cifani 2008: 234.

foundation trench, the *agger* and *fossa* required significant excavation and mounding of excavated earth.

a. *Ashlar masonry*. Estimates vary widely for the cost of placing ashlar blocks in a masonry wall, and further replicative study would be especially beneficial. Abrams' figure of 0.8 skilled PD per m^3 is low but is based upon typically smaller-module stonework and low-elevation structures. In the context of Mediterranean architecture, estimates tend to be higher: Mertens reports that, while working with the anastylosis of the theater at Metapontum, five workmen could place a single block in one day.[17] Pakkanen extrapolates from wages recorded in the Epidaurus building accounts to suggest a figure of 4 PD per m^3 for less-finished ashlar, with an even split between skilled and unskilled labor.[18] These figures from the Greek world may be high for our requirements: tuff was lighter by volume and softer than *poros* limestone, and the roughly hewn finish of the Roman walls with minimal anathyrosis suggests minimal cost in finishing or drafting. DeLaine suggests a formula for the placement of tuff blocks by which it takes three skilled workers and four unskilled workers $0.02 + 0.033d + 0.02h + 0.01$ PD per ton of material, where d is mean distance and h is mean height that each block is moved.[19] I have already incorporated horizontal movement (d) into the model, and I assign a mean lifting distance of half the walls' reconstructed height (5.1 m). That works out to 0.13 PD per ton of material, for 3 + 4 workers. However, lifting and moving were especially arduous tasks, so the figure should be converted to a 5-hour day, producing a rate of 0.31 PD per ton, or 0.39 PD skilled and 0.52 PD unskilled per block of *tufo giallo*. *Tufo del Palatino* needed to be raised to a lower average height (1.38 m), producing a rate of 0.14 PD per ton, or 0.06 PD skilled plus 0.08 unskilled per block.
b. *Excavating, moving, and mounding earth*. Earth moving is perhaps the best-studied of all basic activities involved in architectural production, but the use of comparative data is hindered by the importance of technology and soil type.[20] While the best approximation of excavating Roman soil types can be found in Pegoretti's nineteenth-century building manual, Pegoretti assumes the use of a shovel. Some notion of the difference implied by this technology can be found in Erasmus' timed experiments: workers using only a digging stick excavate 2.6 m^3 in a 5-hour workday, while the same workers using metal shovels excavate 7.2 m^3.[21] Republican agricultural treatises mention various farm implements

17. Mertens 2002: 251.

18. Pakkanen 2014.

19. DeLaine 2001: 258.

20. Xie et al. 2015.

21. Abrams 1994: 47; Erasmus 1965: 285.

similar to a shovel and more or less equipped for excavation.[22] However, literary evidence is difficult to categorize: the *pala* known to Varro (*Ling.* 5.134) and Cato (*Agr.* 4, 6) was for piercing and turning earth in preparation for sowing, but Livy's uses the word to refer to an instrument for excavation (3.26.9: *fossam fodiens palae innixus*). The *rutrum* was a digging implement according to Varro (*Ling.* 5.134) and Festus (Paul. Fest. 321L), but not according to Cato (*Agr.* 37.2). In later periods, the tool for excavating earth for building an *agger* was a pointed implement called a *ferramentum*, as specified by Vegetius (*Mil.* 3.8.8).

It is impossible to say what digging technology existed in the fourth century, but let us assume for the sake of minimizing cost that some sort of implement was available. Pegoretti differentiates excavation rates by depth, with deeper excavation proving more difficult and more costly. To simplify and minimize the calculation further, I use his basic rate and his average soil type, with a worker in a 5-hour workday breaking apart and shoveling up 3.6 m^3 of earth, or 0.28 PD unskilled labor per m^3.[23] As the *fossa* reached a greater depth, the productivity rate would have declined.

Since the *agger* and *fossa* were built complementary to each other, it is likely that soil excavated from the *fossa* was used for the *agger*, and indeed Strabo's description of the walls' construction suggests that Romans themselves believed as much (5.3.7). In my reconstruction, the excavated earth of the *fossa* and the walls' foundations accounts for only 18% of the total *agger* volume, but let us minimize our calculation by assuming that earth for the *agger* was not moved from a further distances than an adjacent *fossa*; there is no reason to assume the illogical importation of earth over long distances. Thus, the *agger* required that earth be loaded into baskets at a rate of 0.05 PD/m^3 and moved an average 46 m at a rate of 0.29 PD/m^3.[24] The energy expended in both tasks suggests an optimal 5-hour workday. Earthwork assembly thus costs 0.34 PD/m^3 unskilled labor, a rate in line with comparative evidence.[25] I disregard smoothing and other finishing processes that would have added additional labor costs, but were not necessary to the *agger*'s function.

22. White 1967: 17–29.

23. While 53% of work was at the 3.6 m^3/day rate, 47% was at the 2.6 m^3/day rate.

24. Pegoretti 1869: 154 assumes the use of wheeled vehicles, but I use the calculation of 0.32 hour/m^3 per 10 linear meters in Erasmus 1965, which replicates moving rates with tumplines; 46 m is the average distance from the *fossa*'s midpoint to the *agger*'s midpoint on the Esquiline.

25. Similar figures from Richardson 2014: 305 attested at Babylonian Larsa.

APPENDIX 2

CATALOG OF PUBLIC BUILDING PROJECTS, 396–168 BCE

This appendix collects all Mid-Republican building projects attested either archaeologically or through literary sources and arranges them in a chronological manner from earliest to latest. Readers will find fuller discussion of various monuments in standard topographical reference works, particularly the *LTUR*, although a few of the monuments found here are not listed there. In particular, those building projects known archaeologically but not necessarily through textual sources are included here along with monuments only known from literary sources, thus giving a more complete urban picture. Another aspect differentiating this catalog is its chronological arrangement, which is meant to give a sense of the city's diachronic development.

Listed in figure A2.1 are all known *public* building projects completed between 396 and 168 BCE insofar as these are construction projects, which drew upon the finances of the Republican state.[1]

There are also a few monuments built by private citizens which seem to have held public status.[2] In light of Polybius' comment at 6.13.3 that the Roman senate's largest domestic expenditure constituted both new building *and* the maintenance of public works, I include all known repair projects, indicated with an asterisk before their entry (*). Those roads and aqueducts whose construction entailed at least some work at Rome itself are listed, even if much of the building effort took place beyond the city. By contrast, I exclude projects such as the Pons Mulvius, which was entirely in the *suburbium*,

1. The *lacus Iuturnae* and also perhaps a significant rebuilding of the Temple of the Castores may have been initiated in 168 BCE, but are thought to have been completed a few years later; cf. Steinby 2012b: 54.

2. E.g. the Temple of Juno Lucina, the shrines of Pudicitia Patricia and Pudicitia Plebeia, and the Fornix Scipionis. The third-century tomb of Fabricius noted at Cic. *de leg.* 2.53; Plut. *q. Rom.* 79 may have been on public land but does not seem to have been considered in any way a public monument, and is therefore excluded.

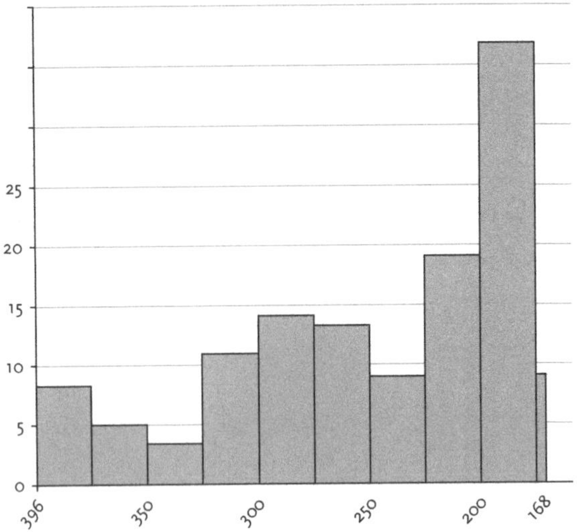

FIGURE A2.1 Public building projects by quarter century, 396–168 BCE.

or censorial construction in the colonies, as attested especially in the early second century BCE. As close as possible, buildings are arranged by their date of dedication. Archaeologically attested projects are dated according to the nearest quarter century, with their date ranges given in parentheses; thus, a structure dated to the mid-third century will be listed under 250 BCE, a late fourth century monument under 300 BCE, and so forth. For this reason, the accompanying histogram (figure A2.1) divides building projects by a quarter-century timespan.[3] Projects with identifiable archaeological remains are indicated with a dagger (†).

In collecting this information, the catalog takes a cautious approach toward making connections between archaeological and textual evidence, and this sometimes leads to multiple entries for monuments whose toponyms others will associate with particular archaeological sites. This will be most evident in the inclusion of the temples of Largo Argentina, which are particularly difficult to identify for reasons discussed in the introduction. Since evidence independent of the literary tradition provides approximate dates for when the Largo Argentina temples were built and restored, however, the structures are listed along with separate notices of the toponyms sometimes assigned to each of them. This perhaps adds additional entries to the catalog; however, the highly fragmentary record of construction during this period has undoubtedly led to the loss of numerous other construction projects, and this catalog still is only likely to represent a portion of actual public building at Rome over this time.

3. As discussed in the introduction, the existence of regular annalist notices for the period after the Second Punic War may partly explain the rise in attested projects on the right side of the graph.

Since many of these entries are based upon highly fragmentary evidence, collecting data of this nature implies a number of choices. Readers more familiar with the scholarly literature will no doubt notice some of these choices in the catalog, but it is also worth spelling several out. In regard to chronology, I do not accept an early fourth-century phase of any significance at the sanctuary of Sant' Omobono, and I follow recent study of the complex in assigning the initial construction of the platform and twin temples to the early fifth century, and thus outside the scope of this study.[4] I do accept that some building activity, likely repair or enlargement, took place in the Vestals' complex in the mid-fourth century as archaeologists now suggest. However, the idea that there are two phases, and not just one, belonging to the fourth century seems to rest on an excessively complex reading of the archaeology.[5] Meanwhile, some cults are attested only by literary sources, while the evidence cannot sufficiently support the existence of a physical temple by the Mid-Republic, and so they are excluded.[6] Likewise omitted are some sanctuaries known to exist by the Mid-Republic, but whose initial construction cannot be securely placed in that period.[7] While I include some *prodigia* such as lightning strikes, whose descriptions seem to imply subsequent repair efforts[8], I exclude references to singular dedications such as the many attested statues in the Forum or sculptural additions to the Capitolium in this period (e.g., Liv. 10.23.12, 35.10.11, 35.41.10, 40.52.7). Several houses are said to be leased or otherwise granted by the state to private individuals. In the case of a *domus aedificata* for Antiochus IV in 190 BCE, this seems to imply public construction, but other instances are less clear and therefore excluded.[9]

---

4. See above p. 63.

5. Arvanitis 2010: 54–59 for the two fourth-century phases. What he calls a second phase consists of a trench "dallo stesso andamento e delle medesime dimensioni" but with no architectural remains.

6. Excluded are cults of Feronia and Juno Curritis in the Campus Martius.

7. Minerva and Luna on the Aventine; Hercules Custos in the Campus Martius; Febris on the Quirinal.

8. Destruction of the doors of the Temple of Luna and sculpture on the Capitolium and in the Circus during a major thunderstorm in 182, described by Liv. 40.2, are not included, since repairs to the Capitolium and Circus are otherwise attested in the following decade, even if not explicitly in relation to storm damage.

9. Ambiguous cases include a house of M.' Curius Dentatus (cf. *de vir. illustr.* 33.10; *LTUR* V.74 [Palombi]; Steinby 2012a: 14); and a house of Ariarathes (cf. Liv. 42.19.6 with Briscoe 2012: 217; the corrupt manuscript of Livy has misled Steinby 2012a: 103).

Number	Name	Date BCE	Location	Procedural	Primary sources	Secondary sources
1	*Temple of Mater Matuta	396	*Forum boarium*	consular vow	Liv. 5.19.6, 23.7; Plut. *Cam.* 5.	*LTUR* II.281–85 (Pisani Sartorio); Cifani 2008: 168–73; Coarelli 1988: 205–18; Diffendale et al. 2016; Holloway 1994: ch. 5; Ioppolo 1971–72; Ioppolo 1989; Pisani Sartorio 1989; Pisani Sartorio and Virgili 1979; *RMR* 100–103; Sommella 1968; Virgili 1977; Virgili 1988.
2	Temple of Iuno Regina	392	Aventine	consular vow, dictatorial dedication	Liv. 5.21–23, 31.3; Dion. Hal. 13.3; Plut. Cam. 6	*LTUR* II.125—6 (Andreussi); Ziolkowski 1992: 76–77.
3	†Substructure on Capitoline	388	Capitoline		Liv. 6.4.12	
4	Temple of Mars	388	Via Appia	*IIviri*	Liv. 6.5.8	*LTUR* Suburbium IV.44–45 (Coarelli); *MAR* 165 (Borbonus); Dubbini 2016; Ziolkowski 1992: 101–4.
5	Altar of Aius Locutius	after 390	Palatine		Liv. 5.32.6, 5.50.5; Varro in Gell. 16.17.2; Cic. *Div.* 1.45.101, 2.32.69 (Aius Loquens); Plut. *Cam.* 14.3–4, 30.4	*LTUR* I.29 (Aronen); Wiseman 2004: 169–70
6	†Circuit Wall	378	city circuit	censorial	Liv. 6.32.1–2	See ch. 4
7	Temple of Iuno Lucina	375	Cispian	private dedication	Plin. *NH* 16.235	*LTUR* III.122–23 (Gianelli); MAR 153 (Thein); Andrews 2015: 47–53
8	*Repair, Temple of Saturn	381 or 370	Forum	*tribunus militum ex s.c.*	Cn. Gellius (FRH 14 F27)	*LTUR* IV 234 (Coarelli)

9	†*Repair, streets in Velia	375–350	Velia			Panella et al. 2014: 180–81.
10	Temple of Concordia	367	Forum	vowed by Camillus, built by senatorial vote	Ov. *Fast.* 1.637–44; Pl. *Cam.* 42.4–6	*LTUR* I.319 (Ferroni); *MAR* 97 (Norena); Momigliano 1942; Gasparri 1979: 16; Maetzke 1991: 69; Ziolkowski 1992: 22–24; Heyworth 2011
11	*Repair of circuit wall	353	city circuit	work done by soldiers	Liv. 7.19–20.9	Cornell 1995: 62 n. 11
12	*Repair of Temple of Apollo Medicus	353	Campus Martius		Asc. in Cic. *Orat.* 90; Liv. 7.20.9	Ciancio Rossetto 1997–98; Delbrück 1907–12; Viscogliosi 1996
13	†Temple of Vesta	(350)	Forum			Argento in Arvanitis, ed. 2010: 74–88; Arvanitis in Arvanitis, ed. 2010: 54–59; Scott 2009: 21–23
14	†Temple of Iuno Moneta	343	Capitoline		Liv. 6.20.13, 7.28.4–6; Ov. *Fast.* 6.183–85	*MAR* 153–54 (Thein); Meadows and Williams 2001; Tucci 2005; Von Hesberg 1995: 77–80; Wiseman 1979; Ziolkowski 1992: 71–73
15	Rostra	338	Forum	triumphal	Liv. 8.14.12; Plin. *NH* 34.20; Varr. *DLL* 5.155	Coarelli 1983 vol. II, 237–57

Number	Name	Date BCE	Location	Procedural	Primary sources	Secondary sources
16	Circus Maximus, wooden carceres	329	Circus Maximus		Liv. 8.20.2; Varro *DLL* 5.153	Humphrey 1986: ch. 4
17	Column of Maenius	318	Forum	censorial	Festus 120 L	*LTUR* I.301–302 (Torelli); Coarelli 1983 vol. II, 39–42
18	Maeniana	318	Forum	censorial	Festus 120 L; Isid. *Orig.* XV.3.11	Coarelli 1983 vol. II, 143–45
19	Tabernae Argentariae	318	Forum	censorial	Liv. 9.40.16; Varro frg. *apud* Non. 853 L	*LTUR* V.10–12 (Papi); Coarelli *FR* II 201–8
20	†*Restructuring and paving of the *comitium*	318	Forum	censorial		Coarelli 1983 vol. I, 119–38; Carafa 1998; Amici 2004–2005
21	†Via Appia to Capua	312		censorial	Str. 5.3.6; Stat. *Silv.* 2.1.12; Liv. 9.29.5–7; Diod. Sic. 20.36.2; *Insc.It.* XIII.3, 79; Front. *Aq.* 5; Eutr. 2.9; Auct. *De vir. ill.* 34	*LTUR* V.130–33 (Patterson); Della Portella 2003; Quilici 1997; Quilici 2004; Spera and Mineo 2004; Wiseman 1970
22	†Aqua Appia	312		censorial	Diod. 20.36; Eutr. 2.9.2; Fest. 23 L; Front. *De Aq.* 5, 18, 65; Liv. 9.29; Pompon. *Dig.* 2.2.36	*LTUR* I.61–62 (Mucci); Ashby 1935: 49–54; Pace 1983: 118–19, tb. 4; Van Deman 1973: 23–28

23	Via Tiburtina/ Valeria	307		censorial	Liv. 9.43.25	*LTUR* V.146–47 (Patterson); Wiseman 1970: 139–40
24	Shrine (*aedicula*) of Concordia	304	Volcanal	aedilician	Liv. 9.46.6; Plin. *NH* 33.17–19	*LTUR* I.320–21 (Ferroni); Momigliano 1942; Ziolkowski 1992: 219–34 (on the resulting legislation)
25	Temple of Salus	302	Quirinal	consular vow, censorial dedication	Liv. 9.43.25, 10.1.9	*LTUR* IV.229–230 (Coarelli); Ziolkowski 1992: 144–48
26	†Temple of Portunus	(300)	*Forum boarium*			*LTUR* IV.151–52 (Buzzetti); Adam 1994; Coarelli 1988: 115–27; Colini and Buzzetti 1986; Ruggiero 1991–92; Del Buono 2009; Diosono 2016
27	†*Repair or enlargement, Velia sanctuary	(300)	Velia below Palatine			Panella et al. 2014: 184–86.
28	†Lower chamber of the *Carcer*/ *Tullianum*	c. 300	NW Forum		Liv. 26.27, 39.22.10; Varr. *DLL* 5.151	*LTUR* I.236–37 (Coarelli); Coarelli 1983 vol II, 62–80; Blake 1947: 35; Catalano, Fortini, and Nanni 2001; Frank 1924: 45–46; Le Gall 1939
29	†Temple C, *Largo Argentina*	(after 300)	Campus Martius			*MAR* 54–55 (Kondratieff); Coarelli 1981; Jackson and Marra 2006; Kajanto 1981; Marchetti Longhi 1932; Strazzulla 1981; Ziolkowski 1986; 1992: 25–28, 94–97

Number	Name	Date BCE	Location	Procedural	Primary sources	Secondary sources
30	Sanctuary of Pudicitia Patricia	before 296	*Forum boarium*	private dedication?	Liv. 10.23.3; Fest. 282L	*LTUR* IV.168–69 (Coarelli); Palmer 1974: 121–23
31	*Paving of the Via Appia from the Porta Capena to the Aedes Martis	296	Via Appia	aedilician	Liv. 10.23.11–12	
32	Sanctuary (*sacellum*) to Pudicitia Plebeia	296	Vicus Longus, Quirinal	private dedication	Liv. 10.23.6–10, Fest. 270L	*LTUR* IV.168–69 (Coarelli); Palmer 1974: 123–25
33	†Temple of Victoria	294	SW Palatine	aedilician vow, consular dedication	Liv. 10.33.9	Cecamore 2002: 120–28; Pensabene 1998: 26–34; Ziolkowski 1992: 172–79
34	Temple of Iuppiter Stator	after 294	Palatine	consular vow	Liv. 10.36.11, 10.37.15–16	*LTUR* V.271 (Arce); Cecamore 2002: 129–44; Coarelli 1983: 21–33; Tomei 1993; Wiseman 2004; Ziolkowski 1992: 87–91
35	Temple of Bellona	c. 293	*Forum boarium*	consular vow	Liv. 10.19.17; Ov. *Fast.* 6.201–8; Plut. *Sull.* 32; Serv. *ad Aen* 9.52; *CIL* I2 192 = *ILS* 54	*LTUR* I.190–92 (Viscogliosi); Coarelli 1967–68; De Nuccio 1995; Ziolkowski 1992: 18–19

36	Temple of Quirinus	293	Quirinal	consular vow and dedication	Liv. 8.20.8, 10.46.7; Varr. *DLL* 5.52; Paul. Fest. 303 L	*LTUR* IV.185–86 (Coarelli); *MAR* 214 (Dumser); Carafa 1993; Manca di Mores 1982–83; Ziolkowski 1992: 139–44
37	Temple of Venus Obsequens	291	Aventine	aedilician vow, consular dedication	Liv. 10.31.9; Serv. *ad Aen.* 1.720	*LTUR* VI.118 (Papi); *PA* 217; Ziolkowski 1992: 167–71
38	Temple of Aesculapius	after 291	Tiber Island	vowed by prescription of Sybilline Books	Liv. 2.5.4, 10.47.6–7, *Per.* 11.2; *de vir. ill.* 22.1–3; Val. Max. 1.8.2	*LTUR* I.21–22 (Degrassi); *MAR* 42 (Harmansah); Brucia 1990: 63–113; Di Manzano, Cecchelli, and Milella 2006–7; Richardson 1992: 4
39	Temple of Iuppiter Victor	c. 290	Quirinal	consular vow	Ov. *Fast.* 4.621; Liv. 10.29.14	*LTUR* III.161 (Coarelli); *MAR* 157 (Dumser); Cecamore 2002: 99–114; Coarelli and Grenier 1986; Ziolkowski 1992: 91–94
40	Temple of Fors Fortuna	289	unknown	consular vow	Liv. 10.46.14	*LTUR* Suburbium III.270–71 (Coarelli); *MAR* 126–27 (Harmansah); Coarelli 1992; Fiorelli 1888; Iacopi 1940; Lanciani and Visconti 1884; Palmer 1981; Richardson 1992: 154–55; Savage 1940
41	Temple of Summanus	278–275	Circus Maximus		Ov. *Fast.* 6.731; Cic. *de Div.* 1.16; Liv. *Per.* 14	LTUR IV.385–86 (Coarelli); Ziolkowski 1992: 154–55

Number	Name	Date BCE	Location	Procedural	Primary sources	Secondary sources
42	*Repair to Temple of Salus and circuit wall?	275	Quirinal		Oros. 4.4.1	*LTUR* IV.229–30 (Coarelli)
43	Temple of Consus	272?	Aventine		Fest. 228 L	LTUR I.321–22 (Andreussi); Ziolkowksi 1992: 24–25
44	†Anio Vetus	270		censorial *ex manubiis;* completed by *IIviri*	Cic. *Att* 4.15.5; Front. *De Aq.* 6, 13; *De Vir. Ill.* 33	*LTUR* I.44–45 (Mari); Andrews and Bernard 2017; Ashby 1935: 54–87; Mari 1991; Gautier di Confiego 2007: 231; Pace 1983: 121–24; Santa Maria Scrinari 1979; Van Deman 1934: 58–59
45	Temple of Tellus	after 268	Oppian	consular vow	Suet. *Gram.* 15; Serv. *ad Aen.* 8.361; Flor. 1.14.2; Val. Max. 6.3.1b; Dion. Hal. 8.79.3	*LTUR* V.24–25 (Coarelli); *MAR* 241 (Dumser); Palombi 1997b: 140–68; Ziolkowski 1992: 155–62
46	Temple of Pales	267	Palatine	consular vow	Florus 1.15	*LTUR* IV.50–51 (Aronen); Ziolkowski 1992: 126; Richardson 1992: 282
47	†Monuments and altars in front of Temples of Fortuna and Mater Matuta	c. 264	*Forum boarium*, Sant' Omobono	consular	epigraphic	*RMR* 103–4 n. 89 (Torelli); Coarelli 1988: 214–15; Degrassi 1963–64; Ioppolo 1963–64; Marcando 1963–64: 43–63; Torelli 1968; Diffendale 2016; Diffendale et al. 2016
48	Temple of Vortumnus or Vertumnus	after 264	Aventine	consular vow?	Fest. 228 L	*LTUR* V.213–14 (Aronen); Torelli 1968; Ziolkowski 1992: 183–85

49	Column of C. Duillius	260	Forum	triumphal	Liv. *Per.* 17; Plin. *NH* 34.11.20; Quint. *Inst.* 1.7.12, 6; Serv. *ad Virg. Georg. 3.29*	*LTUR* I.309 (Chioffi); Degrassi in *Insc. Ital.* XIII 3 nn. 13, 69; Pietilä-Castrén 1987: 30
50	Temple of Tempestas or Tempestates	259	Via Appia, beyond Porta Capena	consular vow ?	*CIL* VI 1286–87 = *ILS* 3 = *ILLRP* 310; Ov. *Fast.* 6.191–94; *Not. Regio* I	*LTUR* V.26–27 (Ziolkowski); Coarelli 1996a, 208–9; Ziolkowski 1992: 162–64
51	Temple of Ianus	258	*Forum holitorium*	consular vow	Tac. *Ann.* 2.49; Fest. 358 L; Serv. *ad Aen.* 7.607	Crozzoli Aite 1981
52	Column of M. Aemilius Paullus	254	Capitoline	triumphal	Liv. 42.20.1	*LTUR* I.307–8 (Palombi)
53	†*Repair and paving of the *comitium*	252	Forum			Coarelli 1983 vol. I, 126, vol. II, 19–20, 55–56; 19–20, 55–56; Carafa 1998; Amici 2004–2005; Amici et al. 2007
54	†Temple A, Largo Argentina	(250)	Campus Martius			Marchetti Longhi 1936; Coarelli 1981: 16–18; Ziolkowski 1992: 25–28
55	Temple of Fides	c. 250	Capitoline		Cic. *Nat. Deor.* 2.61; Plin. *NH* 35.100; Cato *ap.* Cic. *Off.* 3.104; *CIL* XVI *26*	*MAR* 123–24 (Thein); Reusser 1993; Ziolkowski 1992: 28–31

Number	Name	Date BCE	Location	Procedural	Primary sources	Secondary sources
56	*Repair to circuit wall	249		repair after lightning strike?	Ps.-Acron. 5.8	
57	†Temple of Spes	247	*Forum holitorium*		Cic. *de Leg.* 2.28; Tac. *Ann.* 2.49.2	Crozzoli Aite 1981; Frank 1924; Ziolkowski 1992: 52–54
58	†Via Aurelia	241		censorial?	none	*LTUR* V.133–34 (Patterson); Gatti 1940; Carnabuci 1992; Fentress 1984; Wiseman 1970: 133–34
59	Temple of Iuturna	c. 241	Campus Martius		Serv. *ad Aen.* 12.139; Ov. *Fast.* 1.463–64	*LTUR* III.162–63 (Coarelli); *MAR* 158 (Kondratieff); Richardson 1992: 228; Ziolkowski 1992: 94–97; Pietilä-Castrén 1987: 44–48
60	Clivus Publicius	241–238	Aventine	aedilician	Liv. 26.10.6, 27.37.15; Fest. 276 L; Varr. *DLL* 5.158; Ov. *Fast.* 5.297ff.; Tac. *Ann.* 2.49	*LTUR* I.284 (Coarelli); *MAR* 90 (Borbonus and Haselberger)
61	Temple of Flora	241–238	Aventine	aedilician	Fest. 276 L; Ov. *Fast.* 5.277–94; Plin. *NH* 18.286; Tac. *Ann.* 2.49; Vell. 1.14.8	*LTUR* II.253–54 (Papi); *MAR* 124 (Borbonus); Orlin 1997: 101; Ziolkowski 1992: 31–34
62	Temple of Iuppiter Libertas	238	Aventine	aedilician vow	Liv. 24.16.19; Paul. Fest. 108 L	*LTUR* III.144 (Andreussi); MAR 63–64 (Haselberger); Ziolkowski 1992: 85–87

63	Shrine (*delubrum*) of Fons	231	Campus Martius	consular vow?	Cic. *Nat. Deor.* 3.52; *Insc. Ital.* 13.2	*LTUR* II.256–57 (Coarelli)
64	†*Rebuilding of Vestal complex	241–221	Forum	reconstruction after fire	Liv. *Per.* 19.14; Plin. *NH* 7.141; Cic. *Sen.* 30, 61; Val. Max. 8.13.2	Scott 1993; Scott 2009; Arvanitis 2010
65	Via Flaminia	220		censorial	Liv. *Per.* 20; Plut. *q. Rom.* 66	*LTUR* V.135–37 (Patterson); Ashby and Fell 1921; Messineo and Carbonara 1993; Wiseman 1970: 138
66	Circus Flaminius	220	Campus Martius	censorial	Liv. 3.54.15, 3.63.7, *per.* 20; Plut. *q. Rom.* 66; Vitr. 9.8.1	*LTUR* IV.160–61 (Coarelli); *LTUR* I.269–72 (Viscogliosi); *MAR* 86–87 (Pettrucioli); Gatti 1960; 1961; Tucci 1997; Wiseman 1974
67	Taberna in the Compitum Acilii	by 219	Carinae		Plin. *NH* 29.12	*LTUR* I.314–15 (Pisani Sartorio)
68	*Repair of wall	217	circuit wall	dictator and *magister equitum*	Liv. 22.8.6	Säflund 1932: 212, 250–52
69	Temple of Concordia *in arce*	216	Capitoline	Praetorian vow, *locatio* and dedication by *IIviri*	Liv. 22.33.7–8; 23.21.7	*LTUR* I. 321 (Gianelli); Momigliano 1942; *MAR* 96–97 (Thein); Richardson 1978; 1992: 98
70	Piscina Publica	before 215	Aventine		Liv. 23.32.4; Fest. 232L; Amm. Marc. 17.4.14	*LTUR* IV.93–94 (Coarelli); *MAR* 190–91 (Dumser and Haselberger)

Number	Name	Date BCE	Location	Procedural	Primary sources	Secondary sources
71	Temple of Mens	215	Capitoline	vowed on prescription of Sybilline books; dedicated by *IIviri*	Liv. 22.9.9–10, 22.10.10, 23.31.9, 23.32.20	*MAR* 79–80 (Thein); Rodriguez Almeida 1991
72	Temple of Venus Erucina	215	Capitoline	vowed on prescription of Sybilline books; dedicated by *IIviri*	Liv. 22.9.9–10, 22.10.10, 23.31.9, 23.32.20	*MAR* 79–80 (Thein); Rodriguez Almeida 1991
73	†*Repair of Temple of Spes	212	*Forum holitorium*	*IIIviri* appointed after fire	Liv. 24.47.15–16; 25.7.5–6	Crozzoli Aite 1981: 104
74	†*Repair of Temples of Fortuna and Mater Matuta	212	*Forum boarium*, Sant' Omobono	*IIIviri* appointed after fire	Liv. 24.47.15–16; 25.7.5–6	*LTUR* II.281–85 (Pisani Sartorio); Marcando 1963–64: 35–46; Pisani Sartorio and Virgili 1979: 41
75	*Repair of walls	212	Area of *porta Carmentalis*	*Vviri*	Liv. 25.7.5	Säflund 1932: 212–13, 250–52
76	Tomb of Cn. and P. Cornelius Scipio	c. 211		senatorial	Silius Italicus 13.659–60	*LTUR* IV.285 (Coarelli); Steinby 2012, 15 n. 8

77	†*Tabernae Argentariae Novae	209	Forum	censorial repair after fire	Liv. 3.48.5, 26.27.2, 27.11.16, 40.51.5	*LTUR* IV.10–12 (Papi); Freyberger et al. 2007: 495
78	*Quinque Tabernae	209	Forum	censorial repair after fire	Liv. 26.27.2, 27.11.16. Fest. 336 L	*LTUR* IV.266–67 and V.12–13 (Papi); Coarelli 1983 vol. II, 153; Richardson 1992: 375
79	†*Atrium Regium	209	Forum	censorial repair after fire	Liv. 26.27.2, 27.11.16	Carettoni 1948; Freyberger et al. 2007; Gaggiotti 1985; Zevi 1991
80	†*Macellum	209	Argiletum	censorial repair after fire	Val. Max. 3.4.4; Liv. 26.27; 27.11.6	De Ruyt 1983; Tortorici 1991
81	Temple of Honos et Virtus	205	Near *porta Capena*	two consular vows	Cic. *Nat.Deor.* 2.61; Liv. 25.40.3, 27.25.7–9, 29.11.13; Val. Max. 1.1.8	*LTUR* III.31–33 (Palombi); *MAR* 138–39 (Kondratieff); Ziolkowski 1992: 58–60
82	Via circa foros publicos	204	Circus area	censorial	Liv. 29.37.2	*MAR* 259 (Borbonus and Dumser); Coarelli *FB* 12, 31, 34, fig. 20; Ziolkowski 1994: 190–91
83	*Repair of Clivus Publicius	203	N Aventine	aedilician after fire?	Liv. 30.26.5	
84	*Repair to Temples of Summanus and Vulcan	197	Circus Maximus	repair after lightning strike?	Liv. 32.29	

Number	Name	Date BCE	Location	Procedural	Primary sources	Secondary sources
85	Fornices of Stertinius	196	*Forum boarium*	*ex manubiis* by a *privatus*	Liv. 33.27	De Maria 1988: 45–48, 262–63; Shatzman 1972: 168 n. 112; Coarelli 1988
86	Fornix of Stertinius, Circus Maximus	196	Circus Maximus	*ex manubiis* by a *privatus*	Liv. 33.27	De Maria 1988: 45–48, 262–63; Shatzman 1972: 168 n. 112
87	Temple of Faunus	194	Tiber Island	aedilician	Liv. 33.42.10; Liv. 34.53.4; Ov. *Fast.* 2.193–94; Vitr. 3.2.3	*LTUR* II.242 (Degrassi); Richardson 1992: 148
88	†Temple of Iuno Sospita	194	*Forum holitorium*	consular vow, censorial dedication	Liv. 32.30.10, 34.53.3	*LTUR* III.128–29 (Coarelli); Briscoe 1973, 227; Crozzoli Aite 1981, 62–64
89	Temple of Fortuna Primigenia	194	NE Quirinal	consular/*IIvir*	Liv. 29.36.8, 34.53.5–6; Vitr. 3.2.2	*LTUR* II.285–86 (Coarelli); *MAR* 248 (Dumser); Pietilä-Castrén 1987: 67; Ziolkowski 1992: 40–45
90	†Temple of Iuppiter, Tiber Island	194	Tiber Island	praetorian/ consular/ *IIvir*	Liv. 34.53.7, Vitr. 3.23, Ov. *Fast.* 1.293–94; *Insc. Ital.* 13.2.2, p. 111; *CIL* VI 379	*LTUR* V.270 (Di Manzano and Giustini); *MAR* 155 (Harmansah); Brucia 1990: 48–55; Di Manzano, Cecchelli, and Milella 2006–7: passim esp. 126, 134; Richardson 1992: 221, 406
91	†*Repair and enlargement of Atrium Libertatis	194	Forum	censorial	Cic. *Att.* 4.17.7; Fest. 277 L; Liv. 25.7.12, 34.44.5, 37.3.8, 43.16.13; Tac. *Hist.* 1.32	*LTUR* I.133–35 (Coarelli); *MAR* 59–60 (Dumser); Amici 1995–96; Castagnoli 1946; Meneghini 2009: 19, 43–48; Purcell 1993; Rodriguez Almeida 1981: 109–10; Ulrich 1993, esp. 57–58

92	*Repair and enlargement of Villa Publica	194	Campus Martius	censorial	Liv. 34.44.5	*MAR* 273 (Gallia); Richardson 1976a
93	Porticus extra portam Trigeminam emporio ad Tiberim adiecto	193	Emporium area	aedilician	Liv. 35.10.12	*MAR* 118–19 (Harmansah); Cozza and Tucci 2006; Rodriguez Almeida 1984: 24–33
94	Porticus ab porta Fontinali ad Martis aram	193	Campus Martius	aedilician	Liv. 35.10.12	*MAR* 201 (Gallia); Carafa 1993; Coarelli 1997: 251
95	†Temple of Veiovis inter duos lucos	192	Foot of Capitoline	consular vow	Liv. 31.21.12, 34.53.7, 35.41.8; Plin. *NH* 16.216; Gell. *NA* 5.12.8–10; Vitr. 4.8.4; Ov. *Fast.* 3.430	Briscoe 1973 *Comm. ad Liv.* 31.21.12; Colini 1943; Ogilvie 1965: 345
96	Porticus inter lignarios	192	Emporium area	aedilician	Liv. 35.41.9–10	*LTUR* IV.126–27 (Pisani Sartorio); Rodriguez Almeida 1984: 29–33; Palmer 1976–77: 141, 151

Number	Name	Date BCE	Location	Procedural	Primary sources	Secondary sources
97	†Temple and Precinct of Magna Mater including Clivus Victoriae	191	SW Palatine	ordered by Delphic oracle; initiated by censors ex *S.C.*; dedication by *pr. urbanus*	On the temple phases: Liv. 29.37.2, 36.36.3–5. On the ludi: Cic. *Har.* 24	*MAR* 163–64 (Dumser); Coarelli 1977: 12; Pensabene 1998: 34–50
98	Temple of Iuventas	191	Aventine	consular vow, censorial *locatio*, *IIvir* dedication	Liv. 36.36.5–6; Plin. *NH* 29.57	*LTUR* III.163 (Coarelli)
99	House of Antiochus	190		granted by state	Ascon. *in Pis.* 13	*LTUR* II.133 (Papi); Marshall 1985: 105–6
100	Fornix of Scipio	190	Capitoline	private dedication	Liv. 37.3.7	*LTUR* II.266–67 (Coarelli); De Maria 1988: 263 n. 52, fig. 37
101	*Repair of Temple of Iuno Lucina	190?	Cispian	repair after lightning strike	Liv. 37.3.2; Obseq. 1	Andrews 2015: 51
102	†*substructio* super Aequimelium in Capitolio	189	Capitoline	censorial	Liv. 38.28.3	*LTUR* I.20–21 (Pisani Sartorio); Coarelli 1977; Colini 1940: 227–28

103	†Water system overhaul	184	throughout Rome	censorial	Liv. 39.44.4–5; Dion. Hal. 3.67.5	*LTUR* III. 166–67 (Guiliani)
104	Basilica Porcia	184	NW Forum	censorial	Liv. 39.44.7; Plut. *Cat. Mai.* 19.3; Ascon. *Mil.* 2.34	*LTUR* I.187 (Steinby); Coarelli 1983 vol. II, 60–62
105	Temple of Venus Erycina	181	Outside Porta Collina	consular vow, *IIvir* dedication	Liv. 40.34.4; App. *BC* 1.93	*LTUR* V.114–16 (Coarelli); *MAR* 255 (Dumser)
106	†Temple of Pietas	181	*Circus flaminius*	consular vow, *IIvir* dedication	Liv. 40.34.4–6; Val. Max. 2.5.1	*LTUR* IV.86 (Ciancio Rossetto); Ciancio Rossetto 1994–95; Vitti 2010
107	†Basilica Fulvia (later Aemilia)	179	Forum	censorial	Liv. 40.51.5	*LTUR* I.173–75, 183–87 (Bauer); Carettoni 1948; Coarelli 1983 vol. II, 135–38, 203–7; Fuchs 1956; Freyberger 2007; Gaggiotti 1985; Steinby 2012: 54–6
108	Tabernae in the Forum Piscatorium/ Macellum	179	*Argiletum*	censorial	Liv. 40.51.5	*LTUR* II.312–13 (Morselli and Pisani Sartorio)
109	Porticus (and Forum?) extra Portam Trigeminam	179	*Forum boarium*	censorial	Liv. 40.51.6	Coarelli 1988: 16 nn. 12, 25; Lyngby and Pisani Sartorio 1968–69; Rodriguez Almeida 1984: 29–33

Number	Name	Date BCE	Location	Procedural	Primary sources	Secondary sources
110	Porticus post navalia et ad fanum Herculis	179	*Forum boarium*	censorial	Liv. 40.51.6	*MAR* 208 (Haselberger); Coarelli 1988: 16 nn. 12, 25; Lyngby and Sartorio 1968–69; Coarelli 1997: 345–62; Torelli 2006: 588
111	Porticus post Spei ad Tiberim et ad aedem Apollonis Medici	179	*Forum boarium*	censorial	Liv. 40.51.6	Coarelli 1988: 16 nn. 12, 25; Lyngby and Sartorio 1968–69
112	†Pons Aemilius	179 or earlier	Tiber	censorial	Liv. 40.51.4; Plut. *Num.* 9.6	Blake 1947; Coarelli 1988, 139–47
113	Temple of Diana	179	*Circus Flaminius*	consular vow, censorial dedication	Liv. 39.2.8; 40.52	*LTUR* II.14 (Viscogliosi); *MAR* 101 (Kondratieff); Coarelli 1968
114	Temple of Lares Permarini	179	Campus Martius	praetorian/ censorial	Liv. 40.52.4–7; Macrob. *Sat.* 1.10.10	*LTUR* III.174–75 (Coarelli); *MAR* 160 (Kondratieff); Marquez and Gutierrez Deza 2006
115	†Work on Tiber Port	179	Tiber Bank, Forum Boarium	censorial	Liv. 40.51.4	*LTUR* IV.155–56 (Buzzetti); *MAR* 246 (Haselberger); Coarelli 1988: 38–39; Colini 1980; Colini and Buzzetti 1986; Del Buono 2009

116	Whitening columns of Temple of Iuppiter Capitolinus	179	Capitoline	censorial *locatio*	Liv. 40.51.4	
117	†*Enlargement and repair of Temple of Portunus	after 179	*Forum boarium*			Del Buono 2009
118	†Temple of Hercules et Musarum	c. 179	*Circus Flaminius*	dedication *ex manubiis*	Plin. 35.66; Cic. *Arch.* 27; Ov. *Fast.* 6.797–812; Eumenius *Paneg.* 9.7.3 [Bährens]; Serv. *ad Aen.* 1.8; Macr. *Sat.* 1.12.16	*LTUR* III.17–19 (Viscogliosi); Coarelli 1997: 452–84; Gianfrotta 1985; Martina 1981; Richardson 1977
119	†Temple D, Largo Argentina	(175)	Campus Martius			*LTUR* III.136–38 (Manacorda); *MAR* 56 (Kondratieff); Coarelli 1981 18–19; *PA* 294; Richardson 1992: 219
120	†*Repair to Temple of Apollo Medicus	(175)	Campus Martius	aedilician	*CIL* I² 2675c = *ILRRP* 45	Ciancio Rossetto 1997–98; Viscogliosi 1996
121	*Paving of urban streets	174	throughout Rome	censorial	Liv. 41.27.5	

Number	Name	Date BCE	Location	Procedural	Primary sources	Secondary sources
122	Scaena Aedilibus Praetoribusque	174	Forum?	censorial	Liv. 41.27.5	Giuliani and Verduchi 1987: 95–103
123	†*Paving of Clivus Capitolinus	174	Forum to Capitoline	censorial	Liv. 41.27.7	*LTUR* I.280–81 (Wiseman)
124	Porticus ab aede Saturni in Capitolium	174	Forum to Capitoline	censorial	Liv. 41.27.7	
125	†*Work in the Emporium	174	Emporium area	censorial	Liv. 41.27.7–9	*MAR* 118–19 (Harmansah); Cozza and Tucci 2006; Gatti 1934; Mocchegiani Carpano 1985; Richardson 1976b; Rodriguez Almeida 1984
126	*Porticus and roadwork inside the *Porta Trigemina*	174	*Forum boarium*	censorial	Liv. 41.27.9	

127	*Repair and construction in the Circus Maximus	174	Circus Maximus	censorial	Liv. 41.27.6	*LTUR* I.272–77 (Ciancio Rossetto); Humphrey 1986: 70–71
128	Temple of Fortuna Equestris	173	Campus Martius	proconsular vow, *locatio* by *IIviri,* censorial dedication	Liv. 40.40.10, 40.44.8–10, 42.3.1–11, 42.10.5; Vitr. 3.3.2	*MAR* 127 (Kondratieff); Coarelli 1981: 31
129	†Basilica Sempronia	169	Forum	censorial	Liv. 44.16.8–11	*LTUR* I.187–88 (Iacopi); Carettoni and Fabbrini 1961

BIBLIOGRAPHY AND ABBREVIATIONS

ABBREVIATED WORKS

Journal abbreviations follow the conventions of the *American Journal of Archaeology*, while ancient authors and corpora of ancient documents follow those of the *Oxford Classical Dictionary*. Other works cited with frequency are abbreviated as follows:

Crise et transformation = aa.vv. *Crise et transformation des sociétés archaïques de l'Italie antique au Ve siècle av. J.-C.: Actes de la table ronde organisée par l'École française de Rome et l'Unité de recherches étrusco-italiques associée au CNRS* (Rome, 19–21 novembre 1987). Rome: École française de Rome.

FRH = Cornell, T., ed. 2013. *The Fragments of the Roman Historians*. 3 vols. Oxford: Oxford University Press.

HN = Rutter, N. K. 2001. *Historia Nummorum Italy*. London: British Museum Press.

HRR = Peter, H. W. G. 1883. *Historicorum Romanorum Reliquae*. 2 vols. Leipzig: Teubner.

Imag.Ital. = Crawford, M., ed. 2011. *Imagines italicae: A corpus of Italic inscriptions*. 3 vols. London: Institute of Classical Studies, University of London.

Insc.Ital. = Degrassi, A. 1937. *Inscriptiones Italiae*, vol. 13, fasc. 3. Rome: Libreria dello stato

LTUR = Steinby, E. M., ed. 1993–2006. *Lexicon Topographicum Urbis Romae*. 6 vols. Rome: Quasar.

MAR = Haselberger, L., dir., with D. G. Romano, et al. 2002. "Mapping Augustan Rome." *JRA* Suppl. 50. Portsmouth, RI: JRA.

Mommsen *StR* = Mommsen, T. 1871–88. *Römische Staatsrecht*. 3 vols. Leipzig: Herzel.

PA = Platner, S. B. Revised by T. Ashby. 1929. *A Topographical Dictionary of Ancient Rome*. London: Oxford University Press.

RMR = Aa.vv. 1977. *Roma medio repubblicana. Aspetti culturali di Lazio nei secoli IV e III a.C.* Rome: L'Erma di Bretschneider.

RRC = Crawford, M. H. 1976. *Roman Republican Coinage*. 2 vols. Cambridge: Cambridge Press.

RRCH = Crawford, M. H. 1969. *Roman Republican Coin Hoards*. London: Royal Numismatic Society.

RS = Crawford, M. H., ed. 1996. *Roman Statutes*. London: Institute of Classical Studies, University of London.

WORKS CITED

Aberson, M. 1994. *Temples votifs et butin de guerre dans la Rome républicaine*. Mainz: Zabern.

Abrams, E. M. 1989. "Architecture and Energy: An Evolutionary Perspective." *Archaeological Method and Theory* 1: 47–87.

———. 1994. *How the Maya Built their World: Energetic and Ancient Architecture*. Austin, TX: University of Texas Press.

Adam, J.-P. 1994. *Le temple de Portunus au Forum Boarium*. Rome: École Française de Rome.

Adam, A.-M. and A. Rouveret. 1988. *Guerre et sociétés en Italie aux Ve et IVe siècles avant J.-C.: Les indices fournis par l'armement et les techniques de combat: Table-ronde E.N.S. Paris, 5 mai 1984*. Paris: Presses de l'École Normale Supérieure.

Adamesteanu, D. 1956. "Le fortificazioni ad aggere nella Sicilia centro-meridionale." *RendLinc* 11: 358–72.

Afzelius, A. 1942. *Die römische Eroberung Italiens* (340–264 v. Chr.). Aarhus: Muksgaard.

Allen, R. C. 2001. "The Great Divergence in European Wages and Prices from the Middle Ages to the First World War." *EEH* 38: 411–47.

———. 2009. "How Prosperous Were the Romans? Evidence from Diocletian's Price Edict (AD 301)." In *Quantifying the Roman Economy: Methods and Problems*, edited by A. Bowman and A. Wilson, 327–46. Oxford: Oxford University Press.

Amandry, M. 2008. "Le dépôt monétaire de Monte Bibele." In *Tra mondo celtico e mondo italico. La necropoli di Monte Bibele: Atti della tavola rotonda, Roma, 3–4 ottobre 1997*, edited by D. Vitali and S. Verger, 293–98. Bologna: Università di Bologna, Dipartimento di archeologia.

Amici, C. M. 1995–96. "Atrium Libertatis." *RendPont* 65: 295–321.

———. 2004–2005. "Evoluzione archittetonica del Comizio a Roma." *RendPont* 77: 351–79.

Amici, C. M. et al. 2007. *Lo scavo didattico della zona retrostante la Curia (Foro di Cesare): campagne di scavo 1961–70.* Rome: Bonsignori.

Ammerman, A. J. and D. Filippi. 2004. "Dal Tevere all'Argileto: nuove osservazioni." *BullCom* 105: 7–28.

Ammerman, A. J. et al. 2008. "The Clay Beds in the Velabrum and the Earliest Tiles in Rome." *JRA* 21: 7–30.

Ampolo, C. 1976. "L'abitato del Palatino." In *Civiltà Lazio primitive, Palazzo delle Esposizioni, Roma*, edited by M.O. Acanfora, 173–75. Roma: Multigrafica.

———. 1976–77. "Demarato. Osservazione sulla mobilità arcaica." *DialArch* 9–10: 333–45.

———. 1980. "Le condizioni materiali della produzione. Agricoltura e paesaggio agrario." *DialArch* 2: 15–47.

———. 1983. "La storiografia su Roma arcaica e i documenti." In *Tria Corda. Scritti in onore di A. Momigliano*, edited by E. Gabba, 9–26. Como: Edizioni New Press.

———. 2013. "Il problema delle origini di Roma rivisitato: concordismo, ipertradizionalismo acritico, contesti. I." *AnnPisa* 5/1: 217–84.

Anderson, J. C. 1997. *Roman Architecture and Society*. Baltimore, MD: Johns Hopkins University Press.

Andreau, J. 1987. *La vie financière dans le monde romaine: Les métiers de manieurs d'argent (IVe siècle av. J.-C.–IIIe siècle ap. J.-C.). BEFAR* 265. Rome: École française.

———. 2007. "Remarques sur le *quaestus*." In Andreau and Chankowski, eds., 233–52.

———. 2012. "Quelques observations sur les macella." In *Tout vendre, tout acheter. Structures et équipements des marchés antiques. Actes du colloque d'Athènes, 16–19 juin 2009*, edited by V. Chankowski and P. Karvonis, 75–82. Paris: Diffusion De Boccard.

Andreau, J. and V. Chankowski, eds. 2007. *Vocabulaire et expression de l'économie dans le monde antique*. Bordeaux: *Ausonius Editions.*

Andrews, M. M. 2014. "A Domus in the Subura of Rome from the Republic through Late Antiquity." *AJA* 118.1: 61–90.

———. 2015. "Matron, Meretrix, Madonna: An Archaeology and Urban History of the Subura Valley and Cispian Hill in Rome from the Republic through the Early Middle Ages." PhD diss., University of Pennsylvania.

Andrews, Margaret M. and S. G. Bernard. "Urban development at Rome's Porta Esquilina and San Vito over the long durée." *JRA* 30.1: 100–21.

Arvanitis, N., ed. 2010. *Il Santuario di Vesta: la casa delle vestali e il tempio di Vesta; VIII sec. a.C.–64 d.C. rapporto preliminare. Workshop di archeologia classica Qauderni 3.* Rome: Serra.

Ashby, T. 1924. "La via tiberina e i territori di Capena e del Soratte nel periodo romano." *MemPontAcc* 1, 2: 129–75.

———. 1935. *The Aqueducts of Ancient Rome*. Oxford: Clarendon.

Ashby, T. and R. A. Fell. 1921. "The Via Flaminia." *JRS* 11: 125–90.

Astolfi, F., L. Cordischi, and L. Attilia. 1989–90. "Viale del Monte Oppio—via delle Terme di Traiano. Communicazioni preliminari." *BullCom* 93: 59–67.

Aurigemma, S. 1961–62. "Le Mura Serviane, l'aggere e il fossato all'esterno delle mura, presso la nuova stazione ferroviaria di Termini in Roma." *BullCom* 78: 19–36.

Aylward, W. 2009. "Lewises in Hellenistic and Roman Building at Pergamon." In *Bautechnik im antiken und vorantiken Kleinasien: Internationale Konferenz, 13–16 Juni 2007 in Istanbul*, edited by M. Bachmann, 309–22. Instanbul: Ege Yayinlari.

Badian, E. 1965. "The Date of Cleitarchus." *Proceedings of the African Classical Association* 8: 5–11.

———. 1966. "The Early Roman Historians." In *Latin Historians*, edited by T. A. Dorey, 1–38. London: Routledge and Kegan Paul.

———. 1983. *Publicans and Sinners: Private Enterprise in the Service of the Roman Republic*. 2nd ed. Ithaca: Cornell Press.

Bagnall, R. and B. Frier. 1994. *The Demography of Roman Egypt*. Cambridge: Cambridge University Press.

Bairoch, P. 1988. *Cities and Economic Development: From the Dawn of History to the Present*. Translated by C. Braider. Chicago: University of Chicago Press.

Banaji, J. 2010. *Theory as History: Essays on Modes of Production and Exploitation*. Leiden/Boston: Brill.

Bandini, G. and R. Pennino. 2008. "Interventi di restauro e di conserazione recentemente compiuti sulle Mura Serviane alla Stazione Termini." In Barbera and Magnani Cianetti, eds., 116–27.

Bang, P. 2008. *The Roman Bazaar: A Comparative Study of Trade and Markets in a Tributary Empire*. Cambridge: Cambridge University Press.

Barbera, M. 2008. "Le mura di epoca regia e repubblicana: prove di sintesi." In M. Barbera and M. Magnani Cianetti, eds., 12–29.

Barbera, M., M. Pentiricci, G. Schingo, L. Asor Rosa, and M. Munzi. 2005. "Ritrovamenti archeologici in piazza Vittorio Emanuele II." *BullCom* 106: 302–37.

Barbera, M. and M. Magnani Cianetti, eds. 2008. *Archeologia a Roma Termini, Le Mura Serviane e l'area della Stazione: scoperte, distruzioni, e restauri*. Rome: Ministero per i beni e le attività culturali, Soprintendenza speciale per i beni archeologici di Roma.

Barbieri-Low, A. 2007. *Artisans in Early Imperial China*. Seattle: University of Washington Press.

Barbina, P., L. Ceccarelli, F. Dell'era and F. Di Gennaro. 2009. "Il territorio di Fidenae tra V e II secolo a.C." In *Suburbium II. Il suburbia di Roma dalla fine dell'età monarchia all nascità del sistema delle ville (V-II secolo a.C.)*, edited by V. Jolivet, C. Pavolini, M. A. Tomei, and R. Volpe, 325–45. Rome: École française de Rome.

Barker, G. and T. Rasmussen. 1998. *The Etruscans*. Oxford/Malden: Blackwell Publishers

Barker, S. and B. Russell. 2012. "Labour Figures For Roman Stone-Working: Pitfalls and Potential." In *Archeologia della costruzione III, Les chantiers de construction de l'Italie et des provinces romaines*, edited by S. Camporeale, H. Dessales and A. Pizzo, 83–94. Madrid & Mérida: Anejos de Archivo Español de Arqueología.

Baron, C. 2013. *Timaeus of Tauromenium and Hellenistic Historiography*. Cambridge/ New York: Cambridge University Press.

Barresi, P. 2003. *Province dell'Asia Minore: costo dei marmi, architettura pubblica e committenza*. Rome: L'Erma di Bretschneider.

Beck, H. and U. Walter. 2005. *Die Frühen Römischen Historiker*. 2 vols. Darmstadt: Wissenschaftliche Buchgesellschaft.

Bellen, H. 1985. *Metus Gallicus, Metus Punicus: zum Furchmotiv in der römischen Republik*. Stuttgart: Steiner.

Belloni, G. G. 1993. *La moneta romana: Società, politca, cultura*. Rome: La Nuova Italia.

Beloch, K. J. 1926. *Römische Geschichte: Bis zum Beginn der punischen Kriege*. Berlin: De Gruyter.

Benvenuti, V. 2002. "The Introduction of Artillery in the Roman World: Hypothesis for a Chronological Definition Based on the Cosa Town Wall." *MAAR* 47: 199–207.

Bernard, S. 2009. "Alexandrian Tainiai and Land Traffic Patterns: A Note on the Amnesty Decree (P. Teb. I 5) in Light of the Topography." *ZPE* 168: 265–70.

———. 2010. "Pentelic Marble in Architecture at Rome and the Republican Marble Trade." *JRA* 23: 25–54.

———. 2012. "Continuing the Debate on Rome's Earliest Circuit Walls." *PBSR* 20: 1–44.

———. 2013a. "The Transport of Heavy Loads in Antiquity: Lifting, Moving, and Building in Ancient Rome." In *Perspektiven der Spolienforschung: Spoliierung und Transposition*, edited by C. Marcks-Jacobs, S. Altekamp, P. Seiler, 99–122. TOPOI Berlin Studies in the Ancient World. Berlin: De Gruyter.

———. 2013b. "Politics and Public Construction in Republican Rome." *JRA* 26: 513–19.

———. 2014–15. "Varro and the Development of Roman Topography from Antiquity to the Quattrocento." *MAAR* 59/60: 161–79.

———. 2016a. "Workers in the Roman Imperial Building Industry." In *Work, Labour, and Professions in the Roman World*, edited by C. Laes and K. Verboven, 62–86. Leiden: Brill.

———. 2016b. "Debt, Land, and Labor in the Early-Republican Economy." *Phoenix* 70.3–4: 317–38.

———. forthcoming a. "Aedificare res damnosissima: Building and Historiography in Livy Books V–VI." In *Omnium Monumentum Annalium: Historicaal Writing and Historical Evidence in Republican Rome*, edited by C. J. Smith and K. Sandberg. Leiden: Brill.

———. forthcoming b. "Political Competition and Economic Exchange in Mid-Republican Rome." In *Competition in Classical Antiquity*, edited by C. Damon and C. Pieper. Leiden: Brill.

———. forthcoming c. "The Social History of Early Roman Coinage." *JRS* 107.

Bernard, S. G. and S. Pike. 2015. "Isotopic Analysis of Marble from the Stoa of Attalos in the Athenian Agora and the Hellenistic Quarries of Mount Pentelikon." *ASMOSIA* XI: 451–60.

Bertol, A. and K. Farac. 2012. "Aes Rude and Aes Formatum: A New Typology Based on the Revised Mazin Hoard." *VAMZ* 3, XLV: 93–113.

Bidwell, P. 1996. "The Exterior Decoration of Roman Buildings in Britain." In *Architecture in Roman Britain*, edited by P. Johnson with I. Haynes, 19–29. CBA Research Report 94. York: Council for British Archaeology.

Bilic, T. 2015. *Coins of the Roman Republic in the Archaeological Museum of Zagreb*. Zagreb: Tiskara Zelina.

Bispham, E. 2006. "Coloniam Deducere: How Roman was Roman Colonization in the Middle Republic." In *Greek and Roman Colonization: Origins, Ideologies, and Interactions*, edited by G. Bradley and J. P. Wilson, 73–160. Swansea: University of Wales Press.

———. 2007. *From Ausculum to Actium. The Municipalization of Italy from the Social War to Augustus*. Oxford: Oxford University Press.

Blake, M. E. 1947. *Ancient Roman Construction in Italy from the Prehistoric Period to Augustus: A Chronological Study Based in Part upon the Material Accumulated by the Late Dr. Esther Boise Van Deman*. Washington, DC: Carnegie Institute.

Blanck, H. 1966–67. "Zwei Corneliersarkophage." *RM* 73: 72–77.

Bodel, J. 1994. "Graveyards and Groves: A Study of the Lex Lucerina." *AJH* Supp. 11. Cambridge, MA: AJH.

Bogaert, R. 1968. *Banques et banquiers dans les cités grècques*. Leyden: Sijthoff.

Bonamici, M. 1989. "Il marmo lunense in epoca preromana." In *Il Marmo nella civiltà romana: la produzione e il commercio: mostra/seminario, Carrara, maggio-giugno 1989, Museo del marmo*t, edited by E. Dolci, 83–114. Carrara: Internazionale marmi e macchine.

Boni, G. 1900. "Esplorazioni nel Comizio." *NSc*: 295–340.

———. 1910. "Mura urbane tra la Porta Collina e la Viminale." *NSc* 7: 495–513.

Boren, H. C. 1983. "Studies Related to the *stipendium militum*." *Historia* 32: 427–60.

Bourdin, S. 2012. *Les peuples de l'Italie préromaine: identités, territoires et relations inter-ethniques en Italie centrale et septentrionale, VIIIe-Ier s. av. J.-C.* Rome: École française.

Boyance, P. 1940. "Aedes Catuli." *MEFRA* 57: 64–71.

Boyd, T. D. and M. H. Jameson. 1981. "Urban and Rural Land Division in Ancient Greece." *Hesperia* 50.4: 327–42.

Bradley, G. 2017. "The Rome of Tarquinius Superbus: Issues of Demography and Economy." In Lulof and Smith, eds., 123–33.

Bradley, K. 1984. "The Vicesima Libertatis: Its History and Significance." *Klio* 66: 175–82.

Brands, G. 1988. *Republikanische Stadttore in Italien*. Oxford: BAR Intl. Series 458.

Braudel, F. 1982. *Civilization and Capitalism, 15th to 18th Century. Vol. 2: The Wheels of Commerce*. New York: Harper & Row.

Breglia, L. 1952. *La prima fase della coniazione romana dell'argento*. Rome: P. & P. Santamaria.

———. 1965–67. "A proposito dell'aes signatum." *AIIN* 12–14: 269–75.

Bringmann, K. 2003. "Zur Überlieferung und zum Entstehungsgrund der *lex Claudia de nave senatoris*." *Klio* 85(2): 312–21.

Briquel, D. 2008. *La prise de Rome par les gaulois: lecture mythique d'un événement historique*. Paris: Presses de l'Université Paris-Sorbonne.

Briscoe, J. 1973. *A Commentary on Livy Books XXXI–XXXIII*. Oxford: Clarendon Press.

———. 2008. *A Commentary on Livy Books 38–40*. Oxford: Oxford University Press.

———. 2012. *A Commentary on Livy Books 41–45*. Oxford: Oxford University Press.

Broadhead, W. 2001. "Rome's Migration Policy and the So-called Ius Migrandi." *Cahiers du Centre Gustav Glotz* 12: 69–89.

Brown, F. E. 1961. *Roman Architecture*. New York: G. Braziller.

———. 1967. "New Soundings in the Regia: The Evidence for the Early Republic." *Les origines de la république romaine. Entretiens Hardt* 13: 47–60.

Brucia, M. A. 1990. "Tiber Island in Ancient and Medieval Rome." PhD diss., University of Michigan.

Brunt, P. A. 1966. "The Roman Mob." *Past & Present* 35: 3–27.

———. 1971. *Italian Manpower, 225 B.C.–A.D. 14*. Oxford: Clarendon Press.

———. 1980. "Free Labour and Public Works at Rome." *JRS* 70: 81–100.

Bruun, C. 1989. "Statio aquarum." In *Lacus Iuturnae I. Lavori e studi di archeologia pubblicati dalla soprintendenza archeologica di Roma 12*, edited by E. M. Steinby, 127–47. Rome: De Luca.

———. 1991. *The Water Supply of Ancient Rome: A Study of Roman Imperial Administration*. Helsinki: Societas Scientiarum Fennica.

———. 2000. " 'What every man in the street used to know.' M. Furius Camillus, Italic Legends, and Roman Historiography." In Bruun, ed., 41–68.

———. 2010. "Water, Oxygen Isotopes, and Immigration to Ostia-Portus." *JRA* 23.1: 109–32.

———, ed. 2000. *The Roman Middle Republic: Politics, Religion, and History, c. 400–133 B.C. Papers from a conference at the Institutum Romanum Finlandiae, September 11–12, 1998. Acta Instituti Romani Finlandiae* 23.

Buccellato, A., P. Catalano, and W. Pantano, "La site et la nécropole de Castellaccio." In *Rome et ses morts: L'Archéologie funéraire dans l'Occident romaine*, edited by P. Catalano, J. Scheid, and S. Verger, 14–19. Dijon: Les Dossiers d'Archéologie 330.

Buccellato, A and F. Coletti. 2014. "Attivitàdi cava dal suburbio sud ovest di Roma." In *Arqueologìa de la Construcciòn IV. Las canteras en el mundo antiguo: sistemas de explotaciòn y procesos productivos, Actas del congreso (Padova 2012)*, edited by J. Bonetto, S. Camporeale, and A. Pizzo, 105–14. Merida: Taravilla.

Buranelli, S. and R. Turchetti. 2003. *Sulla Via Appia da Roma a Brindisi: le fotografie di Thomas Ashby: 1891–1925*. Rome: L'Erma di Bretscheinder.

Burford, A. M. 1969. *The Greek Temple Builders of Epidauros*. Liverpool: Liverpool University Press.

Burnett, A. M. 1977. "The Coinages of Rome and Magna Graecia in the Late Fourth and Early Third Centuries B.C." *SNR* 56: 92–121.

———. 1978. "The First Roman Silver Coins." *QT* 7: 121–42.

———. 1989. "The Beginnings of Roman Coinage." *AIIN* 36: 33–64.

———. 1998. "The Romano-Campanian Silver." In aa.vv. *La monetazione romano-campana. Atti del X Convegno del Centro internazionale di studi numismatici, Napoli 18–19 giugno 1993*, 19–47. Rome: Istituto numismatico.

———. 2006. "Reflections on the San Martino in Pensilis Hoard." *RN* 162: 37–50.

———. 2012. "Early Roman Coinage and Its Italian Context." *In The Oxford Handbook of Greek and Roman Coinage*, edited by W. E. Metcalf, 297–315. Oxford/New York: Oxford University Press.

Burnett, A. M. and M. H. Crawford, "Coinage, Money, and Mid-Republican Rome: Reflections on a Recent Book by Filippo Coarelli." *AIIN* 60: 231–65.

Burnett, A. M. and A. McCabe. 2016. "An early Roman Struck Bronze with a Helmeted Goddess and an Eagle." In *Nomismata, Studi di Numismatica antica offerti ad Aldina Cutroni Tusa per il suo novantatresimo compleanno*, edited by L. Sole and S. Tusa, 238–74. Ragusa: Edizioni Storia e Studi Sociali.

Burnett, A. M. and M. C. Molinari. 2015. "The Capitoline Hoard and The Circulation of Silver Coins in Central and Northern Italy in the Third Century B.C." In *FIDES, Contributions to Numismatics in Honour of Richard B. Witschonke*, edited by P. G. van Alfen, G. Bransbourg, and M. Amandry, 21–126. New York: American Numismatic Society.

Caballos Rufino, A. 2006. *El nuevo bronce de Osuna y la politica colonizadora romana*. Sevilla: Universidad de Sevilla.

Cam, M.-T., ed. 1995. *Vitruve, de l'Architecture, Livre VII*. Collection Budé. Paris: Les Belles Lettres.

Cama, A. 2011. "L'Appia prima dell'Appia." In Manacorda and Santangeli Valenzani, eds., 265–68.

Cancellieri, M. 1990. "Il territorio pontino e la via Appia." *ArchLaz* 10: 61–71.

Caprioli, F. 2011. "Forma architettonica, linguaggio decorativo e committenza della prima fase del tempio B di largo Argentina." In *Tradizione e innovazione. L'elaborazione del linguaggio ellenistico nell'architettura romana e italica di età tardo repubblicana*. Studi Miscellenai 35, edited by E. La Rocca and A. D'Alessio, 89–107. Rome: L'Erma di Bretschneider.

Capogrossi Colognesi, L. 2012. *Padroni e contadini nell'Italia repubblicana*. Rome: L'Erma di Bretschneider.

Carafa, P. 1993. "Il tempio di Quirino. Considerazioni sulla topografia arcaica del Quirinale." *ArchClass* 45.1: 119–43.

———. 1998. "Il Comizio di Roma dalle origini all'età di Augusto." *BullCom* Suppl. 5. Rome: Bretschneider.

———. 2017. "Latinorum sibi maxime gentem conciliabat (Livio I 49,8). Trasformazione dei paesaggi di Roma e del Lazio dal Regno del Superbo all'inizio della repubblica." In Lulof and Smith, eds., 57–70.

Carandini, A. 1979. *Schiavi e padroni nell'Etruria romana. La villa di Settefinestre dallo scavo alla mostra*. Bari: De Donato editore.

Carandini, A. and P. Carafa, eds. 1995. *Palatium e Sacra Via, 1. Prima delle mura, l'età delle mura e l'età delle case arcaiche. BA* 34.

Carbonara, A. and G. Messineo. 1996. "Via Tiberina: Nuove acquisizioni lungo il tracciato della antica via. II. Cave antiche presso il Fosso di Grotta Oscura e il Fosso del Drago." *BullCom* 97: 294–97.

Carrelli, C. W. 2004. "Measures of Power: The Energetics of Royal Construction at Early Classic Copan." In *Understanding Early Classic Copan*, edited by E. E. Bell, M. A. Canuto, and R. J. Sharer, 113–27. Philadelphia: University of Pennsylvania Press.

Carettoni, G. 1948. "Esplorazioni nella Basilica Emilia." *NSc* 8.2: 111–28.

Carettoni, G. and L. Fabbrini. 1961. "Esplorazioni sotto la Basilica Giulia al Foro Romano." *RendPont* 8: 53–59.

Carnabuci, E. 1992. *Via Aurelia*. Rome: Istituto Poligrafico e Zecca dello Stato.

———. 2012. *Lexicon topographicum urbis Romae. Supplementum V. Regia: nuovi dati archeologici dagli appunti inediti di Giacomo Boni*. Rome: Quasar.

Carter, J. B. 1909. "The Evolution of the City of Rome from its Origin to the Gallic Catastrophe." *PAPhS* 48: 129–41.

Cascino, R., H. Di Giuseppe, and H. I. Patterson, eds. 2012. *Veii. The Historical Topography of the Ancient City. A Restudy of John Ward Perkins's Survey*. Archaeological Monographs of the British School at Rome, 19. London: The British School at Rome, London.

Cassola, F. 1962. *I gruppi politici romani nel III secolo A.C.* Trieste: Università di Trieste, Istituto di Storia Antica.

Casson, L. 1965. "Harbour and River Boats of Ancient Rome." *JRS* 55: 31–39.

Castagnoli, F. 1946. "Atrium Libertatis." *RendLinc* 8.1: 276–91.

———. 1974. "Topografia e urbanisitica di Roma nel IV secolo a.C." *StudRom* 22: 425–43.

Catalano, P., P. Fortini, and A. Nanni. 2001. "Area del Carcer-Tullianum. Nuove scoperte." In *Archeologia e Giubileo: Gli interventi a Roma e nel Lazio nel piano per il Grande Giubileo del 2000*, edited by F. Filippi, 192–96. Naples: Electa.

Catalli, F. 2001. *La monetazione romana repubblicana*. Rome: Istituto Poligrafico e Zecca dello Stato.

Cecamore, C. 2002. *Palatium: Topografia storica del Palatino tra III sec. a.C. e I sec. d.C.* BullCom Supp. 9. Rome: L'Erma di Bretschneider.

Ceci, M. and R. Santangeli Valenzani. 2012. "Area Sacra di Largo Argentina: indagini 2006." *BullCom* 113: 406–16.

Champion, C. 2014. "Livy and the Greek Historians from Herodotus to Dionysius: Soundings and Reflections." In *A Companion to Livy*, edited by B. Mineo, 190–204. Hoboken, NJ: Wiley-Blackwell.

Chan, H.-L. 1992. "The Organization and Utilization of Labor Service Under the Jurchen Chin Dynasty." *Harvard Journal of Asiatic Studies* 52.2: 613–64.

Chassignet, M. 1996–2004. *L'Annalistique Romaine*. 3 vols. Collection Budé. Paris: Les Belles Lettres.

Childe, V. G. 1950. "The Urban Revolution." *The Town Planning Review* 21.1: 3–17.

Chouquer, G. , M. Claval-Léveque, F. Favory, and J.-P. Vallat. 1987. *Structures agraires en Italie centro-méridionale. Cadastres et paysages ruraux*. Rome: École française de Rome.

Christensen, M. 1992. "Appendix: Analysis of stucco samples." In Nielsen and Poulsen, eds., 218–19.

Ciancio Rossetto, P. 1994–95. "Ritrovamenti nel Campo Marzio meridionale." *BullCom* 91: 197–200.

———. 1997–98. "Tempio di Apollo. Nuove indagini sulla fase repubblicana." *RendPontAcc* 70: 177–95.

Cifani, G. 1998. "La documentazione archeologica delle mura arcaiche a Roma." *RM* 105: 359–89.

———. 2001. "Le origini dell' architettura in pietra a Roma." In *From Huts to Houses. Transformation of Ancient Societies*. Proceedings of an International Seminar Organized by the Norwegian and Swedish Institutes in Rome, 21–24 September 1997, edited by J. Rasmus Brandt and L. Karlsson, 55–61. Stockholm: Svenska Institutet i Rom.

———. 2008. *Architettura romana arcaica: Edilizia e società tra Monarchia e Repubblica*. Rome: L'Erma di Bretschneider.

———. 2010. "I grandi cantieri della Roma arcaica: aspetti tecnici ed organizzativi." *AAEA* 57: 35–50.

———. 2013. "Considerazioni sulle mura arcaiche e repubblicane a Roma." *ScAnt* 19.2–3: 204–8.

———. 2015. "Osservazioni sui paesaggi agrari, espropri e colonizzazione nella prima età repubblicana." *MEFRA* 127.2.

———. 2016. "The Fortifications of Archaic Rome: Social and Political Significance." In R. Frederiksen et al., eds., 82–93.

———. 2017. "Small, Medium or Extra-Long? Prolegomena to any Future Metaphysics on the Reconstructions of the Temple of Jupiter Optimus Maximus Capitolinus." In Lulof and Smith, eds., 113–22.

Cifarelli, F. M. 1995. "Un ninfeo repubblicano a Segni con la firma di Q. Mutius architetto." *Tra Lazio e Campania. Quad. Dip. Sc. Ant. Università di Salerno* 16: 159–88.

Cifarelli, F. M. and S. Gatti. 2006. "I Volsci: una nuova prospettiva." *Orizzonti* 7: 23–48.

Claridge, A. 2010. *Rome: An Oxford Archaeological Guide*. 2nd ed. Oxford: Oxford University Press.

Clark, C. and M. Haswell. 1970. *The Economics of Subsistence Agriculture*. New York: Macmillan.

Clarke, L. 1992. *Building Capitalism: Historical Change and the Labour Process in the Production of the Built Environment*. London: Routledge.

Clerici, L. 1943. *Economia e finanza dei Romani: dalle origini alla fine delle guerre sannitiche*. Bologna: N. Zanichelli.

Coale, A. J. and P. G. Demeny. 1983. *Regional Model Life Tables and Stable Populations*. 2nd ed. Princeton: Princeton University Press.

Coarelli, F. 1967–68. "Il tempio di Bellona." *BullCom* 80: 37–72.

———. 1968. "Il tempio di Diana 'in Circo Flaminio' ed alcuni problemi connessi." *DialArch* 2: 191–209.

———. 1977a. "Public Building in Rome Between the Second Punic War and the Gracchi." *PBSR* 45: 1–23.

———. 1977b. "Il comizio dalle origini alla fine della repubblica. Cronologia e topografia." *PP* 32: 166–238.

———. 1978. "Il grande donario di Attalo I." In *I Galli e L'Italia*, edited by P. Santoro, 231–55. Rome: De Luca.

———. 1981. "Topografia e storia." *L'area sacra di Largo Argentina I*. Rome: Comune di Roma, X Ripartizione.

———. 1983. *Il Foro Romano*. 2 vols. Rome: Quasar.

———. 1988a. *Il Foro Boario: Dalle origini alla fine della repubblica*. Rome: Quasar

———. 1988b. "Colonizzazione romana e viabilità." *DialArch* 6: 35–48.

———. 1988c. "Demografia e territorio." In *Storia di Roma*, vol. 1, edited by A. Momigliano and A. Schiavone, 317–39. Torino: Einaudi.

———. 1990a. "Cultura artistica e società." In *Storia di Roma*, vol. 2.1, edited by A. Schiavone, 159–85. Torino: Einaudi.

———. 1990b. "I Volsci e il Lazio antico." In *Crise et transformation*, 135–54.

———. 1991. "Gli emissari dei laghi laziali. Tra mito e storia." In *Gli Etruschi, maestri di idraulica*, edited by M. Bergamini, 35–41. Perugia: Electa.

———. 1992. "Aedes Fortis Fortunae, Naumachia Augusti, Castra Ravennatium: La Via Campana Portuensis e alcuni edifici nella Pianta Marmorea Severiana." *Ostraka* 1: 39–54.

———. 1995a. "Le mura regie e repubblicane." In *Mura e porte di Roma antica*, edited by B. Brizzi, 9–38. Rome: Colombo.

———.1995b. "Vici di Ariminum." In *Mélanges R. Chevallier II. Caesarodunum* 29: 175–80.

———. 1996a. *Revixit ars: Arte e ideologia a Roma dai modelli ellenistici alla tradizione repubblicana*. Rome: Quasar.

———. 1996b. "Legio linteata: l'iniziazione militare nel Sannio." In *La Tavola di Agnone in constesto italico: Convegno di studi: Agnone, 13–15 aprile 1994*, edited by L. del Tutto Palma, 3–45. Florence: Olschki.

———. 1997. *Il Campo Marzio: dalle origini alle fine della Repubblica*. Rome: Quasar.

———. 2012. *Palatium. Il Palatino dalle origini all'impero*. Rome: Quasar.

———. 2013. *Argentum Signatum. Le origini della moneta d'argento a Roma*. Rome: Istituto Italiano di Numismatica.

Coarelli, F. and J.-C. Grenier. 1986. "La tombe d'Antinoüs a Rome." *MEFRA* 98: 217–53.

Colini, A. M. 1940. *Il tempio di Veiove*. Rome: Governatorato di Roma.

———. 1943. *Storia e topografia del Celio nell'antichità*. Rome: Vatican.

———. 1980. "Il porto fluviale del Foro Boario a Roma." *MAAR* 36: 43–53.

Colini, A. M. and C. Buzzetti. 1986. "Aedes Portuni in Portu Tiberino." *BullCom* 91: 7–30.

Colini, A. M. and G. Matthiae. 1966. "Ricerche intorno a S. Pietro in Vincoli." *MemPontAcc* 9: 5–56.

Colonna, G. 1977. "Un aspetto oscuro del Lazio antico: le tombe del VI-V secolo a.C." *PP* 32: 131–65.

———. 1986. "Urbanistica e architettura." In *Rasenna: Storia e civiltà degli Etruschi*, edited by G. Pugliese Carratelli and M. Pallottino, 371–530. Milan: Scheiwiller.

———. 1988. "I Latini e gli altri popoli del Lazio." In *Italia omnium terrarum alumna*, edited by G. Pugliese Carratelli, 411–528. Scheiwiller: Milan.

———. 1990. "Città e territorio nell'Etruria Meridionale del V secolo." In *Crise et transformation*, 7–21.

———. 2016. "Iscrizioni latine arcaiche dal santuario romano delle curiae veteres." *Sc. Ant.* 22.1: 93–109.

Conte, G. B. 1994. *Latin Literature: A History*. Translated by J. B. Solodow. Baltimore, MD: Johns Hopkins University Press.

Cordischi, L. 1993. "Nuove acquisizioni su un'area di culto al colle Oppio." *ArchLaz* 11: 39–44.

Cornell, T. J. 1974. "Notes on Sources for Campanian History in the Fifth Century B.C." *MH* 31: 193–208.

———. 1986. "The Formation of the Historical Tradition of Early Rome." In *Past Perspectives: Studies in Greek and Roman Historical Writing*, edited by I. S. Moxon, J. D. Smart, and A. J. Woodman, 67–86. Cambridge: Cambridge University Press.

———. 1995. *The Beginnings of Rome 1000–264 B.C.* London: Routledge.

———. 2000a. "The City of Rome in the Middle Republic (400–100 BC)." In *Ancient Rome: The Archaeology of the Eternal City*, edited by H. Dodge and J. Coulson, 42–60. Oxford School of Archaeology Monographs 54. Oxford: Inst. of Archaeology.

———. 2000b. "The lex Ovinia and the Emancipation of the Senate." In Bruun, ed., 69–89.

———. 2003. "Coriolanus: Myth, History and Performance." In *Myth, History and Culture in Republican Rome. Studies in Honour of T. P. Wiseman*, edited by D. Braund and C. Gill, 73–97. Exeter: University of Exeter Press.

———. 2004. "Deconstructing the Samnite Wars. An Essay in Historiography." In *Samnium: Settlement and Cultural Change. The Proceedings of the Third E. Togo Salmon Conference of Roman Studies*, edited by H. Jones, 115–31. Providence: Center for Old World Archaeology and Art, Brown University.

———. 2005. "The Value of the Literary Tradition Concerning Archaic Rome." In *Social Struggles in Archaic Rome: New Perspectives on the Conflict of the Orders*, edited by K. Raaflaub, 47–72. Malden, MA.: Blackwell Publishing.

Corretti, A. 2009. "Siderurgia in ambito elbano e populoniese: un contributo dalle fonti letterarie." In *Materiali da costruzione e produzione del ferro. Studi sull'economia populoniese fra periodo etrusco e romanizzazione*, edited by F. Cambi, F. Cavari, and C. Mascione, 133–39. Bari: Edipuglia.

Coudry, M. 2001. "Camille: Construction et fluctuations de la figure d'un grande home." In *L'invention des grands hommes de la Rome antique. Die Konstruktion der grossen Männer Altroms. Actes du Colloque du Collegium Beatus Rhenanus, Augst 16–18 Septembre 1999*, edited by M. Coudry and T. Späth, 47–81. Paris: De Boccard.

Coulton, J. J. 1974. "Lifting in Early Greek Architecture." *JHS* 54: 1–17.

Cozza, L. 1968. "Pianta marmorea severiana: nuove ricomposizioni di frammenti." *QuadTop* 5: 9–22.

Cozza, L. and P. L. Tucci. 2006. "Navalia." *ArchClass* 57: 175–202.

Crawford, M. H. 1970. "Money and Exchange in the Roman World." *JRS* 60: 40–48.

———. 1977. "Rome and the Greek World: Economic Relationships." *EHR* 30.1: 42–52.

———. 1985. *Coinage and Money Under the Roman Republic: Italy and the Mediterranean Economy*. Berkeley: University of California Press.

Cristofani, M. 1984. *Gli Etruschi. Una nuova immagine*. Florence: Giunti Martello.

Crozzoli Aite, L. 1981. *I tre templi del Foro Olitorio*. Rome: L'Erma di Bretschneider.

Cuomo, S. 2011. "A Roman Engineer's Tales." *JRS* 101: 143–65.

Cuomo di Caprio, N. 1971–72. "Proposta di classificazione delle fornaci per ceramica e per laterizi nell'area italiana." *Sibrium* 11: 371–476.

Cuvigny, H. 1996. "The Amount of Wages Paid to the Quarry-Workers at Mons Claudianus." *JRS* 86: 139–45.

Dallai, L. 2009. "Estrazione e circolazione del metallo nell'area medio-tirrenica in epoca romana." In *Materiali per Populonia 8*, edited by F. Ghizzani Marcìa and C. Megale, 197–208. Pisa: ETS.

Damon, C. 2007. "Rhetoric and Historiography." In *A Companion to Roman Rhetoric*, edited by W. Dominik and J. Hall, 439–50. London: Wiley-Blackwell Press.

Davies, P. 2012. "On the Introduction of Stone Entablatures in Republican Temples in Rome." In *Monumentality in Etruscans and Early Roman Architecture: Ideology and Innovation*, edited by M. L. Thomas and G. E. Meyers, 139–65. Austin, TX: University of Texas Press.

———. 2013. "The Archaeology of Mid-Republican Rome: The Emergence of a Mediterranean Capital." In *A Companion to the Archaeology of the Roman Republic*, edited by J. DeRose Evans, 441–58. Chichester, UK: Wiley-Blackwell.

De Bel-Air, F. 2015. "Demography, Migration, and the Labour Market in the UAE." *Gulf Labour Markets and Migration—Explanatory Note* 7: 3–22.

De Ligt, L. 1993. *Fairs and Markets in the Roman Empire:Economic and Social Aspects of Periodic Trade in a Pre-Industrial Society*. Amsterdam: J. C. Gieben

———. 2000. "Studies in Legal and Agrarian History II: Tenancy under the Republic." *Athenaeum* 88: 377–91.

———. 2012. *Peasants, Citizens and Soldiers: Studies in the Demographic History of Roman Italy 225 BC–AD 100*. Cambridge and New York: Cambridge University Press.

De Ligt, L. and L. E. Tacoma, eds. 2016. *Migration and Mobility in the Early Roman Empire*. Leiden: Brill.

De Maria, S. 1988. *Gli archi onorari di Roma e dell'Italia romana*. Rome: L'Erma di Bretschneider.

De Martino, F. 1974. "Intorno all'origine della schiavitù a Roma." *Labeo* 20: 163–93.

———. 1979. *Storia economica di Roma antica*. 2 vols. Florence: La nuova Italia.

———. 1984. "Ancora sulla produzione di cereali in Roma nell'eta arcaica." *PP* 39: 241–62.

De Neeve, P. W. 1984. *Colonus: Private Farm-tenancy in Roman Italy During the Republic and the Early Principate*. Amsterdam: J.C. Gieben.

De Nuccio, M. 1995. "Tempio di Bellona: studi preliminari." *ArchLaz* 12: 71–77.

De Prony, G.-C. 1823. *Atlas des marais pontins*. Paris: Firmin Didot.

De Ruyt, C. 1983. *Macellum: Marché alimentaire des romains*. Louvain: Université Catholique.

———. 2007. "Les produits vendus au macellum." *Food and History* 5.1: 135–50.

De Vries, J. 2008. *The Industrious Revolution: Consumer Demand and the Household Economy, 1650 to the Present*. Cambridge: Cambridge University Press.

Degrassi, A. 1963–64. "Area sacra di S. Omobono. Esplorazione della fase repubblicana. I nomi dei dedicanti del monumento quadrangolare." *BullCom* 79: 91–93.

Del Buono, G. 2009. "Il tempio di Portuno: una nuova periodizzazione per le fasi medio-repubblicane." *BullCom* 110: 9–30.

DeLaine, J. 1995. "The Supply of Building Materials to the City of Rome." In *Settlement and Economy in Italy 1500 BC–AD 1500: Papers of the Fifth Conference of Italian Archaeology*, edited by N. Christie, 555–62. Oxford: Oxbow Books.

———. 1997. "The Baths of Caracalla: A Study in the Design, Construction, and Economics of Large-Scale Building Projects in Imperial Rome." *JRA* Suppl. 25. Portsmouth, RI: JRA.

———. 2001. "Bricks and mortar: exploring the economics of building techniques at Rome and Ostia." In *Economies Beyond Agriculture in the Classical World*, edited by D. J. Mattingly and J. Salmon, 230–68. New York: Routledge.

Delbrück, R. 1907–12. *Hellenistische Bauten in Latium*. 2 vols. Strassburg: Trübner.

Delfino, A. 2009. "L'incendio gallico: tra mito storiografico e realtà storica." *MediterrAnt* 12: 339–60.

———. 2010. "Le fasi arcaiche e alto-repubblicane nell'area del Foro di Cesare." *ScAnt* 16: 285–302.

———. 2014. *Forum Iulium. L'area del Foro di Cesare alle luce delle campagne di scavo 2005–2008: le fase arcaica, repubblicana e cesariano-augustea*. Oxford: BAR Press.

Della Portella, I., ed. 2003. *Via Appia Antica*. Venice: Arsenale.

Di Giuseppe, H. 2010. "Incendio e bonifica prima del Foro di Cesare. Il contributo della ceramica." *ScAnt* 16: 303–20.

———. 2012. *Black-gloss Ware in Italy. Production Management and Histories*. Oxford: BAR Press.

Di Manzano, P., M. Cecchelli and A. Milella. 2006–2007. "Indagini archeologiche nella chiesa di S. Bartolomeo all'Isola Tiberina." *RendPont* 79: 125–76.

Di Mario, F. 2009. "Ardea. L'area archeologica in località Le Salzare-Fosso dell'Incastro." *Lazio e Sabina* 5: 331–46.

———. 2012. "Ardea. Il santuario di Fosso dell'Incastro." In *Sacra nominis Latini: i santuari del Lazio arcaico e repubblicano. Atti del Convegno Internazionale, Roma, Palazzo Massimo, 192–1 febbraio 2009*, edited by E. Marroni, 467–78. Naples: Loffredo.

Diffendale, D. P. 2016. "Five Republican Monuments. On the Supposed Building Program of M. Fulvius Flaccus." In *Ricerche nell'area dei templi di Fortuna e Mater Matuta*. Vol. 1, edited by P. Brocato, M. Ceci, and N. Terrenato, 141–66. Arcavacata: Università della Calabria.

Diffendale, D. P., P. Brocato, N. Terrenato, and A. Brock. 2016. "Sant'Omobono: An interim status quaestionis." *JRA* 29.1: 7–42.

Diosono, F. 2008. *Il Legno: Produzione e commercio*. Rome: Edizioni Quasar.

———. 2016. "La porta e il porto. Il culto di Portunus nella Roma arcaica e repubblicana." In *Vestigia: Miscellenea di studi storico-religiosi in onore di Filippo Coarelli nel suo 80º anniversario*, edited by V. Gasparini, 81–98. Stuttgart: Steiner Verlag.

Diosono, F. and G. Battaglini. 2010. "Le domus di Fregellae: case aristocratiche di ambito coloniale." In *Etruskisch-italische und römisch-republikanische Häuser*, edited by M. Bentz and C. Reusser, 217–31. Wiesbaden: Reichert Verlag.

Dohrn, T. 1972. *Die Ficoronische Cista in der Villa Giulia in Rom*. Berlin: Gebr. Mann.

Dolci, E. 1995. "Considerazioni sull'impiego dei marmi a Luni nella prima età imperial." In *Splendida civitas nostra: Studi archeologici in onore di Antonio Frova*, edited by G. Cavalieri Manasse and E. Roffia, 361–470. Rome: Quasar.

Dondero, I. B. 1950. "Elenco del materiale numismatico ordinato nel medagliere della Soprintendenza alle Antichità del Palatino e Foro Romano." *Antichità* 2, 3: 3–9.

Dondero, I., P. Pensabene, and L. Campus, eds. 1982. *Roma repubblicana fra il 509 e il 270 a.C.* Rome: Quasar.

Drachmann, A. G. 1963. *The Mechanical Technology of Greek and Roman Antiquity: A Study of the Literary Sources*. Copenhagen: Munksgaard.

Drögemüller, H.-P. 1969. *Syrakus: zur Topographie und Geschichte einer griechischen Stadt, mit einem Anhang zu Thukydides 6.96 ff. und Livius 24.25*. Heidelberg: C. Winter-Universitätsverlag.

Du Plessis, P. 2004. "The Protection of the Contractor in Public Works Contracts in the Roman Republic and Early Empire." *Journal of Legal History* 25.3: 287–314.

———. 2012. *Letting and Hiring in Roman Legal Thought: 27 BCE–84 CE*. Leiden: Brill.

Dubbini, R. 2016. "A New Republican Temple on the Via Appia, at the Border of Rome's Urban Space." *JRA* 29.1: 327–48.

Duncan-Jones, R. 1982. *Economy of the Roman Empire: Quantitative Studies*. 2nd ed. Cambridge: Cambridge University Press.

———. 1990. *Structure and Scale Roman Economy*. Cambridge: Cambridge University Press.

Dyer, C. 1989. *Standards of Living in the Later Middle Ages: Social Change in England, c. 1200–1520*. Cambridge: Cambridge University Press.

Egg, M. 1986. *Italische Helme: Studien zu den ältereisenzeitlichen Helmen Italiens und der Alpen*. Mainz: Verlag des Römisch-Germanischen Zentralmuseums.

Elliott, J. 2013. *Ennius and the Architecture of the Annales*. Cambridge: Cambridge University Press.

Elster, M. 2003. *Die Gesetze der mittleren römischen Republik: Text und Kommentar*. Darmstadt: Wissenschaftliche Buchgesellschaft.

Epstein, S. 2008. "Why Did Attic Building Projects Employ Free Laborers Rather Than Slaves?" *ZPE* 166: 108–12.

Erasmus, C. J. 1965."Monument Building: Some Field Experiments." *Southwestern Journal of Anthropology* 21.4: 277–301.

Erdkamp, P. 1999. "Agriculture, Unemployment, and the Cost of Rural Labour in the Roman World." *CQ* 49: 556–72.

———. 2005. *The Grain Market in the Roman Empire: A Social, Political. and Economic Study*. Cambridge: Cambridge University Press.

Evans, J. K. 1981. "Wheat Production and Its Social Consequences in the Roman World." *CQ* 31: 428–42.

Fabbri, M. 2008. "Le 'mura serviane' dalle fonti letterarie alla documentazione archeologica." In aa.vv. *Le perle e il filo: A Mario Torelli per i suoi settanta anni*, 83–100. Rome: Osanna.

———. 2009. "Le mura serviane di Roma fra passato e presente." In aa.vv. *Arch. it.arch: dialoghi di archeologia e architettura, seminari 2005/2006*, 216–38. Rome, Quasar.

Farr, J. M. 2014. "Lapis Gabinus: Tufo and the Economy of Urban Construction in Ancient Rome." PhD diss., University of Michigan.

Farr, J., F. Marra, and N. Terrenato. 2015. "Geochemical Identification Criteria for 'Peperino' Stones Employed in Ancient Roman Buildings: A Lapis Gabinus Case Study." *Journal of Archaeological Science* 3: 41–51.

Feig Vishnia, R. 1987. *State, Society and Popular Leaders in Mid-Republican Rome, 241–167 BC*. New York: Routledge.

Felletti Maj, B. M. 1977. *La tradizione Italica nell'arte romana*. Rome: L'Erma di Bretschneider.

Fentress, E. L. 1984. "Via Aurelia, Via Aemilia." *PBSR* 52: 72–76.

Fentress, E. L. and B. Russell. 2016. "Mud Brick and Pisé de Terre between Punic and Roman North Africa." In *Arqueología de la Construcción V: 5th International Workshop on the Archaeology of Roman Construction. Man-mad Materials, Engineering and Infrastructure*, edited by J. DeLaine, S. Camporeale, A. Pizzo, 131–43. Madrid: Anejos de Archivo Español de Arqueología 77.

Ferenczy, E. 1967. "The Censorship of Appius Claudius Caecus." *Acta Antiqua* 15: 27–61.

Ferrandes, A. F. 2007. "Produzione stampigliate e figurate in area etrusco-laziale tra fine IV e III secolo a.C. Nuove riflessioni alla luce di vecchi contesti." *ArchClass* 57: 73–132.

———. 2016. "Sequenze stratigrafiche e facies ceramiche nello studio della città antica. Il caso delle pendici nord-orientali del Palatino tra IV e III secolo a.C." In *Le Regole del Gioco. Tracce archeologi racconti. Studi in onore di Clementina Panella*, edited by A. F. Ferrandes and G. Pardini, 77–112. *LTUR* Suppl. VI. Rome: Quasar.

Ferri, S. 2002. "Via Giovanni Lanza." *BullCom* 103: 122–25.

Filippi, F., ed. 2008. *Horti et sordes: uni scavo alle falde del Gianicolo*. Rome: Quasar.

Finley, M. 1964. "Between Slavery and Freedom." *Comparative Studies in Society and History* 6: 233–49.

———. 1998. *Ancient Slavery and Modern Ideology*. Edited by B. Shaw. Princeton: Markus Wiener Publishers.

———. 1999. *The Ancient Economy*. Updated edition. Berkeley: University of California Press.

Fiorelli, G. 1888. "Notizie degli scavi: Aprile." *NSc*: 203–68.

Fiori, R. 1999. *La definizione della locatio conductio. Giurisprudenzia romana e tradizione romanistica*. Naples: Jovene.

Firmati, M. 2009. "L'Arcipelago Toscano e la romanizzazione: il contributo delle ultime ricerche." In *Materiali da costruzione e produzione del ferro: studi sull'economia populoniese fra periodo etrusco e romanizzazione*, edited by F. Cambi, F. Cavari, and C. Mascone, 187–93. Bari: Epipuglia.

Fischer-Bossert, W. 1999. *Chronologie der Didrachmenprägung von Tarent, 510–280 v. Chr.* Berlin: De Gruyter.

Fitchen, J. 1986. *Building Construction Before Mechanization*. Cambridge, MA: MIT Press.

Flower, H. 2011. *Roman Republics*. Princeton: Princeton University Press.

Fogel, R. 2004. *The Escape from Hunger and Premature Death, 1700–2100: Europe, America and the Third World*. New York: Cambridge University Press.

Fontaine, P. 2004. "Des 'remparts de Romulus' aux murs du Palatin. Du mythe à l'archéologie." In *Images d'origines. Origines d'une image. Hommages à J. Poucet*, edited by P.-A. Deproost and A. Meurant, 35–54. Louvain-la-Neuve: Bruylant-Academia.

———. 2008. "Mura, arte fortificatoria e città in Etruria. Riflessioni sui dati archeologici." In *La città murata in Etruria*, edited by G. Camporeale, 203–20. Pisa/Rome: Fabrizio Serra.

Forsythe, G. 1990. "Some Notes on the History of Cassius Hemina." *Phoenix* 44.4: 326–44.

———. 2005. *A Critical History of Early Rome. From Pre-History to the First Punic War*. Berkeley: University of California Press.

Frank, T. 1918. "Notes on the Servian wall." *AJA* 22: 175–88.

———. 1924. *Roman Buildings of the Republic. An Attempt to Date Them from Their Materials*. Rome: American Academy of Rome.

———. "Roman Census Statistics from 508 to 225 B.C." *AJP* 51.4: 313–24.

———, ed. 1933. *An Economic Survey of Ancient Rome*. Vol. 1. Baltimore, MD: Johns Hopkins University Press.

———. 1936. "The Topography of Terence, Adelphoe." *AJP* 57.4: 573–85.

Frederiksen, M. 1965. "The Republican Municipal Laws: Errors and Drafts." *JRS* 55: 183–98.

Frederiksen, R., S. Müth, P. I. Schneider, and M. Schnelle, eds. 2016. *Focus on Fortifications: New Research on Fortifications in the Ancient Mediterranean and the Near East. Archaeological Monographs of the Danish Institute at Athens 18*. Oxford: Oxbow.

Frey-Kupper, S. 1995. "Roma–Monete dal Tevere. I rinvenimenti greci." *Bollettino di Numismatica* 25: 33–73.

Freyberger, K. S., C. Ertel, J. Lipps, and T. Bitterer. 2007. "Neue Forschung zur Basilica Aemilia auf dem Forum Romanum." *RM* 113: 493–552.

Freyberger, K. S. and C. Ertel. 2016. *Die Basilica Aemilia auf dem Forum Romanum in Rom: Bauphasen, Rekonstruktion, Funktion und Bedeutung*. Wiesbaden: Reichert Verlag.

Frier, B. 1979. *Libri Annales Pontificum Maximorum: The Origins of the Annalistic Tradition*. Rome: American Academy in Rome.

Fronda, M. P. 2010. *Between Rome and Carthage: Southern Italy During the Second Punic War*. Cambridge: Cambridge University Press.

Fuchs, G. 1956. "Zur Baugeschichte der Basilika Aemilia in republikanischer Zeit." *RM* 63: 14–25.

Fulminante, F. 2014. *The Urbanisation of Rome and Latium Vetus: From the Bronze Age to the Archaic Era*. Cambridge: Cambridge University Press.

Funiciello, R., ed. 1995. *Memorie descrittive della carta geologica d'Italia. La Geologia di Roma, Il centro storico*. Servizio Geologico Nazionale. Rome: Istituto Poligrafico e Zecca dello Stato.

Iacopi, G. 1940. "Scavi e scoperte presso il porto fluviale di S. Paolo." *BullCom* 68: 97–107.

Gabba, E. 1981. "Ricchezza e classe dirigente romana fra III e I sec. a.C." *RSI* 9: 341–58.

———. 1990. "Dallo stato-città allo stato municipale." In *Storia di Roma*, vol. 2.1, edited by A. Schiavone, 697–714. Torino: Einaudi.

Gabrielli, C. 2003a. *Contributi alla storia economica di Roma repubblicana: difficoltà politico-sociali, crisi finanziaria e debiti fra 5. e 3. sec. a.C.* Como: New Press.

———. 2003b. "Lucius Postumius Megellus at Gabii: A New Fragment of Livy." *CQ* 53.1: 247–59.

Gaggiotti, M. 1985. "Atrium regium, basilica (Aemilia). Una insospettata continuità storica e una chiave ideologica per la soluzione del problema dell'origine della basilica." *AnalRom* 14: 53–80.

Gaggiotti, M. 1988. "Pavimenta Poenica marmore Numidico constrata." In *L'Africa romana: atti del V convegno di studio, Sassari 11–13 dicembre 1987*, edited by A. Mastino, 215–21. Sassari: Dipartimento di storia, Università degli studi di Sassari.

Garnsey, P. 1998. "Mass Diet and Nutrition in the City of Rome." In *Cities, Peasants, and Food in Classical Antiquity: Essays in Social and Economic History*, edited by W. Scheidel, 226–52. Cambridge and New York: Cambridge University Press.

Garzetti, A. 1947. "Appio Claudio Cieco nella storia politica del suo tempo." *Athenaeum* 25: 175–224.

Gasparri, C. 1979. *Aedes Concordiae Augustae*. Rome: Istituto di Studi Romani.

Gast, K. 1965. *Die zensorischen Bauberichte bei Livius und die römischen Bauinschriften: versuch eines Zugangs zu livianischen Quellen über Formen der Inschriftensprache*. Göttingen: University of Göttingen.

Gatti, G. 1934. "Saepta Iulia e Porticus Aemilia nella Forma Severiana." *BullCom* 62: 123–49.

———. 1940. "Il viadotto della via Aurelia nel Trastevere." *BullCom* 68: 129–41.

———. 1960. "Dove erano situati il teatro di Balbo e il Circo Flaminio?" *Capitolium* 35: 3–12.

———. 1961. "Ancora sulla vera posizione del teatro di Balbo e del Circo Flaminio." In *Palatino* 5: 17–20.

Gautier di Confiengo, E. 2007. "Il Quartiere di Porta Viminalis: Un contributo alla carta archeologica dell'Esquilino." *BullCom* 108: 221–45.

Gianfrotta, P. A. 1985. "Indagini nell'area della Porticus Philippi." In *Roma: archeologia nel centro*, edited by A. M. Bietti Sestieri, 376–84. Rome: De Luca.

Giardino, C. and F. Lugli. 2001. "L'attività siderurgica nel Giardino Romano." *BullCom* 102: 327–328.

Gilula, D. 1991. "A Walk through Town (Ter. Ad. 573–584)." *Athenaeum* 79: 245–47.

Giuliani, C. and P. Verduchi. 1987. *L'area centrale del Foro Romano*. Florence: Olschki.

Gjerstad, E. 1953–73. *Early Rome*. 6 vols. Lund: C. W. K. Gleerup.

Gliozzo, E. 2007. "The Distribution of Bricks and Tiles in the Tiber valley: The Evidence from Piammano, Bomarzo, Viterbo." In *Supplying Rome and the Empire: The Proceedings of an International Seminar Held at Siena-Certosa di Pontignano on May 2–4, 2004, on Rome, the Provinces, Production and Distribution*, edited by E. Papi, 59–72. *JRA* Suppl. 69, Portsmouth RI: JRA.

Goldthwaite, R. 1980. *The Building of Renaissance Florence: An Economic and Social History*. Baltimore, MD: Johns Hopkins University Press.

Goodman, P. 2007. *The Roman City and its Periphery: From Rome to Gaul*. London: Routledge.

———. 2016. "Working Together: Clusters of Artisans in the Ancient City." In *Urban Craftsmen and Traders in the Roman World*, edited by M. Flohr and A. Wilson, 301–34. Oxford: Oxford University Press.

Graeber, D. 2011. *Debt: The First 5,000 Years*. Brooklyn: Meville House.

Granovetter, M. 2017. *Society and Economy: Framework and Principles*. Cambridge, MA: Harvard University Press.

Gregori G. L. and Nonnis D. 2013. *"Il contributo dell'epigrafia allo studio delle cinte murarie dell'Italia repubblicana."* *ScAnt* 19.2–3: 491–524.

Gros. P. 1996. *L'architecture romaine: du début du IIIe siècle av. J.-C. à la fin du Haut-Empire.* Vol 1. Paris: Picard.

———. 2003. *Vitruve, de l'Architecture, Livre II.* Collection Budé. Paris: Les Belles Lettres.

Gros, P. and M. Torelli. 2007. *Storia dell'urbanistica. Il mondo romano.* 2nd ed. Rome: Laterza.

Guaitioli, M. 1984. "Urbanistica." *ArchLaz* 6: 364–81.

Guidobaldi, M. P. 1999. "La Via Caecilia: riflessioni sulla cronologia e sul percorso di una via publica romana." In *La Salaria in età antica*, edited by E. Catani and G. Paci, 277–90. Rome: L'Erma di Bretschneider.

Halstead, P. 2014. *Two Oxen Ahead: Pre-Mechanized Farming in the Mediterranean.* Hoboken, NJ: Wiley-Blackwell.

Hansen, M. H. 2000. "Introduction: The Concepts of City-State and City-State Culture." In *A Comparative Study of Thirty City-State Cultures: An Investigation*, edited by M. H. Hansen, 7–23. Copenhagen: Kongelige Danske Videnskabernes Selskab.

———. 2006. *The Shotgun Method: The Demography of the Ancient Greek City-State Culture.* Colombia, MO: University of Missouri Press.

Harari, E. 2002. "Ceramic Kilns in Ancient Greece: Technology and Organization of Ceramic Workshops." PhD diss., University of Cincinnati.

Harris, W. V. 1971. *Rome in Etruria and Umbria.* Oxford: Clarendon Press.

———. 1979. *War and Imperialism in Republican Rome: 327–70 B.C.* Oxford: Clarendon Press.

———. 1990. "Roman Warfare in the Economic and Social Context of the Fourth Century B.C." In *Staat und Staatlichkeit in der frühen römischen Republik*, edited by W. Eder, 494–510. Stuttgart: Steiner.

———. 2013. "Defining and Detecting Ancient Mediterranean Deforestation 800 BCE to 700 CE." In *The Ancient Mediterranean Environment Between Science and History*, edited by W. V. Harris, 173–94. Leiden/Boston: Brill.

Haselberger, L. 1994. "Ein Giebelriss der Vorhalle des Pantheon. Die Werkrisse vor dem Augustusmausoleum." *RM* 101: 279–308.

———. 2007. "Urbem adornare: die Stadt Rom und ihre Gestaltumwandlung unter Augustus." *JRA* Suppl. 64. Portsmouth, RI: JRA, 2007.

Hawkins, C. 2012. "Manufacturing." In *The Cambridge Companion to the Roman Economy,* edited by W. Scheidel, 175–94. Cambridge: Cambridge University Press.

———. 2013. "Labour and Employment." In *The Cambridge Companion to Ancient Rome*, edited by P. Erdkamp, 336–51. Cambridge: Cambridge University Press.

Helas, S. 2016. "Polygonalmauern in Mittelitalien und ihre Rezeption in mittel- und spätrepublikanischer Zeit." In R. Frederiksen et al., eds., 581–94.

Heyworth, S. J. 2011. "Roman Topography and Latin Diction." *PBSR* 79: 43–69.

Hin, S. 2008. "Counting Romans." In *People, Land, and Politics: Demographic Developments and the Transformation of Roman Italy 300 BC–AD 14*, edited by L. de Ligt and S. J. Northwood, 187–238. Leiden/Boston: Brill.

———. 2013. *The Demography of Roman Italy: Population Dynamics in an Ancient Conquest Society, 201 BCE–14 CE*. Cambridge: Cambridge University Press.

Hobson, M. 2014. "A Historiography of the Study of the Roman Economy: Economic Growth, Development, and Neoliberalism." In *Proceedings of the Twenty-Third Theoretical Roman Archaeology Conference, King's College, London 2013*, edited by H. Platts, J. Pearce, C. Barron, J. Lundock, and J. Yoo, 11–26. Oxford: Oxbow Books.

Hölkeskamp, K.-J. 1987. *Die Entstehung der Nobilität: Studien zur sozialen und politischen Geschichte der römischen Republik im 4. Jhdt. v. Chr.* Stuttgart: Steiner.

———. 2004. *Senatus Populusque Romanus. Die politische Kultur der Republik-Dimensionen und Deutungen*. Stuttgart: Steiner.

———. 2010. *Reconstructing the Roman Republic: An Ancient Political Culture and Modern Research*. Translated by H. Heitmann-Gordan. Princeton: Princeton University Press.

Hölkeskamp, K.-J. and E. Stein-Hölkeskamp. 2006. *Erinnerungsorte der Antike. Die römische Welt*. Munich: Beck.

Hollander, D. B. 2007. *Money in the Late Roman Republic*. Leiden: Brill.

Holleran, C. 2011. "Migration and the Urban Economy of Rome." In *Demography and the Graeco-Roman World: New Insights and Approaches*, edited by C. Holleran and A. Pudsey, 155–80. Cambridge: Cambridge University Press.

———. 2012. *Shopping in Ancient Rome: The Retail Trade in the Late Republic and the Principate*. Oxford/New York: Oxford University Press.

Holloway, R. R. 1994. *The Archaeology of Early Rome and Latium*. London/New York: Routledge.

Hollstein, W. 1998/99. "Überlegungen zu Datierung und Münzbildern der römischen Didrachmenprägung." *JNG* 48/49: 133–64.

Hölscher, T. 1978. "Die Anfänge römischer Repräsentationskunst." *MDAI* (R) 85: 315–57.

———. 1994. *Monumenti statali e pubblico*. Rome: L'Erma di Bretschneider.

Hopkins, K. 1978. *Conquerors and Slaves*. Cambridge: Cambridge Press.

———. 2002. "Rome, Taxes, Rents, and Trade." In *The Ancient Economy*, edited by S. von Reden and W. Scheidel, 190–230. London: Routledge.

Hopkins, J. 2010. "The Topographical Transformation of Archaic Rome: A New Interpretation of Architecture and Geography in the Early City." PhD diss., University of Texas at Austin.

———. 2016. *The Genesis of Roman Architecture*. New Haven: Yale University Press.

Horden, P. and N. Purcell. 2000. *The Corrupting Sea: A Study of Mediterranean History*. Oxford/Malden: Blackwell.

Hornblower, S. 1997. *A Commentary on Thucydides*. Vol. 1. Oxford: Clarendon Press.

Horsfall, N. 1981. "From History to Legend. M. Manlius and the Geese." *CJ* 76: 298–311.

Howgego, C.J. 1990. "Why Did Ancient States Strike Coins?" *NC* 150: 1–25.

Hülsen, C. 1897. "Der Umfang der Stadt Rom zur Zeit des Plinius." *RM* 12: 148–60.

Hültsch, F. O. 1882. *Grieschische und römische Metrologie*. Berlin: Weidmannsche.

Humm, M. 1996. "Appius Claudius Caecus et la construction de la Via Appia." *MEFRA* 108: 693–746.

———. 2005. *Appius Claudius Caecus: La république accomplie*. Rome: École française de Rome.

Humphrey, J. H. 1986. *Roman Circuses: Arenas for Chariot Racing*. Berkeley: University of California Press.

Hurst, H. and D. Cirone. 2003. "Excavation of the Pre-Neronian Nova via, Rome." *PBSR* 71: 17–84.

Ioppolo, G. 1963–64. "Area sacra di S. Omobono. Esplorazione della fase repubblicana. Due monumenti repubblicani." *BullCom* 79: 68–90.

———. 1971–72. "I reperti ossei animali nell'area archeologica di S. Omobono, 1962–1964." *RendPont* 44: 3–46.

———. 1989. "Il tempio arcaico." In aa.vv. *Il viver quotidiano in Roma arcaica: materiali dagli scavi del tempio arcaico nell'area sacra di S. Omobono*, 29–33. Rome: Procom.

Jackson, M. and F. Marra. 2006. "Roman Stone Masonry: Volcanic Foundations of the Ancient City." *AJA* 110.3: 403–26.

Jackson, M., F. Marra, R. Hay, C. A. Cawood, and E. M. Winkler. 2005. "The Judicious Selection and Preservation of Tuff and Travertine Building Stones in Ancient Rome." *Archaeometry* 47.3: 485–510.

Jaia, A. M. 2013. "Le colonie di diritto romano. Considerazioni sul sistema difensivo costiero tra iv e iii secolo a.C ." In *Mura di legno, mura di terra, mura di pietra: fortificazioni nel Mediterraneo antico. Atti del convegno internazionale, Sapienza Università di Roma, 7–9 maggio 2012. ScAnt*, 19.2/3: 475–89, edited by G. Bartoloni and L. M. Michetti. Rome: Quasar.

Jaia, A. M. and M. C. Molinari. 2011. "Two Deposits of Aes Grave from the Sanctuary of Sol Indiges (Torvaianica/Rome): The Dating and Function of the Roman Libral Series." *NC* 171: 87–97.

Johannowsky, W. 1982. "Considerazioni sullo sviluppo urbano e la cultura materiale di Velia." *PP* 37: 225–46.

Jolivet, V. 1995. "Un foyer d'hellénisation en Italie centrale et son rayonnement (IVe–IIe s. av. J.C-C.): Préneste et la diffusion des strigiles inscrits en grec." In *Sur les pas des Grecs en Occident: Hommages à André Nickels*, edited by P. Arcelin, 445–57. Paris: Errance.

———. 2011. *Tristes Portiques: Sur le plan canonique de la maison étrusque et romaine des origines au principat d'Auguste*. BÉFAR 265. Rome: École française.

Jongman, W. 2007. "The Early Roman Empire: Consumption." In Scheidel, Morris, and Saller, eds., 592–618.

Judson, S. and A. Kahane. 1963. "Underground drainageways in Southern Etruria and Northern Latium." *PBSR* 31: 74–99.

Jursa, M. 2002. "Debt and Indebtedness in the Neo-Babylonian Period: Evidence from the Institutional Archives." In *Debt and Economic Renewal in the Ancient Near East*, edited by M. Hudson and M. Van der Mieroop, 197–221. Bethesda, MD: CDL Press.

———. 2015. "Labor in Babylonia in the First Millennium BC." In *Labour in the Ancient World*, edited by P. Steinkeller and M. Hudson, 345–96. Dresden: ISLET.

Kajanto, I. 1981. "L'inscrizioni." *L'area sacra di Largo Argentina I*. Rome: Comune di Roma, X Ripartizione.

Karlsson, L. 1992. *Fortification Towers and Masonry Techniques in the Hegemony of Syracuse, 4052–11 B.C.* Stockholm: Svenska institutet Rom.

Kay, P. 2014. *Rome's Economic Revolution*. Oxford: Oxford University Press.

Killgrove, K. 2013. "Biohistory of the Republic: The Potential of Isotope Analysis of Human Remains." *European Journal of Post-Classical Archaeologies* 3: 41–62.

Knapp, R. 1980. "Festus 262L and Praefecturae in Italy." *Athenaeum* 58: 14–38.

Kosmin, P. 2014. *The Land of the Elephant Kings: Space, Territory, and Ideology in the Seleucid Empire*. Cambridge, MA: Harvard University Press.

Kraus, C. 1989. "Liviana Minima." *HSCP* 92: 215–21.

———. 1994. "'No Second Troy': Topoi and the Refoundation in Livy, Book V." *TAPA* 124: 267–89.

———., ed. and comm. 1996. *T. Livius, Ab Urbe Condita*. Book VI. Cambridge: Cambridge University Press.

Kroll, J. H. 2008. "The Monetary Use of Weighed Bullion in Archaic Greece." In *The Monetary Systems of the Greeks and Romans*, edited by W. V. Harris, 12–72. Oxford/New York: Oxford University Press.

Kunkel, W. and R. Wittmann. 1995. *Staatsordnung und Staatspraxis der römischen Republik*. Munich: Beck.

Lancaster, L. 1999. "Building Trajan's Column." *AJA* 103: 419–39.

———. 2005. *Vaulted Concrete Construction in Imperial Rome: Innovations in Context*. New York: Cambridge Press.

Lanciani, R. 1871. "Sulle mura e porte di Servio." *Annali dell'Instituto di Corrispondenza Archeologica* 43: 40–85.

———. 1876. "Ara di Vermino." *BullCom* 4: 165–93.

———. 1877. "Miscellenea epigrafica." *BullCom* 5: 161–86.

———. 1892. "Recenti scoperte di Roma e del suburbio." *BullCom* 20: 271–304.

———. 1897. *The Ruins and Excavations of Ancient Rome: A Companion Book for Students and Travelers*. Boston: Houghton Mifflin.

Lanciani, R. and C. L. Visconti. 1884. "Il busto di Anacreonte scoperto negli Orti di Cesare." *BullCom* 12: 25–38.

Laurence, R. *The Roads of Roman Italy: Mobility and Cultural Change*. New York: Routledge, 1999.

Le Gall, J. 1939. "Notes sur les prisons de Rome à l'époque républicaine." *MEFRA* 56: 60–80.

———. 2005. *Il Tevere, fiume di Roma nell'antichità*. Rome: Quasar.

Le Goff, J. 1980. *Time, Work and Culture in the Middle Ages*. Translated by A. Goldhammer. Chicago: Chicago University Press.

Leach, E. 2010. "Fortune's Extremities: Q. Lutatius Catulus and Largo Argentina Temple B: A Roman Consular and His Monument." *MAAR* 55: 111–34.

Lendon, J. E. 2009. "Historians Without History: Against Roman Historiography." In *The Cambridge Companion to the Roman Historians*, edited by A. Feldherr, 41–62. Cambridge: Cambridge University Press.

Levick, B. 1978. "Concordia at Rome." In *Scripta Nummaria Romana: Essays Presented to Humphrey Sutherland*, edited by R. A. C. Carson and C. M. Kraay, 217–33. London: Spink.

Lis, C. and H. Soly. 2012. *Worthy Efforts: Attitudes to Work and Workers in Pre-Industrial Europe*. Boston: Brill.

Liverani, P. 1984. "L'Ager Veientanus in età repubblicana." *PBSR* 52: 36–48.

Lo Cascio, E. 1980–81. "Il primo denarius." *AIIN* 272–8: 335–58.

———. 1981. "State and Coinage in the Late Republic and Early Empire." *JRS* 71: 76–86.

———. 1994. "The Size of the Roman Population: Beloch and the Meaning of the Augustan Census Figures." *JRS* 84: 23–40.

———. 2001. "Il census a Roma e la sua evoluzione dall'età 'Serviana' alla prima età imperial." *MEFRA* 113.2: 565–603.

———. 2009. *Crescità e declino: studi di storia dell'economia romana*. Rome: L'Erma di Bretschneider.

———. 2016. "The Impact of Migration on the Demographic Profile of the City of Rome: A Reassessment." In *Migration and Mobility in the Early Roman Empire*, edited by L. de Ligt and L. E. Tacoma, 23–32. Leiden: Brill.

Loewe, M. 1968. *Everyday Life in Early Imperial China During the Han Period 202 B.C.– A.D. 220*. London: Batsford.

Lomas, K. 2012. "The Weakest Link: Elite Social Networks in Republican Italy." In *Processes of Integration and Identity Formation in the Roman Republic*, edited by S. T. Roselaar, 197–214. Leiden: Brill.

Loreto, L. 1993. *Un'epoca del buon senso. Decisione, consenso e stato a Roma tra il 326 e il 264 a.C.* Amsterdam: A. M. Hakkert.

Luce, T.J. 1971. "Design and Structure in Livy: 5.32–55." *TAPA* 102: 265–302.

Lugli, F. 2001. "Le tombe dell'età del Ferro e l'attività metallurgica dall'età del Ferro al periodo arcaico." *BullCom* 102: 307–20.

Lugli, G. 1926. *Anxur-Terracina. Forma Italiae I.2*. Rome: Danesi.

———. 1933. "Le mura di Servio Tullio e le cosidette mura serviane." *Historia* 7: 3–45.

———. 1957. *La tecnica edilizia romana, con particolare riguardo a Roma e Lazio*. Rome: Bardi.

Lulof, P. J. and C. J. Smith. 2017. *The Age of Tarquinius Superbus: Central Italy in the Late 6th Century. Proceedings of the Conference, The Age of Tarquinius Superbus, A Paradigm Shift?* Rome, 7–9 November 2013. Leuven: Peeters.

Luschi, L. 2008. "L'ariete dei 'manlii': note su una 'tessera hospitalis' dal fucino." *Studi Classici e Orientali* 54: 137–86.

Lyngby, H. and G. Pisani Sartorio. 1968–69. "Indagini archeologiche nell'area dell'antica Porta Trigemina." *BullCom* 80: 5–36.

MacBain, B. 1980. "Appius Claudius Caecus and the Via Appia." *CQ* 30.2: 356–72.

MacDonald, W. 1982. *The Architecture of the Roman Empire*. Vol. 1. New Haven: Yale University Press.

Maddoli, G. 1971. "Il rito degli Argei e le origini del culto di Hera a Roma." *PP* 26: 153–66.

Maetzke, G. 1991. "La struttura stratigrafica nell'area N.O. del Foro Romano come appare dei recenti interventi di scavo." *Archeologia Medievale* 18: 43–200.

Maggiani, A. 2006. "Dinamiche del commercio arcaico: le tesserae hospitalis." *AnnFaina*: 13: 317–50.

Maischberger, M. 1997. *Marmor in Rom: Anlieferung, Lager- und Werkplätze in der Kaiserzeit*. Wiesbaden: Reichert.

Manacorda, D. 2006. "Maestranze alessandrine nella Puglia d'età repubblicana." In *Le vie della storia. Migrazione di popoli, viaggi di individui, circolazione di idee nel Mediterraneo antico (Genova 2004)*, edited by M. G. Angeli Bertinelli and A. Donati, 209–22. Rome: L'Erma di Bretschneider.

Manacorda, D. and R. Santangeli Valenzani. 2011. *Il primo miglio della Via Appia a Roma*. Rome: Roma Tre.

Manca di Mores, G. 1982–83. "Terrecotte architettoniche e problemi topografici. Contributi all'identificazione del tempio di Quirino sul Colle Quirinale." *Studi Classici* 20: 323–60.

Manzelli, V. 2000. "Le mura di Ravenna repubblicana." In *Fortificazioni antiche in Italia. L'età repubblicana*, edited by L. Quilici and S. Quilici Gigli, 7–24. Rome: L'Erma di Bretschneider.

Marcando, L. 1963–64. "Area sacra di S. Omobono. Esplorazione della fase repubblicana. Saggi di scavo sulla platea dei templi gemelli." *BullCom* 79: 35–67.

Marchetti, P. 1993. "Numismatique romaine et histoire." *Cahiers du Centre Gustav Glotz* 4: 23–65.

Marchetti Longhi, G. 1932. "Gli scavi del Largo Argentina I." *BullCom* 60: 253–346.

———. 1936. "Gli scavi del Largo Argentina II." *BullCom* 64: 83–139.

Mari, Z. 1983. *Tibur. Pars tertia. Forma Italiae I.17*. Rome: Danesi.

———. 1991. "Nuovi cippi degli acquedotti aniensi: Considerazioni sull'uso dei cippi acquari." *PBSR* 59: 151–75.

Marquez, C. and M. I. Gutierrez Deza. 2006. "El templo de la Via delle Botteghe Oscure en Roma." In *El concepto de lo provincial en el mundo antiguo. Homenage a la profesora*

Pilar León, edited by D. Vaquerizo and J. Murillo, 301–26. Cordoba: University of Cordoba.

Marra, F., D. Deocampo, M. D. Jackson, and G. Ventura. 2011. "The Alban Hills and Monte Sabatini Volcanic Products Used in Ancient Roman Masonry (Italy): An Integrated Stratigraphic, Archaeological, Environmental and Geochemical Approach." *Earth-Science Reviews* 108: 115–36.

Marra, F. and C. Rosa. 1995. "Stratigrafia e aspetto geologico dell'area romana." *Memorie Descrittive della Carta Geologica d'Italia* 50: 40–112.

Marroni, E. 2010. *I culti dell'Esquilino*. Rome: L'Erma di Bretschneider.

Marshall, B. A. 1985. *A Historical Commentary on Asconius*. Columbia, MO: University of Missouri Press.

Martin, A. 1996. "Un saggio sulle mura del castrum di Ostia (Reg: I, ins. x, 3)." In "*Roman Ostia*" *Revisited. Archaeological and Historical Papers in the Memory of Russell Meiggs*, edited by A. Gallini Zevi and A. Claridge, 19–38. London: British School at Rome.

Martin, S. D. 2002. "Roman Law and the Study of Land Transportation." In *Speculum Iuris: Roman Law as a Reflection of Social and Economic Life in Antiquity*, edited by J.-J. Aubert and B. Sirks. 151–68. Ann Arbor: University of Michigan Press.

Martina, M. 1981. "Aedes Herculis Musarum." *DialArch* 3.1: 49–68.

Mascione, C. and S. Salerno. 2013. "Il sistema difensivo di populonia: nuovi dati sulle mura dell'acropoli." *ScAnt* 19: 411–27.

Massa-Pairault, F. H. 1985. *Recherches sur l'art et l'artisanat Etrusco-Italiques à l'époque Hellénistique*. Rome: École française de Rome.

———. 1988. "Notes sur le problème du citoyen en armes: cité romaine et cité étrusque." In Adam and Rouveret, 51–64.

———. 2001. "Rélations d'Appius Claudius Caecus avec l'Étrurie et la Campanie." In *Le censeur et les Samnites: sur Tite-Live livre IX*, edited by D. Briquel and J.-P. Thuillier, 97–116. Paris: Rue d'Ulm.

Mattei, M. 2014. "Area Sacra di largo Argentina. Indagini archeologiche (2011–2013)." *BullCom* 115: 302–5.

Mattingly, H. B. 1990. "The Roma/Victory Romano Didrachms and the Start of Roman Coinage." In *Ermanno A. Arslan studia dicata*, edited by R. Martini and N. Vismara, 261–90. Milan: Ennerre. Reprinted in H. B. Mattingly, *From Coins to History: Selected Numismatic Studies*, 100–29. Ann Arbor, MI: University of Michigan Press, 2004.

Mauss, M. 1990. *The Gift: The Form and Reason for Exchange in Archaic Societies*. Translated by W. D. Halls. New York: Routledge.

Mayer-Maly, T. 1956. *Locatio conductio: eine Untersuchung zum klassischen römischen Recht*. Vienna: Herold.

Meadows, A. and J. Williams. 2001. "Moneta and the Monuments: Coinage and Politics in Republican Rome." *JRS* 91: 27–49.

Meiggs, R. 1980. "Sea-Borne Timber Supplies Rome." *MAAR* 36: 185–96.

———. 1982. *Trees and Timber in the Ancient Mediterranean World.* Oxford: Clarendon Press.

Meister, K. 2002. "Filisto e la tirranide." In *La Sicilia dei due Dionisi, Atti della settimana di studio, Agrigento 24–28 febbraio 1999*, edited by N. Bonacasa, L. Braccesi, E. De Miro, 453–62. Rome: L'Erma di Bretschneider.

Meneghini, R. 2009. *I Fori Imperiali e I Mercati di Traiano: storia e descrizione dei monumenti alla luce degli studi e degli scavi recenti.* Rome: Istituto Poligrafico e Zecca dello Stato.

Menghi, O. 2008. "Le indagini più recenti e gli aggiornamenti." In M. Barbera and M. Magnani Cianetti, eds., 30–47.

Menghi, O., M. Pales, and M. Di Bernardini. 2006. "La necropoli di epoca repubblicana in via Goito a Roma." *FastiOnline*: 1–10.

Mercuri, A.-M., C. A. Accorsi, and M. Bandini Mazzanti. 2002. "The Long History of Cannabis and Its Cultivation by the Romans in Central Italy, Shown by Pollen Records from Lago Albano and Lago di Nemi." *Vegetation History and Archeobotany* 11.4: 263–76.

Mertens, D. 2002. "Le lunghe mura di Dionigi I a Siracusa." In *La Sicilia dei due Dionisi. Atti della settimana di studio, Agrigento 242–8 febbraio 1999*, edited by N. Bonacasa, L. Braccesi, and E. De Miro, 243–52. Rome: L'Erma di Bretschneider.

———. 2006. *Städte und Bauten der Westgriechen: von der Kolonisationszeit bis zur Krise um 400 vor Christus.* Munich: Hirmer.

Messineo, G. and A. Carbonara. 1993. *Via Flaminia.* Rome: Istituto Poligrafico e Zecca dello Stato.

Meyer, J. C. 1980. "Roman History in Light of the Import of Attic Vases to Rome and Etruria." *Analecta romana Instituti Danici* 9: 47–68.

Michels, A. 1967. *The Calendar of the Roman Republic.* Princeton, NJ: Princeton University Press.

Mignone, L. 2016. *The Republican Aventine and Rome's Social Order.* Ann Arbor, MI: University of Michigan Press.

Milazzo, F. 1993. *La realizzazione delle opere pubbliche in Roma arcaica e repubblicana. Munera e ultro tributa.* Napoli: Edizioni scientifiche italiane.

Millar, F. 1984. "Condemnation to Hard Labour in the Roman Empire, from the Julio-Claudians to Constantine." *PBSR* 52: 124–47.

———. 1989. "Political Power in Mid-Republican Rome: Curia or Comitium?" *JRS* 79: 138–50.

Millett, P. 1991. *Lending and Borrowing in Ancient Athens.* Cambridge: Cambridge University Press.

Mingazzini, P. 1986. "Tre brevi note sui laterizi antichi." In *Paolo Mingazzini: Scritti vari*, edited by G. De Luca, 325–40. Rome: L'Erma di Bretschneider.

Mitchell, R. E. 1966. "A New Chronology for the Romano-Campanian Coins." *NC* 6: 65–70.

———. 1967. "The Fourth Century Origin of Roman Didrachms." *ANS Museum Notes* 15: 41–71.

Mocchegiani Carpano, C. 1985. "Lungotevere Testaccio: resti del porto fluviale." *BullCom* 90: 86–88.

Mogetta, M. 2015. "A New Date for Concrete in Rome." *JRS* 105: 1–40.

Mogetta, M and J. A. Becker. 2014. Archaeological Research at Gabii, Italy: The Gabii Project Excavations 2009–2011." *AJA* 118.1: 171–88.

Molinari, M. C. 1995. "Le monete della meta sudans." *AIIN* 42: 109–60.

———. 2004. "Un ripostiglio di aes grave proveniente dai Colli Vaiticani (Roma)." *BullCom* 105: 115–22.

———. 2011. "A Hoard of Bronze Coins of the 3rd Century BC Found at Pratica di Mare (Rome)." In *Proceedings of the XIVth International Numismatic Congress, Glasgow 2009*, edited by N. Holmes, 828–39. Glasgow: University of Glasgow.

Momigliano, A. 1942. "Camillus and Concord." *CQ* 36.3/4: 111–20.

———. 1950. "Ancient History and the Antiquarian." *JWCI* 13.3/4: 285–315.

Mommsen, T. 1879. *Romische Forschungen*. Vol. 2. Berlin: Weidmann.

———. 1899. *Römische Strafrecht*. Leipzig: Duncker & Humblot.

Moore, T. J. 1991. "Palliata Togata: Plautus, Curculio 462–86." *AJPhil* 112.3: 343–62.

Moormann, E. 2011. *Divine Interiors: Mural Paintings in Greek and Roman Sanctuaries*. Amsterdam: Amsterdam University Press.

Morel, J.-P. 1969. "Etudes de céramiques campaniennes I: L'atelier des petites estampilles." *MEFRA* 81: 59–117.

———. 1987. "La topographie de l'artisanat et du commerce dans la Rome antique." In aa.vv. *L'Urbs: espace urbain et histoire (Ier siècle av. J.-C.–IIIe siècle ap. J.-C.)*, 127–55. Rome: École Française de Rome.

———. 1988. "Artisanat et colonisation dans l'"Italie romaine aux IVe et IIIe siècles av. J.-C." *DialArch* 2.6: 49–63.

———. 2007. "Early Rome and Italy." In Scheidel, Morris, and Saller, 487–510.

Morganti, G. and M. A. Tomei, "Ancora sulla via Nova." *MEFRA* 103.2: 551–74.

Morley, N. 1996. *Metropolis and Hinterland: The City of Rome and the Italian Economy, 200 B.C.–A.D. 200.* Cambridge: Cambridge University Press.

———. 2011. "Cities, Demography, and Development in the Roman World." In *Settlement, Urbanisation, and Population*, edited by A. K. Bowman and A. I. Wilson, 143–60. Oxford: Oxford Press.

Morris, I., R. Saller, and W. Scheidel. 2007. "Introduction." In Scheidel, Morris, and Saller, eds., 1–12.

Mouritsen, H. 2011. *The Freedmen of the Roman World*. Cambridge: Cambridge University Press.

Mrozek, S. 1989. *Lohnarbeit im klassischen Altertum: ein Beitrag zur Sozial- und Wirtschaftsgeschichte*. Bonn: R. Habelt.

Muldrew, C. 2011. *Food, Energy and the Creation of Industriousness: Work and Material Culture in Agrarian England, 1550–1780*. Cambridge: Cambridge University Press.

Nagy, B. 1993. "The Argei Puzzle." *AJAH* 10: 1–27.

Nakassis, D. 2012. "Labor Mobilization in Mycenaean Pylos." In *Études mycéniennes 2010: Actes du XIIIe colloque international sur les textes égéens*, edited by P. Carlier,

C. de Lamberterie, M. Egetmeyer, N. Guilleux, F. Rougemont, and J. Zurbach, 269–83. Pisa: Fabrizio Serra.

Nicolet, C. 1963. "À Rome pendant la seconde guerre Punique: techniques financières et manipulations monétaires." *AnnESC* 18.3: 417–36.

———. 1982. "Il pensiero economico dei Romani." In *Storia delle idee politiche, economiche e sociale*, edited by L. Firpo, 877–960. Turin: Unione tipografico editrice torinese.

———. 1988. *L'Inventaire du monde. Géographie et politique aux origine de l' Empire romain*. Paris: Librarie Arthème Fayard.

Nicosia, E., D. Sacco, and M. Tondo. 2013. "Il santuario di Fondo Decina. Materiale votivo e forme di culto. La spada di San Vittore." *Lazio e Sabina* 9: 483–85.

Niebuhr, G. B. 1827. *Roman History*. Translated by F. A. Walter. London: C. and J. Rivington.

Nielsen, I. and B. Poulsen, eds. 1992. *The Temple of Castor and Pollux*. Rome: De Luca.

Noguera, J. 2012. "La Palma–Nova Classis. A Publius Cornelius Scipio Africanus Encampment During the Second Punic War in Iberia." *Madrider Mitteilungen* 53: 262–86.

Nonnis, D. 2012. *Produzione e distribuzione nell'Italia repubblicana: uno studio prosopografico*. Rome: Quasar.

North, D. C. 1981. *Structures and Change in Economic History*. New York: Norton.

———. 1990. *Institutions, Institutional Change and Economic Performance*. Cambridge: Cambridge University Press.

———. 2005. *Understanding the Process of Economic Change*. Princeton: Princeton University Press.

Northwood, S. J. 2006. "Grain Scarcity and Pestilence in the Early Roman Republic: Some Significant Patterns." *BICS* 49: 81–92.

Oakley, S. P. 1997–2005. *A Commentary on Livy, Books VI–X*. 4 vols. Oxford: Oxford University Press.

Ogilvie, R. M. 1965. *A Commentary on Livy, Books I–V*. Oxford: Clarendon Press.

Olcese, G. and C. Coletti, eds. 2016. *Ceramiche da contesti repubblicani del territorio di Ostia*. Rome: Quasar.

Oliver, J. H. 1932. "The Augustan Pomerium." *MAAR* 10: 145–82.

Orlandini, P. 1965–67. "Gela, depositi votivi di bronzo premonetale nel santuario di Demetra Thesmophoros a Bitalemi." *AIIN* 12–14: 1–20.

Orlin, E. 1997. *Temples, Religion, and Politics in the Roman Republic*. Leiden: Brill.

Özmucur, S. and S. Pamuk 2002. "Real Wages and Standards of Living in the Ottoman Empire, 1489–1914." *JEH* 62.2: 293–321.

Pace, P. 1983. *Gli acquedotti di Roma e il "De aquaeductu" di Frontino*. Rome: Art Studio S. Eligio.

Padilla Peralta, D. 2014. "Divine Institutions: Religious Practice, Economic Development, and Social Transformation in Mid-Republican Rome." PhD diss., Stanford University.

Painter, B. 2005. *Mussolini's Rome. Rebuilding the Ancient City*. New York: Palgrave Macmillan.

Pais, E. 1918. *Storia critica di Roma durante I primi cinque secoli*. Vol. 3. Rome: E. Loescher.

Pakkanen, J. 2014. "The Economics of Shipshed Complexes: Zea, a Case Study." In *Shipsheds of the Ancient Mediterranean*, edited by D. Blackman and B. Rankov, 55–76. Cambridge: Cambridge University Press.

Pallottino, M. 1991. *A History of Earliest Italy*. Translated by M. Ryle and K. Soper. Ann Arbor, MI: University of Michigan Press.

Palmer, R. E. A, 1974. "Roman Shrines of Female Chastity from the Caste Struggle to the Papacy of Innocent I." *RSA* 4: 119–53.

———. 1976–77. "The Vici Luccei in the Forum Boarium and Some Lucceii in Rome." *BullCom* 85: 135–61.

———. 1981. "The Topography and Social History of Rome's Trastevere. Southern Sector." *Proceedings of the American Philosophical Society* 125: 368–97.

Palombi, D. 1997a. "Cic., 2 Verr. V, 19, 48 e Gloss. Ps. Plac. f5 (=GL, IV, p. 61) sulla costruzione del tempio di Giove Capitolino." *BullCom* 98: 7–14.

———. 1997b. *Tra Palatino ed Esquilino: Velia, Carinae, Fagutal: storia urbana di tre quartieri di Roma antica*. Rome: Istituto Nazionale di storia dell'arte.

———. 2010. "Roma tardo-repubblicana. Verso la città ellenistica." In *I giorni di Roma. L'età della conquista*, edited by E. La Rocca and C. Parisi Presicce, 65–82. Milano: Skira.

Panciera, S. 2006. "Aidilis curulis Veliterns locavit." In S. Panciera. *Epigrafi, epigrafia, epigrafisti. Scritti vari editi e inediti (1956–2005) con note complementari e indici*, 587–90. Rome: Quasar.

Panei, L. 2010. "The Tuffs of the 'Servian Wall' in Rome: Materials from the Local Quarries and from the Conquered Territories." *ArcheoSciences* 34: 39–43.

Panei, L. and M. Dell'Orso. 2008. "I tufi delle Mura Serviane: origini e caratterizzazione chimico-mineralogica." In Barbera and Magnani Cianetti, eds., 96–107.

Panella, C. 2010. "Roma, il suburbio e l'Italia in età medio- e tardo- repubblicana: cultura materiale, territori, economie." *Facta* 4: 11–123.

Panella, C., S. Zeggio, and A. F. Ferrandes. 2014. "Lo scavo delle pendici nord-orientali del Palatino tra dati acquisiti e nuove evidenze." *ScAnt* 20.1: 159–210.

Papi, E. and A. Carandini, eds. 1999. *Palatium e Sacra Via II. L'età tardo-repubblicana e la prima età imperiale (fine III secolo a.C.- 64 d.C.). BA 59–60*. Rome: Istituto Poligrafico e Zecca dello Stato.

Parise, N. 1990. "I mestieri bancari nel mondo romano: (a proposito del libro di Jean Andreau)." *Studi Storici* 31.2: 395–97.

Parker, J. H. 1878. *The Primitive Fortifications of the City of Rome and Other Buildings of the Time of the Kings*. 2nd ed. London: John Murray.

Parry, J. and M. Bloch 1989. "Introduction: Money and the Morality of Exchange." In *Money and the Morality of Exchange*, edited by J. Parry and M. Bloch, 1–32. Cambridge: Cambridge University Press.

Patterson, H., H. Di Giuseppe, and R. Witcher. 2004. "Three South Etrurian 'Crises': First Results of the Tiber Valley Project." *PBSR* 72: 1–36.

Pedroni, L. 1993. *Ricerche sulla prima monetazione di Roma*. Napoli: Liguori.

———. 2001. *Ceramica calena a vernice nera. Produzione e diffusione*. Perugia: Petruzzi.

Pegoretti, G. 1869. *Manuale pratico per l'estimazione dei lavori architettonici, stradale, idraulici, e di fortificazione, per uso degli ingegneri ed architetti*. 2nd ed, revised by A. Cantalupi. Milan: Domenico Salvi.

Pekáry, T. 1968. *Untersuchungen zu den römischen Reichstrassen*. Bonn. R. Halbert.

Pelgrom, J. 2008. "Settlement Organisation and Land Distribution in Latin Colonies Before the Second Punic War." In *People, Land, and Politics: Demographic Developments and the Transformation of Roman Italy 300 BC–AD 14*, edited by L. de Ligt and S. J. Northwood, 333–72. Leiden/Boston: Brill.

Pellam, G. 2014. "A Peculiar Episode from the 'Struggle of the Orders'? Livy and the Licinio-Sextian Rogations." *CQ* 64.1: 280–92.

Pellegrini, E., R. Macellari, and R. M. Albanese. 2002. *I Lingotti con il segno del ramo secco: considerazioni su alcuni aspetti socio-economici nell'area etrusco-italica durante il periodo tardo arcaico*. Pisa: Istituti editoriali e poligrafici internazionali.

Pensabene, P. 1998. "Vent'anni di studi e scavi dell'Università di Roma 'La Sapienza' nell'area Sud Ovest del Palatino (1977–1997)." In *Il Palatino. Area sacra sud-ovest e Domus Tiberiana*, edited by C. Giavarini, 1–154. Rome: Bretschneider.

Pensabene, P., E. Gasparini, E. Gallocchio, and M. Brilli. 2015. "'Marmo di Cottanello' (Sabina, Italy): Quarry Survey and Data on Its Distribution." In *ASMOSIA X. Proceedings of the Tenth International Conference of ASMOSIA*, edited by P. Pensabene and E. Gasparini, 629–39. Rome: L'Erma di Bretschneider.

Peppe, L. 1981. *Studi sull'esecuzione personale. 1, Debiti e debitori nei primi due secoli della Repubblica romana*. Milano: Giuffrè.

Perrson, K. G. 2010. *An Economic History of Europe: Knowledge, Institutions and Growth, 600 to the Present*. Cambridge: Cambridge University Press.

Peruzzi, E. 1985. *Money in Early Rome*. Florence: Olschki.

Phelps Brown, H. and S. V. Hopkins. 1981. *A Perspective of Wages and Prices*. London: Methuen.

Pickett, J., J. S. Schreck, R. Holod, Y. Rassamakin, O. Halenko, and W. Woodfin. 2016. "Architectural Energetics for Tumuli Construction: The Case of the Medieval Chungul Kurgan on the Eurasian Steppe." *Journal of Archaeological Science* 75: 101–14.

Pietilä-Castrén, L. 1987. *Magnificentia Publica: The Victory Monuments of the Roman Generals in the Era of the Punic Wars*. Helsinki: Finnish Society of Sciences and Letters.

Piketty, T. *Capital in the Twenty-First Century*. Translated by A. Goldhammer. Cambridge, MA: Harvard University Press.

Pina Polo, F. 2011. *The Consul at Rome: the Civil Functions of the Consuls in the Roman Republic*. Cambridge: Combridge University Press.

Pinsent, J. 1954. "The Original Meaning of Municeps." *CQ* 4.3/4: 158–64.

Pinza, G. 1897. "Sulle mura romane attribuite all'epoca dei re." *BullCom* 25: 228–61.

———. 1905. *Monumenti primitivi di Roma e del Lazio antico*. Monumenti Antichi Lincei, 15.

Pisani Sartorio, G. 1977. "Esame preliminare dei materiali archeologici (scavo 1974–1975): Parte terza." *PP* 32: 55–61.

———. 1989. "La scoperta dei Templi della Fortuna e della Mater Matuta." In aa.vv. *Il viver quotidiano in Roma arcaica: materiali dagli scavi del tempio arcaico nell'area sacra di S. Omobono*, 13–22. Rome: Procom.

Pisani Sartorio, P. and S. Quilici Gigli. 1987–88. "A proposito della Tomba dei Corneli." *BullCom* 92: 247–64.

Pisani Sartorio, G. and P. Virgili. 1979. "Area Sacra di San Omobono." *ArchLaz* 2: 41–47.

Pontrandolfo, A. and B. D'Agostino. 1990. "Greci, etruschi, e italici nella Campani e nella Lucania tirrenica." In *Crise et transformation*, 101–16.

Popkin, M. 2016. *The Architecture of the Roman Triumph: Monuments, Memory, and Identity*. New York: Cambridge University Press.

Poucet, J. 1980. "La Rome archaïque. Quelques nouveautés archéologiques: S. Omobono, le Comitium, la Regia." *Antiquité Classique* 49: 286–315.

———. 2000. *Les rois de Rome. Tradition et histoire*. Brussels: Académie royale de Belgique.

Prag, J. R. W. 2014a. "Bronze rostra from the Egadi Islands off NW Sicily: The Latin Inscriptions." *JRA* 27: 33–59.

———. 2014b. "The Quaestorship in the Third and Second Centuries B.C." In *L'imperium Romanum en perspective. Les savoirs d'empire dans la republique romaine et leur heritage dans l'europe medievale et moderne*, edited by J. Dubouloz, S. Pittia, and G. Sabatini, 193–209. Besançon: Institut des Sciences et Techniques de l'Antiquité.

———. 2016. "Antiquae sunt istae leges et mortuae: The Plebiscitum Claudianum and Associated Laws." *MEFRA* 128-1.

Prag, J. R. W. and J. Crawley Quinn. 2013. *The Hellenistic West: Rethinking the Ancient Mediterranean*. Cambridge: Cambridge University Press.

Purcell, N. 1990. "Maps, Lists, Money, Order, and Power." *JRS* 80: 178–82.

———. 1993. "Atrium Libertatis." *PBSR* 61: 125–55.

———. 2003. "Becoming Historical. The Roman Case." In *Myth, History and Culture in Republican Rome: Studies in Honour of T.P. Wiseman*, edited by D. Braund and C. Gill, 12–40. Exeter: University of Exeter Press.

Quilici, L. 1974. *Collatia. Forma Italiae I.10*. Rome: De Luca.

———. 1990. "Il rettifilo della Via Appia tra Roma e Terracina: la tecnica costruttiva." *ArchLaz* 10.1: 41–60.

———. 1994. "Le fortificazioni ad aggere nel Lazio Antico." *Ocnus* 2: 147–58.

———. 1997. *La Via Appia: regina viarum*. Rome: Viviani.

———. 2004. *La Via Appia: un percorso nella storia*. Rome: Viviani.

Quilici Gigli, S., ed. 1994. *La Via Appia: decimo incontro di studio del Comitato per l'archeologia laziale. ArchLaz* 10.1. Rome: Consiglio nazionale delle ricerche.

Quoniam, P. 1947. "A propos du mur dit de Servius Tullius." *MEFRA* 59: 43–52.

Raaflaub, K. A., ed. 2005. *Social Struggles in Archaic Rome: New Perspectives on the Conflict of the Orders*. Malden, MA: Blackwell Publishing.

Raaflaub, K. A., J. D. Richards, and S. J. Samons. 1992. "Rome, Italy, and Appius Claudius Caecus Before the Pyrrhic Wars." In *The Age of Pyrrhus. Papers delivered at the international conference, Brown University, 8–10 April, 1988*, edited by T. Hackens, N.D. Holloway, and R.R. Holloway, 13–50. Louvain-la-Neuve: Département d'archéologie et d'histoire de l'art Collège Erasme.

Rakob, F. 1983. "Opus caementicium und die Folgen." *RM* 90: 359–72.

Rakob, F. and D. Heilmeyer. 1973. *Der Rundtempel am Tiber in Rom*. Mainz: Zabern.

Rathbone, D. W. 2009. "Earnings and Costs: Living Standards and the Roman Economy." In *Quantifying the Roman Economy: Methods and Problems*, edited by A. Bowman and A. Wilson, 299–326. Oxford: Oxford University Press.

Rawson, E. 1990. "The Antiquarian Tradition: Spoils and Representations of Foreign Armour." In *Staat und Staatlichkeit in der frühen römischen Republik*, edited by W. Eder, 158–73. Stuttgart: Steiner.

Reece, R. 1982. "A Collection of Coins from the Centre of Rome." *PBSR* 50: 116–45.

Regoli, C. 2012. "Alcune considerazioni sulla stratigrafia del settore I (scavi 1974–76)." In *Nuove ricerche nell'area archeologica di S. Omobono a Roma*, edited by P. Brocato and N. Terrenato, 79–94. Arcavacata di Rende: Università della Calabria.

Rendeli, M. 1989. "Vasi attici da mensa in Etruria. Note sulle occorrenze e sulla distribuzione." *MEFRA* 101.2: 545–79.

Reusser, C. 1993. "Der Fidestempel auf dem Kapitol in Rom und seine Ausstatung: ein Beitrag zu den Ausgrabungen an der Via del Mare und um das Kapitol 1926–1943." *BullCom* Suppl. 2. Rome: L'Erma di Bretschneider.

Ricci, G. 2002. "Un laboratorio tessile a Ponte Milvio: indagini 2001–2002." In *Il Santuario della Musica e il Bosco Sacro di Anna Perenna*, edited by M. Piramonte, 89–95. Milan: Electa.

Richard, J.-C. 1975. *Les origines de la plebe romaine. Essai sur la formation du dualisme patricio-plébéien*. Rome: École française de Rome.

———. 1990, "Historiographie et histoire: L'expedition des Fabii a la Cremere." In *Staat und Staatlichkeit in der frühen römischen Republik*, edited by W. Eder, 174–99. Stuttgart: Steiner.

Richardson, L., Jr. 1976a. "The Villa Publica and the Divorum." In *In Memoriam Otto J. Brendel: Essays in Archaeology and the Humanities*, edited by L. Bonfante and H. von Heintze, 159–62. Mainz: Zabern.

———. 1976b. "The Evolution of the Porticus Octaviae." *AJA* 80: 57–64.

———. 1977. "Hercules Musarum and the Porticus Philippi in Rome." *AJA* 81: 355–61.

———. 1978. "Concordia and Concordia Augusta. Rome and Pompeii." *PP* 33: 260–72.

———. 1992. *A New Topographical Dictionary of Ancient Rome*. Baltimore, MD: Johns Hopkins University Press.

Richardson, J. H. 2004. "Dorsuo and the Gauls." *Phoenix* 58.3/4: 284–97.

———. 2008. "Rome's Treaties with Carthage: Jigsaw or Variant Traditions?" In *Studies in Latin Literature and Roman History* 14, edited by C. Deroux, 84–94. Brussels: Latomus.

———. 2012. *The Fabii and the Gauls: Studies in Historical Thought and Historiogrpahy in Republican Rome*. Stuttgart: Steiner.

Richardson, S. 2014. "Building Larsa: Labor-value, Scale, and Scope of Economy in Ancient Mesopotamia." In *Labour in the Ancient World*, edited by P. Steinkeller and M. Hudson, 237–328. Dresden: ISLET.

Richter, O. 1885. *Über antike Steinmetzzeichen*. Berlin: G. Reimer.

———. 1901. *Topographie der Stadt Röm*. Munich: C. H. Beck.

Ridgway, D. 1992. *The First Western Greeks*. Cambridge: Cambridge University Press.

Riemann, H. 1969. "Beitrage zur römischen Topographie." *RM* 76: 103–21.

Roberts, L. 1918, "The Gallic Fire and the Roman Archives." *MAAR* 2: 55–65.

Robinson, O. F. 1992. *Ancient Rome: City Planning and Administration*. London: Routledge.

Rodgers, B. S. 1986. "Great Expeditions: Livy on Thucydides." *TAPA* 116: 335–52.

Rodgers, R. H., ed., and comm. 2004. *Frontinus De Aqueductu Urbis Romae. Cambridge Classical Texts and Commentaries 42*. Cambridge: Cambridge University Press.

Rodriguez Almeida, E. 1981. *Forma Urbis marmorea. Aggiornamento generale*. Rome: Quasar.

———. 1984. *Il Monte Testaccio: ambiente, storia, materiali*. Rome: Quasar.

———. 1991. "Nuovi dati dalla Forma Urbis marmorea per le mura perimetrali, gli accessi e i templi del Colle Capitolino." *BA* 8: 33–44.

———. 1991–92. "Diversi problemi connessi con la lastra n. 37 della Forma Urbis Marmorea e con la topografia in circo e in campo." *RendPont* 64: 3–26.

Roselaar, S. T. 2010. *Public Land in the Roman Republic: A Social and Economic History of Ager Publicus in Italy, 396–89 BC*. Oxford: Oxford University Press.

———. 2011. "Colonies and Processes of Integration in the Roman Republic." *MEFRA* 123.2: 527–55.

Rosenstein, N. 2004. *Rome at War: Farms, Families, and Death in the Middle Republic*. Chapel Hill, NC: UNC Press.

Rotondi, G. 1962. *Leges publicae populi romani. Elenco cronologico con una introduzione sull'attività legislative dei comizi romani*. Hildesheim: G. Olms.

Rouveret, A. 1994. "La ciste Ficoroni et la culture romaine du IVe s. av. J.-C." *Bulletin de la Société des Antiquaires de France*: 225–42.

Ruggiero, I. 1990. "La cinta muraria presso il Foro Boario in età arcaica e medio repubblicana." *ArchLaz* 10: 23–30.

———. 1991–92. "Ricerche su tempio di Portuno nel Foro Boario." *BullCom* 94: 253–86.

Russell, B. 2013. *The Economics of the Roman Stone Trade*. Oxford: Oxford University Press.

Säflund, G. 1998 (Repr. of 1932 edition). *Le mura di Roma repubblicana*. Rome: Quasar.

Saller, R. 2005. "Framing the Debate Over Growth in the Ancient Economy." In *The Ancient Economy: Evidence and Models*, edited by J. G. Manning and I. Morris, 223–38. Stanford, CA: Stanford University Press.

———. 2012. "Human Capital and Economic Growth." In *The Cambridge Companion to the Roman Economy*, edited by W. Scheidel, 71–89. Cambridge: Cambridge University Press.

Salomies, O. 2014. "The Roman Republic." In *The Oxford Handbook of Roman Epigraphy*, edited by C. Bruun and J. Edmondson, 153–78. New York: Oxford University Press.

Santa Maria Scrinari, V. 1969. "Tombe a camera sotto via S. Stefano Rotondo." *BullCom* 81: 17–24.

———. 1979. "Brevi note sugli scavi sotto la chiesa di S. Vito." *ArchLaz* 2: 58–62.

Santangeli Valenzani, R. 1994. "Tra la Porticus Minucia e il Calcarario. L'area sacra di Largo Argentina nell'altomedioevo." *Archeologia Medievale* 21: 57–98.

Sassatelli, G. 1977. "L'Etruria padana e il commercio dei marmi nel V secolo." *Studi Etruschi* 45: 109–47.

Savage, S. M. 1940. "The Cults of Ancient Trastevere." *MAAR* 17: 26–56.

Savunen, L. 1993. "Debt Legislation in the Fourth century B.C." In *Senatus populusque Romanus: Studies in Roman Republican Legislation*, edited by U. Paananen, 143–59. Helsinki: Institutum Romanum Finlandiae.

Schatzmann, A. 2015. "An Ancient Highway to the Tufa Quarries: New Considerations on a Forgotten Monument North of Rome." In *Hypogea 2015. Proceedings of International Congress of Speleology in Artificial Cavities*. Rome, March 11–17 2015: 211–22.

Scheidel, W. 2003. "Germs for Rome." In *Rome the Cosmopolis*, edited by C. Edwards and G. Woolf, 158–76. Cambridge: Cambridge University Press.

———. 2004. "Human Mobility in Roman Italy, I: The Free Population." *JRS* 94: 1–26.

———. 2005. "Human Mobility in Roman Italy, II: The Slave Population." *JRS* 95: 64–79.

———. 2007. "Demography." In Scheidel, Morris, and Saller, 38–66.

———. 2012. "Approaching the Roman Economy." In *The Cambridge Companion to the Roman Economy*, edited by W. Scheidel, 1–21. Cambridge: Cambridge.

———. forthcoming. "Slavery and Forced Labor in Early China and the Roman World." In *All Under Heaven: Eurasian Empires in Antiquity and the Middle Ages*, edited by H. J. Kim, F. Vervaet and S. Adali. Cambridge: Cambridge University Press.

Scheidel, W. and J. Friesen. 2009. "The Size of the Economy and the Distribution of Income in the Roman Empire." *JRS* 99: 61–91.

Scheidel, W., I. Morris, and R. Saller, eds. 2007. *The Cambridge Economic History of the Greco-Roman World*. Cambridge: Cambridge University Press.

Schingo, G. 1996. "Indice topografico delle strutture anteriori all'incendio del 64 d.C. rinvenute nella valle del Colosseo e nelle sue adiacenze." In *Meta Sudans I. Un'area sacra in Palatio e la valle del Colosseo prima e dopo Nerone*, edited by C. Panella, 145–58. Rome: Istituto poligrafico e Zecco dello Stato.

Schiöler, T. 1994. "The Pompeii-groma in New Light." *Analecta Romana* 22:45–60

Schröck, K. 2012. "Stone Setting Practiced by the Masons of the Naumburg and Meissen Cathedrals: A Comparative Look at Stone Setting Techniques." In *Masons at Work*, edited by R. Osterhout, R. Holod, and L. Haselberger. Digital publication: http://www.sas.upenn.edu/ancient/publications.html.

Schulze, W. 1991. *Zur Geschichte lateinischer Eigennamen*. Updated reprint edition. Hildesheim: Weidmann.

Scott, R. T. 1993. "Excavations in the Area Sacra of Vesta 1987–1989." In *Eius virtutis studiosi: Classical and Postclassical Studies in Memory of Frank Edward Brown, 1908–1988*, edited by R. T. Scott, 160–81. Washington, DC: National Gallery of Art.

———. 2009. *Excavations in the Area Sacra of Vesta (1987–1996)*. Ann Arbor, MI: University of Michigan Press.

Serafini, C. 1943–45. "Tesoretto di monete d'età repubblicana rinvenuto sul Campidoglio." *Bullcom* 71: 109–12.

Sewell, J. 2010. "The Formation of Roman Urbanism, 338–200 B.C.: Between Contemporary Foreign Influence and Roman Tradition." *JRA* Suppl. 79. Portsmouth, RI: JRA.

Shatzman, I. 1972. "The Roman General's Authority Over Booty." *Historia* 21: 177–205.

Shaw, B. D. 1975. Debt in Sallust." *Latomus* 34.1: 187–96.

———. 2006. "Seasonal Mortality in Imperial Rome and the Mediterranean: Three Problem Cases." In *Urbanism in the Preindustrial World: Cross-cultural Approaches*, edited by G. Storey. Tuscaloosa, 86–109. Alabama: University of Alabama Press.

Shear, T. L. 1993. "The Persian Destruction of Athens: Evidence from the Agora Deposits." *Hesperia* 62.4: 383–482.

Shipley, G. 2000. *The Greek World after Alexander, 323–30 B.C.* London: Routledge.

Shoe Merritt, L. T. 2000. *Etruscan and Republic Roman Mouldings*. 2nd ed. Philadelphia, PA: University Museum, University of Pennsylvania.

Sijpesteijn, P. 1964. *Penthemeros-certificates in Graeco-Roman Egypt*. Leiden: Brill.

Silver, M. 2012. "The Nexum Contract as a 'Strange Artifice.'" *Revue international des droits de l'antiquité* 59: 217–38.

Simon, H. 1983. *Reason in Human Affairs*. Stanford, CA: Stanford University Press.

Sironen, T. 1997. "Un graffito in latino arcaico su un frammento di terracotta da Fregellae." *ZPE* 115: 242–44.

Skutsch, O. 1953. "The Fall of the Capitol." *JRS* 43: 77–78.

———. 1973. "On the Fall of the Capitol Again: Tacitus, Ann. 11.23." *JRS* 68: 93–94.

Smelser, N. J. and R. Swedberg. 2005. "Introducing Economic Sociology." In *The Handbook of Economic Sociology*, 2nd ed., edited by N. J. Smelser and R. Swedberg. Princeton, NJ: Princeton University Press.

Smith, C. J . 2006. *The Roman Clan: The Gens from Ancient Ideology to Modern Anthropology*. Cambridge: Cambridge University Press.

Sommella, P. 1968. "Area sacra di S. Omobono: Contributo per una datazione della platea dei templi gemelli." *QITA* 5: 63–70.

———. 2005. "La Roma Plautina (con Particolare Riferimento a Cur. 467–485)." In *Lecturae Plautinae Sarsinates VIII: Curculio, Sarsina, 25 Settembre 2004*, edited by R. Raffaelli and A. Tontini, 69–106. Urbino: Quattro-Venti.

Sordi, M. 1960. *I rapporti romano-ceriti e l'origine della "Civitas sine suffragio."* Rome: L'Erma di Bretschneider.

———. 1984. "Il campidoglio e l'invasione gallica del 386 a.C." In *I santuari e la Guerra nel mondo classico*, edited by M. Sordi, 82–91. Milan: Vita e pensiero.

Spagnoli, E. 2007. "Evidenze numismatiche dal territorio di Ostia antica (età repubblicana—età flavia)." In aa.vv. *Presenza e circolazione della moneta in area vesuviana, Atti del XIII Convegno organizzato dal Centro Internazionale degli Studi numismatici e dall'Università di Napoli Federico II, Napoli 30 maggio–1 giugno 2003*, 233–388. Rome: Istituto italiano di numismatica.

Specchio, P. 2011. "L'insula della Salita del Grillo all'interno dei Mercati di Traiano a Roma." In *Il future nell'archeologia. Il contributo dei giovani ricercatori–Atti del IV convegno nazionale dei giovani archeology tuscania (VT), 12–15 Maggio 2011*, edited by G. Guarducc and S. Valentini, 349–58. Rome: Scienze e lettere.

Spera, L. and S. Mineo. 2004. *Via Appia I. Da Roma a Bovillae*. Rome: Istituto poligrafico e Zecca dello stato.

Spurr, M. S. 1986. *Arable Cultivation in Roman Italy c. 200 B.C.–c. A.D. 100.* London: Society for the Promotion of Roman Studies.

Stanco E. A. 2009. "La seriazione cronologica della ceramica a vernice nera etrusco-laziale nell'ambito del III secolo a.C." In *Suburbium II. Il suburbia di Roma dalla fine dell'età monarchia all nascità del sistema delle ville (V-II secolo a.C.)*, edited by V. Jolivet, C. Pavolini, M. A. Tomei, and R. Volpe, 157–93. Rome: École française de Rome.

Starr, C. 1980. *The Beginnings of Imperial Rome: Rome in the Mid-Republic*. Ann Arbor, MI: University of Michigan Press.

Staveley, E. S. 1959. "The Political Aims of Appius Claudius Caecus." *Historia* 8.4: 410–33.

Steinby, E. M. 2012a. *Edilizia pubblica e potere politico nella Roma repubblicana.* Milan: Jaca.

Stek, T, and Pelgrom, J., eds. 2014. *Roman Republican Colonization. New Perspectives from Archaeology and Ancient history*. Papers of the Royal Netherlands Institute in Rome. Vol. 62. Rome: Palombi Editori.

———. 2012b. *Lacus Iuturnae. II, Saggi degli anni 1982–85*. Rome: Institutum Romandum Finlandiae.

Stibbe, C. M. et al. 1980. *Lapis Satricanus: Archaeological, Epigraphical, Linguistic and Historical Aspects of the New Inscription from Satricum*. The Hague: Staatsuitgeverji.

Storchi Marino, A. 1991–92. "Il rituale degli Argei tra annalistica e antiquaria." *Annali dell'Istituto Italiano per gli Studi Storici* 12: 263–308.

———. 1993. "Quinqueviri mensarii: censo e debiti nel IV secolo." *Athenaeum* 81: 213–50.

Strazzulla, M. J. 1981. "Le terrecotte architettoniche. Le produzioni dal IV al I sec. a.C." In *Società romana e produzione schiavistica, 2. Merci, mercati e scambi nel Mediterraneo*, edited by A. Gardina and A. Schiavone, 187–207. Bari: Laterza.

Strong, D. E. 1968. "The Administration of Public Building in Rome During the Late Republic and Early Empire." *BICS* 15: 97–109.

Suolahti, J. 1963. *The Roman Censors: A Study on Social Structure*. Helsinki: Suomalainen Tiedeakatemia.

Syme, R. 1956. "Seianus on the Aventine." *Hermes* 84.3: 257–66.

Tacoma, L. E. 2016. *Moving Romans: Migration to Rome in the Principate*. Oxford: Oxford University Press.

Tan, J. 2017. *Power and Public Finance at Rome, 264–49 BCE*. Oxford: Oxford University Press.

Taylor, R. 2003. *Roman Builders: A Study in Architectural Process*. Cambridge: Cambridge University Press.

Taylor, L. R. 2013. *The Voting Districts of the Roman Republic: The Thirty-Five Urban and Rural Tribes*. Reissue. Ann Arbor, MI: University of Michigan Press.

Tchernia, A. 2007. "Le *plebiscitum Claudianum*." In Andreu and Chankowski, eds., 253–78.

———. 2016. *The Romans and Trade*. Oxford: Oxford University Press.

Temin, P. 2004. "The Labor Market of the Early Roman Empire." *Journal of Interdisciplinary History* 34: 513–38.

———. 2013. *The Roman Market Economy*. Princeton: Princeton University Press.

Termeer, M. 2010. "Early Colonies in Latium (ca. 534–338 BC). A Reconsideration of Current Images and the Archaeological Evidence." *BABesch* 85: 43–58.

———. 2016. "Roman Colonial Coinages Beyond the City-State: The View from the Samnite World." *Journal of Ancient History* 4.2: 158–90.

Terrenato, N. 2014. "Private Vis, Public Virtus. Family Agendas During the Early Roman Expansion." In Stek and Pelgrom, 45–60.

Terrenato, N. et al. 2012. "The S. Omobono Sanctuary in Rome: Assessing Eighty Years of Fieldwork and Exploring Perspectives for the Future." *Internet Archaeology* 31: online publication, http://dx.doi.org/10.11141/ia.31.1.

Theander, C. 1951. *Plutarch und die Geschichte*. Lund: C. W. K. Gleerup.

Thomsen, R. 1961. *Early Roman Coinage: A Study of the Chronology*. Copenhagen: Nationalmuseet.

———. 1980. *King Servius: A Historical Synthesis*. Copenhagen: Gyldendal.

Thouret, G. 1880. "Ueber den Gallischen Brand. Eine quellenkritische Skizze zur älteren römischen Geschichte." *Neue Jahrbücher für classische Philologie*. Suppl. XI: 93–178.

Tomei, M. A. 1993. "Sul tempio di Giove Statore sul Palatino." *MEFRA* 105: 621–59.

———. 1998. "Cave e cavità sotterranee del monte Palatino." In *Il Palatino. Area sacra sud-ovest e Domus Tiberiana*, edited by C. Giavarini, 155–76. Rome: Bretschneider.

Torelli, Marina. 1978. *Rerum Romanarum fontes ab anno CCXCII ad annum CCLXV a.Ch*. Pisa: Giardini.

Torelli, M. 1968. "Il donario di M. Fulvio Flacco nell'area sacra di S. Omobono." *QuadTop* 5: 71–76.

———.1978. "Il sacco gallico di Roma." In *I Galli e l'Italia, Catalogo della mostra*, edited by S. Paolo, 226–29. Rome: De Luca.

———. 1980. "Innovazioni nelle techniche edilizie romane tra il I sec. a.C. e il I sec. d.C." In aa.vv. *Tecnologia, economia, e società nel mondo romano, Atti del convegno di Como, September 1979*, 139–61. Como: Banca Popolare Commercio e Industria.

———. 1981. "Colonizzazioni etrusche e latine di epoca arcaica: un esempio." In *Gli Etruschi e Roma. Incontro di studio in onore di Massimo Pallottino*, 71–82. Rome: Bretschneider.

———. 1988. "Aspetti ideologici di colonizzazione romana più antica." *DialArch* 6: 65–72.

———. 1992. "Paestum romana." In aa.vv. *Poseidonia-Paestum. Atti del XV convegno di studi sulla Magna Graecia: Taranto-Paestum, 9–15 Ottobre 1987 edited by A. Stazio and S. Ceccoli*, 33–130. Taranto: Istituto per la storia e l'archeologia della Magna Grecia.

———. 2000. "C. Genucio(s) Clousino(s) prai(fectos). La fondazione della praefectura Caeritum." In Bruun, ed., 141–76.

———. 2006. "Ara Maxima Herculis. Storia di un monumento." *MEFRA* 118: 573–620.

Tortorici, E. 1991. *Argiletum. Commercio, speculazione edilizia e lotta política dall'analisi topográfica di un quartiere di Roma di età repubblicana*. Rome: Bretschneider.

Trigger, B. G. 1990. "Monumental Architecture: A Thermodynamic Explanation of Symbolic Behaviour." *World Archaeology* 22.2: 119–32.

Tsiolis, V. "The Baths at Fregellae and the Transition from Balineion to Balneum." In *Greek Baths and Bathing Culture: New Discoveries and Approaches*, edited by S. Lucore and M. Trümper, 89–112. Leuven: Peeters.

Tucci, P. 1994–95, "Considerazioni sull'edificio di via di Santa Maria de' Calderari." BullCom 96: 95–124.

Tucci, P. L. 1997, "Dov'erano il tempio di Nettuno e la nave di Enea?" *BullCom* 98: 15–42.

———. 2005. "'Where high Moneta leads her steps sublime'. The 'Tabularium' and the Temple of Juno Moneta." *JRA* 18: 6–33.

Ulrich, R. B. 1993. "Julius Caesar and the Creation of the Forum Iulium." *AJA* 97.1: 49–80.

———. 2007. *Roman Woodworking*. New Haven: Yale University Press.

Vagi, D. 2014, "Rome's First Didrachm in Light of the foedus Neapolitanum and the equus October." In *Essays in Honour of Roberto Russo*, edited by P. G. van Alfen and R. B. Witschonke, 73–94. Zurich: Numismatica Ars Classica

Vaglieri, D. 1907. "Scoperte al Palatino. Prima, seconda, terza, quarta relazione." *NSc*: 185–206.

Van Deman, E. B.1973. *The Building of the Roman Aqueducts*. Washington, DC: McGrath Pub. Co. Reprint.

Vandermersch, C. 2001. "Aux sources du vin romain, dans le Latium et la Campania à l'époque médio-républicaine." *Ostraka* 10.1–2: 157–206.

Vecchio, L. 2009–12. "I laterizi bollati di Velia." *Minima Epigraphica et Papyrologica* 12–15: 63–114.

Viglietti, C. 2011. *Il limite del bisogno. Antropologia economica di Roma arcaica.* Bologna: Il mulino.

———. 2017. "Tarquinius Superbus and the Purchase of the Sibylline Books. Conflicting Models of Price Formation in Archaic Rome." In Lulof and Smith, eds., 49–56.

Villaronga, L. 1993. *Tresors monetaris de la peninsula ibèrica anteriors a August: Repertori i anàlisi.* Barcelona: Filial de l'Institut d'Estudis Catalans.

Vine, B. 1993. *Studies in Archaic Latin Inscriptions.* Innsbruck: Institut für Sprachwissenschaft der Universität Innsbruck.

Virgili, P. 1977. "Scavo Stratigrafico (1974–1975)." *PP* 32: 20–34.

———. 1979. "Discussione." *ArchLaz* 2: 124.

———. 1988. "Area sacra di S. Omobono: Una cisterna fra i templi gemelli." *ArchLaz* 9: 77–81.

Virlouvet, C. 1995. *Tessera Frumentaria: les procédures de la distribution du blé public à Rome. Rome: École Française de Rome.* Rome: École Française de Rome.

Viscogliosi, A. 1996. *Il tempio di Apollo "in Circo" e la formazione del linguaggio architettonico augusteo.* Rome: L'Erma di Bretschneider.

Vitale, R. 1999. "La monetazione romano-campana. Studi e prospettive." *Rivista storica del Sannio* 11: 19–52.

Vitali, D. and G. Kaenel 2000. "Un Helvète chez les Etrusques vers 300 av, J.-C." *Archäologie der Schweiz* 23.3: 115–22.

Vitti, M. 2010. "Note di topografia sull'area del teatro di Marcello." *MEFRA* 122: 549–83.

Volpe, R. 2009. "Vini, vigneti ed anfore in Roma repubblicana." In *Suburbium II. Il Suburbio di Roma dalla fine dell'età monarchica alla nascità del sistema delle ville,* edited by V. Jolivet, C. Pavolini, C. Tomei, and R. Volpe, 369–81. Rome: École française de Rome.

———. 2012. "Republican Villas in the Suburbium of Rome." In *Roman Republican Villas: Architecture, Context, and Ideology,* edited by J. A. Becker and N. Terrenato, 94–110. Ann Arbor, MI: University of Michigan Press.

———. 2014. "Dalle cave alla Via Tiberina alle mura repubblicane di Roma." In *Arqueologia de la construcción IV. Las canteras en el mundo antiguo: sistemas de explotación y procesos productivos, Padova, 222–4 novembre 2012,* edited by J. Boneto, S. Camporeale, A. Pizzo, 61–73. Merida: Anejos de Archivo Español de Arqueologia.

Volpe, R. and G. Caruso. 1995. "Mura serviane in piazza Manfredo Fanti." *ArchLaz* 12: 185–91.

Volpe, R., V. Bartoloni, F. Pacetti, and S. Santucci. 2014. "Sepolcro degli Scipioni. Indagini nell'area archeologica (2008, 2010–2011)." *BullCom* 115: 175–91.

von Fritz, K. 1950. "The Reorganisation of the Roman Government in 366 B.C. and the So-Called Licinio-Sextian Laws." *Historia* 1.1: 3–44.

von Gerkan, A. 1958. Review of *La Tecnica edilizia Romana*, by G. Lugli. *Göttingische Gelehrte Anzeigen* 212: 627.

von Hesberg, H. 1995. "Ein Tempel Spätrepublikanischer Zeit mit Konsolengesims." In *Modus in rebus. Gedenkschrift für Wolfgang Schindler*, edited by D. Rössler and V. Stürmer, 77–80. Berlin: Gebr. Mann.

von Reden, S. 2007. *Money in Ptolemaic Egypt: From the Macedonian Conquest to the End of the Third Century BC*. Cambridge: Cambridge University Press.

———. 2010. *Money in Classical Antiquity*. Cambridge: Cambridge University Press.

Waelkens, L. 1998. "Nexum et noxalité." In *Le monde antique et les droits de l'homme, Actes de la 50e session de la Société internationale Fernand de Visscher pour l'Histoire des droits de l'Antiquité, Bruxelles 16–19 septembre 1996*, edited by H. Jones, 89–94. Brussels: Uitgave.

Walbank, F. W. 1957–79. *A Historical Commentary on Polybius*. 3 vols. Oxford: Clarendon Press.

Walsh, K. 2013. *The Archaeology of Mediterranean Landscapes: Human-Environment Interaction from the Neolithic to the Roman Period*. Cambridge/New York: Cambridge University Press.

Ward-Perkins, J. B. 1962. "Etruscan Engineering: Road-Building, Water Supply, and Drainage." *Latomus* 58: 1636–43.

Warmington, E. H. 1935–40. *Remains of Old Latin*. 4 vols. London: W. Heinemann.

Watson, A. 1975. *Rome of the Twelve Tables: Persons and Property*. Princeton, NJ: Princeton University Press.

Weber, M. 2000. *Wirtschaft und Gesellschaft: Die Stadt*. Heidelberg: Mohr Siebeck.

Welwei, K.-W. 2000. *Sub corona vendere. Quellenkritische Studien zu Kriegsgefangenschaft und Sklaverei in Rom bis zum Ende des Hannibalkrieges*. Stuttgart: Steiner.

White, K. D. 1967. *Agricultural Implements of the Roman World*. Cambridge: Cambridge University Press.

———. 1975. *Farm Equipment of the Roman World*. Cambridge: Cambridge University Press.

Williams, D. 2011. "Note sulla circolazione monetaria in Etruria meridionale nel III secolo a.C." In *Proceedings of the 14th International Numismatic Congress, Glasgow 2009*, edited by N. Holmes, 1103–14. Glasgow: International Numismatic Council.

Williams, J. H. C. 2001. *Beyond the Rubicon: Romans and Gauls in Republican Italy*. Oxford: Oxford University Press.

Wilson, A. I. 2008. "Machines in Greek and Roman Technology." In *The Oxford Handbook of Engineering and Technology in the Classical World*, edited by J. P. Oleson, 285–318. Oxford: Oxford University Press.

———. 2009. "Indicators for Roman Economic Growth: A Response to Walter Scheidel." *JRA* 22: 71–82.

———. 2011. "City Sizes and Urbanisation in the Roman Empire." In *Settlement, Urbanisation, and Population*, edited by A. K. Bowman and A. I. Wilson, 161–95. Oxford: Oxford University Press.

Winter, N., I. Iliopoulos, and A. Ammerman. 2009. "New Light on the Production of Decorated Roofs of the 6th c. B.C. at Sites in and around Rome." *JRA* 22.1: 6–28.

Winters, F. 1997. "The Use of Artillery in Fourth-Century and Hellenistic Towers." *Echos du monde classique* 41: 247–92.

Wiseman, T. P. 1970. "Roman Republican Road Building." *PBSR* 38: 122–52.

———. 1974. "The Circus Flaminius." *PBSR* 42: 3–26.

———. 1979. "The Legends of the Patrician Claudii." In *Clio's Cosmetics: Three-Studies in Greco-Roman Literature*, 104–39. Leicester: Leicester University Press.

———. 1986. "Monuments and the Roman Annalists." In *Past Perspectives. Studies in Greek and Roman Historical Writing*, edited by I. S. Moxon, J. D. Smart, and A. J. Woodman, 87–100. Cambridge: Cambridge University Press.

———. 1995. *Remus: A Roman Myth*. Cambridge: Cambridge University Press.

———. 1998. "A Stroll on the Rampart." In *Horti Romani. Atti del convegno internazionale, Roma, 4–6 maggio 1995*, edited by M. Cima and E. La Rocca, 13–22. Rome: L'Erma di Bretschneider.

———. 2004. "Where was the 'nova via'?" *PBSR* 72: 167–83.

———. 2008. *Unwritten Rome*. Exeter: Exeter University Press.

Wolski, J. 1956. "La prise de Rome par les Celtes et la formation de l'annalistique romaine." *Historia* 5: 24–52.

Woodman, A. J. 1988. *Rhetoric in Classical Historiography*. London: Taylor and Francis.

Woodward, D. 1995. *Men at Work: Labourers and Building Craftsmen in the Towns of Northern England, 1450–1750*. Cambridge: Cambridge University Press.

Woytek, B. E. 2014. "Monetary Innovation in Ancient Rome: The Republic and Its Legacy." In *Explaining Monetary and Financial Innovation: A Historical Analysis*, edited by P. Bernholz, 197–226. Cham: Springer.

Wrigley, E. A. *Energy and the English Revolution*. Cambridge: Cambridge University Press.

Xie, L., S. L. Kuhn, G. Sun, J. W. Olsen, Y. Zheng, P. Ding, Y. Zhao. 2015. "Labor Costs for Prehistoric Earthwork Construction: Experimental and Archaeological Insights from the Lower Yangzi Basin, China." *American Antiquity* 80: 67–88.

Yavetz, Z. 1958. "The Living Conditions of the Urban Plebs in Republican Rome." *Latomus* 17: 500–17.

Zanker, P., ed. 1976. *Hellenismus in Mittelitalien. Kolloquium in Göttingen vom 5. Bis 9. Juni 1974*. Göttingen: Vandenhoeck und Ruprecht.

Zeggio, S. 2006. "Dall'indagine alla città: un settore del Centro Monumentale e la sua viabilità dalle origini all'età neroniana." *ScAnt* 13: 61–122.

Zehnacker, H. 1980. "Unciarium fenus (Tacitus, Annales VI.6.16)." In *Mélanges P. Wuilleumier*, 353–62. Paris: Belles Lettres.

Zevi, F. 1991. "L'atrium regium." *ArchClass* 43: 475–87.

———. 1993. "Per l'identificazione della Porticus Minucia frumentaria." *MEFRA* 105.2: 661–708.

———. 1996. "Sulle fasi più antiche di Ostia." In *"Roman Ostia" Revisited. Archaeological and Historical Papers in the Memory of Russell Meiggs*, edited by A. Gallina Zevi and A. Claridge, 69–89. Rome: British School at Rome.

———. 2007. "Minucia frumentaria, crypta Balbi, circus Flaminius: Note in margine." In *Res Bene Gestae. Ricerche di storia urbana su Roma antica in onore di Eva Margareta Steinby*, edited by A. Leone, D. Palombi, and S. Walker, 451–64. Rome: Quasar.

Ziolkowski, A. 1986. "Les temples A et C du Largo Argentina. Quelques considérations." *MEFRA* 98: 623–41.

———. 1992. *The Temples of Mid-Republican Rome and Their Historical and Topographical Context*. Rome: Bretschneider.

———. 1994. "I limiti del Foro Boario alla luce degli studi recenti." *Athenaeum* 82: 184–96.

———. 1999. "La scomparsa della clientele arcaica: un'ipotesi." *Athenaeum* 87: 369–82.

———. 2005. "The Aggeres and the Rise of Urban Communities in Early Iron Age Latium." *Archeologia* 56: 31–51.

———. 2015. "Reading Coarelli's Palatium, or the Sacra via yet again." Review of *Palatium. Il Palatino dalle origini all'impero*, by F. Coarelli. *JRA* 28: 569–81.

INDEX